LENIN: A POLITICAL LIFE

Copyright © 1991 by Robert Service

Manufactured in Great Britain

Library of Congress Cataloging-in-Publication Data
(Revised for vol. 2)

Service, Robert.
  Lenin, a political life.

  Includes bibliographical references and indexes.
  Contents: v. 1. The strengths of contradiction—v. 2.—Worlds in collision.
  1. Lenin, Vladimir Il'ich, 1870–1924. 2. Heads of
state—Soviet Union—Biography. 3. Revolution—Soviet
Union—Biography. 4. Soviet Union—Politics and
government—1894–1917. 5. Soviet Union—Politics and
government—1917–1936. 1. Title.
DK254.L4$4324 1985   947.084′1′092   84–43044
ISBN 0–253–33325–3 (cloth: v. 2)
  1 2 3 4 5 95 94 93 92 91

LENIN: A POLITICAL LIFE

Volume 2
Worlds in Collision

ROBERT SERVICE

Indiana University Press
Bloomington and Indianapolis

To Adele

Contents

List of Plates

All photographs reproduced with the kind permission of the School of Slavonic and East European Studies, University of London, except no. 15, reproduced with kind permission of Punch Publications.

Notes and Acknowledgements

This second volume follows Vladimir Ilich Lenin from the doldrums of his career in 1910 to its stormy triumph in 1917–18. Before the First World War he struggled to obtain supremacy over the Bolshevik faction. He scored several victories, but these were never such as to give him sustained control; and often they caused divisions which weakened his influence. He changed his base of operations from Western Europe to the Habsburg-ruled region of Poland in 1912 in order to increase contact with the Russian socialist movement. But his impact on the legal labour movement and even on groups of Bolshevik activists remained intermittent, and few people uninvolved in politics in Russia had heard of him. The outbreak of war brought him still greater set-backs. He sought refuge again in Switzerland and could keep only frail links with his party comrades in the Russian empire; his only consolation was that his standing among far-left socialists in the rest of Europe, or at least among certain groups of them, was enhanced. The transformation in his prospects came about unexpectedly through the February Revolution of 1917. Lenin returned to Russia in April. The Bolsheviks were already set to become a major mass party; they rallied to him and to his policies, and strove to win the soviets of workers, soldiers and peasants to their side. They denounced the liberals who formed the first Provisional Government, as well as the other socialist parties who entered a coalition with the liberals. In the October Revolution, the Bolsheviks seized power in Petrograd in the name of the soviets; by spring 1918 they held governmental authority throughout urban Russia.

I have learnt a great deal in writing these chapters. Lenin's mind was exercised by most contemporary themes in the social sciences; and even those which eluded his attention are not irrelevant to this study, since they throw light on the quality and direction of his thought. Intellectual life has moved on since Lenin's day; and, indeed, its movement has been conditioned in crucial ways by positive and negative reactions of thinkers to the experience of the October Revolution. All this notwithstanding, the intellectual range of Lenin's interests deserves respect.

This is not the same as sympathy with all his assumptions, ideas and projects. The volume is intended as an accurate record of Lenin's thought which indicates both its strengths and its weaknesses, and it has become increasingly evident to me that the weaknesses of description, logic and prediction were especially remarkable in 1917. There is a difference between a serious thinker and a coherent, convincing thinker. Lenin sincerely wanted socialist revolution and thought long and hard about problems. But the final result was analytically uneven and, when assessed as a programmatic whole, unsuccessful. Another purpose of this volume, which became a more prominent theme in the course of research, is to demonstrate our need to distinguish the various layers of Lenin's audiences. Recent studies of his political and economic thought have sought to identify his intellectual purposes in their own terms; but some have started from the unjustified premise that Lenin always spoke or wrote his mind. He would have been a much less effective politician if this had been true. Lenin fudged and obscured issues when convenient, knowing well how to cut his ideas to suit the cloth of his listeners or readers at the time. Undoubtedly the Bolsheviks came to power because they took up the grievances of workers, soldiers and peasants and in some measure reflected their demands; but the party leadership also deliberately modified its policies so as to avoid the loss of working-class support: there was manipulativeness at work as well as genuine utopianism.

Nor must we be transfixed by that tricky old question about Lenin: was he first and foremost a thinker and only secondly a politician, or was the diametrical opposite the case? The answer can never be either wholly one alternative or wholly the other. There were times when ideological considerations held the upper hand, and times when practical ones did. On no occasion did ideology completely exclude pragmatism, or vice versa. This was surely one of the reasons for his pre-eminence among Bolsheviks and for his emergence as a leader of a revolution that survived against the odds.

Political genius though he was, however, Lenin's impact has been exaggerated in most general accounts. He was a man of his times, and little sensible about Lenin can be said without reference to what his rivals were saying. His relationships with Bukharin, Luxemburg, Martov, Stalin and Trotski have been expounded in several monographs (even though the roles of Bukharin and Stalin are subjected to some reassessment in this volume). It is my intention to cast the net wider and to catch under-researched figures such as Kamenev, Milyutin, Maslov, Radek, Semkovski, Zhordania and Zinoviev – and to examine what they said for themselves and not merely what was said by Lenin about what they said. This enables us to take the true measure of Lenin's impact and originality as a thinker. The consequence is a lessening of the importance attributable to his ideas; but this is hardly surprising since so many Sovet and Western accounts, especially textbooks, have taken his demiurgical role as axiomatic. For example, the conventional notion that Lenin perennially dominated Bolshevik agrarian policy is nonsense. Similarly, it is wrong to suppose that his writings on the characteristics of the Romanov state or on twentieth-century imperialism were his unique invention. Even so, it is undeniable that he wielded a major influence and that his ideas were not without novelty. Bolshevik thought was tremendously affected by the *April Theses* of 1917.

The contemporary debates about the Russian economy and society were in many ways more subtle than those among the generations of historians which followed the October Revolution. Yet the hurricane of political change in the early years of the twentieth century posed enormous problems of understanding. No leader possessed our benefit of hindsight. Some politicians had a clear view of particular events or trends; it is remarkable how much they managed to comprehend about possibilities in such volatile circumstances. But none of them, Lenin included, perceived the full complexity of developments in the country. (Let us remember that Lenin, if he was a manipulator, also succeeded in manipulating himself.) The crisis in Russian state and society pressed down hard on all Russia's politicians, and no single party's proposed solutions were adequate to the crisis. No fast-acting and painless solutions were available: truly this was Russia's tragedy in 1917.

But what of Lenin's impact as a practical leader? I had assumed that a drastic reduction of his reputation would emerge from the documents. A maturing body of writing has pointed to his difficulty even in communicating with his fellow factionalists before the First World War (and the recently-published minutes of the Prague Conference demonstrate the suspicion directed at him). This volume highlights the proliferation of his problems during the War. Even in 1917-18, when his authority grew rapidly, he could not win every intra-party struggle. In addition, he often refined existing opinion rather than created it *ex nihilo*. Yet these qualifications can be pushed too far. Lenin was a political giant; he was never an ordinary figure in the array on the Bolshevik tapestry. This is most easily discernible in the key decisions on Bolshevik strategy at the April Conference of 1917, at the Central Committee meetings in October 1917 and in the debates on war and peace in early 1918. He was victorious mainly through his persuasiveness in the open discussions typical among Bolsheviks in 1917. But the pattern of accountability in the party also had gaps, and Lenin in October and November used the organisational looseness to push for decisions to be taken without wide consultation. And yet the latitude for political action to occur was not boundless. Most general books on Lenin overrate his practical authority. I hope therefore to indicate the political framework inside and outside the party which made his exceptional impact possible at all. Lenin, for all his brilliance, could not have advanced to the position of governmental premier if conditions both in his party and in Russian public life had not been what they were.

This brings us to questions about his activity that are much neglected. We need to look carefully at the kinds of work that involved him in 1910-18. Lenin, despite the claims made about him through the extravagances of demonography and hagiography, was a human being. Twenty four hours existed for his use each day. His intellect, while being outstanding, was finite and his energy was not (quite) boundless. It becomes clear that certain arenas of theory, propaganda and organisation were more favoured by him than others. The division of functions among Lenin and his close comrades also needs to be considered. The Bolshevik Central Committee was a collectivity of talents and jobs.

The issue arises whether the good and bad that arose from the October Revolution of 1917 are attributable to Lenin. He crudified Bolshevik opinion in significant ways. He also channelled ideas in specific directions. The Council of People's Commissars (or Sovnarkom) headed by Lenin, however, was massively affected by his presence. He decisively increased intolerance to the point of mass terror. But the current of the party's ideas would not have become stagnant without him; and, in the conditions of military defeat and the breakdown of liberal politics and capitalist economics in 1917, the likelihood of the emergence of a radical socialist option was strong. If Lenin had never existed, a socialist government would probably still have ruled Russia by the end of the year. The

Provisional Government was ceasing to govern by early autumn. In addition, the Bolshevik party had a mainly democratic internal structure and could ignore Lenin when it saw fit. The altering of certain aspects of central party strategy in spring and summer 1917 were done largely without the direction of Lenin, and sometimes occurred against his expressed desires. It was also a stroke of fortune for his party that Lenin was hiding in Finland in September when he was urging his party to seize power before there was a realistic chance of holding on to it. In practical politics, then, Lenin's contribution was ambivalent. His zeal as a revolutionary in quest of power outmatched his skills at analysing what, in the long term, could be achieved in contemporary Russian conditions; and he was not devoid of irresponsibility.

In examining these points, I have tried to provide an historical narrative and analysis as well as to address issues which arise generally in the socal sciences. The chapters draw extensively upon the growing secondary literature on the political, social and economic history of the period. Accounts of social conditions in the period covered by this second volume have lately proliferated. We ought never again use the dreary formula of 'Lenin, the party and the masses'. The economic conditions of 1917, the war-weariness and the foreign and military situation: with these there would still have been a revolution in Russia. But they helped to create a situation in which it was precisely a far-left socialist like Lenin, and not a socialist of less extreme views, or a liberal, who came to the top. The relation of the high politics of Russia to the socio-economic environment is a crucial interest of this second volume.

It must be repeated that this is only a sketch of a political life. There is no sector of Lenin's thinking or activity which would not merit an account at least as long as this volume. Concision and compression have been essential aims. Several topics have deliberately been made to stand larger in the chapters in this volume than in previous accounts. I have tried to provide the years 1914-16 with the due proportion of attention they have commonly lacked. Much space is also given to Bolshevik conferences and congresses, since the stenographic record gives an immediacy of evidence absent from even the best memoirs – and most memoirs on Lenin must be about the least revealing for any major world politician. Furthermore, I have tried to offer an account not only of Lenin's grand treatises but also of his lesser-known and smaller works including letters, memoranda and jottings; and to examine his silences, which were frequently as eloquent of his purposes as were his explicit recommendations. Not all the corners of his career can yet be flooded with light. Let us please remember that the full access to documents is still unattainable despite the publishing campaigns in the late 1950s and since the mid-1980s. Furthermore, the secondary literature covers many important themes in politics, culture and intellectual debate only thinly. Patches of the period under review are still dimly-lit.

Several friends have helped me immensely by criticising the full version of these chapters: Franscesco Benvenuti, Bob Davies, Israel Getzler, Geoffrey Hosking, Eero Loone, Bob MacKean, Evan Mawdsley, Alexander Rabinowitch and Arfon Rees. They kindly diverted themselves from their own work, and their comments have led to substantial improvements. Everyone writing on the Soviet Union, its past and its present, has a busy life. I am deeply grateful to the above-mentioned scholars who have been so generous with their time and expertise.

Work on this volume was supported by a research award from the University of Keele in spring 1983 and a grant from the British Academy to visit Finnish libraries in summer 1986. I have been lucky to work at the University of Keele and, latterly, at the University of London. Regular conversations with Genia Lampert and Arfon Rees at Keele; with Olga Crisp, John Channon, Geoffrey Hosking, Judith Schapiro and – on his frequent visits – Israel Getzler in London; with Jyrki Iivonen in Tampere and with Vladimir Buldakov in Moscow have greatly enhanced my understanding of the revolutionary period in Russia. In addition, the School of Slavonic and East European Studies signed a research exchange with the Academy of Sciences in Moscow in December 1988. The fact that Lenin and the Russian Revolution have at last begun to become a topic for scholarly discussion between Western and Soviet scholars is already yielding positive results, to the benefit of scholars in both countries. Above all, my wife Adele Biagi has shared our house with the bulging fifth edition of Lenin's collected works (which, to her obvious consternation, are now officially recognised to be far from 'complete'); she has also discussed the themes and contents over many years. Her comments, coming from someone with a background in British history, has assisted invaluably in the maintenance of a comparative analytical perspective. Our children – Emma, Owain, Hugo and Francesca – have grown up with Lenin, learning to recognise his image as quickly as anyone born in the USSR. They have been as intrigued as their father was to sit on the couch (now stored in

Tampere) whereon Lenin supposedly composed his *State and Revolution*, or to visit the beer-hall in Munich where Lenin and Krupskaya sometimes refreshed themselves. As they have got older, they have shown the sort of interest in Lenin that any historian would appreciate. I am grateful to all of them, especially for their help in the last stages of preparation of the draft.

Dates are given according to the Julian calendar until the end of January 1918; thereafter they follow the Gregorian: the exception to this are important dates in European history, which are given according to the Gregorian calendar even for the pre-1918 years. Transliteration of Russian names follows the pattern of the first volume. I should like to add that what I thought would be the last draft of this volume was finished in winter 1987–88. But just then President Gorbachev's political reforms began to yield up new documentary publications and a further draft was made. We now have the invaluable Prague Conference minutes as well as the records of the early sessions of the Soviet government; further significant letters have been published from the Lenin archives. It is to be hoped that free access to these and other holdings will be accorded. Such a reform would be fraught with difficulties: Lenin remains an ingredient in the cement used by the Soviet political leadership to keep the edifice of the Soviet political system intact. The dangers of eroding the myth of the Soviet state's founding father are readily apparent, but the task will have to be tackled: an increasingly sophisticated, frustrated and restless society cannot be treated to fairy stories for ever. The latest purveyor of the Lenin myth has been Mikhail Gorbachev. It is unclear, at the time of writing, how far criticism of Lenin will be allowed to go in conditions of *glasnost'*; but many critics are beginning to enter the public discussion. Meanwhile Gorbachev has remoulded 'Lenin' for public presentation. Lenin's image is being linked to untrammelled power for the soviets; to universal democratic rights; to informal groups and to forms of 'pluralism'; to the eradication of 'legal nihilism'; to exalted status for peasants and their agricultural accomplishments; and to small-scale economic units.

Such a Lenin is not totally unhistorical. But, to say the least, the presentation is heavily biased. Readers of this volume may well conclude that often it was certain opponents of Lenin, especially among the Mensheviks and the Socialist Revolutionaries, who first highlighted themes which were redeveloped in the post-1985 *perestroika*. Yet it is not my purpose here to engage in polemics over historiography. I should also like to emphasise that colleagues in the USSR are starting to get to grips with complex and tormented questions of the country's history which they were once compelled to avoid. Lenin is a topic of common central concern; and it is recognised that the significance of Lenin for our times must be assessed in conjunction with an understanding of his own life and times. This volume is a contribution to the debate.

London   RJS
March 1990

1 All or Nothing: 1910–1912

CONFLICTS IN THE CENTRAL COMMITTEE

The political life of Vladimir Ilich Lenin was avidly scrutinised by the subjects of the former Russian empire from 1917, and foreign politicians and commentators strove to stay abreast of his career. Few statesmen had attracted an examination of this intensity. Not since the days of Napoleon Bonaparte had an individual so deeply intrigued and exercised world opinion. This extraordinary fascination was evoked by the nature of the new regime's projects. The first socialist state had been born. The objective of pan-European revolution was triumphantly proclaimed. The natural reflex of contemporaries was to enquire what sort of man had led the Bolshevik march on power. Faulty communications inside Russia and the disruption caused in Europe by the battles on the Western and Eastern fronts made it difficult to gather information on him; but his articles in *Pravda* provided much material. Many decrees of the new Soviet government were written by him; he also granted occasional interviews. Books which he had written before the First World War were republished with large print-runs. Diplomats reported back to their governments from Petrograd. Few observers doubted that the main inspirer of the October Revolution was Lenin. His declaration that the era of European socialist revolution was imminent, and that the Bolsheviks of Russia would inaugurate it, caused ubiquitous frissons of excitement.

And yet seven years earlier, in 1910, none of Lenin's contemporaries had any presentiment of what the future held in store for him. Before the First World War his name had become a synonym, among Russian revolutionaries, for intolerance. But no one had to take him unduly seriously until 1917. The consensus had been that he was a troublemaker who would come to no good end; and that he was causing most trouble inside his own Russian Social–Democratic Labour Party. It had crossed nobody's mind that Lenin would soon be a realistic contender for supreme power in his native land.

1

Lenin had not expressed such a thought; he had not even given the impression that a pan-European socialist revolution was an imminent possibility.[1] In the pre-war days his priority had been to exert authority within the Russian Social-Democratic Labour Party. He genuinely detested the entire political and social order of capitalism in his country and abroad; his will to rid society of oppression and exploitation gave meaning to his life. But his energies in emigration were focused on the party's internal struggles, and he took an aggressive fanaticism to the extreme. The Central Committee at its January 1910 plenum had tried to restrain him. A straitjacket of stipulations, designed with him in mind, had been applied. Lenin and his Bolsheviks were not explicitly censured, but were asked to dismantle their separate factional centre. Their newspaper, *Proletari*, had to cease publication. They were also to hand over the finances acquired by them from N. P. Shmidt's legacy to three German socialist trustees. The Central Committee, based mainly in the Russian empire, was to resume charge of a reunited party; and a general party newspaper, *Social-Democrat*, was to be refounded. Bolsheviks were to desist from their polemics against the Liquidators and the Ultimatumists. The Liquidators were Russian Marxists who refused to belong to illegal party organisations on the grounds that the police had broken them up and the State Duma and the legal labour movement offered greater chances of political advance. The Ultimatumists, on the other hand, were committed to the illegal party organisations and wished those party members who had secured election to the State Duma (or parliament) to be constrained to speak strictly within the guidelines of party policies. Liquidators and Ultimatumists were detested equally by Lenin, who wanted both a strengthening of the illegal committees and the flexible use of the Duma as a forum for party propaganda.[2]

Other Bolsheviks at the plenum had not demurred at the plenum's decisions. On the contrary, they too hoped that Lenin would mend his ways. But they had not gone through the learning process of an all-out contest with Lenin. Yuli Martov as a Menshevik had endured this experience, and was less optimistic about the chances of the straitjacket remaining secure. He had co-operated in the plenum because he had always assumed that a united party was desirable. No Menshevik was truly optimistic about the prospects of unity. But all of them recognised that the alternative was to do nothing at all, and allow Lenin to call them splitters and enemies of the party.[3]

Immediately after the plenum, Lenin started to pick the locks. He did so, but not like some political Houdini, out of sight and with a showman's mystery: he relished the display. First of all he needled Martov, his fellow editor of *Social-Democrat*, by trying to include critical comments on the Menshevik deputies to the State Duma. Only a flurry of letters with the Polish representative on the editorial board obviated total rupture. On 13 February 1910, invoking his authority as co-editor of *Social-Democrat*, he published an article ironically entitled 'Towards Unity'. It renewed the onslaught on Liquidationism and Ultimatumism, and the verbal formulas were only slightly less ferocious than in the previous year.[4] In March he went further, by accusing Martov of wanting to relax the party's control over its members in the legal labour movement in Russia.[5] He taxed Martov's associate, Fedor Dan, with exuding 'a Liquidationist spirit' (even though the Mensheviks heartily supported the maintenance of the underground party committees).[6] There was cunning in this. The January 1910 plenum, though calling off any campaign against Liquidationism, proposed that the Liquidators ought to be persuaded to alter their views. Lenin contrived to imply that the Menshevik leaders had overturned the plenum's resolution. This, in his estimation, freed him to resume his earlier themes. He announced that the Bolsheviks would re-establish a factional organ, which he wanted to call *The Workers' Newspaper*.[7] Publication began on 30 October 1910 and, under Lenin's control, an open struggle was resumed against all opponents of Bolshevism.

Not even this satisfied Lenin. By December 1910 he was requesting the remittance of the Shmidt monies to his faction and to his alone.[8] His demand was aimed at abrogating the arrangements made at the January 1910 Central Committee. He did not describe them as such. Many fellow Bolsheviks among the Marxist *émigrés* distrusted his intense anti-Menshevism, and these still desired party unity. They wanted to keep up the fight against the Mensheviks without driving them into a separate party. It was a tactical finesse that Lenin scorned.[9] Only a few close supporters, such as Grigori Zinoviev wanted an organisational split, and even he was far from approving the whole gamut of Lenin's proposals to deal with non-Bolshevik groups in the party.[10] The Mensheviks had become accustomed to calling him the chief of Bolshevism. Now, at Central Committee meetings, they beheld the delicious spectacle of Bolsheviks haranguing their leader.[11] To be sure, Lenin's position strengthened in the course of 1910. But this was small satisfaction for him; he had surged back only to where he had been in 1909 – hardly a year he recalled with pleasure.[12]

In the emigration as well as in the Russian empire, moreover, the feeling persisted that greater attention should be paid to activity and propaganda in Russia. Lenin was regarded as one of those many émigrés whose Alpine disputations distracted the party from its objective of making revolution in St Petersburg.[13] The Russian secret police undertook sophisticated measures to hunt down leading revolutionaries. In autumn 1910, two Bolshevik members of the Central Committee fell into their clutches. The Central Committee had created an inner subcommittee, the Russian Bureau, to direct its affairs from inside the empire; and two further Bolsheviks belonging to it were arrested at the end of the same year.[14] Bolsheviks remained on the Central Committee, but none of these were enthusiasts for Lenin's factionalism. As Lenin ruefully noted, they were Bolshevik Conciliators.[15] Their insistence on keeping a united central apparatus was so much to his distaste that he claimed that they constituted a separate faction.[16] No less irritating was the support they had from the Polish and Latvian representatives in the Central Committee.[17] And, although Lenin wished the Bolsheviks to form a separate party, it was as yet impolitic to articulate such a desire.[18] By December 1910 he had concluded that another Central Committee plenum might break the stalemate. Its membership in emigration contained more Bolsheviks than Mensheviks, and Lenin presumably counted upon winning some Conciliators to his side. The Menshevik leaders did not demur, but subtly suggested that the location of the plenum should be in Russia. They were playing upon the idea, which was not peculiar to Mensheviks, that the main aptitude of the émigrés lay in fomenting internal party conflict.

Lenin punched back. The real intention of the Mensheviks, he contended, was to facilitate the round-up of the Central Committee by the Okhrana (or political police).[19] This counter-attack was his most shameful statement in these years. Mensheviks impassively asked him to explain what made him think that they wished to assist the imperial régime. Again Lenin aimed his blows low. Menshevik strategy, he asserted, neglected the illegal party organisations; and Mensheviks allegedly confined themselves to the legal framework of politics erected by the emperor, Nikolai II and his Chairman of the Council of Ministers, P. A. Stolypin, in 1907. It was therefore no coincidence that no Menshevik member of the Central Committee had recently been caught and imprisoned.[20]

The Okhrana's ability to set one faction against another in the Russian Social-Democratic Labour Party by a judiciously selective policy of arrests should not be underestimated; but Lenin's imputation of deliberate connivance by the Mensheviks was scandalous. Yet an unexpected result of the altercations was a sudden consensus that a Central Committee plenum should be convoked. Lenin wanted it in order to aggravate disputes and insulate all Bolsheviks from the rest of the party; the other leaders, from the Mensheviks through to the Bolshevik Conciliators, desired it so as to eliminate factionalism once and for all. Lev Trotski urged that a fresh initiative should be made and that a full Party Conference, with properly elected delegates from local groups in Russia, should be organised.[21] The endless disputes after the Central Committee plenum of January 1910 demonstrated that a comprehensive examination of the party's condition was necessary. But his proposal was considered too expensive in time and finance. Trotski's émigré journalism, with articles excoriating the 'Leninists' for their intransigence and sectarianism, increased his influence.[22] It was little relief to Lenin that his opponent had no organised followers in Russia. To some extent this was Trotski's deliberate choice; he wanted to stand outside and above factional squabbles, and made no attempt to set up yet another faction. Trotski was a talented pamphleteer and organiser. His pleas for party unity were bound to have an impact on the forthcoming Central Committee meeting.

Consequently Lenin inveighed against him more than any other Russian Marxist, in 1910–11[23] accusing him of 'adventurism'.[24] He also invented a nickname for him: 'little Judas'.[25] Trotski was Jewish; and, in most contexts, such nomenclature would have carried an anti-semitic resonance. This was not Lenin's conscious intention.[26] Rather, it was an attempt to liken Trotski to a character called Little Judas, in a well-known nineteenth-century Russian novel, who, in a family whose members were engaged in perpetual animosities, indefatigably tried to create an unnatural atmosphere of sweetness and light. Trotski's ultra-leftism in the sphere of Marxist political strategy did not prevent him from rallying to those Mensheviks in Russia who had hit upon the idea of collecting signatures for a workers' petition for the government to grant full freedom of association.[27] Trotski saw that this would constitute only a 'partial' reform of the political system; but, unlike the Bolsheviks, he argued that a 'petition campaign' would enhance the standing of socialism amidst the working class.[28] According to Lenin and Zinoviev, such a standpoint merely brought Trotski together with the Liquidators in an unholy and unprincipled alliance.[29] Trotski's ideas were distorted by his Bolshevik critics: he continued to assert that both violent and peaceful political methods ought to be undertaken by the party.[30]

And yet he would have stood a better chance of inhibiting Lenin's disruptiveness if the Mensheviks had not been so inept. The long-heralded plenum of the Central Committee met for a whole week starting on 28 May 1911. No Menshevik leader was willing to repeat what they regarded as the charade of January 1910. B. Gorev, their representative, walked out when his faction's views were ignored. Then Mark Liber from the Jewish Bund joined him when the meeting opted to maintain pressure on the so-called Liquidators.[31]

The Bolsheviks, for neither the first not the last time, were being helped by the voluntary exodus of their enemies. Supported by the representatives of both the Polish and Latvian autonomous sections of the All-Russian Social-Democratic Labour Party, they called for the convocation of a Conference in the near future. A Foreign Organisational Commission was chosen to co-ordinate activity outside Russia, and a Technical Commission was to handle the party's treasury. Meanwhile a Russian Organisational Commission was to direct the party in the Russian empire.[32] The Bolshevik Conciliator, A. I. Lyubimov, and the Pole Leo Jogiches, had held the ring at the meeting, and Lenin went on complaining of their prominence.[33] His influence was therefore neither unchallengeable nor unchallenged. But he had recovered much strength in the central party apparatus and was in better shape to win his future fights than a year before. The Mensheviks, for comprehensible reasons but with scant sense of tactics, had stormed out. The resistance to Lenin's onslaughts in the following months was bound to be weaker; and the composition of the forthcoming Party Conference was ever likelier to produce a triumph for him. His grand objective was evidently to set up a totally separate party. The odds against achievement were shortening.

THE RUSSIAN SOCIAL-DEMOCRATIC LABOUR PARTY IN RUSSIA

No organisational commotion was worthwhile even to Lenin unless there was hope of revolutionary unrest in the Russian empire; and, for Marxists, expectations centred on the industrial working class.

Employers launched an offensive after the upheaval of 1905–6. Real wages were lowered; unemployment persisted; strikes diminished. Prime minister P. A. Stolypin allowed only limited freedom for trade unions. They were disallowed from establishing national networks, and non-workers were prohibited from belonging to their executive boards.[34] The police, guarding against infiltration by subversives, closed down about six hundred such unions before 1911.[35] Initially it was the Mensheviks who won most elections to trade union boards. The Bolshevik ambition to use the legal labour movement as a means of communicating with and guiding the working class was still only weakly realised.[36]

But the tide was on the turn. Industrial production grew sharply from around 1908, and the Russian recession was surmounted. Estimates suggest that output rose by an annual average of 6 per cent in the decade before the First World War.[37] Government contracts for armaments, especially in the reconstruction of the Russian fleet annihilated by the Japanese at Tsushima in 1904, stimulated the metallurgical sector.[38] But the factories were also expanding production for non-defence needs: textile enterprises continued to constitute the largest industry and, together with those connected with food-processing, supplied about a half the value of the empire's total industrial output.[39] Investment poured in from abroad. mines and manufacturing plants acquired the most modern technology; Russia obtained some of the vastest factories, with the largest labour forces in Europe.[40] The workforce took advantage of this expansion. They had been taught by the revolution of 1905–6 to hate the political system; and skilled workers in particular were less threatened by unemployment. Strikes returned to the scene. Official records state that the number rose to 2404 in 1913.[41] The unrest occurred, as had been usual, without being co-ordinated by the trade unions. Nor were the revolutionary parties the instigators. The Party of Socialist Revolutionaries had made efforts to recruit workers to its ranks in this period. But the Okhrana found it no more difficult to crush such endeavours than it had done with Russian Social-Democratic Labour Party.[42]

Bolsheviks saw that the opportunities for political advance were none the less increasing; and the need to enhance involvement in the labour movement, both legal and illegal, was conventional wisdom.[43] Lenin was no better informed about the increasing unrest than any other émigré leader. The reunification of the various factions in Western Europe had deprived him of a separate agency of communication. Bolshevik activists moved between Russia and the emigration; but it was generally agreed that the Okhrana had shattered many of the old links.[44]

Lenin's objective was to use the instrumentalities available since the May 1911 meeting of the Central Committee to convoke a Party Conference; and to ensure that the Conference should take place entirely under Bolshevik auspices. He was convinced that a tightly-centralised party offered the best chance to take advantage of Russian labour unrest. Serge Ordzhonikidze, as leader of the Russian Organisational Commission, chose agents to accompany him to Russia to make the arrangements.[45] He was far from merely being Lenin's stooge. While being enthusiastic about the idea of a Conference, he disliked Lenin's preoccupation with the intrigues of émigré politics.[46] A Russian political focus and geographical base of work was Ordzhonikidze's aim, and his opinions were shared by countless Bolshevik underground activists.[47] The fact that Lenin had repeatedly called for the maintenance of the illegal party apparatus did not assuage their resentment (and Lenin was as yet protected against their wrath only by the police's effectiveness in severing contact between Russia and the emigration). His critics noted how little service he had recently given to such an apparatus. Certainly he had founded *Workers' Newspaper*; but it did not pass unnoticed that he only produced eight issues in 1911. Lenin's qualities as a propagandist were accepted. Yet the lack of material which was truly accessible to ordinary workers or even rank-and-file party members caused exasperation.[48]

Not that anyone entirely denied the contribution made by Lenin. In 1911 the Central Committee allocated funds to the opening of a 'party school' in the village of Longjumeau outside Paris.[49] The aim was to select promising undergrounders, pay their passage out from Russia and offer them intensive lecture-courses on Marxism and party strategy before releasing them back to their underground duties. Not all of them were Leninists. Ordzhonikidze, I. I. Shvarts and Boris Breslav were among the ten Bolshevik activists who attended as students alongside members of the other factions. Lenin was an inveterate pedagogue and spoke in the characteristic pose of a schoolmaster, with thumbs pressed hard into the armholes of his waistcoat. He delivered fifty-six lectures at Longjumeau, his topics including general disquisitions on political economy as well as more detailed offerings on his favourite theme: the agrarian question in the Russian empire. Some students wished that he had addressed questions of practical revolutionary activity, but on the whole he received a positive reception.[50]

Furthermore, the condition of the underground committees was so dire that no one could reasonably turn Lenin into the sole scapegoat. Ordzhonikidze and his fellow Longjumeau graduates, Breslav and Shvarts, who were working for the Russian Organisational Commission, found widespread 'disarray' and 'collapse'.[51] This was the situation, according to Ordzhonikidze, in 'the majority of Russian provinces'.[52] Contacts between one town committee and another were minimal; and even within towns there were few ties among the various Bolshevik groups.[53] So were Lenin's interfactional polemics completely irrational? Not quite, at least in his own terms. In St Petersburg a group of Liquidators had scorned the underground committees and founded a legal journal, *Nasha Zarya* ('Our Dawn') in 1910. Its editorials stressed the gains obtainable by workers engaging in protests within the framework of imperial legality.[54] For Lenin, such initiatives would deflect Marxists from taking proper advantage of the resurgence of labour unrest. Yuli Martov, Fyodor Dan and the other Mensheviks expressed the same opinion, but only in private. Their refusal to denounce *Nasha Zarya* became grist to Lenin's mill.[55] Thus Lenin saw himself as a super-optimist. The fact that in 1910 there were only about 10,000 organised Russian Marxists, including all the various factions,[56] did not depress him. He felt that the revolution of 1905–6 had demonstrated how quickly a mass party could be formed. Even under the régime of Nikolai II, he sounded an exultant note: 'The party is the conscious, progressive layer of a class, its vanguard. The power of this vanguard is 10, is 100 times greater than its number.'[57]

Lenin also adduced the history of the German Social-Democratic Party as evidence. Pointing out that only one in fifteen German workers had become a party member, he emphasised that the party's impact on the German working class was, nevertheless, enormous.[58] The German Social-Democratic Party was the Second Socialist International's major force. And Lenin proclaimed that in Russia, too, 'a small party core' exercised 'an extraordinarily strong influence over the vast masses of the workers'.[59] Already, too, the Russian working class had accomplished wonders in less than two decades. It was marching towards its destiny, which was 'the very great global task of liberating humanity'.[60]

Trotski retorted that, if it did not really matter that so few party members existed, Lenin's rancour and schismatism in the party's affairs was all the more pointless;[61] and others, too, maintained that, while the Liquidators were misguided to rely exclusively on legal operations, Lenin was exhibiting a sectarian obsessiveness.[62] Trotski's explanation was that the Marxist movement was dominated by intellectuals.[63] He failed to recognise that the recruits to pro-Bolshevism since the 1905–6 revolution had mainly been workers.[64] But he was right about the damage done by disputatious middle-class intellectuals in this period. Several Bolshevik groups in Russian drew the same conclusion. Compromises with other factions were not unknown. Ordzhonikidze, for example, reported approvingly that Bolshevik groups in the capital had been collaborating with Ultimatumists.[65] This was bad enough from Lenin's viewpoint (although he knew nothing about it until later, since communications had broken down). Worse still was the situation in Samara, where Bolsheviks and Liquidators co-operated.[66] Separate factional groups were at work, but these did not belong to separate parties; and there were plenty of Marxists endorsing radical but differing strategies who found a basis for collaboration. With so few groups in existence and with a remorseless political police, it made little sense not to avoid unnecessary splintering of the ranks.

The German philosopher Friedrich Nietzsche had considerable vogue among many thinkers in Russia and the rest of Europe around the turn of the century. His notion that an heroic individual, through the power of personality and will, could pull the mass of society into dynamic motion out of stasis was influential. Lenin's refusal to reply directly to Trotski's argument convinced his enemies that his persistent schismatism had no intellectually respectable rationale; they increasingly regarded him as a would-be Nietzschean 'superman'. His goatee beard appeared to confirm the validity of the daemonic image.

Like almost all Russian Marxists, Lenin ridiculed this intellectual tradition.[67] Not once did he mention Nietzsche in his entire published output.[68] But Lenin's adversaries claimed that, even if unknowingly, he had ingested the Nietzschean drug. The legally-published St Petersburg Marxist newspaper *Luch* ('Ray') railed against 'the dictatorship in the party of supermen with a cynical attitude to the masses'.[69] This was exaggeration (but no worse than the exaggerated prosecutions that Lenin brought against his victims). A direct connection with Nietzsche can neither be proved nor disproved. And yet his associate Zinoviev, while denying that Lenin was either egocentric or dictatorial, confided the following considerations to his notebook: 'But did he have a consciousness (a sensation) that *he* had been 'called'? *Yes*, he did. Without this he would not have become Lenin.'[70] Zinoviev conceded that, in the period when Lenin was struggling for political 'recognition', the relationship of individuals with 'him personally (i.e. not precisely *personally* but politically and theoretically) was *the criterion* of the measure of things for him'. Indeed, according to Zinoviev's revealing memoir, Lenin felt himself 'responsible for the whole of humanity' and saw himself as 'the leader (in the *best* sense of the word) of the working class and the party'.[71]

Consequently, loyalty to this man of destiny and to his ideas was more important, in his own eyes, than the quest for a united party which would include opponents as well as followers. His self-confidence was accompanied by an intolerance bolstered by the introspective conditions of the émigré disputes that typified the Russian revolutionary movement. Even so, Lenin's willingness to split his faction again and again went beyond the norm. Of course, he could not speak openly about his sense of personal vocation; this was alien to the comradely and collectivist ethic of Marxism. Instead he talked about the destiny of 'the proletariat', not about his own; and he tried to submerge his identity in the cause of the Marxist revolutionary movement, proclaiming that 'we, the workers' were marching towards a world socialist order.[72]

Yet this verbal flourish did not convince the Bolshevik deputies to the Third State Duma. There were only five of them even though several other social-democratic deputies sometimes voted with them rather than with the five Menshevik deputies. All were hostile to organisational divisiveness. Speaking and acting in consort with the eleven Menshevik deputies, they did what they could to embarass the government by using the Duma as a forum for denunciation of P. A. Stolypin and his Cabinet. Their leading figure was N. G. Poletaev, who tried to persuade Lenin to moderate his anti-Liquidator campaign. Lenin was angry; but, located in the emigration and lacking any sanction to compel Poletaev's obedience, he could only persuade and cajole. Poletaev, however, knew his own mind and would not budge.[73] In vain Lenin put the following proposition to him: 'One cannot sit between two stools; it's a matter of being either for or against the Liquidators'.[74]

Poletaev, a fitter by trade and the Duma deputy for St Petersburg province, could also incommode Lenin politically. His seat in the Duma gave him a degree of immunity from arrest, and he was able to take an active role in the editing of the Bolshevik legal journal *The*

Star. Without Poletaev's permission, Lenin's articles would remain unpublished.[75] In addition, Poletaev believed that the surest way to outmatch the Liquidators in the capital was to establish a Bolshevik daily newspaper. The post-1905 reforms included the disbandment of pre-publication censorship. Newspapers continued frequently to be banned; but the scope of acceptable political discourse was widened. Open calls for the violent overthrow of the state were still impossible, but suitably indirect language could keep a revolutionary organ in existence for months before the Ministry of the Interior might intervene.[76] Poletaev's suggestion evidently did not preclude a campaign in the newspaper for political objectives of Bolshevism. Despite his theoretical support for the exploiting of all legal as well as illegal opportunities, Lenin was not keen. His reasons, as expressed in a letter to Maksim Gorki in May 1911, highlighted suspicions about Poletaev and his friends. Gorki was bombarded with details about Poletaev's insufferable indulgence to the Liquidators and to the Mensheviks. In a rare confession of his intention to break with the Mensheviks, Lenin stated that unification 'with Mensheviks like Martov is *absolutely* hopeless'.[77] Lenin also claimed, mistakenly, that increased repression of the press was in the offing; and not too subtly he tried to dissuade Gorki from subsidising Poletaev's scheme.

There must have been further reasons too. The failure to support Poletaev was consonant with Lenin's reluctance to write articles for popular consumption. Lenin had written fly-sheets for workers in the 1890s; and his pamphlet 'To the Village Poor' in 1900 was a model of its kind.[79] But his literary work had tended to be limited to intra-party theoretical work since then. He aimed at a readership composed of party members, and indeed party members initiated in the current debates over Marxism. Poletaev's project surely also incurred his disfavour since, if successful, it would further weaken his exigous authority over his faction's activity in the Russian empire. Ordzhonikidze and his associates on the Russian Organisational Commission, so far from supplying directives to the underground party committees, frequently could not even discover their whereabouts.[80] Lenin's dream of a tightly co-ordinated and centralised party was as distant from fulfilment as ever. No wonder he was horrified by Poletaev. A St Petersburg daily newspaper would rob *Workers' Newspaper*, printed in Paris, of its usefulness to the illegal Bolshevik organisations in Russia; and Lenin's influence would decline.

THOUGHTS ON RUSSIA

Lenin's isolation in the West was not all his own fault; it was also the price paid by all émigrés for their freedom. Moreover, he endeavoured to stay in touch with contemporary intellectual debates. Russian public discussion was effervescent in books, journals and newspapers. Lenin kept up with current publications, and himself contributed to them. Daily journalism did not interest him. He barely mentioned Stolypin's assassination in 1911; nor did he expatiate upon the notion, which was common not only to revolutionaries but also to conservatives like Prince Yusupov at the Imperial Court itself, that the dynasty was lapsing into decadence. There is no trace in Lenin's writings of the gossip about the empress Aleksandra, and he said little even about the self-styled 'holy man' Grigori Rasputin.[81] He despised all such discourse as tittle-tattle. Instead, he focused on the concerns of a follower of Karl Marx and Friedrich Engels. He continued to study Russian economic development, and to ponder the implications for the struggle between social classes. He watched the agrarian sector keenly. His confidence that the Stolypin land reforms would fail was growing. At political gatherings he could talk of 'the complete dissolution of the economic position of the peasantry',[82] and he repeated that mass destitution was an unavoidable consequence of the government's policy.[83] According to Lenin, Russia's internal market would therefore remain needlessly restricted. He added that only a minority among the peasant households leaving their commune became independent farmers. Most sold up straightaway; poverty had driven them to break their communal ties.[84]

Scholarship in recent years has by and large confirmed this gloomy verdict on Stolypin's agrarian measures.[85] It must be added that Lenin was doing little other than expressing the conventional contemporary wisdom among revolutionaries about the government's strategy in the countryside; and that he was very far from thinking that Marxists had to hasten their accession to power for fear that the programme of Stolypin might succeed. He still perceived the landed nobility's existence as an obstacle to economic maturity. His idiosyncracy, at least when judged alongside the Mensheviks, was that he continued to deny that rural capitalism had reached a dead end.[86]

Thus he stuck to certain basic tenets of his analysis, and found himself subject to a deal of Menshevik teasing. Petr Maslov had ceased to worry himself with what Lenin wrote; he had either gained his own confidence over the years, or had decided that there was no point in aiming criticisms at a Lenin who had resolved to ignore incommodious empirical data. But N. Cherevanin entered the controversy, claiming that Lenin had never answered those critics of his *Development of Capitalism in Russia* who had stated that his statistics did not conclusively demonstrate his contention that an inter-generational process of differentiation of the peasantry into rival classes of rural bourgeoisie and rural proletariat was in existence.[87] Lenin ignored Cherevanin. It was left to another Bolshevik, A. Y. Finn-Enotaevski, to defend him. It is an interesting vignette in the history of Russian intellectual thought; for Finn-Enotaevski declared that, in the 1908 second edition of the book, Lenin had acknowledged that recently-published figures on horse ownership had caused him to retract the assertions of the first edition.[88] Lenin had made no such retraction; on the contrary, he had asserted that the new figures bolstered his original case. The episode is yet another sign that Lenin's ideas could be understood in ways diametrically opposite to those which he really held (and that this was not a phenomenon peculiar to the years after his death); it also shows that the Bolsheviks were not devoid of theorists such as Finn-Enotaevski who already perceived that rural life was more complex than as portrayed by the Lenin of the 1890s.

Such realism among Bolsheviks came to the fore only after 1921, when an anti-Bolshevik peasant revolt pushed Lenin into introducing a New Economic Policy granting large economic and social concessions to the peasantry. All this, of course, lay in the future. In the years immediately before 1917, Lenin's main initiative in the field of economic theory lay in his comparisons of the features of agricultural development in Russia and the USA. It irritated him that, over a decade after the publication of his *Development of Capitalism*, many commentators persisted in imagining that Russia's pre-capitalist social vestiges made her unique.

Through the 1890s he had accumulated notes on German economic development. Karl Kautsky's works were read assiduously; and Lenin admired his attacks on Eduard David, who argued against Marx's assumption that large-scale capitalist agricultural estates might not turn out to be as competitive on the world market as small, owner-occupied farms.[89] Unfortunately, as Cherevanin gleefully indicated, Kautsky began to moderate his stridency, conceding that the prognostications of the demise of small-scale agriculture had not been scientifically based.[90] Lenin again opted to remain discreetly silent, filling his notebooks before and after the 1905–6 revolution with data on German and Danish farming.[91] In 1915 he was to read academic works on the USA's agriculture, and was gratified to discover that even the world's most dynamic economy contained, in the southern states, Negro tenant farmers who would starve to death unless they combined their farming with labour on nearby modern agricultural estates. The parallel with the Russian empire was close.[92] Georgi Plekhanov, Petr Maslov and Lev Trotski in their books on Russian economic development had emphasised the *sui generis* path taken in Russia; and Trotski in particular had stressed the coexistence of backward peasant villages and highly-advanced large-scale factories.[93] Lenin delighted in arguing that such phenomena coexisted elsewhere. Not for the first time, he overstated his case. For in the USA's north east, where most industrial enterprises were based, a more technologically-developed capitalist agriculture existed than in the south. But there was a kernel of truth in his argument.

He also wrote passionately about the empire's class structure. There were, he said, two bourgeoisies in Russia. One was already mature: urban-based, it was headed politically by the Kadet and the Octobrist parties and was inclined to either liberal or moderate conservative aims. Lenin saw it as a ruling class. But he appended the qualification that it shared power with 'the Purishkeviches': his polemical shorthand for the wealthier among the traditional landed nobility.[94] This first bourgeoisie, furthermore, was only 'a narrow layer'. The second by contrast was 'broad': its members were mostly peasants, and Lenin stressed that it had not reached maturity.[95] Only the beginnings of an analysis were being afforded here. Assertion had displaced argument. Yet the substance of his commentary signalled a shift of emphasis in his interpretation of Russian economic conditions. His loudly-proclaimed estimates of the 1890s were being muted. 'In Russian capitalism,' he proclaimed before the First World War, 'the features of Asiatic primitiveness, bureaucratic bribery and deals by financiers sharing their monopolistic incomes with leading civil servants are still boundlessly strong.'[96] *The Development of Capitalism* was largely without such fulminations.

Lenin now scorned economists claiming too much for Russian industrial progress. The Menshevik, O. A. Ermanski (whose viewpoint was thought eccentric even by most Mensheviks), was a case in point. Ermanski, comparing Russian and German official statistics, concluded in 1912 that the concentration of capital in Russian industry was greater than in Germany.[97] Lenin revelled in pulling another economist's data to bits; he indicated that Ermanski failed to include the output of home-based workers and artisans in his arithmetic for Russia; and that he consequently overrated the modernity of her industry.[98] The criticism was perceptive, but also marked the limitations of Lenin's own economic enquiries. No longer was he pioneering interpretative investigations. Rather, he reacted to the books of others. His statements, even if we allow for the many practical demands upon his time, were often very cursory. His categories for the bourgeoisie were crude. Not for him the social subdivisions of capitalism in the towns described by the Austrian Marxist Rudolph Hilferding.[99] At least until 1914, Lenin portrayed industrial production as falling under the control of a united class. Hilferding's talk of rival commercial, industrial and financial segments of capitalism as yet did not appeal to him. He was happier when taking the battle to the middle classes. In 1912, newspapers in Russia were exercised by one of their recurrent debates about foreign capitalist penetration and domination; xenophobia was rampant. Lenin scathingly pointed out that innumerable Russian firms and their owners profited from the influx of alien capital; and he urged that those Duma deputies who played the 'patriotic' card should have their stocks and shares investigated to see whether they stood to benefit from a change in the regime's financial policy.[100]

And yet the very strangest gap in Lenin's pre-war writings lay elsewhere. Notwithstanding his economic expertise and social concern, he failed to produce much material on the conditions of Russian industrial labourers. A few scant words on the wage rises won through the struggles of 1905 appeared; but they were the commonplace of contemporary journalism.[101] He noted the same about agricultural workers since 1906.[102] Was this skimpiness accidental? It seems a significant lapse for a writer with the special bias towards the 'proletariat' that being a Marxist involves. Probably the reason was political. Lenin wanted a revolution and wanted all workers to take part in it; he may well have felt that the image of a working class displaying a variety of skills, material conditions and aspirations would have impeded his general objective.

Nor did Lenin do much to sharpen his recent ideas on the changing nature of the Russian imperial state. Since the revolution of 1905–6 he had noted the régime's adaptiveness, and had argued that official policies constituted a series of manoeuvres which balanced the interests of the bourgeoisie and the landed gentry. This, in Lenin's presentation, was a form of 'Bonapartism'. The state, by playing off these two major property-owning classes against one another, was achieving a degree of autonomy from them.[103] The extent of such autonomy was not defined; but he emphasised that the autocracy continued to rely heavily upon the gentry and the bourgeoisie and, he implied, could not afford to alienate both classes at once.[104] In 1912, however, he proposed that the state's latitude for manoeuvre might be so great as to permit it to move completely athwart the interests of the gentry. He drew attention to the survival, despite all the reforms after 1905–6, of the empire's 'colossal bureaucratic apparatus'. He asserted: 'This apparatus has independent interests; when these interests so demand, the autocracy moves against its very best allies, the gentry, the star chamber and so on.'[105] Lenin ridiculed the notion of fellow Bolshevik M. S. Olminski in his booklet, *The State, Bureaucracy and Absolutism in Russian History*, that the Romanov state was the plaything of the gentry's interests.

Thus Lenin's analysis was starting to entwine itself with a venerable strand in Russian socialist, liberal and even some conservative intellectual thought from the previous century.[106] The bureaucracy, accordingly, was regarded as an entirely parasitic excrescence. Mensheviks, too, had tended to accept this view. Feudalism in Russian was state-created and not, as it had been in Western Europe, 'organic'.[107] Lenin's reconsiderations should therefore serve as a warning against the belief that his thought before the First World War was internally wholly consistent.[108] Moreover, his remark showed an awareness of the huge and independent power that a ruthless state might wield in the teeth of much public hostility; and his actions after the October Revolution of 1917 exemplified his own willingness to deploy such power if the opportunity came his way.[109]

THE PRAGUE CONFERENCE

At any rate, Lenin said little and published less on the topic of the Russian imperial state; and, apart from Olminski's book, it was many years before Marxists in general began to tackle the thorny questions of the forms and intricacies of state power.[110] His single piece of sustained political analysis took a more limited subject: the Duma. He wrote to M. A. Savelev in 1911 requesting data on the electoral procedures used for the Third State Duma in 1907. These researches resulted in a pamphlet on the Fourth Duma elections of mid-1912.[111] At its core were Lenin's speculations on the reasons why the Kadets, as the leading liberal party, acquired so few seats. The Octobrists, who wished to work again for an alliance between themselves and the government, were the largest group, with 94 seats; and the next biggest was constituted by parties even further to the political right. The newly ultra-right political complexion of the parliamentary chamber, according to Lenin, was the product of the calculations and manipulations of the authorities.[112] But an illiberal majority was already secured by the political system introduced by Stolypin's counter-reforms in 1907, and yet the prescience and fine-tuning required for the manufacturing of a particular electoral result for the Fourth Duma was surely beyond the capacity of the Ministry of the Interior.[113] A more cogent explanation is that opinion among most members of the property-owning classes, especially the gentry in the countryside, had spontaneously moved rightwards; and perhaps there was a despondency among many middle-class voters which expressed itself in abstention from the elections. The Russian empire bestrode a superficially modified autocracy. But it was not a régime of total control.[114]

Lenin's 'conspiracy theory' of the Fourth Duma elections divulged much about his own instincts about elections and majorities. The Central Committee in May 1911 had called for a Party Conference.[115] The convoking organs were the new Foreign and Russian Organisational Commissions. Lenin made a cobra-like attack upon the Bolshevik Conciliators. His timing and tactics were brilliant. Lenin arranged with Sergo Ordzhonikidze, as leader of the Russian Organisational Commission of the Central Committee, for an ultimatum to be delivered to the Foreign Organisational Commission to place itself under the Russian Organisational Commission's sovereignty.[116] This was bound to cause a furore. The Polish social-democratic leader Leo Jogiches, provoked beyond endurance by the disputes among the Russians, withdrew his Polish associates from the Central Committee. The Russian Social-Democratic Labour Party was left to its own devices. Lenin gratefully accepted the opportunity to call together his emigration-based supporters in Paris in December 1911, and the consequence was the establishment of a Committee of the Foreign Organisation which was to supplant the Foreign Organisational Commission in co-ordinating all party organisations abroad.[117]

Such manipulations were blatantly factional; no non-Bolshevik was given a place on the new body. But Lenin calculated that he needed an appearance of procedural legitimacy even if it really was a charade. His objective was the confection of a 'Party Conference' which would be not merely a predominantly Bolshevik assembly but an assembly consisting mainly of Bolsheviks who supported Lenin's strategy. Most were also of the younger generation and were practical organisers rather than theorists. Prague was chosen as the venue. It was close to the Russian imperial frontier, and yet it lay within the Habsburg empire and offered a safe refuge for foes of the Romanov autocracy; and it was distant from the major centres of Russian Marxist émigrés in Western and Central Europe. Ordzhonikidze, a hard-working and ruthless Bolshevik, operated efficiently. Assisted by Bolsheviks such as L. P. Serebryakov and B. A. Breslav, he 'toured' Russia arranging the election of Conference delegates.[118] Democratic procedures were disregarded. Ordzhonikidze blatantly aspired to the arrangement of a Bolshevik-dominated Conference; he invited a few Party Mensheviks (who were close to Plekhanov and opposed Martov's gentleness with the so-called Liquidators), but only with the purpose of giving the impression that the Conference was more open to the party as a whole than it really would be.[119] Trotski was alerted to these developments. He and his friends discerned that Lenin aimed to reconstruct a Central Committee under his personal control and, by means of the Conference, claim that it presided over the entire party. Only Trotski was willing to organise the necessary counter-measures. From Paris he put out the word that the Conference would be illegitimate. Instead he called for a fresh effort to be made to reunite all factions and announced that a Conference would be held in Vienna.[120]

Yet the competition for delegates was scarcely intense, not least because Lenin's Bolsheviks did not want their rivals to come to Prague. The stage-managed Conference opened on 5 January 1912. There were eighteen delegates. Nearly all were Bolsheviks. Two representatives from Plekhanov's Party Mensheviks turned up and stayed, and Ordzhonikidze was used by Lenin as his 'expert' in handling them at the Conference. No other faction except the Bolsheviks and the Party Mensheviks was present.[121] For most purposes, the Prague Conference, which the Bolsheviks dubbed the Sixth Party Conference, was a Bolshevik Factional Conference.[122]

This did not mean that it was a Conference made in Lenin's image. Ordzhonikidze had had little contact with the emigration while gathering delegates in the Russian empire; and, while admiring most of Lenin's general policies, he detested his schismatic excesses. Worse still, from Lenin's viewpoint, was the fact that six delegates had come under the assumption that other factions were being invited. These delegates, including some of Lenin's professed sympathisers, sent last-minute invitations to the non-Russian 'national parties' within the Russian Social-Democratic Labour Party as well as to the émigré newspapers of Trotski, Plekhanov and the Vperedists.[123] Ordzhonikidze informed fellow delegates that Lenin might walk out if the recipients of these late invitations turned up.[124] Lenin could have spared himself his rage. Everyone who had been invited in this way refused to lend legitimacy to the Prague proceedings.[125] A reassured Lenin came to recognise that these same invitations could be used to amplify the fictional story that he had genuinely sought to involve all factions in the Prague Conference. He learnt to accept the presence of the two Party Mensheviks who had arrived under the aegis of Ordzhonikidze and the Russian Organisational Commission, since they could not outvote the Bolsheviks.[126] His pressing worry was that the Okhrana might discover the whereabouts of the Conference. The party had experience of delegates being arrested shortly after returning from Congresses and Conferences. Lenin implored delegates not to send postcards from Prague in case of interceptions by the Russian police.[127] He could not know that his precautions were in vain. Two Bolsheviks at the Conference, R.V. Malinovski and A.S. Romanov, were agents of the Okhrana and reported on all that went on.[128]

Luckily for Lenin, neither Malinovski nor Romanov had instructions to impede his progress in Prague. Nevertheless he did not advance smoothly with all his schemes; and his opponents in the emigration (as well as subsequent historians) exaggerated the ease and extent of his victories. He had to sustain much criticism. Firstly, there was worry about his obvious disdain for the Polish, Latvian and Bundist organisations. The Menshevik Y.D. Zevin was trenchant on this point;[129] and there was spirited dispute as to whether the Conference's decisions should be binding upon the non-Russian organisations.[130] Yet Lenin and Zinoviev, after modifying parts of their proposed official statement, persuaded the other delegates to cast the blame for the non-attendance of the non-Russians on the non-Russians themselves.[131]

Ensuing discussions were replete with imprecations against the sustained 'factional conflict' in the emigration. Ordzhonikidze based his tactics upon a Conference consisting mainly of Russia-based activists, and Lenin had to listen to P. A. Zalutski's criticisms of émigré squabbling.[132] Ordzhonikidze demonstratively praised the anti-Lenin *Vpered* activists in St Petersburg who had attacked Menshevik Liquidators (and he later talked of the possibility of *rapprochement* between Bolsheviks and Mensheviks).[133] Other delegates, apparently, referred in detail to Lenin's unpleasant polemics against other Russian Marxists, including even the Bolshevik Conciliators.[134] Lenin was unbowed. For him, it was 'a struggle to the death'. He adjured his small audience to recognise what he saw as the reality: 'We now have two parties – that is a fact!' Let there be, he demanded, no more moaning, no more complaining.[135] E. N. Onufriev, F. I. Goloshchekin and O. I. Pyatnitski answered him with further criticisms of the role of the emigration.[136] The least barbed objection was that Lenin and his fellow editors had not been producing material of sufficiently 'popular' quality; and the call for a switch of line was incorporated in a resolution.[137] Ordzhonikidze again rubbed salt in his leader's wounds by stating that co-operation between Bolsheviks and Mensheviks would be easier if only there did not exist '"the damned emigration" and the leaders who, sitting around in Paris or San Remo and understanding nothing, write directives and produce splits.'[138] He later added the following combative gloss: 'We know that the emigration has failed, all along, to give us anything of value.' He added, more starkly: 'The emigration is nothing.'[139] S. S. Spandaryan went further, saying that those who wanted to do party work should do the work in Russia proper. The polemical antics of the émigrés, he added, had even resulted in arrests of activists at home.[140]

Most of the following debates were focused on the Russian labour movement. Topics ranged from the worsening material plight of workers (as well as peasants) to the imperial government's project for social insurance.[141] But periodically the resentment of the émigrés resurfaced. Lenin tried to treat it casually: 'Why is this all so laughable?' But tempers were frayed, and he tried to explain the troubles abroad by reference to objective political conditions, stating that the polemics were 'the result of a struggle of two currents'. He contended that a fiercer fight with the Liquidators would leave the party stronger.[142] Ordzhonikidze took offence, especially at Lenin's insinuation that the anti-émigré noises were merely tearful laments. 'And Lenin,' he declared, 'has not answered a single question of ours.' Goloshchekin took Ordzhonikidze's side. There was even a proposal, possibly from M. S. Gurovich, that the Committee of the Foreign Organisation should be disbanded.[143]

This particular suggestion was rejected; but so, too, was Zinoviev's motion on 'party organisation abroad', which embodied an attempt to provide the Committee of the Foreign Organisation with complete approval.[144] Delegates, while allowing the body to survive, would agree only to describing it as 'one of the party organisations abroad'; they also specified that all foreign organisations should communicate with Russia exclusively through the Central Committee and should submit entirely to its authority. The Central Committee was to be based mostly in Russia: the final resolution defined it pointedly as 'the Russian centre of social-democratic work'.[145] Everyone, including Lenin, agreed that an emphasis on work in the legal channels of the labour movement was required. Trade unions, sickness insurance schemes and even lecture clubs should be given a priority.[146] Lenin stressed that such organisations need not be tightly-structured. The formalist of *What Is To Be Done?* criticised those who were devoted to formalism in the party underground, and even Zinoviev himself thought this new position to be exaggerated.[147] Zevin, a non-Bolshevik, was more blunt. He asked how Lenin's recommendation for a party founded mainly upon work in 'legal societies' was reconcilable with his demand for intensified struggle with the Liquidators; and he charged Lenin with underestimating the real difficulties of even legal activity in the Russian labour movement.[148] Goloshchekin concurred with the Menshevik speaker, adding that Lenin had painted an 'idealistic picture'. And he resented what he took to be Lenin's criticisms of the Bolshevik party activists in Russia.[149] Only Onufriev supported Lenin.[150]

And Lenin, perhaps recognising that his advocacy of legal work might continue to be misunderstood, suggested that a clause on the need to strengthen the illegal party apparatus be included in the Conference resolution on party organisation.[151] A tiny episode; but it showed that he perceived that his own enthusiastic but one-sided presentation could lead to his being misunderstood. He also regretted certain phrasings of the motion proposed by his assistant Zinoviev. Lenin advised the replacement of a clause which embodied outright opposition to the elective principle in party work; his grounds were not philosophical but those of political tact.[152] In any case, there was universal agreement that legal organisational opportunities ought to be explored more energetically. The Conference was united on that point.[153]

Zinoviev introduced debate on the other vital question, namely how to organise the party for the forthcoming electoral campaign for the State Duma.[154] Lenin could safely leave such functions to him. The political line followed Lenin's: that 'the party' should put up its own candidates in the workers' curiae without pacts with other parties. In practice this would mean that factions of the Russian Social-Democratic Labour Party which did not accept the legitimacy of the Prague Conference ought to be shunned.[155] In addition, Lenin and Zinoviev persuaded the Conference to oppose the Menshevik-supported campaign to collect signatures for a 'petitition' for the right of freedom of association to be granted in Russia. Such a campaign, he declared, was Liquidationist claptrap; and a further resolution was passed asserting that the Liquidators had 'definitively placed themselves outside the party' – a device already used by Lenin in 1908 to 'expel' Aleksandr Bogdanov from the Bolshevik faction without using the word expulsion.[156] Lenin also successfully urged the Conference to insist that the party's deputies in the State Duma should denounce the Kadets more vigorously and should accentuate the slogans of a democratic republic, the eight-hour day, and confiscation of gentry-owned land.[157] After three weeks of discussion, the Conference constituted itself as the supreme and legitimate assembly of the entire Russian Social-Democratic Labour Party.[158] The only objector was the Party Menshevik Zevin – and even he failed to walk out of the proceedings.[159]

A collective snook was therefore cocked at other factions of the Russian Social-Democratic Labour Party. Lenin's victories on policy were large; and the non-Bolshevik Marxist press quickly reported on the proceedings in such terms. Indeed, many commentators at the time, and many more since 1912, dated the essential formation of a Bolshevik party from the Prague affair. The formation of a self-styled Central Committee, staffed mainly by pro-Lenin Bolsheviks, was truly a watershed in the history of the Russian Marxist movement. The designation of *Workers' Newspaper* as the Central Committee's 'official organ' confirmed the demise of attempts to compromise with Trotski and the other aspirants to a broadly-based party unity.[160]

Yet the Conference delegates did not see themselves as mere auxiliaries in Lenin's war. It is usually overlooked that the Committee of the Foreign Organisation, which had been the initial channel for the planning of the Conference and which had been especially important to Lenin in 1911, had been confirmed not as the supreme émigré party body but simply as 'one of the party organisations abroad'. Hardly a fulsome recommendation. The resolution on the emigration also specified that foreign-based organisations should rally round the Central Committee.[161] Delegates were trying to prevent supreme operational power from falling into Lenin's grasp. The Central Committee was meant to govern the party, and was not to be encumbered with undesirable emigrant subcommittees. Thus foreign-based party organisations were required to rally round not the Committee of the Foreign Organisation but the Central Committee.[162] The seven elected members of the Central Committee, moreover, were not as solidly pro-Lenin as is usually thought. In the first place, D. M. Shvartsman was one of them. As a Party Menshevik, he was obviously welcomed by several delegates as proof that they were not aiming at the formation of a totally homogeneous, sectarian mini-faction.[163] Secondly, many of the 'Leninists' had criticised the émigrés at the Conference; and they included newly-elected members of the Central Committee Ordzhonikidze, Spandaryan and Goloshchekin.[164]

Only two émigrés, in fact, belonged to the Central Committee: Lenin and Zinoviev. The last of the seven members was R. V. Malinovski, an as yet unmasked police spy; and his posture at the Conference is unclear from the published minutes. But the general tendency to fire shafts of warning at Lenin about his future behaviour is transparent in the debates, the resolutions and the elections even though Lenin, with characteristic imperturbability, ended the Conference with a rousing speech.[165]

RUSSIANS AND POLES (AND LATVIANS, LITHUANIANS AND JEWS)

Lenin wasted no time in justifying the Prague Conference to his opponents. A brisk sentence or two expressing relief that the 'party' had been hauled out of the mess that had enveloped its central apparatus was the extent of his pleading.[166] He did not quite stop harrying the non-Bolshevik émigrés; but he was no longer preoccupied by them after Prague. Rather, he was a happy spectator of their chaos. Trotski had not given up trying to call a rival gathering of the Russian Social-Democratic Labour Party, properly open to all factions, in Vienna. Mensheviks retained their dislike of Trotski's ideas on revolutionary strategy, a dislike reinforced by personal animus. But on this occasion they would co-operate with him. Twenty-three delegates arrived in Vienna for the start of proceedings on 23 August 1912.[167] Seven months had passed since the Bolshevik venture in Prague. It is scarcely astounding that Lenin, faced with such evidence of inefficiency and parlousness, withheld his fire. To have attacked too fiercely might have rallied the opposition. The 'August Bloc' in Vienna included a range of Russian social-democrats, from a pair of Bogdanovists through to a representative of the so-called Liquidators. Apart from hostility to Lenin, nothing united them strongly. They also lacked the Bolshevik understanding of the tactical importance of nomenclature. Decently but self-defeatingly, they declined to describe their new supreme party body as the Central Committee and opted for a less forceful name: the Organisational Committee. In practice, the proclaimed unity was seen to be weak even by the delegates; the 'Bloc' was a complete misnomer.[168]

Among their resolutions were words of condemnation of the Prague Conference. But everyone must have known that the missiles aimed at Lenin would not wound him. 'I have no fear,' he had announced, 'of a condemnation of factional struggle.'[169] He laughed out loud at some anti-émigré remarks by even fellow Bolsheviks in Prague.[170] Shortly after the Conference he began to behave as he always had done. He was like a St Sebastian who has burst from his bonds, pulled the arrows from his body and shot them in the direction of his assailants.

The attack on him at Prague had been heavy; but it was concentrated upon his factionalism: and it certainly did not include any criticism of his attitude to the non-Russian constituent parts of the Russian Social-Democratic Labour Party.[171] Lenin was mightily pleased that he no longer had to worry about the official central leadership of the Social-Democracy of the Kingdom of Poland and Lithuania, which had belonged to the Russian Social-Democratic Labour Party (not to mention the Jewish Bund and the Social-Democracy of the Latvian Region) since 1906.[172] Disagreements between Lenin and Leo Jogiches, the Polish social-democratic leader, were of long standing. At the Second Party Congress, in 1903, Lenin and the *Iskra* group had argued that the subject nations of the Romanovs should be offered the right of self-determination. This alienated the Social-Democracy of the Kingdom of Poland and Lithuania. Leo Jogiches and Rosa Luxemburg, instructing their representatives at the Congress by letter, argued that Polish independence was an irrelevance in a capitalist world which was making economic nonsense of all frontiers. Lenin's refusal to budge discouraged the Social-Democracy of the Kingdom of Poland and Lithuania from joining the Russian Social-Democratic Labour Party at the Second Congress.[173] Lenin at first did not regret this situation; for the Polish social-democrats objected to Bolshevik attitudes to party organisation, and Luxemburg had entered the Bolshevik–Menshevik controversy about the party rules on the Menshevik side.[174]

And yet there was much agreement about general revolutionary strategy. There were also good working contacts between Lenin and other Polish leaders such as A. Warski and Jan Hanecki;[175] and neither Lenin nor Luxemburg allowed their disputes over party organisation to get in the way of personal friendship.[176] As the divisions between the Bolsheviks and the Mensheviks deepened over strategy in 1905, Lenin warmed again to talk of the incorporation of the Polish social-democrats of the Romanov empire in the Russian Social-Democratic Labour Party. At the Fourth Party Congress in April 1906 an agreement was reached, and the Polish social-democrats entered the larger party with rights of autonomy in the territory covered by its existing organisations and with automatic representation in the central party apparatus.[177] At the Fifth Congress in 1907, the Polish social-democrats constituted roughly a sixth of the party's entire membership;[178] their radicalism was vital to the success of Bolshevik policies at the Congress. Subsequently, in a Central Committee of twelve persons, the Poles Warski and F. E. Dzierzynski were supporters of Lenin against Menshevik strategy; and Jogiches on the editorial board of *Social-Democrat* was equally anti-Menshevik. At the International Socialist Congress in Stuttgart in 1907 Luxemburg, Martov and Lenin collaborated closely.[179]

Nevertheless Polish social-democrats were soon irking Lenin again. Niggles about strategical distinctions never disappeared. The Bolshevik preference for an alliance between 'the proletariat and the peasantry' struck Jogiches as being too close to Russian populist (or agrarian–socialist) ideas. Jogiches spoke instead of 'the proletariat supported by the peasantry', arguing that an emphasis on the primacy of the urban working class was more appropriate to Marxism.[180] The disagreement amused the Mensheviks. And it annoyed Lenin, but not to the point of rupture; indeed he came, in 1917, to see the uses of deploying a programmatic slogan very similar to that of Jogiches.[181] Much more serious, for Lenin before the First

World War, was Jogiches's devotion to the retention of Bolsheviks and Mensheviks in the same party. Bolshevik organisational schismatism was hated by the Poles, and Jogiches would never lend support to Lenin's calls to exclude the Mensheviks from the central party leadership even though Jogiches opposed Menshevik political strategy.[182] The Polish social-democrats, moreover, deftly retained the balance of power in the central party apparatus.[183] Lenin was frustrated by this. Jogiches, on the other hand, was incensed by the attitude taken by Lenin to the other main socialist party in Poland: the Polish Socialist Party. A former section of the Polish Socialist Party, the PPS-Lewica, appeared to Lenin to be moving towards a Marxist programme; and, unlike Jogiches and the Polish social-democrats, these socialists were sensitive to the need to embrace the national aspirations of the Polish population.[184] Relations between Lenin and Jogiches worsened. At the January 1910 Central Committee plenum, the Polish influence helped to prevent the passage of his divisive motions.[185]

Lenin sought pretexts for a definitive conflict with Jogiches. This was not difficult. In his own organisation, Jogiches was as authoritarian and intolerant as Lenin and he entirely lacked the Bolshevik leader's more attractive personal qualities.[186] Jogiches resented what he regarded as the unnecessarily enthusiastic co-operation between Lenin and Warski, who was replaced on *Social-Democrat* on Jogiches's orders by Z. Leder.[187] Not only Warski attracted Jogiches's anger. His oppressive personality and methods offended many others, and he had even threatened his former lover, Rosa Luxemburg, with a gun. Luxemburg somehow managed to continue to work with him.[188] But there was a growing hostility towards him in certain underground organisations in Poland itself. Warsaw-based social-democrats were especially discontented. The split between Lenin and Jogiches widened in November 1911, when Jogiches ordered that no Polish social-democrat should any longer serve on the board of *Social-Democrat*. The decision reflected Jogiches's impatience with the aggressive policies being pursued by the Bolsheviks in calling a schismatic party conference for January 1912.[189]

But the Warsaw organisation saw Lenin as a protector of their interests, and Lenin received news that a complaint had been made by it against Jogiches's decision to boycott the Prague Conference.[190] Previously the objections to Jogiches had been formulated mainly by individuals. By the end of 1911, Jogiches's highhandedness had

driven A. M. Malecki, Hanecki and Leder to resign from the Polish
official leadership. Political disputes were also involved. Jogiches,
unlike Lenin, wanted nothing to do with the legal trade unions
established after 1905; and, like Lenin, a growing number of Polish
social-democrats wanted a rapprochement with the left wing segment
of the Polish Socialist Party.[191] Other talented Poles were also hostile
to Jogiches: F. E. Dzierzynski, J. Unszlicht and Karl Radek; and
these, too, hoped for closer relations with the Bolsheviks while
retaining doubts about Lenin's divisive scheming.[192] Jogiches in
1911 had not totally despaired of dealing with the Lenin problem
by seeking an accommodation with Bolshevik Conciliators. A. I.
Rykov was an obvious choice, and a spirited correspondence ensued
until the Prague Conference broke off such possibilities.[193] Jogiches
then moved against his Polish opponents. In May 1912 he and his
adherents formally declared the Warsaw organisation disbanded.[194]
He also delivered Malecki and Unszlicht up to a 'party court'; and
Radek, too, suffered this fate on the alleged grounds of stealing party
funds.[195]

The fissures in the Social-Democracy of the Kingdom of Poland
and Lithuania brought cheer to Lenin, relieving any lingering
difficulty in explaining the need for a supposedly unifying Party
Conference in Prague; they also removed a good deal of responsibility for the party split from his shoulders. They were used as a
pretext for continued meddling in Polish socialist affairs. Until 1912,
Jogiches had interfered more in Russian business than Lenin in the
affairs of Polish organisations. In the remaining years of European
peace the dissentient figures in the Polish section of the party drew
closer to Lenin; he frequently advised them on tactics for dealing
with Jogiches and took their side in the International Socialist
Bureau.[196] Meanwhile, Dzierzynski, counselling Lenin to leave
Switzerland, suggested that Krakow in Austrian-ruled Poland would
afford him a better base for contact with Russia.[197]

The political friendship of Lenin and this handful of leading Polish
social-democrats helped to deflect attention from the most remarkable consequence of the Prague Conference: namely the fact that the
territorial base of the Russian Social-Democratic Labour Party – or
at least the part of it led by Lenin – had diminished.[198] The 'party'
could no longer properly claim to have organisations in Poland.
Since neither the Jewish Bund nor the Social-Democracy of the
Latvian Region had agreed to join Lenin's venture in Prague (and
Lenin had not given them an invitation in any event!), huge areas in

the western part of the Romanov lands were similarly uncovered. Nor did the Armenian organisations, which had been affiliated to the Russian Social-Democratic Labour Party since 1907, attend.[199] Geographically, therefore, Lenin's claim to authority was more restricted to Russia proper than before. Many Bolsheviks themselves, of course, were not Russians. Iosif Stalin and Sergo Ordzhonikidze were Georgians; Y. M. Sverdlov, G. E. Zinoviev and L. B. Kamenev were Jews, and Lenin had allies such as the Poles opposed to Jogiches. It must be stressed that he broke his ties with the Bund and the Social-Democracy of the Kingdom of Poland and Lithuania for reasons quite innocent of chauvinism. Lenin wanted freedom to make his own policies, direct his own organisations, run his own party, and looked on the concessions made to the various national organisations in 1906 as productive of 'federalism of the worst sort'.[200] Clear-cut centralism in a party definitively under his personal control was his objective, and he thought nothing of splitting the existing party in order to achieve it.

The unintended consequences of his actions in Prague, however, were at least as important in the longer term as those which he planned. Those Poles who stayed as his allies were destined to play a role alongside Lenin in the realignment of forces within the European socialist left in the First World War. As it happened, Lenin kept most of them at arm's length before mid-1914. The alliance was on conditional terms. Many of the Poles were critics of the German Social-Democratic Party, and Lenin did not abrogate his loyalty to Kautsky until then.[201] But it was Hanecki who helped to secure an exit visa from Austria-Hungary for Lenin in 1914; it was Radek's assistance that meant much to Lenin in the struggle against the European 'official' socialist parties in 1915-16,[202] and, in 1917, Hanecki and Radek were a source of information and possibly of funds channelled through to the Bolsheviks from the German government. Failure to take account of the longstanding two-way links between Lenin and these Polish socialists for years allowed the myth to endure that Hanecki and Radek were German spies.[203]

LEISURE AND ITS DISCONTENTS

No longer needing to appease Jogiches, Lenin could write more openly on the 'national question'; and, since Radek and Jogiches agreed in their hostility to the slogan of Poland's independence, the

Lenin–Radek relationship was always tense.[204] Lenin, even at his most Machiavellian, was also a man of belief. There was a quasi-religious quality in some of his utterances. Marx, for Lenin, was beyond criticism. Lenin evidently needed a rock of certainty in his life. This did not prevent him from interpreting Marx with a freedom, even a licentiousness, that astounded his Marxist opponents. Yet nobody near to him remembered him as having shown an awareness of the liberties he frequently took in interpreting Marxian texts; and, while Lenin was wrong to claim his analyses as being the only true development of Marxism, he was frequently justified in declaring that his adversaries had traduced Marx's intentions.[205] Each debate has to be examined on its merits, but the main point is that Marxism had never been a complete, unambiguous and coherent system of thought. The extraordinary feature of Lenin's treatment was its near-metaphysical lack of doubt in Marx and Engels; no prominent Marxist gave so overtly unquestioning a commitment. Despite being a militant atheist, he unembarrassedly composed the following apophthegm: 'Marx's teaching is omnipotent because it is true.'[206]

The words are worth dwelling upon: they are the language of a zealot. They have a lapidary naïveté; their content and rhythm are catechistic. They presume unchallengeability and bring together the realm of power with the realm of ideas. They scoff at those wretches, the infidels, who fail or refuse to see the light and recognise the verities of Marx and Marxism.

Lenin fought for Marx as his 'teacher', but chose carefully where to make a stand. Marxism was under a remarkable intellectual attack by a number of German politicians and academics. Robert Michels, studying political parties, wrote of the 'iron law of oligarchy'. He postulated that democratic regulations in any party could not prevent the domination of the rank-and-file membership by its central leaders; and he asserted that even socialist leaders would become seduced by the attractions of authority and material well-being and would tacitly drop revolutionary objectives. They would undergo *embourgeoisement*. Michels and his fellow German sociologist, Max Weber, in addition considered 'bureaucracy' to be intrinsic to modern industrial cultures. It was consequently utopian for Marxists to think that patterns of government could be drastically transformed by political revolution.[207] Michels and Weber were impugning the practices and objectives of the German Social-Democratic Party. In reply, Kautsky did not deny that hierarchical administrations and established leaderships were crucial for effective large organisations; but he felt that processes of election and consultation would curb abuses.[208] Rosa Luxemburg was less complacent. She stressed that Marx's optimism was realistic only if the 'party masses' impeded the inclination of their leaders towards compromise with the *status quo* in Germany.[209] Lenin held back from the fray. Perhaps this was just another pragmatic decision; his instinct was always to avoid appearing embattled or apologetic.[210] But a thinker's quality is revealed as much by his silences as by his statements; and Lenin's failure to address the pertinent questions raised by Michels and Weber damages his reputation as a political theorist even for his own epoch.

His efforts on Marx's behalf in the last few years before the First World War were mainly in the field of economics. He stood by the Marxian theory of 'immiseration'. Quite what Marx meant with his ideas on the inevitability of mass impoverishment is still disputed. Some have claimed he thought that, under capitalism, workers would become ever poorer in absolute terms. This was difficult to square with the empirical data on wage rises in many countries.[211] Lenin, following Kautsky and several other Marxist theorists, regarded him as having predicted only that the working class would become 'relatively' impoverished. Subsequent macroeconomic statistics, according to Lenin, had confirmed the forecast: the proportion of Germany's wealth in the hands of workers fell as year succeeded year, and an average labourer's wage did not increase as fast as an average employer's profits.[212] But the comment presumably seemed to Lenin, on reflection, too much like a retreat; and he added that German wages were not rising in real value and that inflation was soaring more steeply.[213] This could have constituted a return to the first version of Marx's immiseration theory; but Lenin refrained from proposing the trend as a general norm. He simply made his remark and moved on.

Marx exhilarated him, and those studies of Lenin which entirely deny his Marxist commitment are profoundly erroneous. But he was also excited by the latest technological developments. (Curiously, he had not paid them much heed before 1905.) He read with enthusiasm that a certain William Ramsey had invented a process for extracting gas from coal.[214] Electricity, too, fascinated Lenin. Living in an age when even well-appointed factories were dirty and dangerous, and when the drudgery of housework was considerable, he sensed that electrical power could do inestimable good in easing the burdens of day-to-day existence and in improving standards of hygiene.

Mankind, he felt, stood at the dawn of an era. Yet he assumed that the popular benefits of electricity, even in advanced industrial countries, would not become available until after a socialist revolution.[215] Lenin did not foresee the mass purchases of electrical goods under capitalism. If he proved to be a poor prophet, however, we must remember that the marketing of Hoover vacuum cleaners was in its infancy at his time of writing. His attitude to electricity was in any case paralleled by his notions about other 'bourgeois' discoveries and trends. The time-and-motion specialist F. W. Taylor was greatly in vogue before the First World War, with followers in Russia as well as in the more economically-developed countries. Lenin's reaction to Taylor's 'scientific management' was negative (and it was only after the Bolsheviks had seized power in the October Revolution that he started to perceive Taylorism's advantages).[216] Taylor, he asserted, simply wished to strengthen capitalist exploitation. Ignore fashion and have faith, have socialist faith: these were Lenin's guidelines.

He and Nadezhda Krupskaya, like most better-off revolutionaries from Russia, lived a life that was middle-class in style. Many commentators have dealt severely with the paradox. How could a man who talked so fervently about the coming of a classless society continue to enjoy such an existence? In photographs, Lenin was always neatly dressed. It was almost *de rigueur* for Marxist leaders from Russia to wear three-piece suits, and knee-length overcoats were usual on cold days. Homburg hats were typical. While pursuing revolutionary politics, Lenin did not aspire to what might be called a 'counter-culture'; and in any case it made sense, if he wanted to avoid deportation as a politically undesirable foreigner, to appear as conventional and respectable as he could.

Furthermore, a middle-class ambience covered a range of living conditions. For most of his career before the February Revolution of 1917, Lenin had to live in rented rooms, and fairly cheap rented rooms at that. Royalties from his books, his Central Committee stipend and emergency subsidies from his mother meant that he would never starve.[217] He seems never to have mastered the typewriter. Perhaps this was yet another sign of his social background: in that epoch, typing attracted even worse pay and lower prestige than today. Lenin wrote out his articles in longhand, and he must have written very fast if the quantity of published output, notes, drafts and excerpts copied from library books is any guide. But the final typing was done by professionals. The young Bolshevik, V. A. Karpinski was among these and, in later years, gratefully recalled how Lenin always insisted upon paying him at the going rate. Karpinski knew that Lenin, as an economist, divided the Russian peasantry into poor peasants, middle peasants and kulaks. Lenin, according to Karpinski's only half-joking memoir, operated like a middle peasant. He hired the labour of others but did not exploit them.[218] Not being a 'poor peasant' who had to toil away over a ramshackle Cyrillic typewriter, Lenin nevertheless was not a wealthy kulak-*littérateur* like Georgi Plekhanov.

Yet Lenin also expected value for money. Everyone from the typist to the print-worker learnt that he insisted on a speedy, efficient job. His letters bulged with detailed instructions about textual alterations.[219] Lenin lived in an age when typesetting and copy-editing was done to a much higher standard than is characteristic today; and since he was dealing with small publishing firms run by fellow revolutionaries he could exert some control over the process of publication. He justifiably thought of himself as a leading Marxist political writer. Asked to supply a list of such authors, he mentioned G. E. Zinoviev, L. B. Kamenev, V. V. Vorovski and a certain 'V. Ilin': his own *nom de plume* for his legally-published books.[220] Little things like his answer say much about him. Nobody who did not already know would have guessed that his list contained only Bolsheviks. Ever the politician.

2 Storms Before the Storm: 1912–1914

KRAKOW

Residence in Switzerland and France was endured stoically by Russian émigrés. They had left their motherland involuntarily; and most of them regarded Geneva, Berne and Zurich as the least hateful of alternative bases. At first glance it is mystifying that they did not gravitate towards citadels of Europe's contemporary avant-garde, such as Vienna. Why did they, in the main, avoid lengthy stays in centres of economic power such as London or Berlin? The main reason was that Switzerland's constitution provided an unusual degree of civic tolerance. Russian revolutionaries attracted little attention from the authorities. The snowy winters were bittersweetly reminiscent of home. The mountains were strange, certainly, to inhabitants of the Russian empire unless they happened to come from the Caucasus. Yet all the émigrés, whatever their geographical origins, adored the Alps. Hill-walking was as popular among them as among Swiss townsfolk – in those days it was only a few aristocratic Britons who were mountaineering enthusiasts. Swiss orderliness could grate upon the sensibilities of Russians (although this was never Lenin's reaction!), but in general earned its due esteem. The efficiency of libraries and postal services was a godsend to these bibliophile rebels. Russian socialists as Second International members also found the country well situated for communications with Central, Western and Southern Europe. A large Russian community inhabited Switzerland. Before the First World War, 10,000 of Nikolai II's subjects lived there. They even had their own bookshops, restaurants and printing presses.

There was no joy for Lenin in deciding, in June 1912, to move to Austria-Hungary. He had spent several months of the previous year in France, teaching at the party school at Longjumeau and editing *Workers' Newspaper* and setting up his notorious Committee of the Foreign Organisation in Paris.[1] In March 1912 he still intended to remain in France for the entire summer; the plan was to leave the capital, where accommodation prices were high, and move to its 'more pleasant and peaceful' environs in the small town of Fontenay.[2] By May he had changed his mind, getting Krupskaya to make enquiries about leaving France and about taking her mother with them. But instead of moving back to Switzerland, Lenin and she were planning to relocate the base of their operations in Galicia, the Habsburg-ruled territory of historic Poland. Enquiries were made about prices and passport regulations, and about the intensity of the local police's interest in Russian revolutionaries.[3]

And yet Lenin and Krupskaya were still considering spending summer 1912 in Geneva prior to any firm decision on their long-term residence.[4] Not even the police shooting of 170 striking workers in the Lena goldfields in Siberia in April, and the surge of demonstrations against the government, had tempted him into moving eastward more quickly. And yet by the latter half of June they were in Galicia.[5] The decision was formally explained by Lenin as being motivated by a desire to study the 'local agrarian conditions' and to learn the Polish language.[6] This pretence was needed to satisfy the authorities in the Galician capital of Krakow. A more plausible explanation came in a letter to the writer Maksim Gorki. Lenin affirmed that Krakow afforded faster communications with St Petersburg. It was possible to receive Russian newspapers within three days, and easier to contribute to and collaborate with the editors of the legal Bolshevik press.[7] Krupskaya was to recall that Lenin was drawn to Galicia especially by his wish to influence the affairs of the factional daily newspaper, *Pravda*, which had at last been issued in the capital on 22 April 1912 under N. G. Poletaev's aegis.[8] An announcement that a daily would be appearing had been made by the St Petersburg Bolsheviks on 15 January (while the Prague Conference was taking place);[9] and the Prague delegates had supported schemes for an intensification of efforts in the legal press.[10] Lenin's belatedness in moving from Paris could well have been a further sign of his disapproval of the project. Once established, however, *Pravda* had to be controlled! Perhaps, too, police agents were right that Lenin was already looking forward to the working of the Fourth State Duma.[11] The Third Duma's natural time-span ran out in June 1912, and elections were arranged for the Fourth's convocation by November. Again, it was easier to co-operate with Bolshevik Duma deputies from Krakow than from Geneva or Paris.

But Lenin may have had little choice. The Prague Conference had ordered that increased emphasis and resources be devoted to party activity in Russia. Lenin's letter to Gorki specified that the Central Committee subsequently set up a Foreign Bureau in Galicia,[12] and this could signify that he had moved under some pressure. Be that as it may, Lenin came to feel glad about the transfer. The opportunity for mountain-walking in the Tatras; the similarities of everyday life to conditions in the Russian empire; the physical separation from the atmosphere of internecine factional struggle in France and Switzerland, which took its toll on Lenin despite his relish for it; and the greater chances for Russia-based Bolsheviks to travel out to meet him: all these factors contributed to a feeling that the Galician sojourn was only 'a semi-emigration'.[13]

He also developed a casualness about the émigré central press, which was remarkable for a politician who had been perpetually involved in campaigns to dominate it. *Workers' Newspaper* was issued only twice in 1912; publication of *Social Democrat* continued, but less frequently than before. Only three issues appeared in 1913. Lenin continued to contribute; but the main work was entrusted to L. B. Kamenev in Paris.[14] In the year before moving to Galicia Lenin was contributing fewer articles to the *Workers' Newspaper* and *Social-Democrat* than to the Russia-based newspaper *The Star* and the new periodical *Enlightenment*.[15] Nor were he and other émigré Bolsheviks alone in re-orientating their literary endeavours. The Mensheviks took more drastic action when Fyodor Dan risked returning not merely to a cross-border zone like Galicia, but to Russia proper. On 31 December 1912 he arrived in St Petersburg, amazed that the informal assurances from the authorities about his safety had been honoured.[16] Dan assumed the editorial direction of *Luch*. Martov joined him ten months later, after a semi-amnesty for political offenders had been announced as part of the official celebrations of the Romanov dynasty's tercentenary.[17] The motivations of the Ministry of Internal Affairs are uncertain; but perhaps the fact that no Bolshevik had up to then been similarly treated indicates that the Okhrana wanted to boost the more moderate forces of Marxism in an attempt to check the growing radicalism of the workers' movement. Lenin, astounded that Dan had even managed to visit Menshevik deputies in the State Duma, confessed his bafflement about the 'game' being played by the authorities.[18]

The Zinovievs accompanied Lenin and Krupskaya to Krakow, and both couples quickly found apartments in the city. Finance and predilection drew them quickly to the countryside. In March 1913,

Lenin opted for a house near the summer resort village of Zakopane, which lay close by the town railway station of Poronin and a hundred kilometres from Krakow.[19] To maintain contact with Krakow and the outside world, Lenin walked twice daily to the post office in nearby Bialy Dunajec.[20] In October 1913, after a delightful summer which allowed him to travel abroad with Krupskaya as well as to enjoy the peace of the Polish countryside, he moved back to Krakow.[21]

The Bolsheviks were not the only anti-Romanov revolutionaries in the area. Polish socialists too appreciated the convenience of the Krakow region for the preparation of subversive activities across the frontier. Not only the Social-Democracy of the Kingdom of Poland and Lithuania but also the Polish Socialist Party had representatives there, and they made a lively contribution to open political debates in Krakow. The Polish Socialist Party was as internally divided as the Social-Democracy of the Kingdom of Poland and Lithuania. Josef Pilsudski, the future vanquisher of the Red Army in the Soviet–Polish war in 1920 and dominant Polish politician in the inter-war period, led a faction which controlled the party's Combat Organisation. He had taken a group of activists into the Russian empire in 1908 and robbed a train carrying 200,000 roubles.[22] Pilsudski was already more nationalist than socialist, and Lenin preferred to talk mainly to the left-wing elements who had left the Polish Socialist Party to form the PPS-Lewica. Yet the two men knew about each other in Galicia: they often drank coffee in the same café. Nevertheless they scrupulously avoided conversing even when their elbows brushed against each other. That their private contacts were closer is probable, since Zinoviev subsequently suggested that Pilsudski's men helped the Bolsheviks with their security precautions. In addition, Pilsudski had been sentenced to exile in connection with the 1886 conspiracy of Lenin's elder brother Aleksandr to assassinate the Russian emperor. The past, as well as the present, linked them together.[23]

Thus the émigré Bolshevik leadership was not the exclusive source of concern for the Romanovs in Galicia. Indeed, it was Pilsudski, not Lenin, whose extradition was requested by the St Petersburg authorities.[24] It was Pilsudski's military units which exercised in the streets and fields around Zakopane;[25] and Lenin, always being alert to the practical requirements of armed revolution, cannot have failed to have been impressed by Pilsudski's project to twin revolutionism with nationalism. It is not too fanciful to suppose that the Galician sojourn greatly reinforced Lenin's feeling that Russian social-democrats should take the 'national question' in the Romanov empire more seriously.

Lenin, however, did not confine himself to Galicia. Trips were also made to countries to the West. He accepted an invitation to Leipzig to give a lecture in April 1913;[26] and in June he accompanied Krupskaya on a longer trip to Berne in Switzerland in search of medical treatment for her worsening thyroid problem. Doctor Kocher had been recommended by the Krakow social-democrat and physician S. O. Bagocki.[27] Lenin took a dislike to Kocher, calling him capricious in his arrangements.[28] After Krupskaya's operation, which was only a temporary success, the couple returned to Galicia in late July. Life was hectic but pleasurable. The elections to the Fourth State Duma had resulted in victory for six Bolsheviks and were marred, in Lenin's view, only by the fact that seven Mensheviks also were elected. Visits to Galicia by Bolshevik Duma deputies occurred sporadically through 1913, and on two occasions these coincided with Central Committee meetings in Krakow and Poronin.[29] Lenin offered plenty of advice to the deputies.[30] As for the Central Committee, meetings took place more often than in the past: seven took place between November 1912 and the end of 1913. All occurred in Galicia,[31] and Lenin, naturally, played a prominent role. Letters to and from Galicia rose in number.[32] *Pravda* and the Duma deputies were the addressees most frequently contacted, but communication was kept up also with many other Bolshevik supporters in the Romanov lands. Krupskaya's address-book was being rapidly filled and by mid-1914 it contained 271 names of contacts in the Russian empire, and included Bolsheviks for nearly every province of the Romanov empire.[33]

And yet, for all its advantages over Switzerland, Galicia was not wholly favourable for international political organisation. Krupskaya soon complained that the postal service to Russia was 'inconvenient'; and she sometimes resorted to sending bundles of mail to Bolsheviks in Berlin for further dispatch. She intimated that Vladimir Ilich, who expected to travel to Berlin in January 1914, would refund the expenditure.[34] The flow of news, moreover, between non-metropolitan towns in Russia and Galicia was intermittent. Lenin railed at those who would not write regularly.[35]

Revolutionaries in the Russian political underground, harassed by a life on the run from the Okhrana, responded frostily to his imprecations. The Central Committee distributed its members between a Russian Bureau and a Foreign Bureau. The Foreign Bureau, since only Lenin and Zinoviev were based in the emigration, sounded grander than it really was; and the joint sessions of the émigrés and the Russian undergrounders prevented Lenin from claiming to speak in the name of all Bolsheviks without consultation.[36] Russia-based correspondents felt that he had a cheek to accuse them of failing to write and his own assiduity was called into question.[37] He was also deemed to be insufficiently energetic in supplying the drafts of official party statements (for example, about the trade unions) which were requested from St Petersburg by the Duma deputies and others.[38] His factitiousness, not surprisingly, still irked the undergrounders. With the exception of Malinovski, the Bolshevik Duma deputies rejected his calls for a clean split from the Menshevik deputies; they were willing to sit in the Duma under the chairmanship of Menshevik N. S. Chkheidze[39] (and Malinovski wanted a split only because the Okhrana wanted it). Most of the Bolshevik Duma deputies even wanted a merger of Bolshevik *Pravda* and Menshevik *Luch*.[40] The editors of *Pravda* too proved capable of standing up to Lenin. References to 'Liquidators' were sometimes cut from his articles,[41] and M. S. Olminski directly reproved him for polemical excesses.[42] Lenin muttered that *Pravda* was a 'sleepy old spinster'.[43] The editors were undeterred; 47 out of 331 submitted articles were turned down before the First World War.[44]

Without ever becoming dominant, on the other hand, Lenin's influence grew stronger. The numbers can be turned upside down: *Pravda* accepted as many as 284 submitted articles out of 331.[45] In addition, the *Pravda–Luch* merger did not take place; and, if *Pravda*'s editors were irritated when he did not supply them with commissioned articles, he cannot have been entirely a *persona non grata* in the first instance. Even his refusal to follow the precedent of Dan and Martov by returning to Russia had its advantages. Central Committee meetings might be held in his Galician house; and, in his domestic surroundings and in face-to-face meetings, he was a match for most opponents. As the host, he had a psychological edge. Unsophisticated undergrounders, some of them never having been abroad before, were not in the best position to resist being browbeaten.

And Lenin made the most of his advantages. The Prague Conference had empowered the Central Committee to co-opt new members; and among those who first gained membership in this way was Iosif Stalin, who was regarded by Lenin as 'the marvellous Georgian' and who allied himself with Lenin in the debate on the 'national question'.[46] In autumn 1912, Stalin was chosen by a Central Committee meeting to go to St Petersburg and take charge of *Pravda*.[47] *Pravda*'s rising readership figures made the Central Committee, and especially Lenin, keen to guide its editorial policies. *Workers' Newspaper*, accordingly, was closed down in August 1912.[48] Yet Stalin declined to be as aggressive towards the Mensheviks as Lenin desired. Not for the last time, Lenin acted to correct Stalin's line. A Central Committee meeting delivered an implicit rebuke to Stalin and sent yet another of its co-opted members, Yakov Mikhailovich Sverdlov, to join Stalin as co-editor.[49]

Unfortunately for them as well as for Lenin, both Sverdlov and Stalin were arrested in February 1913, but their replacement as editor, Miron Chernomazov, was greatly to Lenin's liking. Taking over in May 1913, Chernomazov took exactly the polemical posture traditionally demanded by Lenin; and fifty articles by Lenin appeared in the initial two months of his editorship.[50] Chernomazov, however, was a police agent, his instructions being not only to stir up inter-factional enmity but also to publish overtly anti-régime material which would give a pretext for the authorities to shut down the newspaper. *Pravda*'s circulation dropped; the stress on factionalism proved to be unpopular among workers who had never accepted the need for two separate Marxist parties and who had always wanted a less theoretical and more popular style and format for the newspaper;[51] and the shut-downs of production were hardly designed to retain such readers as the newspaper had already attracted.

In the Duma fraction, Bolsheviks such as M. K. Muranov and G. I. Petrovski held out for months against the demand by Lenin and their fellow deputy (and Okhrana agent) Malinovski for a split with the Mensheviks. At Poronin in September 1913, ten months after taking their seats in the Duma, they finally acceded to his arguments:[52] in October, Bolshevik and Menshevik deputies sat apart. Petrovski and Muranov possibly looked at the growing turbulence in the form of workers' strikes and demonstrations, and judged that the Mensheviks were displaying insufficient revolutionary zeal. The Menshevik daily, *Luch*, staffed by Liquidators among others, was *Pravda*'s chief Marxist rival newspaper and tended to discourage strikes.[53] The police had crushed an attempt to establish a daily which would follow a more orthodox Menshevik line. But the persuasiveness of Lenin, and indeed of Malinovski who worked alongside them, must also have contributed to the Bolshevik deputies' eventual decision to break with their Menshevik counterparts.

The year 1913 had done much to compensate for the difficulties of 1912. Lenin had exerted considerable authority in Central Committee, in the Bolshevik Duma fraction and in *Pravda*. Yet his impact was small outside these central party bodies. Strikes increased. The Lena shootings had engendered a lasting bitterness. Trade union boards lost an ever greater number of Mensheviks;[54] and *Luch*'s allegations about 'playing at strikes' evoked an effusion of sarcasm from Lenin.[55] He boasted in public about the election of Bolsheviks to the union boards. But he coupled this with a private acknowledgement that the unions exerted scant influence on the labour movement.[56] No evidence has emerged, to this day, that the strikes were mainly union-led; outbreaks of industrial conflict were sporadic and localised. Furthermore, the illegal party apparatus was in no better shape than before 1912. The Russian Bureau, as chosen after the Prague Conference, was in prison or exile except for Malinovski.[57] Local Bolshevik bodies experienced no general renaissance. Acting as Central Committee secretary, Krupskaya received doleful messages from the Russian empire.[58] And, even though *Pravda*'s print-run on the occasion of its second anniversary momentarily reached 130,000 copies, the largest-selling popular paper for the working man and woman remained the somewhat scurrilous and largely unpolitical *Gazeta-Kopeika*. The working class's antagonism towards the monarchy, the police and the employers was intense; but the Okhrana was efficient. The Bolsheviks had no answer to the police's interventions.

THE 'NATIONAL QUESTION'

Lenin, despite frequent invitations from *Pravda*, wrote next to nothing about the trade unions; there was to be no equivalent of *What Is To be Done?* for the legal labour movement. His energies in the realm of theory, between the Prague Conference and mid-1914, were spent on the so-called national question. In the first half of 1913 he drafted 'theses' which were incorporated in a resolution of a Central Committee meeting in Poronin in September. His most controversial recommendation related to the future of the Russian empire. He went further than any Russian Social-Democratic Labour Party leader in taking account of the national aspirations of non-Russians, and demanded that 'the nations oppressed by the tsarist monarchy' should be granted 'the right of self-determination, i.e. of secession'.[59]

Socialists in the Romanov lands had typically hoped to maintain a multi-national state once the monarchy had been removed. Lenin the centralist and internationalist *par excellence* agreed, but argued that tactical subtlety was required. He condemned 'Great Russian' chauvinism and castigated Romanov absolutism as 'the most reactionary and barbaric state system in Europe and in Asia'. The monarchy's overthrow should be followed by a declaration of educational and cultural equality for all nationalities; and 'broad regional autonomy and completely democratic local self-government' should be realised. These concessions, he hoped, would dispel distrust of the Russians among the non-Russian nationalities and would actually diminish the likelihood of secessionist movements. Lenin, moreover, did not want the 'right of secession' to be confused with the 'wisdom of secession'. As a socialist internationalist, he aimed to keep workers together in mass organisations regardless of national origin. He raged against the bourgeoisie for using nationalism as a means of deflecting the working class from an appreciation of its best interests; and he suggested that any particular decision on secession should be assessed 'from the viewpoint of the interests of societal development as a whole and the interests of the class struggle of the proletariat for socialism'.[60] He did not promise to grant national independence even if a native popular movement called for it. The Central Committee resolution, despite broaching the topic of secession, was therefore not a little vague and gave few political hostages to fortune.[61]

In the Russian Social-Democratic Labour Party, it had been the Jewish Bund which had most persistently highlighted the national question; but, since Jews did not inhabit a territory where they were the demographic majority and where they could form a nation state, the Bundists did not aspire to secession for Jewish people. Instead they called for 'national–cultural autonomy' within a multi-national state. The August 1912 gathering of non-Bolshevik factions convoked by Trotski had approved this very slogan.[62]

The concept of national–cultural autonomy had been deeply influenced by Austrian Marxists, who lived in the other great empire on the European continent: Austria-Hungary. The pioneering work, *The National Question and Social-Democracy*, had been written by Otto Bauer and published in Vienna in 1907.[63] Other Marxists, including Lenin, had stated their preferences in policy without much theoretical investigation of the definition and conditions of nationhood. Bauer filled the lacuna. His book attacked the almost universal conventional notion that modern nations had been centuries-old phenomena embracing whole peoples. He stressed that a number of contingent factors could make and unmake nations: wars and conquest; geographical dispersal; alien cultural penetration. He argued, too, that until recently it had only been the upper echelons of any society which had a sense of their nationality; and that the peasantry in particular was characteristically without true national feeling. For Bauer (as for some later non-Marxist theorists), it was industrialisation and the establishment of a national educational system which drew a people into a common basic sense of nationhood. As a Marxist, he anticipated a time when national differences counted for nothing in human relationships. But his contention was that, for years ahead, social-democrats would have to take account of nationalism as an important political factor. The development of a capitalist economy and culture was bound to strengthen national feelings.[64]

Lenin read Bauer's book immediately after its appearance, but made no open comment on it for six years.[65] He came back to the national question in 1912–13, and vehemently attacked the Austrian Marxists. This should not be allowed to disguise how much had been learned by Lenin from Bauer, especially on the contingent nature of nationhood. Lenin also started to emphasise, as he had not done before reading the work of Bauer (as well as of Karl Kautsky), that nationalism would neither disappear for a lengthy epoch nor rule out the possibility of economic and cultural advance for newly-independent nations.[66]

Yet Lenin, as was his wont, concentrated on the points of disagreement between himself and Bauer. *The National Question and Social-Democracy*, while allowing for national independence as a goal for several peoples, emphasised the practical impediments in areas such as the Habsburg empire where the national groups were territorially intermingled in bewildering complexity. No independent territory for an individual nation was feasible without including unwilling minorities from other nations on the same territory. Bauer recommended that the old empire, instead of being broken up into separate chunks, should be transformed into a socialist federation; and he wanted each national group in the federation to have elective, representative institutions to protect its 'extra-territorial national autonomy'.[67] The Jewish Bund in the Russian Social-Democratic

Labour Party had always leant in this direction and successfully advocated it in Vienna in August 1912.[68] The Polish social-democrats under Jogiches and Luxemburg added an economic dimension to the feeling that multinational states should be maintained. Luxemburg asserted that Poland's industrial development was tied into relations of production and commerce which would be disrupted without access to foreign capital and foreign markets; and that national independence would be industrially retrogressive and damage the interests of the Polish working class.[69] Bauer did not have Jogiches's absolute hostility to national independence movements in Europe; but that did not stop Lenin from banding them together in his polemics against them.[70]

Lenin's main criticism was that the respective proposals of both Bauer and the non-Bolshevik factions at Trotski's Vienna gathering in August 1912 were inherently bureaucratic, inefficient and anti-centralist. They would, he argued, increase rather than diminish the divisions in the international proletariat. The counter-scheme sketched in Lenin's theses of 1913 rejected extra-territorial proposals for the national question and insisted that nationally-discrete territories at local level were the best assurance that multinational states would not break up into fragments.[71]

The replies of Lenin's opponents have fallen into undeserved neglect. Nor was it only the Bundists and the Polish social-democrats who prolonged the dispute. Both the outstanding Georgian Menshevik leader and theorist Noi Zhordania and Trotski's sympathiser S. Semkovski declared that Lenin had under-estimated the complexity of the problems highlighted by Bauer. Ethnic intermingling was as intense in the Romanov as in the Habsburg empire, and Lenin was unjustified in portraying Bauer as having been overly influenced by the peculiar demographic features of the Habsburg lands. Zhordania confined his comments mainly to the Transcaucasus: Georgians, Azeris and Armenians lived throughout its regions; and Armenians were supposedly not even a majority in historic Armenia.[72] In the Ukraine, as Semkovski added, there were Jews, Kalmyks, Tartars, Greeks and Russians as well as Ukrainians.[73] The various national groups had their rivalries, even hatreds. Lenin had written breezily about protection of the minorities; but, apart from equality of language rights, he had been extremely unspecific. Lenin treated Semkovski and Zhordania with vituperation concerning their extra-territorial ideas; but he presented no defence against their objections to his own theses. His nonchalance is all the more remarkable in view of his residence in Galicia, where there was a striking demographic mixture of Poles, Jews, Ukrainians and Germans. His silence was perhaps a pragmatic device; a response to Zhordania and Semkovski would only have drawn further attention to his argument's weak spots. But it was hardly an adequate intellectual approach.

Lenin in power was to appreciate the need to go beyond dealing with the national question through autonomous nationally-based territorial units. For example, Jews in the Ukraine and Armenians in Georgia had never lived a life so free from tension as in the 1920s. The Soviet central government took steps to ensure that Ukrainian and Georgian national dominance in the Ukraine and Georgia did not impinge on the cultural freedoms of other nationalities. Nevertheless, even when we recognise that Stalin in the 1930s exacerbated all the country's problems over the national question, the Nagorno–Karabakh dispute which erupted in 1988 indicates that failure to protect the interests of minority groups can have explosive consequences.[74]

At all events Zhordania, rightly impugned Lenin in 1913 for trying to terminate debate before discussions had run their course.[75] Lenin was, in fact, more forthcoming in the other half of the dispute: in his polemic against Luxemburg and Jogiches. Possibly he found these Poles hard to dismiss so abruptly because they were not Mensheviks or Trotskyists. Moreover, he knew that most leading Bolshevik theorists sympathised with Luxemburg's analysis.[76] Some were Russian neophytes like Nikolai Bukharin and Georgi Pyatakov; others were non-Russians such as the Georgian Filip Makharadze and the Jewish Evgeniya Bosh.[77] Lenin could not afford not to engage them in an exchange of opinions. He continued to assert that there might be occasions when secession would have to be refused on the grounds of harming the working class of a given nation.[78] He still refused to advocate national independence as a general rule.[79] A letter to Kamenev in 1913 included the following sentence: 'It is necessary to wage a struggle for truth against the separatists and opportunists from the Bund and from the Liquidators.'[80] Publicly he was less intemperate; but his theses contained the notion that the bourgeoisies of Finland and Poland were pro-tsarist and that liberation would come to the Finnish and Polish proletariats only through alliance with the Russian proletariat.[81] He made a similar argument about the Ukraine in the November–December 1913 issue of *Enlightenment*.[82] He avoided repeatedly both outright support for and outright opposition to Finnish, Polish and Ukrainian independence. A myriad of unpredictable factors, he affirmed, would have to be taken into account.[83]

Even so, he never ceased to feel that retention of all the Romanov nations within a multinational political unit might be impossible. He asserted, against Luxemburg, that Poland and Finland were notably suitable cases for independence since they were the 'most cultured and most separate' entities in the Russian empire.[84] Alone of leading Bolshevik theorists, Stalin came to Lenin's assistance before the 1914–1918 war.[85] Indeed, Stalin provided easily the most comprehensive Bolshevik analysis of the national question. Lenin supplied mainly fragmented materials, whereas Stalin leaned heavily on Kautsky and produced definitions, bibliographical surveys and arguments aplenty.[86] And yet even Stalin, writing in *Enlightenment* from March 1913 onwards, was more eager to excoriate the Bund than to argue the positive case for Lenin's policy. The right of secession as a right appeared in Stalin's article, but only fitfully.[87]

But it was close enough to Lenin's views for Lenin to be enormously grateful.[88] Stalin had given useful theoretical assistance, and his lengthy pieces in *Enlightenment* relieved Lenin of the necessity to work up his own fragments into a sustained piece of work. Not that these fragments are without interest. He suggested, for example (and here he, too, followed Kautsky), that the nation state was the normal vehicle for capitalist economic development.[89] This was hard to reconcile with the industrial success of the United States of America with its multi-ethnic immigrant population. But Lenin glossed over the difficulty.[90] Secondly, Lenin firmly rejected federalism in all its guises. This should be noted in contrast with his later practice, after coming to power, when he felt compelled to conclude that the country was ungovernable without federal administrative arrangements.[91] And, thirdly, he proposed that the ultimate objective for Marxists was not merely a *rapprochement* of the nationalities, but a 'fusion' which would permanently eradicate national differences and consciousness.[92] Under Stalin in the 1930s this objective became, as Lenin had never intended, a pretext for a programme of 'Russification'; nor did the tendency entirely vanish after Stalin's death. A fourth point, though, is much more to Lenin's credit: after the October Revolution of 1917, Lenin's government confirmed the independence of Poland (which was in any case under German occupation) but also gave it to Finland (which was not). On the other hand, independence was summarily refused to the Ukraine.

The Red forces sent out from Russia had no orders to conduct a Ukrainian plebiscite.[93]

SCANDALS

Lenin none the less continued to exude exceptional self-confidence. Nor did he worry at all about his own motives and comportment. He acquired his reputation as a polemicist in the 1890s and, upon emigrating, became notorious for unfairly bending the party's rules in his favour. He always complained when his opponents trespassed the slightest regulation of procedure; but this never prevented him from believing that his own acts of trespass were necessitated by a higher revolutionary duty.

Outside politics he observed contemporary public propriety; but he did not insist on these personal standards among his associates. An early example was the so-called Bauman affair. N. E. Bauman was a social-democratic activist exiled to Vyatka province in 1899, where he had an affair with the wife of a fellow revolutionary. The unfortunate woman became pregnant. So far from showing sympathy or even common tactfulness, Bauman openly mocked her; and a cartoon ridiculing her plight was circulated among comrades. In despair she hanged herself. Her suicide note drew attention to the need to insist on high standards of behaviour, on a social level, among revolutionaries whose party wished to transform the life of society. The Bauman affair was adjudicated by the *Iskra* board at the instigation of the cuckolded comrade in early 1903. To his colleague's disgust, Lenin refused to countenance the party's right to interfere and certainly not to discipline Bauman for bringing disfavour upon Russian Marxists.[94] He argued that the party's task was to make revolution against the Romanov monarchy and to vet the morality of comrades only when and in so far as their actions affected the implementation of the task. He welcomed Bauman enthusiastically as a future Bolshevik, using his services as a troublemaker from the floor at the Second Party Congress.[95] Bauman's death in 1905 inspired Lenin to write a fulsome obituary dedicated to 'the eternal memory of a fighter in the ranks of Russian social-democracy'.[96]

The choice of an undesirable personage such as Bauman as not only an acceptable but even a respected associate boded ill for the behaviour of Bolsheviks when (as, admittedly, hardly seemed very likely before the First World War) they took power in Russia. Doubts continued to arise about Lenin's judgement of individuals; and his mode of behaviour tacitly encouraged others to act in a similar manner. The disputative tricks of Grigori Zinoviev and P. A. Krasikov were sharpened, even if not originally learned, at the feet of a master polemicist. Stalin, too, elaborated such a skill.

Lenin did not have our retrospective vantage point and could not anticipate the full range of horrors breeding in the mind of Stalin. Yet he can surely be faulted for a persistent blindness to the unpleasant characteristics of his associates. It was only as he lay dying, in 1922–23, that he acquired a recognition of Stalin's 'crudity'. For years, Lenin had in any case spoken warmly of the efficiency of the guillotine in the French Revolution.[97] He perceived in his boisterous comrades the incarnation of the 'proletarian' ruthlessness vital to the making of a revolution. This was part and parcel of his support for the armed robberies conducted by Bolsheviks in the Russian empire in 1906–9 as well as his condoning of the marriage of Bolsheviks A. M. Andrikanis and V. K. Taratuta to rich heiresses, in quest of their heirlooms.[98] Practical activists and practical results were Lenin's objectives: the criteria for assessing the means to these ends were prudential, not moral for him. In 1914, furthermore, it became abundantly clear that Lenin's prudence could not be taken for granted; and it was not Stalin but a more pressing evil, R. V. Malinovski, who demonstrated this. Malinovski, Central Committee member and Bolshevik spokesman in the State Duma, vanished from St Petersburg in mid-May.[99] The intensifying rumours that he was an Okhrana informer were confirmed for everyone but Lenin.

Lenin had spurned them as a slur on Malinovski and an attempt to sow dissension among Bolsheviks loyal to him. This was psychologically easier to do when it was the Mensheviks who castigated the Duma deputy. But in 1912 the young Bolshevik theorist Nikolai Bukharin arrived in Krakow.[100] Bukharin plainly meant Lenin well, and Lenin was pleased to welcome a comrade who regarded himself as a 'pupil'; but Bukharin was convinced that the stories about Malinovski and his undercover role for the Okhrana were accurate.

The business of unmasking a police spy was never a matter of arithmetical precision. It proceeded by calculations of logarithmic probability. Miron Chernomazov was eventually fired from Pravda in February 1914 on evidence which was far from being conclusive.[101] He had not been caught talking to police contacts or receiving police money or instructions; he was rumbled because his outrageous behaviour had repeatedly given the Ministry of Internal Affairs an excuse to close down Pravda. The Okhrana, which advised him on tactics, had overplayed its hand. Malinovski, however, was more cautious and the police were more circumspect in their handling of him; he was not asked to fulfil the role of a cantankerous hothead. Yet the circumstantial data against him was pretty strong. He was better off than his Duma stipend permitted; he enthusiastically backed Lenin's schismatic schemes among Bolsheviks even in that first year after the Prague Conference when other pro-Lenin Bolshevik leaders, such as Stalin, were loathe to endorse them without qualification; and arrests of comrades were made which were only explicable either by boundless ill-luck or by the existence of a highly-placed police agent: nobody seriously suspected Lenin, Zinoviev or Kamenev. Malinovski was one of the very few others who was in a position to know the secrets of the faction's inner sanctum.[102] Bukharin gamely went over the details with Lenin in Krakow; and he sent letters corroborating the accusations. But Lenin intransigently refused to accept the case.[103]

Even when Malinovski absconded in 1914, Lenin refused to acknowledge reality. It would have been an unpleasant undertaking. Lenin, at the Prague Conference, had prided himself on his anti-police precautions. When two candidates tied for the last place in the elections to the Central Committee, he had suggested that the voters in the second ballot should whisper their choice in his ear; and he had also insisted that the list of the Central Committee's members should not be announced at the Conference.[104] All in vain. Malinovski, as a Central Committee member, conveyed the list without further ado to his secret employers. Again, in 1913, Lenin had written to Kamenev: 'We have suffered some heavy arrests. Koba [Stalin's other main pseudonym] has been taken. I've discussed the measures now required with Malinovski.'[105] To have recognised Malinovski for what he was would have led to a bout of self-reproach which was not congenial to Lenin. Scarcely a major factional decision had been taken without the two of them conferring. Malinovski had been the Bolshevik chief's eyes, ears and even mouth in Russia. Lenin was reluctant to acknowledge that his surrogate had exerted these same organs in the service of the head of the Okhrana.

This blunder of Lenin's was not his worst error. His incorrect prediction of European socialist revolutions in 1917–18 was a misjudgement of epochal significance, compelling him to sign the treaty of Brest–Litovsk. By comparison, the Malinovski affair was petty and ephemeral.[106] Nevertheless a party boss ought to be capable of sounder assessment of character. The problem was not that Malinovski had flattered him but that he had fooled him. Such was Lenin's naïveté that, even after Malinovski had disappeared and left political activity (and therefore left the party in the lurch), he claimed that Malinovski had been the victim of slander. Lenin believed what he wanted to believe. Firing off telegrams to Paris, he tried to challenge the emergent consensus that comrade Malinovski was a police agent. Duma deputy G. I. Petrovski had initially informed Lenin that the 'Liquidators' were sowing the rumours,[107] but Lenin sensed that Petrovski would not long stand by Malinovski. A telegram was sent from Krakow adjuring the Bolshevik Duma fraction not 'to get nervous'; its members were asked to refrain from expelling Malinovski from the fraction. Why? Lenin's reasoning was strictly pragmatic: 'Everything is over with Malinovski, everything's finished. He's finished. Suicide.'[108] By this he meant that Malinovski had killed off his own career and that the party's task was to forget him and get on with other business at hand.

Yet Malinovski had retained credence in his ability to delude Lenin. He craftily fled directly to Galicia and requested a party trial to clear his name. A commission was formed, with Lenin and Zinoviev as members and Jan Hanecki as chairman. There was still no watertight case against Malinovski, who threatened to commit suicide unless acquitted. The commission sat for weeks and had not completed its work when the First World War began. Lenin avoided stern words of censure; he could not bring himself to disbelieve Malinovski even while conceding that, after several exposures of police *provocateurs*, 'everything was possible'.[109] Krupskaya was willing, by 4 June, to condemn Malinovski's 'scoundrelish escapade';[110] but she, too, contended that the Liquidators could 'not adduce a single fact or even anything like a fact' against the Duma delinquent.[111] Lenin, judging by his dismissive remarks about Bukharin's being 'credulous about gossip' in 1916,[112] continued to feel that the entire affair was a provocation concocted by as yet unidentified enemies of Bolshevism; he even wrote to Malinovski, after he fell into German captivity in the war, in pursuit of further collaboration.[113]

DEBATES ON WAR AND IMPERIALISM

If Lenin's choice of associates was widely thought to be faulty, his attitude to imperialism and militarism caused small resentment in his party. There was debate about both subjects in European social-democracy in the two decades before the First World War. Lenin read the literature, but did not essay a major contribution of his own. We can surely sympathise: the demands on his time as leader and theorist were already enormous. Yet the abstention is also significant. Lenin made choices about his priorities in apportioning his time; by writing much about the national question in the Russian empire and little about the inter-imperial questions of colonies and war, he signalled an ordering of importance.[114]

The Bolshevik I. I. Skvortsov-Stepanov produced a lengthy two-part essay on imperialism for the journal *Enlightenment*; but he elaborated few new ideas and, as with other Russian Marxists, drew his inspiration on this issue mostly from theorists elsewhere in Europe.[115] Among these the most prominent were Karl Kautsky, Eduard Bernstein, Rudolf Hilferding, Rosa Luxemburg and Karl Radek. All had been impressed by the scramble for colonies in the late nineteenth century. They noted the support for imperialism from liberals as well as conservatives. Ideologies of 'racial superiority', they observed, were proliferating. They also perceived that the major industrial powers of Europe and North America had reduced virtually the entire remainder of the world to the condition of colonies, or at least semi-colonies, and were locked into rivalries about the existing division of 'the spoils'. Armaments industries were fostered to enhance the national interests of the imperial powers, and militaristic attitudes were widely encouraged. The prospect of war between contending coalitions of the world's imperial powers thrust itself forward.

Only Bernstein, of the above-mentioned writers, felt that that colonial expansion might have a generally progressive effect. The others found his opinion unpalatable. Luxemburg and Radek welcomed the fact that the conquests of colonies created larger economic units (and they opposed socialists like Lenin who were willing to contemplate their break-up in the future under the aegis of European socialist governments). Yet both Luxemburg and Radek condemned Bernstein's perception of capitalist imperialism as anything other than a brutal and brutalising process.[116]

The first to undertake a serious analysis of the causes of imperialism was Karl Kautsky, who summarised his arguments in his book *Socialism and Colonialism*, in 1907. Karl Marx and Friedrich Engels had described capitalism's propensity to produce a greater quantity of industrial goods than the market for such goods could sustain, and they identified this as a reason for recurrent economic crises. Their contention was that the potential for 'consumption' was likely to be insufficient in each capitalist society. Marxologists continue to debate whether Marx and Engels believed that such underconsumptionist factors would be the crucial cause of capitalism's ultimate demise. A neat summary of their thought is impossible since, as on other questions, they appear not to have attempted a definitive answer for themselves. Be that as it may, Kautsky took up the theme of underconsumption with alacrity. Already in 1884, he was writing that contemporary large-scale capitalists experienced a need to find overseas markets for their surplus goods. According to Kautsky, the acquisition of colonies provided a nation's industry and finance with a secure base for such trade, and the underlying cause of modern imperialism and modern militarism was capitalism itself.[117] Thus he attacked the gentler interpretation of the overt 'revisionists' such as Bernstein and the various German right-wing social-democrats who found talk of revolution disturbing.

Kautsky wrote in a period of growing nationalism at home. After the Franco-Prussian war of 1870, there had been no major continental military conflict involving Germany; and Chancellor Bismarck had usually contented himself with diplomatic pressure to achieve his international ends. German political influence in central Europe increased as the position of the Habsburg monarchy in Austria-Hungary became unstable, and the industrial might of Germany grew. There were also moves towards the establishment of a German empire in Africa. Togoland and parts of south-west Africa were conquered in 1884–85. Germany's lateness in becoming an imperial power meant that few countries remained for easy annexation, and Britain's imperial ambition had not faded, as wars against the Boers showed. This stimulated the Prussian-staffed high command and the Rhenish 'iron barons' to build up a navy capable of taking on the British; and Kautsky denounced the encouragement given to militarist values in Germany.[118]

Lenin read Kautsky's articles in *Die Neue Zeit*, but barely added to the literature. A few desultory remarks appeared in the 1890s.[119] The notable exception was his statement in *The Development of Capitalism* that the absence of an overseas empire would not prevent capitalist economic development. Russian capitalists, he suggested, could continue in business even without colonies across the oceans because they already possessed conquests which offered a ready-made market for their industrial products.[120] But in *Iskra*, in 1900, he added that domestic industrial expansion could be enhanced by guaranteed access to trade with China; and that this was the reason for the imperial government's entanglement in the Russo-Chinese crisis in 1900. Lenin was equally in line with Kautsky's argument when he added that Russian armaments manufacturers had an interest in promoting an expansionist foreign policy.[121] A few similar statements came from Lenin before 1904,[122] when Russia went to war against Japan. He attributed the Russian military adventure especially to pressures from industrialists and merchants who, knowing that the Russian working class and peasantry had been impoverished under the impact of industrial growth, needed to seek other outlets for their goods.[123] It was, to that date, his least qualified promotion of underconsumptionist economic theory. Evidently Lenin was no less ambiguous about it than was Marx.

About one thing, he was distinct: victory for Japan was desirable; and a large number of Russian socialists held the same opinion. In Lenin's view, the Russo-Japanese war was a struggle 'between a despotic and backward government and politically free and culturally fast progressing people'.[124] Lenin's judgement on the extent of freedom in Japan may be challenged; but, in the tradition of Marx and Engels, he took sides in a given war by the criterion of the respective political and economic 'progressiveness' of the two belligerent states.[125] Yet he largely overlooked such subjects, until in 1907 he attended the Stuttgart Congress of the Second Socialist International. Kautsky, for the German Social-Democratic Party, wrote passionately about the rise of militarism in Europe; and Lenin, Martov and Rosa Luxemburg wanted to shape a framework for action in the event of a general European war.[126]

Luxemburg, with Lenin's consent, took on the main task of sharpening the draft resolution of August Bebel, the German social-democratic leader.[127] Bebel's formulations were airily vague.[128] Luxemburg's successful amendments described militarism as the chief instrument of 'class oppression' in Europe and demanded that, if war were to break out, the crisis should be used 'to accelerate the fall of the bourgeoisie'.[129] Lenin was content. Both he and

Luxemburg would have preferred an even firmer resolution; but he, unlike Luxemburg, accepted that a more strongly-worded formulation would gravely damage Europe's greatest mass socialist party, the German Social-Democratic Party, in its dealings with the German government.[130] He still took Kautsky's professions of revolutionary commitment at their face value, and ignored the warnings of Rosa Luxemburg, Karl Liebknecht and other far-left commentators on German socialism. In any case, neither Luxemburg nor Lenin was the fieriest participant at Stuttgart. Gustave Hervé, a French leftist, had demanded that the outbreak of a European war should be met with a 'military strike' and a 'popular insurrection'. Lenin argued that Hervé's proposal would bind the Second International to an inflexible policy and would in any case disclose tactics to the forces of capitalism. Hervé also seemed to adhere to pacifist ideas. Lenin (and here he left Luxemburg behind) emphasised that 'revolutionary wars' might be necessary.[131]

After Stuttgart, Lenin returned to questions on imperialism only fitfully. The emergence of nationalist movements in Persia, Turkey, India and China attracted his attention, and in 1908 he asserted that European socialism was obtaining 'an international ally' in Asia.[132] In addition, he affirmed that wars could arise from economic competition and that militarism was the child of capitalism.[133] Occasional remarks on international crises were forthcoming; like all political commentators, he wrote about the Balkans. In 1908 he still thought that the crowned heads of the houses of Habsburg, Hohenzollern and Romanov would effect a peaceful, anti-democratic settlement.[134] In 1912, when war broke out between Bulgaria and the Ottoman empire, he mentioned the dangers of a geographical extension of the conflict. A Congress of the Second International was held in Basle while the war raged; but he did not attend, preferring to dispatch Kamenev to represent the Bolshevik standpoint. In general, Lenin welcomed the Basle Congress's adherence to the Stuttgart Congress's anti-war policies, and left the matter at that.[135]

On imperialism, it was the Austrian social-democrat Rudolf Hilferding who broke fresh ground. His *Finance Capital*, published in 1910,[136] focussed on the growth of industrial cartels and monopolies in each national economy and the increasing dependence of industrialists on the financial support of the banks as the need to expand fixed-capital investment grew. Increasingly, according to Hilferding, the nation's industrial sectors jointly pursued their respective interests since a small number of banks controlled the whole process. Moreover, the difficulties of maintaining profits on the domestic market stimulated a quest for foreign outlets and for foreign sites for factories where both labour and land were cheap. The most dependable receptacle for such 'capital exports' was the colony. Thus contemporary capitalism was linked to the rise of the power of the banks and in turn to imperialism, racialism and anti-democratism.[137] Hilferding's book was recognised to be not only a massive contribution to Marxist theory but also a contemporary economic classic.[138] It is not known when Lenin read it; but he probably knew its contents soon after publication. He had always kept abreast of continental socialist debates, and was in any case a voracious reader. And yet, even if he had read the book, he refrained from comment.

This contrasted with two other 'East Europeans', Karl Radek and Rosa Luxemburg. Hilferding had suggested that each imperialist nation's economy would undergo periodic crises and that the only practical alternative was socialism; and he maintained that this would be not an unduly difficult transition since, with the concentration of banking capital, a socialist government would merely need to nationalise the handful of central banks in order to inaugurate socialism.[139] This emphasis on economic measures with little reference to politics was to call forth criticism from Lenin in the First World War.[140] But it was left to Radek and Luxemburg to tackle Hilferding at the time.

In 1911, Radek published a lengthy pamphlet, *German Imperialism and the Working Class*, in Bremen. He described imperialism as 'capitalism in its latest stage of development' – a phrase picked up by Lenin after 1914.[141] His pamphlet was a call to revolution and was less scholarly in tone than Hilferding's book. It also discussed German imperialism in darker terms. Radek noted that German workers were gaining material benefit from German colonial exploitation,[142] and was not complacent about the working class as the unchallengeable constituency of socialists. He also emphasised the massive investment in the development and production of armaments in Germany in recent years; his prognosis of the prospects of peace were pessimistic.[143] Radek stressed the increasing inadequacies of parliaments in restraining governments. Lenin read Radek's pamphlet and took notes, but again he did not reveal his opinion;[144] nor did he comment on the possibility, mooted by Kautsky from 1911, that the imperial nations might mitigate their rivalry and avoid war by reaching a concordat for the peaceful collective exploitation of all colonial peoples.[145] This idea, which became known as the theory of 'ultra-imperialism', caused Lenin to put pen to paper only after 1914. Luxemburg was quicker to react. Her *Accumulation of Capital*, which appeared in 1913, surveyed the evolution of capitalism and examined Hilferding's arguments. She had also noted the shifts in Kautsky's thinking, which indeed led him by 1914 to deny that capitalism was inherently militarist.[146]

Luxemburg denounced such views. She also felt that Marx's *Capital*, with its claim that capitalism in any given country brought poverty to the mass of its population, had never explained capitalism's longevity and continued growth.[147] How, in fact, did capitalism reproduce itself? Luxemburg's answer, supported by reproduction-cycle diagrams, was that industrial capitalism must discover and hold on to foreign agrarian societies as its major market and as a location for cheap production. Lenin, having failed to be disconcerted by Hilferding and Radek, was annoyed with Luxemburg. Firstly, he objected to her temerity (as he saw it) in correcting Marx. This, as a true believer, he could forgive in nobody; and he jotted down diagrams which, he thought, were more closely in line with Marx's.[148] The second irritation for him was that Luxemburg referred to the Russian socialist debates of the 1890s, contending that 'V. Ilin' (which was Lenin's main legal pseudonym) had been wrong to criticise populists such as V. P. Vorontsov and N. F. Danielson who maintained that the absence of foreign markets hobbles the growth of a nation's capitalism. She also asserted that the populist emphasis on the importance of the growth of industrial consumer goods in the initial phase of capitalist development was wholly justified.[149]

Lenin was enraged, standing by his old positions and taking offence at her few complimentary remarks about his *Development of Capitalism*. These were, he opined, 'oracle-like' condescension.[150] Luxemburg's book would probably have pulled him at last into the theoretical battle over imperialism, albeit within the narrow field of capital-reproduction cycles. He drafted a plan for an article in March 1913.[151] He congratulated Anton Pannekoek and Otto Bauer (whom, on the national question, he so despised) for attacking Luxemburg in their reviews.[152] But his campaign against Luxemburg was limited to brief sallies as other worries intervened. He pointed out that even large imperial states such as Russia could be net importers of finance capital. This was in order to prove that Luxemburg's neat contrast between the industrial imperial powers and the rest of the world did not entirely fit reality.[153] He also continued to write pieces intermittently on international developments in 1913–14; and his journalism included remarks on militarism, on banking capital, immigration to Europe, and on the corrupting effects of nationalism.[154] But his thinking required the jolt of the First World War to shake him into a full-blooded consideration of the issues. And, while deploring nationalism, he continued to believe that the European working class would respond positively to the revolutionary movement; and that even the 'English proletariat' was awakening from its alleged political quiescence. Radek's stress on the spread of imperialist ideas among workers was ignored.[155]

THE INTERNATIONAL SOCIALIST BUREAU

Europe's leading Marxist writers were familiar with the theories of Lenin. But the level of acquaintance was low outside that group; only a few eccentrics with a highly-developed interest in Marxian theory or with an idiosyncrasy for staying in touch with the Russian Social-Democratic Labour Party's affairs could have filled an area bigger than a postage stamp with their knowledge about Bolshevism. Lenin and Krupskaya rented a succession of apartments in central and eastern Europe in streets where the neighbours had no idea of Bolshevik politics and, as likely as not, would not have cared to acquire one either.

Nonetheless there was one political forum on the Continent where Lenin was not only famous but also a major and obtrusive figure: the International Socialist Bureau. He became the bane of the Bureau's deliberations, and he reciprocated in his thoughts about the Bureau. The International Socialist Bureau was drawn from the various national parties belonging to the Socialist International. This was not the First Socialist International of Karl Marx and Mikhail Bakunin, but the Second, which had existed since 1889. Lenin had briefly been one of the Russian Social-Democratic Labour Party's representatives on the International Socialist Bureau (ISB) in October 1905; but his departure for Russia forced him to resign the post.[156] The Central Committee elected him again as an ISB representative in June 1907;[157] and he held this office after the Socialist International Congress in Stuttgart in August. His work was mostly confined to correspondence, since the ISB's members did not have to reside in Brussels, its base. Lenin attended Bureau sessions in the autumns of 1908 and 1909.[158] Up to that time, despite annoying its members on account of his schismatic antics inside Russian socialism, he had not disturbed the Second Socialist International as a whole. This tranquillity started to come to an end with the January 1910 Central Committee plenum, which reunited the factional leaderships of Russian social-democracy and turned over the disputed funds from the legacy of N. P. Shmidt to an arbitrational 'court' of Karl Kautsky, Franz Mehring and Clara Zetkin. All three were prominent figures in the Socialist International, and their deliberations about Russian social-democratic finances dragged the ISB into the morass of Bolshevik–Menshevik disputes.[159]

Not approving of the outbreak of peace with the Mensheviks at the January 1910 plenum, Lenin felt uneasy about what the arbitrators might do with the money. By November 1910 he was claiming that it rightfully belonged only to the Bolsheviks.[160] He journeyed to Berlin to lobby Kautsky in person,[161] and he called for a Central Committee plenum to discuss the delay in the arbitrators' decision, but he could not yet get a sufficient number of Central Committee members to back him.[162]

Lenin refused to relent, visiting Berlin in March 1911 with N. G. Poletaev, the Bolshevik editor of *The Star*, to negotiate with Kautsky and his two colleagues.[163] He badgered Kautsky by letter in May and met Zetkin in Stuttgart in June.[164] In fact, it was only in July 1911 that, finally, he transferred the money into Zetkin's keeping. Neither Zetkin nor the other two arbitrators could forget that Lenin wished to split the Bolsheviks from the Mensheviks, and that a definitive release of the money to two separate factions would hasten such a division. Abstention from a definitive ruling, coupled with piecemeal grants in response to requests from each faction, was considered preferable; but it was a thankless task nevertheless, especially with a Lenin who had a record of nagging away interminably and had a lawyer's training into the bargain. The arbitrators had to tread circumspectly, and they knew it. Lenin looked into the German laws on private financial arbitration and planned to hire professional lawyers.[165] Arbitrators Kautsky and Franz Mehring had already had enough of the entanglement in Russian socialism. By October 1911, both had pleaded ill-health and resigned their position.[166] Lenin wrote officially to Clara Zetkin that the original arbitrational agreement had therefore lapsed and that, unless she immediately returned the money to him, legal proceedings would be initiated. He appended a more informal letter, excusing the formal tone of his request but asking her what else he could do in the given situation.[167] Zetkin tried to temporise. She was unwilling to act unaccompanied as an arbitrator and, as Lenin could see, was not averse to supposing that the Bolsheviks had better legal title to the money than the Mensheviks;[168] but still she declined to take a decision. In annoyance, Lenin carried out his threat to turn to the lawyers. He took advice from the Swiss socialist and advocate Karl Zraggen;[169] and in May 1912 he resorted to Georges Ducos de la Haille, a French socialist as well as a barrister, offering him payment of 5000 francs on condition that the case against Zetkin was successfully completed by August 1912.[170]

His insistence on haste was caused not only by the perennial shortage of cash suffered by all Russian revolutionary groups, but also by his dread that further delay would increase the possibility of the ISB's becoming involved.[171] Bolsheviks G. L. Shklovski and L. B. Kamenev ran errands in the judicial business over following months since Lenin had meanwhile decamped to Galicia; but the telegrams, letters and official statements by Lenin on the Shmidt money did not abate. The bemused Ducos de la Haille predictably got nowhere in the time appointed – not that this was condoned by Lenin, who wrote to complain in September 1912.[172] Lenin sought another lawyer. The snag was that Lenin had entrusted all the original documents to Ducos's safekeeping, and he perceived that Ducos might refuse to give them up without receiving some compensation for his work. In March 1913, admitting to his own 'hyper-suspiciousness', Lenin requested Kamenev not to pay out any cheque until he had received the necessary documents.[173] Then the Stuttgart advocate A. Kahn was drawn into the case, and Ducos de la Haille was informed that he would have to share his fees with him; Zraggen, too, was pulled back in for assistance.[174] In December 1913, Lenin's trepidations were realised: the Socialist International started to take an interest in the Bolshevik–Menshevik dispute. Karl Kautsky, the ex-arbitrator and long-time commentator on Russian socialist affairs, spoke at an ISB session in London. Declaring that the Russian Social-Democratic Labour Party had ceased to exist, he felt justified in calling for a meeting of 'all factions of the Russian labour movement' in the Romanov empire which accepted the social-democratic party programme.

The ISB accordingly urged the calling of a gathering which might effect 'a mutual exchange of opinions'.[175] Lenin foresaw that this could lead not only to a financial settlement quite unsatisfactory to him but also to moves towards the party's organisational reunification. He was alarmed by the noises made recently by Rosa Luxemburg in this direction in *Vorwärts*. Luxemburg's attitude had always been the same as Zetkin's.[176] Now it was Lenin's turn to temporise. The ISB's invitation to Bolsheviks and Mensheviks to exchange opinions could not be resisted unless he was willing to appear to be the party splitter he really was; and, in any case, socialist lawyers such as Zraggen (who was now regarded as 'very weak and cowardly' by Lenin)[177] did not wish to obstruct the ISB's plan.

Lenin's ploy was to accept the invitation to 'a mutual exchange of opinions' of the Russian factions while expressing objection to Kautsky's characterisation of the Russian Social-Democratic Labour Party.[178] Meanwhile 'all kinds of reconnaissance' should be undertaken to find out the political line-up and agenda.[179] What about the Shmidt money? Lenin's room for manoeuvre had shrunk, and he strove for general recognition that the financial question and the question of party reunification should be kept separate; he remarked that Kautsky, too, had once conceded that directly 'political' considerations were not at stake in the controversy over Shmidt's legacy.[180] He also repudiated any offer from the German Social-Democratic Party to mediate further in the matter.[181] Simultaneously, he endeavoured to seem as well-intentioned as possible. He beavered away at the statistics of the votes for Bolsheviks and Mensheviks at the 1912 State Duma elections and at the respective print-run of Bolshevik and Menshevik newspapers. His motivations were only barely disguised: Lenin wanted to seize and retain the mantle of legitimacy for the Bolshevik-controlled 'party' he had inaugurated at the Party Conference in Prague in 1912; and he had no intention of going to the ISB's proposed 'exchange of opinions' meeting in order to give up his grasp on a Bolshevik-dominated Central Committee. But this would require a barrage of preparatory propaganda to convince the ISB that the Bolsheviks were indeed the sole representatives of organised Marxism in the Russian empire and that the Mensheviks comprised only a gaggle of unattached émigrés and anti-party, Russia-based 'Liquidators'.[182]

He discerned that the wrangling had dragged the party's name in the mud across Europe; and he frequently emphasised that he had no personal financial interest in the judicial to-and-fro. But the patience of the ISB was wearing thin. With so many issues to be resolved in the Socialist International, it was irritating for so much time and effort to be put into Russian affairs. But no concession was forthcoming from him. To have yielded over the money would have increased the hated possibility of party reunification. Lenin had not attended the ISB meeting in December 1913, and he made clear that he would absent himself from international gatherings in the months to come.[183]

RUSSIA IN 1914

And so, in the first half of 1914, Lenin faced organisational problems both international and Russian. One complicating factor was of his own making. Since July 1913 he and the Central Committee had been talking about holding a Party Congress.[184] This was another device to arrogate legitimacy for the Bolsheviks as the principal constituent members of the Russian Social-Democratic Labour Party. Although Conferences could and did take major decisions on behalf of the party, Congresses were considered more authoritative. Lenin wanted to follow up the Prague Conference with a Krakow Congress.[185] His calculations were not publicly revealed, but can easily be guessed: he was 'going for broke'. In order to win his forthcoming struggles in the Socialist International, he had to call a Congress which would 'demonstrate' that the Mensheviks had no significant following in Russia; and he had the confidence, or rather the gall, to plan to manipulate the Congress rules to produce the desired political composition of delegates. The ISB had to be presented with a plausible performance if he was to get away with his scheme. The Central Committee reconvened in Krakow from 2 April 1914 and approved a proposal to convoke the Sixth Party Congress in Krakow in August, just before the time when the Socialist International was scheduled to hold a Congress in Vienna. The Krakow delegates would be able to travel on to Vienna to lobby for the Bolshevik cause.[186]

This was characteristic bluff and skulduggery from Lenin. As with the Prague Conference arrangements, various commissions were appointed to ensure that Bolsheviks commanded the selection and vetting of delegates.[187] Lenin had either learned from Prague or bowed to advice from colleagues: a genuine invitation would be issued in a timely fashion to the Poles, Latvians and Lithuanians so as to avoid the criticisms of his neglect of the non-Russian segments of the party in 1912. But they still would not receive a fair proportion of available seats at the Congress. There would be between sixty and ninety seats. The Poles would receive only five, the Latvians two or even one, and the Lithuanians one. The Jewish Bund would be invited, but the letter would deliberately be dispatched so as to arrive too late. It was not even clear that the 'national' parties would be allowed to vote at this Sixth Congress in Galicia.[188]

Lenin knew full well that his Congress's self-proclamation as the party's supreme assembly would be challenged by all non-Bolsheviks. Among his tasks in 1914 was the continued gathering of quantitative data on the support for Bolshevism in Russia. As regards newspapers, he noted that *Pravda*'s print-run had ascended to a fairly regular 40,000 whereas the Menshevik-edited *Luch* had attained less than half of this figure.[189] He highlighted the activity of the Bolshevik deputies to the Fourth State Duma, and emphasised that the Bolsheviks had swept the board in the workers' constituencies in St Petersburg and Moscow, whereas the Mensheviks had scored victories in more peripheral areas and often through electoral pacts with liberals. Much was also made about the election of Bolshevik activists to trade union boards. His claim, which may have been somewhat exaggerated, was that at least sixteen out of the capital's twenty boards had moved towards the Bolsheviks.[190] In the absence of a freely-conducted survey of popular opinion, Lenin fell back on arithmetical extrapolations. He asserted that four-fifths of the Russian imperial urban working class were consciously pro-Bolshevik.[191] This was trumpery even by Lenin's standards. The extrapolations came from the limited sample of *Pravda*'s circulation alongside the elections to the capital's trade unions. The data, in other words, were in effect confined largely to St Petersburg's skilled workers, which was far from being typical of the Russian empire's urban society and economy. Someone who had been born in the Volga town of Simbirsk and had, in his *Development of Capitalism in Russia*, castigated others for their sloppy statistics must have been aware of the mathematical sleight of hand here.

Working-class unrest, however, certainly increased in 1914. Strikes in enterprises surveyed by the official factory inspectorate rose to 3534 from 2404 in the previous year (and the number of strikers to 985,655 from 502,442).[192] The Ministry of Internal Affairs was seriously concerned. Workers were enraged with both employers and government, and anti-Romanov street demonstrations were organised in St Petersburg. It was claimed that the slogans carried on several banners mentioned demands for a democratic republic, confiscation of gentry-owned land and an eight-hour day. These were Bolshevik slogans,[193] but it is a moot point whether acquaintance with Bolshevism went beyond this or indeed whether most workers on demonstrations acquired their ideas directly from Bolsheviks. *Pravda* editorials; speeches by the Bolshevik Duma deputies; public statements of Bolshevik trade unionists: all these had to be cautiously formulated so as not to attract punitive actions by police and censor.

Unconstrained discussion of Bolshevik ideas occurred only in the Russian political underground, in Siberian exile and in the emigration. Lenin and Krupskaya had no illusions about the weakness and low morale in the illegal party apparatus. In February 1914, Krupskaya wrote bluntly: 'The illegal organisation is pulverised.'[194] Regional centres had vanished; local urban organisations were cut off from each other. Almost all experienced activists had been 'taken out of circulation'.[195] Reports from Russia, such as we know them from published documents, confirm her judgement. The Moscow comrades talked of 'a complete break-up' of party groups.[196] Lenin put the problem in a nutshell (but did so in a private letter, presumably to avoid further demoralisation among his followers in Russia): 'The revolutionary mood arising in recent times in Russia has the tendency to keep growing but, being insufficiently guided in the absence of well-established underground organisations, can become powerless and aimless.'[197] The Bolshevik leader was not the only politician to wring his hands. Mensheviks and Socialist Revolutionaries had still less to cheer about; and the Kadets, while suffering less from the Okhrana's attentions, had little serious hope of attracting workers to their cause. The trade unions seem to have had as many difficulties as before. The labour movement, illegal and legal, was severely harassed.[198]

And yet this did not expunge working-class discontent. The ruthless suppression of strikes, sometimes with Cossack cavalrymen riding into pickets, caused lasting embitterment; and conditions in the factories worsened for the labour force as employers in St Petersburg and elsewhere imposed new working practices to raise productivity.[199] The industrial scene was a tinder-box awaiting ignition. The authorities persisted with their policy of restricting the freedom of trade unions. As always, the huge size of many factories and accompanying feelings of 'alienation' among workers created difficulties; and the appalling environment, with its under-provision of housing and poor sewage and recreational facilities, increased the probability of political crisis. Workers, denied easy opportunities to join trade unions or political parties, found other places to discuss their grievances: groups of men gathering in taverns, many of them coming from the same towns or villages and feeling able to trust each other, talked about their misfortunes. There were also heated debates between shifts at the factories.[200]

Such circumstances made it likely that strikes would erupt without warning and take both revolutionaries and government by surprise. Lenin recognised this; and, when he was not busy explaining to the International Socialist Bureau that the Bolsheviks were in better shape and had greater support than the Mensheviks, urged his comrades to do their utmost to re-establish the illegal party apparatus. Krupskaya's notebook continued to acquire names,[201] but it was of limited practical use since the police were so skilful in capturing revolutionaries. Signs of vigorous communication between the Central Committee and the Russian political underground are few. In three out of the first six months of 1914, apparently, Lenin did not even write to the Bolshevik Duma deputies; and these deputies, overburdened with Duma activities and other speaking and writing engagements, seldom visited him. Petrovski seems to have done so twice.[202] There was also the usual pressure on Lenin to cool his polemical ardour. At the turn of the year a Central Committee session in Galicia had passed a resolution that *Pravda* should avoid abusing so-called Liquidators: a veiled censure of Lenin and his friends.[203] Dissatisfaction with Lenin was also expressed in his discharge of technical duties. Despite the stress laid by the Prague Conference upon the legal labour movement, Lenin failed, as before, to supply the requested articles and advice on the subject.[204] Even the second anniversary of the Lena goldfields massacre did not inspire him to compose a suitable piece. E. F. Rozmirovich wrote from St Petersburg, by then more in sorrow than in anger: 'My closest friends are grumbling that you're doing nothing for them. They're upset.'[205]

By 1914 Lenin, too, had come to see that his *protégé* Chernomazov's zest for polemics was causing more harm than good; and that the Ministry of Internal Affairs was being provided with regular excuses to shut down *Pravda*. Lenin acceded to Chernomazov's removal and was able, because of the shortage of competent journalistic talent in the capital, to secure agreement for his associate Kamenev (who no longer had *Workers' Newspaper* to edit in Paris) to take over *Pravda*'s direction in February 1914. Kamenev was also expected to liaise with the Bolshevik Duma deputies as

Fyodor Dan did for the Menshevik deputies.[206] Kamenev's appointment soothed Lenin; and, for the first time since its foundation, *Pravda* ceased to give him worry.[207]

Nor was the Central Committee as troublesome to Lenin as it once had been. The Bolshevik underground members who had been elected at Prague and had objected to his methods – Ordzhonikidze, Goloshchekin, Spandaryan – had been arrested; and the sole Central Committee member from the Party Mensheviks, D. M. Shvartsman, dropped out entirely from Central Committee work: and he too was put in prison in 1914.[208] Meanwhile Zinoviev and, until his abscondment, Malinovski supported Lenin on most questions. Several activists were co-opted to fill the gaps: I. V. Stalin, I. S. Belostotski, Y. M. Sverdlov, G. I. Petrovski, A. E. Badaev and A. S. Kiselev. None of them, with the exception of Stalin,[209] stood up to Lenin as Ordzhonikidze and his friends had done. At any rate Lenin was accorded much scope for initiative, at least in regard to the politics of the emigration. The International Socialist Bureau's December 1913 decision to invite all factions of the Russian Social-Democratic Labour Party to an 'exchange of views' meeting in Brussels lay on the table.[210] For some months, Lenin was unruffled. His constantly-updated collection of data purporting to demonstrate the conscious support of most workers in Russia for Bolshevism was periodically issued;[211] and, since the International Socialist Bureau had called for the meeting, he left it to the Bureau to convoke it. The delay seemed to guarantee that his own 'Sixth Congress' would occur in advance of the Brussels meeting and that a new Central Committee, formed under Lenin's guidance, would be created.

But this *fait accompli* was pre-empted by the Bureau's sudden scheduling of the inter-factional 'exchange of views' meeting for July.[212] Things became stickier for Lenin when the Malinovski scandal erupted and, as might easily have been predicted, non-Leninists in the party were raising a hue and cry about Lenin's convoking his own Party Congress.[213] The Congress plan was shunted quietly to the side; all efforts were centred on the ISB's Brussels gathering. Lenin felt he was not the faction's ideal spokesman: he would lose his temper and his opponents would have a chance to interrogate him. He implored Inessa Armand to fulfil the role,[214] offering to supply a report and a speech if she would deliver them.[215] He had been outmanoeuvred. The Brussels meeting opted to hold a Party Congress to reunify the party; and the Executive

Committee of the International Socialist Bureau, whose representatives attended, concluded that no irreconcilable basic disagreements divided the various Russian factions.[216] Armand, having been told by Lenin that 'the essential thing is to prove that only we are the party', abstained in the vote on a unifying Congress.[217]

Lenin worked to extricate himself from the mess. He went on collating information on the respective strengths of the Bolsheviks and Mensheviks in the legal labour movement in Russia.[218] From 29 June to 6 July he held a meeting in Poronin of his closest supporters. Zinoviev, Petrovski and Kiselev attended as Central Committee members, and N. P. Glebov-Avilov and A. N. Nikiforova took part as leading Bolshevik activists in Russia.[219] Kiselev later wrote that the talk was mainly about the Brussels meeting, the forthcoming Congress of the Second International in Vienna and the Russian State Duma.[220] Lenin's subsequent letter to Bolshevik Duma deputy, F. N. Samoilov, who was convalescing in Switzerland, referred only to the trouble engendered by the decisions of the International Socialist Bureau. He predicted that the 'workers of Russia' would take no notice of the Brussels meeting.[221]

The absorption in intra-party concerns was extreme. Summer 1914 witnessed renewed labour unrest in the Romanov empire: a general strike was organised by workers in Baku in June; and, from 4 July, strikes and demonstrations began in St Petersburg. Barricades went up in some suburbs. The employers hit back and were actively supported by the Ministry of Internal Affairs.[222] It is impressive that the Bolshevik supreme leadership, which had insisted that the Mensheviks underrated the revolutionary potential of the working class, sat around on Lenin's veranda in Poronin oblivious of the disorder in St Petersburg. Even more noteworthy is that, with war about to break out in central Europe and to envelope all the major powers on the Continent, the chieftains of Bolshevism assumed that the major international issue for them was how to comport themselves at the Vienna Congress of the Second International.[223]

3 *Ad Extirpanda*: 1914–1915

THE JULY CRISIS

The First World War, breaking out in summer 1914, sealed the fate of old Russia. Probably there would eventually have been a revolution. Having survived his ordeals of 1905–6, the emperor had tried to restore his autocratic powers and had been suspicious of his premier Petr Stolypin's co-operation with the State Duma. Yet the imperial state had lost its ability to repress all opposition at will. The monarch's truculence narrowed the ground for political compromise and evolution; it also made more likely the ultimate success of the more radical among his opponents. The nature of an anti-Romanov revolution would very probably have been different if Russia had not gone to war. In mid-1914, before the war, there was no economic crisis. Agricultural production and the trade in farm products had never been greater, and industrial output was expanding. Social conflicts were fierce but not uncontrollable. Thus the major catalysts for the Bolshevik party to advance to power, as it did in 1917, were weak. No doubt the Bolsheviks would have exerted much influence in the course of any conceivable revolution even in a Russia which was at peace and was economically buoyant; but they surely would not have become the monopolistic party of government. It is worth recalling that in 1914 they did not intend to initiate a socialist revolution, and that Lenin declared that the next stage in the country's development would be bourgeois. Perhaps he would have changed his mind; the ease with which he did so in 1917 indicates his changeability, and the Bolshevik strategy of 1905 for a bourgeois revolution had always carried strong traces of a zeal for socialist reforms.[1]

But this is all hypothetical. Russia had no revolution, bourgeois or socialist, in 1914; but she entered a war in central Europe which acquired a near-global character in the following three years. The scale of casualties was unprecedented. Millions of people perished in combat or behind the lines; and the epidemic of Spanish influenza, which killed further millions after 1918, was all the more deadly in consequence of the material and social hardships induced by the fighting. Political structures crumbled; the crowned rulers of Russia, Germany and Austria-Hungary lost their thrones. Economic devastation prevailed throughout Europe.

Lenin, like every other leader of the Second International, had sometimes predicted a continental war; indeed this was the common prognosis of most politicians and commentators regardless of political orientation. But such predictions were frequently offered somewhat casually. Zinoviev was to recall that Lenin had no idea that the European war really was fast approaching.[2] Moreover, even those commentators who thought war to be near at hand were astounded by the actual timing of the outbreak and by the longevity and intensity of the subsequent fighting. German Chancellor Bethmann Hollweg sensed 'a doom greater than any human power hanging over Europe'. But in the fateful summer of 1914 few actors in the international drama, whether ministers or diplomats, had a sense of the cataclysm awaiting their nations. The revolutionaries were no less caught off their guard. Lenin in his articles in July 1914 anticipated a verbal international conflict among socialists, not a military international conflict between two great coalitions of European states; he was describing Lilliput and not Brobdingnag. His bemusement by the declaration of war was a typical condition (even though it must be added that he was extraordinary in taking so little notice even of the July diplomatic crisis). Were it not for the egregious claims about his perspicacity made by official historians in the USSR, the matter would not need to be belaboured. The speed of the transformation of a regional diplomatic crisis into continental war was staggering; and mobilisation of whole societies and economies, and not merely the combatant armies, in pursuit of victory was unprecedented in wars among great powers.

The event that produced the crisis was the Austrian Archduke Franz Ferdinand's assassination by a Serbian nationalist in Sarajevo on 28 June. On 23 July, Austria-Hungary delivered her ultimatum to neighbouring Serbia. Unless the Serbs agreed to humiliating political conditions, war would ensue between Serbia and the Austro-Hungarian empire. The Russian government declared support for the Serbs. On 31 July, the German government announced that, unless Russia agreed to demobilise her forces, Germany would take military action on Austria-Hungary's side. Russia, encouraged by intimations of support from Britain and France, held firm. Germany declared war on Russia. Britain and France entered the hostilities against Germany and Austria-Hungary. By the second week of August the mightiest states of Europe were lined up against each other. The Allies, including Russia, confronted the Central Powers.

Russia's relations with Austria-Hungary had deteriorated over the previous decade; and Germany's pretensions in both Eastern Europe and the Near East had intermittently heightened tension between St Petersburg and Berlin. Accommodation was reached about the plan for a German-built railway from the Turkish seaboard to Baghdad. But the economic competition to be expected from Germany in traditional Russian trading areas such as Persia remained a source of worry. Russian business in several key industrial sectors was also suffering at the hands of German firms in the Russian domestic market. In addition, Russian foreign policy from the 1890s moved closer towards the embrace of the French. The Paris-raised loan of 1906 had been crucial to the survival of the Romanov dynasty. Both Russian and French politicians opposed the expansion of German power in Europe. Germany, at the same time, resented the lack of a large overseas empire and felt baulked by the British in her quest to wield a worldwide power commensurate with her industrial and military strength. Ideas about the nation's honour and vital interests affected not only governing and proprietorial groups but also broad social classes. Russian fears about Germany were complemented by German fears about Russia. German army leaders advised that the achievements of Russian industrial development were such that, if Germany's security was to be guaranteed, Russian power had to be destroyed by a pre-emptive war.

By 1914, the Russian emperor judged that his country's prestige and geopolitical interest in the Balkans were at stake. Russia had publicly given way to Austrian threats in the recent past. Austria-Hungary's annexation of Bosnia and Herzegovina in 1908 had evoked protests from Serbia; but Russia had stepped back from armed conflict on the Serbian side. Relations with both Austria-Hungary and Germany never fully recovered. And Britain too, which since the mid-nineteenth century had avoided being ensnared in Europe's rivalries, was alarmed by Germany: the build-up of the German fleet agitated the British government, and in 1904 an *entente* was formed between Britain and France.

A mystery endures about Lenin's attitude in the pre-war years. To be sure, he predicted a continental war. And yet he was little bothered by the vicissitudes of European diplomacy or even regional wars in Europe. Only the barest comments were elicited from him on the Balkan wars of 1912 and 1913, which were fought by Turkey and the successor states to the Ottoman empire in south-eastern Europe. Unlike Trotski, who worked as a war correspondent in the Balkans in 1912–13 and covered the fighting, he did not recognise – except in the most cursory fashion – that a military conflict in the Balkans might light a holocaust of mutual destruction among the Great Powers.[3] It is only halfway towards an explanation to suggest that he was absorbed in party-political thoughts and activity; it remains to be explained why he allowed such an absorption to take place. Obsessive as he was about controlling Bolshevik affairs, he seldom let them expunge everything else from his mind. Perhaps, like many other Marxists, his belief in the probability of European war inhabited a rarified, intellectual plane; he showed little vital concern. Before 1914 he had written several anti-militarist articles and had lobbied in the Second International at the Stuttgart Congress.[4] But the articles were brief. And he had left it to L. B. Kamenev to put the anti-militarist case at the Basle Congress of the Second International in 1912, when the first Balkan war was raging.[5]

Consequently, his intellectuality about the prospect of a general continental war was shattered only by the outbreak of the First World War itself. The armies of the two sides mobilised according to long-laid national plans, and Europe's railways were loaded with men, weapons, horses and fodder. The German authorities, entertaining low expectations of Austria-Hungary as their ally, encouraged Turkey to join the Central Powers. This added to Russia's difficulties, compelling her to fight simultaneously on two fronts. Yet Germany, facing Russia to the east and France and Britain to the west, had the same problem to a greater degree. Speedy conquests were essential to German strategy: Belgium and Holland were invaded, and troops poured into northern France before British regiments could cross the English Channel. But the line on the Western front steadied and then held firm. Masses of men, rapidly trained and equipped, dug themselves into trenches. The no-man's land between the two sides was turned into a lunar landscape of destruction. To the east, it was the Russians who temporarily held the initiative. The armies of the Romanovs swept out from 'Russian' Poland through to eastern Prussia. Galicia, where Lenin was living, was overrun in autumn 1914.

ARREST AND RELEASE

Lenin and Zinoviev unknowingly had chosen to live in what was to be the path of the Russian advance. The additional danger for the two Bolshevik leaders was that, as Russian subjects, they and their wives might come under suspicion in Austrian-ruled Poland as being spies. Imprisonment by either Russians or Austrians could happen at any time,[6] so they planned to leave Habsburg territory as fast as was legally possible: war hysteria afflicted all combatant countries; it was not unknown for aliens to be lynched. Anti-Russian sentiment was rife among local Poles. All Russian emigrants could expect to be contacted by the police authorities in Krakow sooner or later and Lenin was an obvious object of mistrust. His daily habits were far from reassuring to policemen; he owned a Browning pistol. Why did someone claiming to have come to Galicia to study agricultural conditions have need of such a weapon? He also went climbing regularly in the hills near the border: could he be keeping a rendezvous with his St Petersburg spy-masters? Lenin, Krupskaya and the Zinovievs none the less refused to panic. They saw it was too late to make a dash across the vast domains of the Austro-Hungarian empire to seek sanctuary in any neutral country: they were a thousand kilometres by rail from the Swiss border and almost as far from the nearest ferry port to Scandinavia. Lenin conferred with Zinoviev, and both of them relied heavily on their acquaintances. Bagocki for advice on how to avoid trouble.

They bore up well. Bagocki was to recall that Lenin was agitated less by his personal situation than by the Second International leadership's reaction to the war. His worst moment came when he read the Krakow newspapers on 5 August.[7] Reports from the German Reichstag told that the social-democrats had voted war credits to their government. Lenin rightly stated that this implicitly breached the assumptions of the Second International's anti-war policy.[8] To be fair, a minority of the Reichstag social-democratic fraction under Hugo Haase had privately objected to the fraction's attitude to war credits; and Kautsky, who did not belong to the Reichstag, sided with Haase. Both Haase and Kautsky continued to seek an end to the fighting without themselves being arrested. But such behaviour was not the outright opposition that Lenin demanded.

According to S. Bagocki, Lenin stated bluntly: 'This is the end of the Second International . . . From today I shall cease being a social-democrat and shall become a communist.'[9] There would have been ructions in the International even if war had not broken out; and Lenin might have been willing to disaffiliate his Bolsheviks from membership. He now planned something much more grandiose: the construction of an entirely separate 'Third' International.[10] His inclination hardened as it became evident that not only the German social-democrats but nearly all other socialist parties in Europe declined to oppose their respective country's entry into the war. Most French and British socialists saw the war as a tragic national necessity. Only few brave spirits denounced it. Karl Liebknecht, social-democratic deputy in the German Reichstag, took this course in 1915 and was arrested; and Pierre Brizon in France had to tread warily to escape the same fate. Not all socialist groups were swept up by the pro-war and patriotic frenzy. Minority factions in Britain, France and Germany took an openly anti-war stand; opposition was stronger in Italy and among the Czechs. But generally the French Socialist Party and the British Labour Party supported the Allied war effort even while retaining objections to their governments and speaking up for better treatment of the workers. Lenin renamed social-democrats 'social-chauvinists', seeking to emphasise their rupture with ideals of internationalism and anti-militarism.[11]

It was among the socialists of the Romanov empire that hostility to the war was strongest and most pervasive. The antagonism to the monarchy was profound in Russia, and the chasm between socialists and the rest of political society was vast. In most other countries there were moves by socialists towards an attenuation of social strife until the war ended. In the Romanov lands, however, not many socialists aspired at a 'civil peace', a '*Burgfrieden*' or '*une union sacrée*'. Lenin's instinctive refusal to condone the Russian imperial government's engagement in war was paralleled by the reactions of many others.

Most Bolshevik leaders, including those hostile to Lenin, fulminated against the dynasty and its military objectives; only a few, such as G. A. Aleksinski called for a patriotic defence against the Germans who were accused of imperialist aggression. And yet the will to volunteer to fight for the Allies was not absent even from the Paris-based Committee of the Foreign Organisation, which lost several members to the French armed forces. Among these it was the wish to protect democratic France rather than to defend Russia which was the motivation. The Committee of the Foreign Organisation collapsed in disarray.[12] Among the Mensheviks, there were similar divisions. Martov, Dan, and Pavel Akselrod were as antagonistic as Lenin to the waging of the war.[13] Even A. N. Potresov and Maslov, who called for a war of national defence against German militarism, declined to lend overt support to Nikolai II; they would defend the country but would lend no succour to the government.[14] This appeared to be Georgi Plekhanov's standpoint, but in practice he suspended his tirades against the monarchy for fear of destabilising the war effort.[15] The Mensheviks who took an unashamedly 'patriotic' position were a minority of their faction. The Socialist Revolutionaries, too, were riven by disputes; but Viktor Chernov and most leaders opposed support for the Russian war effort. The general desire to hold to an 'internationalist' perspective prevailed among most socialist activists regardless of party allegiance.[16]

And yet the anti-war Russian revolutionaries were initially out of step with popular sentiment in the Russian empire. Not only the middle and upper classes but, so far as can be judged, all sections of the population believed that Germany and Austria-Hungary had to be resisted. Workers who had been striking or demonstrating in St Petersburg in July were voluntarily back at work in August. Leading socialist opponents of the war, if they were in the emigration, chose Switzerland, Sweden or the United States of America as their haven for the duration of hostilities, but few émigrés faced quite the dilemmas of Vladimir Ilich Lenin and his colleagues, caught as they were on the territory of Russia's military foe.

On 7 August 1914 Lenin received his first visit from the authorities. After a superficial search, his statistical notes on the agrarian question were confiscated on suspicion that they might be a spy's coded messages. Lenin remarked ruefully that his party correspondence was left untouched. He was ordered to present himself next day at the railway station and to travel to Nowy Targ for the completion of further enquiries. Lenin contacted his Polish friends. Jan Hanecki sent a telegram to S. Marek, a social-democratic parliamentarian in Austria-Hungary, to seek his intercession on Lenin's behalf. Lenin himself telegraphed the Krakow police, asking them to confirm to the police in Poronin and Nowy Targ that he was an émigré revolutionary who had entered the country legally.[17] Off he set for Nowy Targ on 8 August. On the same day Marek telegrammed to Nowy Targ police station that 'Lenin-Ulyanov' was known to him personally and was 'blameless and trustworthy'.[18] This did not prevent Lenin's arrest on arrival in Nowy Targ at eleven o'clock that morning, and he remained in custody until 19 August. The interrogations, which were facilitated by material sent by the police in Krakow,[19] bore out Lenin's testimony. The sole untoward aspect of his case, in the eyes of the Nowy Targ investigators, was Lenin's illegal possession of the Browning pistol (which was removed from him).[20] Visits by Hanecki and Krupskaya were allowed; but the Nowy Targ police, despite being convinced that Lenin's story was genuine, were unwilling to take responsibility for his release. Bureaucratic red-tape was not peculiar to the Romanov lands.

Krupskaya took the initiative. On 11 August she wrote to the Austrian social-democratic leader and parliamentarian Viktor Adler in Vienna to request his intervention.[21] She made the same plea to parliamentary deputy G. Diamand on 14 August.[22] Adler and Diamand responded helpfully, declaring to the Ministry of Internal Affairs in Vienna that the suspected Russian spy Lenin was well-known throughout Europe for his dedication to the 'struggle against Russian tsarism'.[23] Lenin's referees exaggerated his fame, but their words had the desired effect. On 19 August the case against Lenin was abandoned and the Krakow authorities instructed the Nowy Targ police to release him.[24]

Lenin returned to Bialy Dunajec. On 20 August, after sending his thanks to Adler and Diamand, he made arrangements to leave for Switzerland. According to Hanecki, Lenin retained the fear that his life might be in danger from the villagers.[25] In any case, he desired a freedom for his politics that was unavailable to a Russian emigrant in Austria-Hungary. The journey required official permission in wartime, and while waiting, Lenin studied the German socialist press with increasing exasperation.[26] Herman Greulich, the Swiss social-democratic leader, contacted Adler to enquire how he could help Lenin financially with his travel plans. This was ironical; within a few years Greulich would be regarded by Lenin as a deadly betrayer of socialism.[27] On 16 August, Lenin and Krupskaya received the necessary documentation from Krakow to travel to Vienna, and they set off in company with Krupskaya's mother,[28] but further external assistance was needed. Not having a passport,[29] Lenin could not take a train across the Swiss frontier, but he invoked the name of Greulich and left for Switzerland on 21 August.[30] The Ulyanovs travelled in the company of Zinoviev and his wife Lilina.[31] They arrived in Zurich on 23 August. Behind them they left a region of Eastern Europe which was to be marched over by the armies of

Russia, Germany and Austria-Hungary. They also had to abandon the largest part of the Bolshevik faction's archive of books, pamphlets, manuscripts and letters.[32]

Later, when the Bolsheviks had consolidated their power in Russia, a search was made in Nowy Targ for them. Ten hundred-weights of these materials were discovered.[33] But the temporary loss, while hardly being insignificant for a politician and a bibliophile, was compensated in Lenin's mind by the knowledge that he could resume his struggle against the Romanov dynasty without let or hindrance. Lenin wrote to Adler to thank him warmly for his assistance.[34]

ANNOUNCING A POLICY

Settling again in Switzerland, Lenin was a leader with an even smaller following than in the pre-war period. The struggle for influence would have to be resumed virtually from scratch. Contact with Russia had disappeared and the central émigré apparatus had ceased to exist; and the Central Committee was a fiction; Lenin and Zinoviev were its only members at liberty; and the Committee of the Foreign Organisation was a shambles. The situation with the press was disastrous: *Pravda* had been closed down by the authorities shortly before the declaration of war, and the Bolsheviks themselves had discontinued the foreign-based *Workers' Newspaper* in 1912 and *Social-Democrat* in 1913. Krupskaya's address book could not be used after the Malinovski affair since the assumption had to be that the Okhrana had had access to its contents. Lenin and Zinoviev, while still rejecting the case against Malinovski (and even proceeding to correspond with him when, as a Russian soldier, he was captured and placed in a German prisoner-of-war camp), could not take risks with the lives of Bolsheviks in Russia.[35] The restoration of communications with the underground party committees had to be undertaken with care. The postal services were in any case impeded by the Western and Eastern military fronts which stretched from north to south across Europe; and even correspondence with sympathetic émigrés in Britain and France had to be handled cautiously in view of the alertness of governments in London and Paris to anti-war propaganda. Political conditions had grown more difficult even in Switzerland, where the authorities would not allow forms of activity likely to compromise its neutrality in wartime.[36]

Lenin's early need was to rally support in the Swiss emigration, beginning with the Geneva 'section' of the Bolshevik Foreign Organisation. The section, which had fewer than a dozen members, welcomed him and Zinoviev warmly.[37] They had contacts with Bolsheviks elsewhere in Switzerland, and the news spread that the two most eminent Bolsheviks had arrived safely. All wanted to end the uncertainty about party policy. The time had passed when it would have been possible to implement the Stuttgart recommendation that potentially belligerent governments should be held back from war by the threat of counter-actions by the massed labour movement; the war already raged at full spate. But the question arose as to what to do about it now that it had started. Lenin fell back on his experience in the underground movement in Samara and St Petersburg in the 1890s. He wrote out his ideas and then had them typed and circulated as carbon copies to fellow Bolsheviks in Switzerland.

Apparently he had written an 800-word draft of 'Tasks of Revolutionary Social-Democracy in the European War', before reaching Switzerland, in the last days of August 1914.[38] The themes were fundamental to all his wartime work. Lenin's readers amounted to a few hundred at most, and the overwhelming majority of those were émigrés.[39] But the contents had an historic significance; they were pillars in the formation of Lenin's Bolshevism and of the official ideology of the early Soviet state. Lenin began and ended by cursing the German Social-Democratic Party. Socialism and the revolution, he declared, had been betrayed. The German government had deluded its country's social-democrats by assuring them that its war aims were entirely defensive and non-expansionist; and even Kautsky was giving Bethmann Hollweg the benefit of the doubt until it could be proved otherwise. But Lenin maintained that neither the Central Powers nor the Allies should be analysed so generously. The war was not a struggle between the just and the unjust; on both sides it was 'a bourgeois, imperialist, dynastic' conflict.[40] Its origins, according to Lenin, lay in the international struggle for markets; it was also an attempt to divide the international working-class movement and to prevent revolution. Socialists ought to respond by preparing for a 'revolutionary war'. Workers of each nation should be adjured to rise up against their national middle class. 'Centrists' such as Kautsky who tried to bridge the rift between leftists and rightists in European socialist parties would fail; but centrism itself was so damaging that its proponents should be refused membership of the Socialist International. The working classes of Europe had been misled; they had long been 'hostile to opportunism and chauvinism', but had been gulled into acquiescing in governmental policies through the connivance of social-democratic party leaderships.[41]

Among anti-war Bolsheviks such words caused little dissension. To them it was self-evident that the Second International's pre-war commitments had been abrogated by its most prestigious leaders, and that further collaboration, even with Kautskyite centrists, was intolerable.[42] What caused controversy was Lenin's attitude to Russia. He summed up his position: 'From the viewpoint of the working class and the toiling masses of all the peoples of Russia, the lesser evil would be the defeat of the tsarist monarchy.'[43] The exceptional character of this sentence cannot be savoured unless we momentarily suppress our hindsight about his later career. Here was an émigré revolutionary, lacking finances, organisation and personnel, declaring to his colleagues that propaganda should be directed at telling the largely patriotic population in Russia to welcome the country's conquest. No Menshevik or Socialist Revolutionary, however opposed to the Russian government and to the war, took this line; and few Bolsheviks did either.[44]

Like many socialists of the Russian empire, Lenin had advocated 'defeatism' in the Russo-Japanese war of 1904–5.[45] His prediction that defeats would induce revolutionary crisis had been correct. He repeated it in 1914, but there was a significant difference in the circumstances: nobody in 1904 expected the Japanese, if victorious, to occupy Russia. German war aims in 1914 were not definitively formulated; but political commentators in Russia, from governmental spokesmen through to Marxist theorists, anticipated that the German armed forces would dismember the Russian empire and reduce the Russian state to a semi-colonial dependency of Germany. Secret treaties were, in fact, signed in 1915. The Central Powers decided that Austria-Hungary would obtain a sphere of influence in south-eastern Europe while Germany would acquire one in Russia; Turkey would be rewarded by annexations in Romanov lands adjacent to the Ottoman empire. The Allies made agreements which were also rapacious. Russia signed a treaty to take over the Straits of Dardanelles and the British and French conspired to break up the Habsburg empire and to rob Germany of her colonies. Russia's dire potential plight after a German victory was eloquently sketched by Lenin's adversary Petr Maslov.[46] And yet Lenin remained willing to

call for Russia's defeat even though he repeatedly asserted, with the
mechanical reliability of a gramophone, that all belligerent states
were bent upon territorial expansion and political and economic
dominion. No wonder Lenin's differential attitude to the Russian
and German war effort policy was regarded as illogical by Bolshevik
activists who read his writings or listened to him in Switzerland.[47]

Lenin's chance to argue for his eccentric notions came on 6
September when the Bern section's members had arranged a meeting. There were so few of them that they could easily have met in
someone's flat; but such was their edginess that, in contrast with their
pre-war practice in Switzerland, they convened secretly in some
woods outside the city. It was as if they were in autocratic Russia,
not democratic and tolerant Switzerland. No advertisement of the
meeting was made.[48] The presence of Bolshevik Duma deputy F. M.
Samoilov, who had been convalescing abroad and was set to return
to Russia shortly after the gathering, must also have been a factor;
the Bern Bolsheviks would not have wished to compromise
themselves and Samoilov in the eyes of the Swiss authorities by
holding a session of overtly political character.[49]

No definitive decision on policy, of course, could be taken by the
Bolsheviks of Bern alone; but Samoilov's attendance gave Lenin a
chance to relay his policies back to Russia. In fact, the other five
Bolshevik Duma deputies, quite without Lenin's intervention, had
behaved with commendable adherence to the spirit of Stuttgart and
Basle by demonstratively walking out of the State Duma session
which voted war credits to the Russian government on 26 July
1914.[50] Menshevik deputies also had opposed the Russian declaration of war and left the chamber. A joint criticism by Menshevik and
Bolshevik deputies was read out by the Menshevik, V. I. Khaustov.
Like the revolutionary émigrés, however, the Bolsheviks in Russia
had to elaborate policy for the duration of the war. Samoilov's return
to St Petersburg with Lenin's recommendations inevitably caused
controversy. It was decided that a survey of Bolshevik opinion
through the empire was needed. Leading Bolsheviks in the capital
were known to take an anti-war line. But Lenin's defeatist demands
were contentious. A meeting of the Duma deputies and other
Bolshevik leaders, including Kamenev, was held at Ozerki outside
St Peterburg. But the Okhrana broke up the discussions on 4
November, found incriminating material (which included Lenin's
recommendations) and arrested all participants. At the subsequent
trial, in February 1915, Kamenev disowned Lenin's defeatism.

Bolshevik Duma deputies such as G. I. Petrovski and M. K. Muranov refused to break ranks; and Lenin's regret at their exile to Siberia was alleviated at least somewhat by the evidence that Bolsheviks in Russia were ready to take a stand on their anti-war principles.[51]

In October 1914, Lenin travelled to Geneva and Zurich to talk with other Bolsheviks.[52] Plans were made, with the assistance of V. A. Karpinski, to revive *Social-Democrat*. Finances were still tight, and only around 2000 copies could be printed: each issue amounted to only two sides of a single sheet of paper. Most copies, moreover, were sent to addresses in western and central Europe.[53] Communication with Russia remained hazardous. Even so, a few copies reached Petrograd. The first wartime issue of *Social-Democrat*, no. 33, was made on 1 November. The front page included a manifesto on the party's attitude to the war. The Bolshevik central émigré apparatus had rapidly begun to re-emerge.

Debate with fellow Bolsheviks in Switzerland induced changes in Lenin's stance on the war. Karpinski asked why, if social-democrats were 'internationalists' who hated the governments of all belligerent countries, did Lenin prefer a German victory over Russia? Karpinski also queried Lenin's rhetoric. Was it fair, he asked, to describe the Russian armies as 'Black Hundred bands'. Did Lenin really contend that all Russian soldiers, conscripted from the peasantry and the working class, were like the reactionary antisemitic thugs of the pre-war Black Hundreds?[54] Lenin excised the slur from his statements. More importantly, he ceased to advocate 'defeatism' exclusively for Russia. He still suggested in *Social-Democrat* that the Russian regime was the worst of Europe's regimes and that Russia's defeat was more desirable than that of any other nation.[55] But he also declared that socialists of every country should call for their respective government's military defeat.[56] Thus Lenin urged multilateral defeatism. This exculpated him of the charge that his internationalism was belied by anti-Russianism, but it exposed him to the accusation of misunderstanding how wars are waged. How could all governments be simultaneously defeated? Lenin brushed the question aside. Instead he insisted that defeat for any nation was likely to engender revolution. The objective, then, was not military defeat for its own sake but the creation of conditions for a political upheaval. Socialist seizures of power would become possible.[57]

Lenin added that the politics of each belligerent state had become inextricably linked to the politics of all the others. Socialism could not be expected 'to complete its victory within the framework of a fatherland'.[58] The introduction of socialism had to be conceived in terms of Europe as a whole. The struggle would ultimately be fought between the Continent's working classes and its middle classes, and national borders would mean nothing in such conflicts: class war would envelop Europe. Before 1914, Lenin had said that the outbreak of conflict among the European powers should be countered by socialists who would launch a revolutionary war. He had not specified what this would involve. In 1914 his meaning became clearer as he proposed a new slogan: European civil war![59]

Plekhanov treated such proposals as the product of a deranged mind. He did not deign to examine the practical details, or rather the lack of them. For Plekhanov, Lenin had become an insane sloganeer instead of a serious politician. But if Plekhanov would not argue with Lenin, Lenin relished the chance to debate with Plekhanov, who travelled from France on 10 October 1914 to address a Russian émigré gathering in Lausanne. Lenin attended, and not wanting Plekhanov to withdraw because of his presence, he buried his face in some papers at the back of the hall until the proceedings began. Plekhanov's speech lasted an hour and a half. At its end, Lenin stood up to denounce what he regarded as mere chauvinism and to claim that Plekhanov had parted company forever with Marxism.[60] The significance of the confrontation was considerable. This was the first time that Lenin had shown unconditional disrespect to Plekhanov to his face and at a public meeting.[61] His aggressiveness was not confined to Russians. He no longer had the slightest respect for any leading Marxist in Europe.[62] He lashed out at the German Social-Democratic Party, and named names. Kautsky's refusal to condemn Kaiser Wilhelm, according to Lenin, was as heinous as Plekhanov's argument in favour of Russian national self-defence.[63] Another precedent had been set. For the first time, apart from small gatherings of Bolsheviks, Lenin had publicly castigated Karl Kautsky. A psychological Rubicon had been crossed.

It was Lenin's extremism that resulted in his Bolshevik friends remaining isolated from other Russian Marxists in emigration who equally abhorred Plekhanov's 'defencism'. Martov and Trotski in Paris were among these. Lenin declared his opinion frankly: 'It would not be a bad thing if the Germans took Riga, Tiflis and Helsingfors!'[64] They too expected the war to induce Europe's long-awaited socialist revolution. Lenin did not initially oppose a *rapprochement*. He remarked of Martov: 'This writer is now doing what a social-democrat should do.' Praise indeed, by Lenin's standards. Martov must have pinched himself to check that he was not hallucinating. Lenin also dubbed *Golos* ('The Voice') as the best in Europe.[65] Again, Martov must have blinked in astonishment. But there was a snag. Martov and Trotski rejected any call upon workers in Russia and elsewhere to work for the military defeat of their respective countries as unrealistic. They urged a more flexible policy. Both men saw that the popular desire for peace in Europe would strengthen as the rigours of war worsened; and they wanted social-democrats to join all movements, socialist or not, that expressed this desire.[66] Martov in particular had a profounder understanding of the barbarism unleashed by the war.[67] Lenin's almost puerile stridency about 'European civil war' had no echo in their statements.[68] More particularly, Martov and Trotski did not despair of winning over other socialists who did not yet directly oppose their governments. Kautsky, for them, was not yet a lost soul.[69] N. S. Chkheidze, leader of the Menshevik Duma fraction, was equally keen to avoid a premature split in the ranks of European socialism. The Menshevik Duma deputies, unlike their Bolshevik counterparts, were not arrested; and it irritated Lenin that Chkheidze retained opportunities for legal propaganda. His heart hardened fast against compromise with non-Bolsheviks in the Russian Social-Democratic Labour Party. The fact that neither Chkheidze nor Martov would break organisational ties with straightforward 'defencists' such as P. P. Maslov confirmed Lenin's inclination to reject all thought of negotiating with the Mensheviks.[70]

The Bolsheviks would go it alone among Russian social-democrats. *Social-Democrat* was designated as the organ of the Central Committee. Lenin turned the paucity of surviving Central Committee members to his advantage. He tacitly reasoned that he and Zinoviev, if only they remained at liberty, were perfectly entitled to set up a new central newspaper howsoever they wanted. For the same reason, no doubt, he was in no hurry to co-opt new Central Committee members. He and Zinoviev could cheerfully continue to call themselves the Foreign Bureau of the Central Committee and take decisions in the Central Committee's name.[71] Lenin also aimed to have tight control over the Committee of the Foreign Organisation. Its fund-raising and co-ordinating functions would be useful: and presumably Lenin did not want it to emerge as a rival Bolshevik body. Its collapsed condition made this easier. He therefore planned to call a conference of all Bolshevik foreign sections in Bern in

February 1915 and secure the re-election of the Committee of the Foreign Organisation.[72]

'THE COLLAPSE OF THE SECOND INTERNATIONAL'

Lenin was signalling, for the first time in his career, that the establishment of socialism in Europe's advanced industrial countries had become an immediate possibility and objective. He did not say why he came to this attitude, and he may well have made up his mind before defining what objective circumstances encouraged this optimism. It was to his notebooks, as late as 1916–17, that he confided such thoughts.[73] In the meantime, he worked to found a Third International and to win socialist allies in Europe. Two major pamphlets were written. The first was *The Collapse of the Second International*. Published in early June 1915, it attacked the positions of Martov, Trotski and Kautsky. Lenin kept track of Kautsky's articles, and incorporated further criticisms as he composed both pamphlets. Kautsky had allegedly brought about 'an unheard-of prostitution' of Marxism and was a *Mädchen für alle*.[74] The second pamphlet, *Socialism and the War*, was co-authored in August 1915 with Zinoviev. Again, the imagery was florid with sexual innuendo; Lenin was not so prim in print as in his outward behaviour. *Collapse of the Second International* stated the formal case that the parties of the Second International at Stuttgart in 1907 and at Basle in 1912 had undertaken to oppose their countries' entry into a continental war, and to use any such military conflict for 'the acceleration of the fall of capitalism'.[75] This commitment, according to Lenin, had been infringed. He indicated that the Basle Manifesto had been composed with precisely the kind of war which broke out in 1914 in mind. The war was not a traditional struggle for national independence or for a limited redrawing of territorial boundaries. It was 'imperialist'; it was a fight to the death between two armed coalitions of powers bent upon global domination.[76] The talk of the Allies about the need to liberate Belgium was rhetoric. Germany's communiqués about her desire to assist Austria-Hungary in her legitimate wish to fend off Serbian aggression was eyewash: the war was about worldwide political and economic hegemony.[77]

In Lenin's presentation, the Basle Manifesto had predicted that the outbreak of a European war would be accompanied by a revolutionary situation; and he argued that this had been confirmed by events in July–August 1914. Supposedly, revolution in Europe had been possible. There had been a 'crisis' in governing circles; there had been a sharp worsening of material conditions; there had been a 'raising of the activism of the masses'.[78] This analysis suffered from certain defects. Neither at Stuttgart nor even at Basle had the Second International stipulated unconditionally that a declaration of war should be met by the immediate organisation of a revolution.[79] Consequently, Lenin could not nail down his specific charges. But he was correct in less formal terms: the Basle Manifesto had certainly given the impression that the parties belonging to the Second International would oppose all governments daring to plunge the Continent into war. The voting of war credits was an unmistakable infraction of the International's decision. A minority of Europe's socialists had sustained the line of International; the majority, as Lenin increasingly pointed out, had broken it.

A second defect lies in Lenin's contention that a European revolutionary situation existed. Undoubtedly there was political trouble for the Russian imperial authorities, especially in St Petersburg, in the month before the declaration of war. But the unrest faded rapidly after the emperor declared war on Germany and Austria-Hungary. Still less was a revolutionary situation discernible in other countries. Neither the Allies nor the Central Powers exhibited serious tensions within their ruling élites. Nor was there much opposition to the national war effort among the various social classes. On the contrary, it was a moment of near-universal patriotism in Britain, France and Germany; even Austria-Hungary experienced little disturbance apart from among the Czechs and a few other national minorities.[80] The labour movement across Europe had been active before 1914 in strikes and protests; but calls and support for revolutionary action were remarkable for their scarcity. Lenin also asserted that there had been a drastic deterioration of wages and conditions before 1914; but several groups within the working class were better off than ever before. In fairness to Lenin, it must be acknowledged that other groups were worse off and that standards of living differed from country to country. But lower wages and poorer conditions do not demonstrate the existence of a revolutionary situation. Lenin's assertions were based on inadequate sociology and shaky argumentation.

His commentary on the German Social-Democratic Party, too, was unreliable. He did not bother with the ascendant party leaders who voted in favour of war credits in the Reichstag; for him, they were beneath contempt. Lenin was instead infuriated with Kautsky, Haase and their 'centrist' colleagues who refused to break unequivocally with the rest of their party. Kautsky felt that a summons to the German workers to take to the streets would fall on deaf ears; he saw no point in inviting arrest for an obviously doomed adventure.[81] He, unlike Lenin, recognised the patriotic mood of the German working class.

In addition, *The Collapse of the Second International* maintained that Kautsky was merely trying to cast the blame on 'the masses'. Only the party leaders, according to Lenin, were in a position to act with sufficient knowledge and decisiveness in the swiftly-changing conditions of pre-war crisis. The masses could not act if firm guidance failed to be supplied. The difficulties for the workers became greater once war had been declared: censorship was imposed; conscription was introduced, and the penalty for disobedience was death.[82] Other Russian Marxists, however, believed that Lenin and Zinoviev idealised German working-class attitudes. According to the right-wing Menshevik, P. P. Maslov, the German government could count on most German social-democrats to approve of expansionist war policies;[83] and his left-wing Menshevik colleague A. S. Martynov added that the notion that German workers were infused with revolutionary zeal was the result of looking at Germany with spectacles tinted with 'Jacobinism' and 'oriental messianism'.[84] Plekhanov highlighted how isolated the German far-left socialists under Karl Liebknecht were in the German Social-Democratic Party, and he suggested that German socialism's doctrines would quickly be 'revised' in favour of a more explicit nationalism in the event of a German victory in the war.[85] Other leaders of the Russian Social-Democratic Labour Party, such as Trotski and Bukharin, were less scathing about the German workers and maintained faith in the imminence of a German socialist revolution.[86] Yet they also perceived that patriotic support for the war effort was a serious impediment to the achievement of that objective. Lenin referred to the problem only glancingly; the greater problem, in his view, was constituted by the sins of the party leadership.[87]

Consequently Lenin's demand for the abandonment of the Second International and the establishment of a Third had few supporters outside Bolshevik circles. Martynov declared that only political 'sectarians' would delight in the Second International's permanent demise.[88] Plekhanov was nearer to Lenin in washing his hands of the

Second International; but Lenin could not found a Third International with a Plekhanov, who stoutly defended the necessity for Germany to be defeated. And so Lenin was compelled to explain why the break with the German Social-Democratic Party had to be final. Here he borrowed several arguments from Robert Michels, whom he had mocked for years.[89] Command over German socialism, according to Lenin, had been taken by the party's permanent paid officials; and he claimed that these tacitly rejected revolutionary policies and had undergone a process of *embourgeoisement*. He refused to accept Michels's analysis in its entirety, and continued to scorn him in public utterances.[90] Lenin denied that all organisations, regardless of political orientation, eventually give rise to bureaucratic practices in response to the technical requirements of fast, informed and co-ordinated decision-making. It was only the economic side of Michels's work that he incorporated; and he did this mainly by borrowing from the researches of Grigori Zinoviev (who was less reluctant to acknowledge his intellectual debt to Michels).[91] Zinoviev alleged that the German Social-Democratic Party's officials were supported mainly by the skilled and better-paid workers, who outnumbered the unskilled in the party's ranks. Following Michels, Zinoviev added that 'petit-bourgeois' recruits to the party, such as innkeepers and clerks, were a rising proportion of the membership. This whole 'labour aristocracy' benefited from the German economy's expansion and objectively had a stake in the expansionist foreign policy espoused by Bismarck and his successors in Berlin. There was therefore a firm social base for the development of the party's 'opportunism' in 1914.[92]

Reproducing the outline of Zinoviev's detailed sketch, Lenin suggested that such socioeconomic factors explained the party's abandonment of revolutionary commitments and the implicit adoption of a strategy of peaceful and piecemeal reforms. The ascendant party leadership called itself social-democratic. It was actually, in Lenin's abusive caricature, a congeries of 'social-chauvinists'. It had become a 'political detachment of the bourgeoisie'.[93]

Where Zinoviev and Lenin marched intellectually, not only Michels but also European social-democratic leftists such as Rosa Luxemburg and Anton Pannekoek had gone before.[94] The rightward shift of the German Social-Democratic party was not imaginary. The question for sociologists today is whether a mainly economic explanation is sufficient, and the answer must surely be no. At last

Lenin had shed the complacent optimism about the German Social-Democratic Party so evident in *What Is To Be Done?*. In organisational questions he remained predominantly a practical political leader in search of practical solutions; the broader issues of contemporary political sociology passed him by. His naïveté prevailed for several further years, and in many ways never left him. Nor, as regards the particular circumstances of the war, was he ever to admit that political constraints bore down heavily upon Kautsky and his colleagues in the conditions of state power and popular opinion of Wilhelminian Germany. But to expect anything else of Lenin is to misunderstand his mood and aims in 1914. He wanted to stake out a political ridge to be won. He wanted to construct a beacon for guidance to others. He exaggerated and distorted, and his zeal led him into simplistic intellectualising. In *Socialism and the War* he made his objective explicit. He wanted 'A Marxist International without and *against* the opportunists'.[95] Under such a slogan, no non-Marxist would belong. Not even Marx had required a self-professedly Marxist International, and only Lenin and friends suggested the formation of an International which would exclude Marxists deemed to have incorrect opinions.

STRUGGLES AMONG BOLSHEVIKS: 1915

Lenin, getting his second wind after the shocks of mid-1914, was pleased. The first full year of war was nearly catastrophic for Nikolai II's government. The Russian armies advancing into East Prussia were rebuffed. Catastrophe ensued at the battle of Tannenberg and a retreat deep into Romanov territory was undertaken. 'Russian' Poland was overrun by German forces; and Galicia, too, was returned to the Austrians in summer 1915. Disasters in the field were compounded by difficulties in the factories. A shortage of munitions was growing. And, after the initial rallying around the government after the declaration of war, industrial conflict returned. The emperor agreed to permit the establishment of 'war-industry committees', which would include representatives of both employers and workers. The intention was to surmount the technical impediments to factory production for the army's requirements, and to lessen the tensions which produced strikes. Not only liberal but also socialist politicians exploited the committees for their own ends. Even so, the government's administratative problems compelled its consent to the establishment of a central organ uniting zemstva and municipal councils. Hospitals at the front line were set up from private charitable funds. Gossip about the empress Aleksandra's Germanophile leanings and unfounded rumours about her liaison with the 'holy man' Grigori Rasputin spread everywhere. The Kadets and other liberals sensed their opportunity and demanded 'a government of public confidence'; they especially sought the dismissal of the aged and reactionary premier I. L. Goremykin and his Cabinet in favour of liberally-inclined ministers.[96] The emperor would not yield so much. He appointed himself commander-in-chief in summer 1915, taking full responsibility for the war effort. The Eastern front steadied and became almost as static as the Western front; trench warfare techniques were employed with efficiency. The factories increased production. The Kadets talked subversively in private but acted loyally. The war-industry committees were shunned by the Bolsheviks; it was mainly the right-wing exponents of Menshevism, under Kuzma Gvozdev who joined, and these were committed to national defence. Industrial conflict occurred frequently in the last months of 1915. But the Okhrana coped adequately, strike leaders were arrested and Bolshevik party groups were hunted down with notable zeal.

None the less Lenin and his associates felt that the chances of revolution in Russia had increased. The problem for them was to communicate with their fellow factionalists from abroad. In mid-October 1914 Lenin had initiated a scheme whereby Aleksandr Shlyapnikov, a Petersburg Bolshevik leader, would move to Stockholm to operate as courier between Switzerland and Russia. Shlyapnikov was an able underground organiser. He also had valuable experience of working abroad, having been employed as a craftsman in the Hendon aircraft works in north London. Towards the end of the year, Shlyapnikov had written to Lenin revealing that support for his attitude to the war was growing among Bolsheviks in Russia. He made arrangements for the regular dispatch of *Social-Democrat* to Petrograd (as St Petersburg was renamed, to avoid its Germanic linguistic connotations).[97] Shlyapnikov also spoke at the Congress of Swedish social-democrats in November. Yet Lenin's hopes about Shlyapnikov were soon dashed. Shlyapnikov and his colleague and lover, Aleksandra Kollontai, also asked Lenin to move to Scandinavia to facilitate better contact with St Petersburg. They themselves went to Oslo and left the Bolshevik transport arrangements in ruins. Communication with Russia ceased for weeks.[98] At such a distance it was hard for Lenin to dissuade them from being so unco-operative (and he was subsequently, when it was too late, to recognise the cogency of their request).[99] There were also troubles in the Swiss emigration. The conference of all the émigré Bolshevik sections, scheduled for the beginning of 1915, was delayed by the 'uncooperative' attitude taken by a small section living near the village of Baugy outside Lausanne. These included young theorists such as Yuri Pyatakov and Nikolai Bukharin. While accepting many strategical notions put forward by Lenin, they objected to his pre-war writings on national self-determination and disliked his neglect of the peace movement.[100] They refused to attend unless Lenin guaranteed to give them the floor at the conference to put their case. At last, on 14 February 1915, the proceedings commenced.[101]

In general, the conference was a victory for Lenin. The war was defined as imperialistic; all socialists were called upon to oppose their governments; multilateral defeatism was accepted as policy; and the idea that a democratic peace was achievable without revolution across Europe was rejected.[102] These ideas were, in fact, acceptable to the Baugy group; and Lenin agreed to trim his proposals of the bits that offended them. Definitive resolution of the disputes between them was postponed.[103] Bukharin and Pyatakov continued to argue against the right of national self-determination on grounds made familiar by Rosa Luxemburg. To their mind, in the age of imperialism, there was no possibility of a sealed-off national economy; and, in the political sphere, the creation of new nation states would only impede the spread of internationalist sentiments among Europe's workers. The Baugy Bolsheviks added an inflection to Luxemburg's argument which would have annoyed her. If national economies were becoming inextricably enmeshed with each other, then revolution in any single country would have immediate and profound repercussions elsewhere. There was therefore no longer much point in Russian social-democrats emphasising the reforms to be demanded when the Romanov autocracy should fall. Instead they should take a European perspective and stress socialist objectives.[104] Bukharin came perilously close to repudiating the old Russian Marxist premise that Russia's next revolution would be a 'bourgeois' one. This, as yet, was heresy for Lenin.[105]

Yet Bukharin and Pyatakov did not carry the conference with them; and Lenin had pragmatic reasons for not exacerbating or advertising his conflict with the Baugy group. Bukharin and

Pyatakov had independent financial means, and agreed at the conference to place them at the Central Committee's disposal. This was a powerful incentive to Lenin to dispel fractiousness. In addition, Bukharin disowned any aim to drop the demands for reforms embodied in the party programme since 1903.[106] Bukharin, in his own view, simply desired a switch of the party's focus of work from a Russian bourgeois revolution towards a European socialist revolution; he did not deny that the forthcoming revolution in Russia would be bourgeois. Lenin was the sort of theorist who, in the Middle Ages, would have become cantankerous about the number of angels who could stand on the point of a needle, but for once he saw the sense in amicably talking matters over with Bukharin at leisure.[107]

Social-Democrat's future was secured. In 1915 it appeared roughly once a month. Fourteen issues appeared in 1915, carrying twenty four pieces by Lenin; he oversaw all stages of its production.[108] He had none of the problems which had plagued him about *Pravda*. There was even sufficient money to found a journal, *Kommunist*, with the assistance of Bukharin and Pyatakov. Indeed it was more their project than Lenin's.[109] *Kommunist* was intended to provide a forum of Marxist intellectual discussion and to attract participation from left-wing, anti-war socialists from other countries. Articles were commissioned from Karl Radek and the Dutchman Anton Pannekoek. Such collaboration was crucial if Lenin's Bolsheviks were to appear as something greater than a tiny Russian sect. Bukharin was also willing to help repair the damage done by Shlyapnikov's self-removal. After the Bern conference of Bolshevik émigrés, Bukharin moved to Scandinavia.[110] In fact, Shlyapnikov quickly returned to his transport duties. Switzerland was so much the centre of international socialist debates in the war that Lenin may have seen Bukharin's transfer as a mode of ridding himself of a rival. Yet a price had to be paid. Scandinavia was bound to remain the main clandestine transit point for Bolshevik newspapers and correspondence *en route* to Russia; the linkmen and couriers for the Bolshevik Committee had a marvellous opportunity to manipulate the Bolshevik faction's activity. Perhaps Lenin trusted in Bukharin's manifest good nature and continuing high regard for him.

Furthermore, Lenin had other things to preoccupy him. He was not alone in seeing the need for a European anti-war initiative; and, while he called for action, others acted. The International Socialist Bureau was virtually inoperative. Based in Brussels until 1914, it had

had to be evacuated to The Hague. The dissensions besetting its members discouraged its secretary Camille Huysmans from holding meetings.[111] The obvious tactic for Lenin and Pannekoek was to create their own international co-ordinating body. But the actual call for this came from the Swiss socialist Robert Grimm and the Italian Odino Morgari. Martov had similar thoughts. In spring 1915, Grimm announced the convoking of an anti-war socialist gathering.[112] The location was to be the Swiss Alpine village of Zimmerwald. A march had been stolen on Lenin. It was evident that several non-Bolshevik Russian Marxists such as Martov and Trotski would also be invited. There was also the likelihood that the Socialist Revolutionaries would be present. Lenin's joy at the news was not undiluted.[113]

'THE NOTEBOOKS ON PHILOSOPHY'

Lenin's expressions of pleasure in 1915 were directed at matters more arcane. He returned, after a break of half a decade, to his philosophical studies. Day after day was spent in the Bern Public Library. He had been shocked that several theorists previously enjoying his approval had adopted policies on the war which he deemed to be inimical to the traditions, commitments and interests of the international socialist movement. Foremost among these was Plekhanov. When writing *Materialism and Empiriocriticism* in 1908–9, Lenin had been intellectually close to Plekhanov. His aim had been not only to denigrate Aleksandr Bogdanov as a politician but also to indicate the kind of philosophy acceptable to Marxists: and Plekhanov's influence on Lenin's chapters had been strong.[114] Now Plekhanov represented everything Lenin found politically distasteful. Lenin believed that 'correct' policy should stand upon 'correct' premises in philosophy, and he was moved to re-examine the philosophical issues at stake. His present objective was to discover what misinterpretations of Marxian epistemology and ontology had provoked the alleged political betrayal made by Kautsky, Plekhanov and other leaders of the Second International in 1914. It was in character for Lenin to jot this down, even in his private notes, in terms of the mistakes of others; at no point did he directly criticise his own statements in *Materialism and Empiriocriticism*. And yet, implicitly, the endeavour was also an attempt to see where he himself had been mistaken.

Shortly before the outbreak of war he had signed a contract to write a short biographical piece on Karl Marx and already planned to include a summary of Marxian philosophy. He began the work, in peacetime, in July 1914.[115] The biography was completed by November; but Lenin had by then started to fill many new notebooks on philosophy. He continued with this into 1915. The main texts he studied were works by Aristotle, G.W.F. Hegel and L.A. Feuerbach: all to trace Marxism to its theoretical underpinnings.

This, obviously, was not casual toil. He was serious enough about his labours to read Aristotle's *Metaphysics* in a German–Greek parallel-text edition, checking the original Greek where the German translation seemed unconvincing.[116] Lengthy excerpts from Hegel's *History of Philosophy* and *The Philosophy of History* were also made by him. Altogether he filled twenty-three notebooks. Lenin, like most leading Russian revolutionary intellectuals, found such tasks of self-education congenial (although few equalled his multilinguistic competence). Both Plekhanov and Martov re-engaged their minds with philosophical issues after 1914.[117] The fact that Lenin overlooked the wartime writings of his adversaries indicates how deeply submerged he had become in his own theoretical quest. He was behaving like a typical Russian revolutionary intellectual in setting himself the objective of achieving a comprehensive 'world-view'; politics alone was not enough. But his private delight in reading these philosophers was paralleled by a commitment to publish his resultant thoughts. Contrary to a widely-held opinion, it is the merest accident that the considerations in *The Notebooks* were published only posthumously. In 1915 he had started to draft a forbiddingly substantial item, 'Towards the Question of the Dialectic.'[118] Had it not been for his other concerns in 1916 and the occurrence of the February Revolution in 1917, he would have tried to see it into the press.

Lenin impugned Plekhanov for attacking Kant's epistemology 'more from the vulgar-materialist than from the dialectical-materialist viewpoint'.[119] Plekhanov had done a service, in Lenin's view, by attacking Kantianism. In fact, Plekhanov after 1914 came to discern healthy sides in Kantianism; he even praised the call for moral imperatives in politics, and claimed that Marx's deployment of terms such as 'duty' and 'right' had displayed the same attitude.[120] Lenin overlooked Plekhanov's startling change of heart. It fell to Martov to attack Plekhanov in the press for undermining the 'scientific' principles of socialism with its amoral notions of historical inevitability and impersonal socioeconomic forces.[121] What Lenin held against Plekhanov was a mistake of longer standing: namely his neglect of the importance of Hegel. Lenin pointed out that Marxists in general had attended more to the writings of Feuerbach and G. Büchner than to the Hegelian dialectical method espoused by Marx himself.[122]

Lenin chuckled at this discovery, making the following remark in his notebooks: It is impossible to achieve a complete understanding of Marx's *Kapital* and especially its first chapter without first thoroughly studying and understanding all of Hegel's *Logic*. Consequently not one Marxist has completely understood Marx in the past half-century.[123] These words have often been treated as a stupendously arrogant dismissal of other Marxists.[124] Such an interpretation is not entirely accurate; for Lenin claimed not that everyone had no understanding whatsoever of Marx, but that no one had 'complete' understanding. He did not despise previous Marxology in its entirety. Nevertheless he certainly hinted that only he had the capacity to gain the necessary 'complete' understanding. Arrogance enough, perhaps. Even so, he must also be given credit for perceiving that leading Marxist theoreticians after Marx and Engels had not examined, nor even properly recognised, Hegel's influence upon Marx. According to Lenin, their philosophical outlook consequently lacked dynamism, supplying a rationale not for authentic Marxists but for those who were politically passive. The writings of both Plekhanov and Kautsky could therefore be seen as avoiding essential questions about how to transform the world. Supposedly they merely 'reflected' the world.

He omitted to specify that these objections could be levelled with even greater cogency at *Materialism and Empiriocriticism*. He was seldom lavish in purveying self-criticism, and his *Notebooks* contain no explicit explanation as to how his own views had changed. What, then, did he find in Hegel? Very important was Lenin's examination of Hegel's ideas about cognition. Lenin altered his reflection theory of knowledge. In a striking rupture with *Materialism and Empiriocriticism*, he declared that the mind was not akin to a camera: 'Cognition is the reflection of nature by man. But it is not a simple, not a direct, complete reflection, but a process of a series of abstractions, of the formation, of the construction of concepts, laws, etc.; and these concepts, laws, etc. (thinking, science = 'the logical idea') also comprehend conditionally, approximately the universal pattern of an eternally moving and developing nature.'[125]

This inelegant declaration was an off-the-cuff note not yet refined for publication; its galloping style gives a good impression of the excitement experienced by Lenin at the time. He wanted to emphasise that knowledge cannot be total, but only partial. Our concepts therefore have to be 'hewn, chopped, supple, mobile, relative, reciprocally-linked, united in opposites in order to embrace the world'.[126] This led Lenin to a further modification. In *Materialism and Empiriocriticism* he had written about the brain as an unmediated register of external phenomena. In his wartime notebooks, however, he accorded a more or less autonomous significance to concepts and laws and categories, and dropped his previous analysis of human thought as a mere physiological reflex.[127] He stressed that cognition should be understood in terms not only of mind and matter but also of concepts. Plekhanov had said this all along, and had been ridiculed by Lenin's *Materialism and Empiriocriticism* for doing so.[128] None the less, Lenin also went beyond Plekhanov in 1915 by asserting that the validity of concepts and categories was testable only by their usefulness when applied to real situations. 'Practice' was the sole litmus-paper test. This, according to Lenin, was Hegel's view; and a rereading of Marx's *Theses on Feuerbach* convinced him that Marx himself had held the same opinion.[129]

An emphasis on practical experimentation was hardly new among Russian Marxists; it had been characteristic of Lenin's old philosophical adversary, Aleksandr Bogdanov, in *Empiriomonism*.[130] The closeness of standpoint is still more remarkable when Lenin's reconsiderations about ontology are taken into account. Lenin now focused on the universe's infinite complexity. Causality was not simple: no phenomenon results exclusively from the action of any other single phenomenon. Instead the world encompasses innumerable interactions in space and time, and the attribution of causal influences must therefore be exceedingly intricate.[131]

Bogdanov had elaborated his ideas from a dialogue between Marx's *Theses on Feuerbach* and the neo-Kantianism fashionable among many Austrian and Russian Marxists around the turn of the century. Lenin's philosophical development had taken a different track: through a rereading of Marx alongside a study of the works of Hegel which had influenced Marx himself. Nevertheless the resultant outlooks are remarkably similar. A further contention of Lenin's reinforces this impression. Throughout his notes on Hegel, he enthused about what he took to be proof that 'leaps' take place in nature. At 0° C, for example, water changes its quality and becomes ice.[132] The idea of 'contradictions' and 'breaks' and 'interruptions of gradualness' were brought to the forefront of Lenin's philosophical work.[133] They had previously been evident mainly in his political practice and his political ideas; but they had been banished from his epistemological work. In the war, he brought his philosophy abreast of his politics. Bogdanov would no doubt have relished the spectacle of his opponent being drawn into a refutation of the very arguments aimed at Bogdanov in 1909. But Lenin's work was committed to the pages of his notebooks. The rethinking of his epistemology and ontology remained unpublished and was unknown to others.

Yet the shift in Lenin's thought did not occur on all fronts. Those accounts postulating a complete revolution in his philosophy after 1914 are misleading. For Lenin still detested Kant, and still used 'Kantian' as a term of abuse.[134] He sustained his hatred quite without feeling obliged to re-examine Kant's works. Lenin at his best was never more than a gifted reader of other philosophers' works. He made no contributions of his own; and, as his continued casual contempt for Kant indicates, his competence was patchy.

Important differences between the respective standpoints of Lenin and Bogdanov anyway remained. Lenin's publication of a second edition of *Materialism and Empiriocriticism* in 1920 was not fortuitous.[135] Several tenets of his earlier book stayed intact in the *Notebooks on Philosophy*. Lenin's jottings reaffirmed the independent existence of the external world. They also stated that man's abstract conceptions derive from 'a knowledge of the pattern of the objective link of the world'.[136] (Let us remember that this infelicitous phrasing occurs in work-in-progress notes.) In addition, Lenin repeated that philosophy was divided into two principal camps, materialism and idealism;[137] Bogdanov thought such affirmations to be neither provable nor worthy of discussion. Lenin, moreover, continued to categorise Hegel as a philosophical idealist while recognising his intuitive 'genius' and stating that Hegel had produced the 'embryos of dialectical materialism'.[138] Indeed Lenin declared, albeit to himself: 'Intelligent idealism is nearer to intelligent materialism than is stupid materialism.'[139] But this was still far from being a wholehearted endorsement of Bogdanov's ideas. The old Lenin reappeared in his draft philosophical article of 1915, when he triumphantly proclaimed the attainability of 'living, fruitful, true, powerful, omnipotent, objective, absolute human knowledge'.[140]

When all is said and done, Lenin failed to achieve internal coherence in his newer philosophical views. Accretion, rather than basic reconstruction, had taken place. The lately-added layers of thought display a greater awareness of epistemological subtleties. But they are like a new wing built on to a house without thought for the architectural strains imposed.

This matters for the fate of Soviet philosophy in ensuing decades. In seeking to maintain the appearance of Marxist 'orthodoxy', writers in the USSR through to the mid-1980s had to trace the lineage of their notions from Lenin. The fact that his ideas were left in such a hotch-potch makes them less restrictive for later Soviet philosophers. Lenin's self-contradictions and explorations allow an astute scholar to select a wide range of ideas as sources of professed influence.[141] This is one principal reason why Soviet philosophical discourse has not been devoid of interesting and inventive qualities. The *Notebooks on Philosophy* do not constitute even a minor intrinsic contribution to twentieth-century epistemology and ontology. Nor do they contain an accurate account of the history of European philosophy.[142] In particular, the relationship between Hegel and Kant is misrepresented. The two German philosophers, who were crucial to Lenin's understanding of the continental tradition, were never as distant from each other as he claimed. Nor did he pick up the theme of 'alienation', developed by Marx on the basis of Hegel's ideas. This brings us back to our point of entry. While exploring, Lenin was bent on discovering what would be congenial for him. He sought and found a rationale for adaptability in politics. Lenin's philosophical cerebrations did not precede and predetermine his politics. No doubt there was some mutual influence between the politics and the philosophy; but, in the main, it was the politics which produced the philosophy, and not vice versa.

For Lenin, the toil in the Bern Public Library was well worthwhile; the abundance of exclamation marks, whether in approval or exasperation, are sure signs that he was invigorated by the experience. He also gained reassurance. His reading convinced him that it was not sensible to expect to make no mistakes as a leader. This opinion is offered towards the end of the *Notebooks*, coming as a tangential remark in his commentary on Aristotle's *Metaphysics*: 'The approach of mind (man) to a particular thing is . . . complex, divided, zigzaggish, *including within itself* the possibility of a flight of fantasy from life . . . It is stupid to deny the role of fantasy even in the strictest science.'[143] This is reminiscent of Lenin's invocation in *What Is To Be Done?*: 'It is necessary to dream.'[144] But he went further in 1915. He referred to a statement by the Russian democrat

D. A. Pisarev of the mid-nineteenth century that even 'a bad dream can have its uses'.[145] Pisarev's meaning was that a man's vision, even if proved wrong by experience, may have brought about practical human benefit before its incorrectness is demonstrated. Here was confirmation of the need to take risks, to take a gamble. Here was a frame of mind which sustained a lonely politician, far from home and distant from power; and which, in 1917, left him uninhibited in promoting his party's seizure of the reins of government.

4 War's Divisions: 1915–1916

ATTACHMENTS AND DETACHMENTS

Seven million soldiers were slaughtered in the First World War, and thirteen million civilians perished through the diseases and malnutrition brought on by the fighting; the imperturbability of the statesmen involved became notorious to later generations. A stiff-upper lip mentality was not peculiar to the British; the idea that the burdens had to be endured without complaint was shared by the other Allies and by the Central Powers. A feeling that national honour was at stake was potent. Nor could the ruling élites in each belligerent state ever forget that defeat would almost certainly bring their rule to an end. Most conscripts, moreover, were drawn from Europe's working classes and peasantries. The dangers of discontent with the worsening conditions in town and countryside were obvious to ministers. The upper and middle classes were affected also, since military officers were killed in their tens of thousands. The politicians knew this; but their offices were in London, Paris, Berlin, Vienna and Petrograd, hundreds of miles from the muddy, dispiriting, blood-stained trenches. Ministerial visits by a Lloyd George or a Clemenceau were fleeting episodes. Furthermore, the various military high commands were baffled by the stationary form taken by the war on both Western and Eastern fronts. In the first couple of years of the fighting it seemed that there was no strategic alternative to the man-hungry trench cross-fire that raged on both fronts.

Lenin's *sang froid* about the mass homicide was far from making him unusual among political leaders. It was widespread among those holding office. Parliamentarians in opposition were a more varied bunch; and some, including revolutionaries such as the German social-democrat Karl Liebknecht felt an emotional as well as an intellectual repugnance about the war. Yet others, who were probably the majority, qualified their opposition to their governments by indicating that they would use their armies in a similar way even if their war aims were different. They saw themselves as facing up to the political and military realities of the time.

Lenin had predicted the war's outburst in a detached frame of mind, and from 1914 detested its actual occurrence in a similarly abstract fashion. He showed emotion about the military conflict only intermittently; and, when he did, anger and not pity was his dominant sensation. His outbursts were seldom directed at the war's consequences for the wretches in the trenches or even at the responsibility of governments. His preferred target was the behaviour of fellow socialists, and none annoyed him more than Karl Kautsky.[1] He lived through 1915 and 1916 in a state of constant and even near-hysterical irascibility, such was his sense of betrayal on the part of the Second International and most of its leaders. There were only rare periods of remission from his anger. Lenin's pen-portrait of the death of Marxism's co-founder contains an example of sentimentalism with few parallels in his works: 'On 14 March 1883 Marx quietly fell asleep forever in his armchair.'[2] This was the language of obituaries in popular newspapers. In a letter to Inessa Armand in January 1917, Lenin gave a slightly less clichéd but even more startling tinge to his feelings. He was still, he averred, 'in love with Marx'.[3] He informed Inessa that none of Marx's critics had managed to quench his ardour.[4] Yet his affections for Marx had a jealous side; he was never more vicious in disputes than with other Marxists who challenged his interpretation of Marxism. The altercations with Kautsky and with Menshevik theorists over social-democratic attitudes to the war were but one manifestation among many during Lenin's long relationship with Marx.

It was ironical that Lenin's profession of love for Marx was made in a letter to Inessa. Tales were told in the Russian Marxist emigration that Lenin was sexually promiscuous. Lidiya Dan, Martov's sister, claimed that his extramarital adventures started in middle age.[5] It was widely supposed that Inessa had been among his mistresses. She was an attractive woman, five years younger than Lenin. She was also married and had children; and her commitment to the revolutionary cause was firm. Lenin had met her for the first time in 1911, and there can be no doubt that he quickly developed affectionate feelings towards Inessa.[6]

That there was also a sexual liaison between them is not clearly demonstrated. It is indisputable that Inessa participated in a *ménage à trois* with Lenin and Krupskaya in 1912,[7] but so long as Lenin remains an iconic figure for the Soviet state, the revelation of the full truth will be fraught with difficulties of a political nature.[8] Yet much circumstantial evidence points in a positive direction: in particular, Krupskaya apparently hinted that she was ready to accept such a situation. She had a strong inner strength, and continued to be on warm terms with Inessa's children.[9] Nevertheless any possible relationship between Lenin and Inessa can hardly have been an all-consuming passion even though it would imply a chilling of feelings between Lenin and Krupskaya. Lenin's duties to Krupskaya could in any case not be ignored. Her health was deteriorating: the chronic thyroid illness showed itself with severity, and surgery was for a time contemplated. Lenin's own health was not perfect either. Pictures of him after the outbreak of war show him looking older than his forty-four years. But the greatest impediment to a lasting love affair with Inessa was the driving force in Lenin's life: his preoccupation with politics and all that this meant – literary invective, organisational attentiveness, philosophical speculation and economic study. Time for pleasures of the flesh was exiguous in this man's supremely political life.

Inessa's beauty shines out of all the extant photographs; only Lidiya Dan rivalled her amidst the Russian revolutionary sorority. But by 1915, to judge by the published record, the heat of his letters to her had cooled. He began to sign with the non-familiar version of 'Yours' in Russian, and often he gave his name not as Vladimir or Volodya but baldly as 'V.U.', his mere initials.[10] On the other hand, he often used this signature even in letters to his mother, in poor health in wartime Russia. Lenin could do little to help at all, marooned as he was in neutral Switzerland. His younger brother had become a doctor, and tried to guide her medical regimen, but in 1914 she was already 73 years old. Her family's difficulties never ceased; at the beginning of the war she had to contend with the fact that her daughter Mariya, also a Bolshevik, was arrested in Petrograd;[11] and exile to Vologda province ensued. Vladimir Ilich's mother spent her last remaining years in this far-northern city, with its dark and icy-cold winter months.

Not that Ulyanov-Lenin lacked his share of personal worries. His original intention was to live out the war in Bern. On arrival, he faced financial circumstances less happy than before 1914. As an economist he expected, and as an apartment-tenant dreaded, a rise in the cost of rented rooms if the anticipated influx of refugee French revolutionary socialists should occur.[12] Yet French socialism by and large did not oppose French involvement in the war, and the wave of Gallic immigrants to Switzerland failed to take place. This, for Lenin, was the only desirable consequence of the 'collapse of the Second International'. But problems with money were not dispelled. In 1915 he could not travel to make speeches unless a fee, however small, was promised. This was not money-grubbing but necessity. He would write to friends asking for an overnight stay to be arranged in as cheap a couple of rooms as possible, preferably with self-catering facilities to cut down expenditure on café food.[13] He was not as robust as previously; but his stamina was sustained by his anger and sense of duty. Yet it was a hermetically-contained existence. With all his talk about Russia, he met no Russian who had seen military combat until shortly before the February Revolution of 1917. He saw nothing of the barbed wire and the trenches and, though everyone read about them, wrote little on them. His isolation was greater than for others, like Trotski and Martov, who were based in Paris. They at least saw the trainloads of conscripts going off to the front, and equally saw the wounded soldiers returning and the wrecked families who had lost their menfolk.

Perhaps this inexperience accounts for Lenin's blithely innocent use of military metaphors. There was an incongruity of scale, at the height of the the First World War, in designating 'a war upon the opportunists and the social-chauvinists' as the priority of the moment. His over-statements, too, were egregious. He bracketed the German army commander Paul von Hindenburg and the British left-wing socialist H.M. Hyndman as politically indistinguishable,[14] as if Hyndman, who gave merely conditional support to the British Government in 1914, espoused any single great power's militarist subjugation of the Continent. Lenin was writing off everyone who disagreed with him on any major policy.

He presented this as a cut-and-dried affair. Those who, in his view, had failed the supreme test of July–August 1914 could never be trusted again. Great events can break individuals on their wheel, and this is what he thought had happened to the German Social-Democratic Party leadership. Repeatedly he returned to the figure of Kautsky. Lenin assumed that the socialist 'centrists' were most dangerous to his policy because they might win left-wing socialists to the path of moderation and, eventually, of a betrayal as great as that already perpetrated by the ascendant party leaders. But this was only part of Lenin's motivation. The other reason was that he had esteemed Kautsky so highly. Despite the various pre-war disagreements, Lenin had continued to admire Kautsky's economic expertise, and had taken his revolutionary strategy for Germany at its face value. Lenin regarded Kautsky's words from 1914 as mere rhetoric, as the worst sort of hypocrisy.[15] And, although Hugo Haase was a more influential figure among the centrists of the German Social-Democratic party in the war, it was Kautsky who drew Lenin's unrelenting fire. The obverse side of the coin was that Lenin tacitly took a higher view of his own stature inside European revolutionism. Among younger revolutionaries who had a benign estimation of him, he was becoming akin to an elder statesman. He began to talk of 'us, the old men'.[16] As a senior politician, he felt a duty to contact young socialists. Opportunities were limited in wartime, nevertheless he snatched his chances to address meetings of the young Swiss socialists in the Zürich Volkshaus.[17]

As he passed on the torch, he attempted to keep his words simple and maximalist; but his prognoses were not without nuances and qualifications. In his moods of pessimism he conceded that the European revolution might not occur until after the end of the present war. Politics, he stressed, was a volatile process. He foresaw, too, that this might not be the last world war: an unconventional prediction in its time and a typically hard-headed pronouncement from him.[18] Lenin could not abide the cant of those governmental ministers and political commentators who trumpeted that the military conflict was a war to end all wars. Intermittently, he was also perspicacious about Germany. Laying aside his apocalyptic over-simplifications, he once even recognised that Germany was not in fact characterised by a revolutionary crisis.[19] But such an acknowledgement was unique among his public comments. Not surprisingly, few colleagues in Switzerland took much notice of the remark.

THE ZIMMERWALD CONFERENCE

Robert Grimm and Odino Morgari were the first European socialists trying to organise an international anti-war conference who, in Lenin's opinion, could not be ignored. The earliest of such initiatives had come with a meeting of representatives from the Allied countries in London in February 1915 and a meeting in Vienna for socialist parties from the Central Powers in April 1915. But these gatherings had the obvious weakness that Germans and Austrians were not speaking with Britons, French and Russians. A second kind of enterprise was embodied in efforts made by socialists from neutral countries to contact each other. In September 1914, a group of Swiss and Italian socialists met in Lugano and agreed to prepare a conference, under Hermann Greulich's direction. The Danish and Swedish parties were moving in the same direction; for them, as for their friends in Switzerland and Italy, the immediate priority was to prevent the spread of the war to their countries. Steadily, however, the ambition of many participants widened and the idea of a gathering of anti-war socialists of all nations was born. The International Socialist Bureau's lethargy incensed such socialists. The Bureau, which was transferred to The Hague after Belgium's conquest by the German armies, did little more than conduct routine discussions after 1914.[20]

Grimm decided to be bold. Encouraged by the Lugano arrangements and spurred on by Russian Marxists such as Martov,[21] he convoked a conference of all socialists who opposed their governments, rejected policies of 'civil peace' and wanted an end to the war. Grimm and his fellow conferees were heartened by the news in December 1914 that a German social-democrat, Karl Liebknecht, had broken instructions by voting against war credits in the Reichstag. A strongly anti-war group was forming around Liebknecht in the Reichstag, and Rosa Luxemburg outside. It was a tiny minority of the German Social-Democratic Party, but a breach in the wall of party unity had been made.[22]

Hugo Haase and Karl Kautsky regarded both of them as demagogues. And yet they, too, were disconcerted by the growing evidence of the German government's expansionist war aims. Unlike Liebknecht, they refrained from open criticism of the party's policy on the war but hoped to steer it towards a demand for a peace without annexations.[23] Exposure of governmental intentions, undertaken by Haase in spring 1915 in respect of Bethmann Hollweg, was not confined to Germany. In Britain, the Independent Labour Party remained a thorn in the side of the authorities, and the Conféderation Générale du Travail and the Section Française de l'Internationale Ouvrière had a rising number of anti-war activists. Many socialists in the Russian political underground persisted in their actions against the Romanov government despite the campaigns of arrest and exile. Italy's government moved towards war on the

Allied side in summer 1915, but the Italian Socialist Party contained several thousand anti-war members. In June 1915 Liebknecht deepened the rift among German social-democrats by suggesting in a pamphlet that the party's policy of 'civil peace' (*Burgfrieden*) for the war's duration ought to be abandoned; he drew support from twelve Reichstag members. He also helped to found *Die Internationale* with the aim of disseminating his ideas more widely; but his conscription into the army prevented him from accepting Grimm's invitation to join the anti-war socialist conference in Switzerland.[24]

Proceedings commenced on 5 September 1915. Thirty-eight people assembled in the centre of Bern and embarked on four charabancs to travel the six miles to the mountain village of Zimmerwald. No one pretended that it was a large gathering, or even that all the participants were on friendly terms with each other: long-standing animosities divided socialists from the Romanov empire in particular. But international socialist gatherings were accustomed to disputes among Russians, and the passengers in Bern resolved to be cheerful. The joke went the rounds that, half a century after the First International's foundation, all Europe's internationalists could still be accommodated in just four charabancs.[25]

The Russian Social-Democratic Labour Party, the Italian Socialist Party and the Balkan Socialist Federation sent official representatives (although the Russians made their customary insistence on sending separate factional representatives); these were necessarily but a small minority of European socialist organisations. Most other major parties, having voted war credits for their respective governments, were shunned. Thus the ascendant leaderships of the German Social-Democratic Party, the French Socialist Party and the British Labour Party received no invitation. Yet the list of participants would have been longer if the governments of belligerent states had not been obstructive. Some delegates, such as Bruce Glasier of the Independent Labour Party in Britain, could not obtain travel documents.[26] French anti-war socialists managed to send representatives; but these made their journey at a time of jingoism at home, and were not sure whether they would be permitted to return safely.[27] Even Robert Grimm, editor of *Berner Tagwacht*, was in an anomalous position. The Swiss Social-Democratic Party instructed him to attend in the capacity of a private observer; his colleagues, despite having done much to call the Conference, wanted to minimise any possible offence to their government.[28]

Not even a quartet of charabancs would have been needed if Lenin had had his way. He had joined in the planning for the Conference, urging that only those groups who unconditionally wanted to vote against war credits should be invited.[29] This was unacceptable to Grimm and most others. Grimm's hope remained that German social-democratic 'centrists', perhaps even Haase and Kautsky in person, would attend. In the event, ten German social-democratic leaders arrived; and only one of them, Julian Borchardt, advocated Liebknecht's outright opposition to war credits.[30] Lenin tried also to limit the nature of the Russian delegation. He stiffened the resolve of Zinoviev, his representative in the formal pre-Conference negotiations, not to make too many concessions to Trotski as leader of the Paris-based *Nashe Slovo* ('Our Word') group.[31]

Lenin's rationale for the Conference was tacit but plain: the fewer the participants, the bigger the proportion of the far left. Even Lenin, however, needed allies. European revolution could not be undertaken solely by Russians. The comradely spirit between the Bolsheviks and the Polish left-wing social-democrats grew. Of these Poles, Karl Radek displaced Hanecki and others as the central figure in Lenin's calculations. Radek was not a practical organiser like Hanecki, but a leading Marxist pamphleteer, and the Conference's labours would be taken up with issues of policy. Lenin and he got together in Bern in July. Independently of each other, both had been composing material to be presented to the Conference. Lenin had a draft resolution. It castigated the 'social-chauvinists' who supported the slogan of 'defence of the fatherland', describing their policy as a 'betrayal of socialism'. It called for a break with the official socialist leaderships which took such a line, and it indicated that Kautsky and the German 'centrists' were also to be categorised as advocates of social-chauvinism.[32] Radek's proposed theses were not as specific or rebarbative. In his initial draft he neither mentioned social-chauvinism nor referred to the offending socialist leaders by name. Radek was vague too about practicalities. His theses did not explicitly demand a rejection of war credits and of socialist participation in belligerent governments.[33]

These omissions were caused more by oversight than by deliberate intent, and Radek was content to accept several modifications demanded by Lenin. Yet he would not yield entirely. His revised version did not include approval of the tactic of defeatism; Radek remained baffled that the Bolsheviks had approved such a policy at their émigré conference in Bern in February 1915. Nor did Radek's second draft uphold the principle of national liberation movements, and he persisted in opposing Lenin on the question of nationalities. In addition, Radek refused to call for a break with the official socialist parties,[34] he was not persuaded about the wisdom of alienating the entire German Social-Democratic Party even though he had a longer record of hostility to Kautsky than had Lenin; and he would not condone Lenin's cold-shouldering of Trotski.[35]

Radek had a mordant wit and was in awe of nobody (and in the 1930s he was to pay the ultimate price for this under Stalin). He was also a potentially uncomfortable ally for the Bolsheviks inasmuch as he had an intimate knowledge of Bolshevism not shared by many far-left socialists in Europe. He had perennially objected to Lenin's sectarian leanings, and referred scathingly to the Bolsheviks as 'an orientation of a tiny group of revolutionaries'.[36] It was the sort of quip which, as Radek knew, got deep under Lenin's skin. But Lenin's only response at the time was to resume his collation of data from Russia to emphasise how much stronger the Bolsheviks were than the Mensheviks. He could not afford to alienate Radek entirely since not only would this confirm the veracity of Radek's quip but also a rare non-Bolshevik ally would be lost at Zimmerwald. There was no alternative but to agree to differ on several matters and to restrain mutual criticisms in public. Both found this difficult; Lenin never liked losing a comma or semi-colon from his proposed drafts, and Radek, a gregarious and gossipy soul, was a stranger to self-discipline. Radek and Lenin sent their materials to the various socialist emigrant groups in Switzerland. Letters were also dispatched to far-left socialist leaders abroad in order to make the left as strong as possible at the Conference.[37]

But it was already clear that the Zimmerwald Left, as such leaders became known, would constitute a minority. A private meeting was held a day before the Conference's first session. A joint strategy for the Left was thought essential, and Bolsheviks and Polish social-democrats were past masters of the skills of the organisational cabale. E. Höglund from Norway; J. Borchardt from Germany; J. Berzins from the Leftish social-democrats; T. Nerman from Norway: these were to prove to be usefully eloquent allies at Zimmerwald. Radek was undaunted by the Left's numerical weakness. Nor was he bashful about competing directly with Lenin for the Zimmerwald Left's favour. A vote was taken, and Radek's drafts were taken as the basis for the Zimmerwald Left's submission to the Conference. Lenin continued to contribute amendments. But it had been made plain to him that he had better take a careful view of the art of the possible if he was not to be entirely isolated; and, in the end, eight signatories put their hands to the Left's draft manifesto.[38]

Grimm opened the Conference. Rehearsing the sins of omission of the International Socialist Bureau, he explained the steps taken by Italian and Swiss comrades in arranging the gathering at Zimmerwald. He carefully eschewed calling for a Third International, and stressed the need for joint socialist action for peace. He described the Conference as a means of bringing together the Left and the so-called Centre in international socialism.[39] Lenin was on his best Conference behaviour. This meant that on the first day he totally refrained from speech, leaving Zinoviev to act as Bolshevik spokesman. It was Georg Lebedour, a German centrist to Kautsky's left, who introduced acrimony by challenging the validity of Borchardt's mandate to the Conference. Lenin could scarcely contain himself. Borchardt was a crucial member of the Zimmerwald Left since he was its only German. A flurry of notes passed between Lenin and Lebedour (or possibly an associate of Lebedour's). Lenin wrote: 'You want to exclude the *only* German group standing on the viewpoint of the *leftists*, and you don't want to say this openly.'[40] Lebedour was equally frank in reply: 'But you're still here! And there are three of you! And we're not driving you out.'[41] Lebedour's attitude reflected an undercurrent of feeling that subjects of the Romanov empire were represented unduly well at the Conference. In truth there were eleven of them in all; and it was hardly in Lenin's interest to deepen the squabble over mandates.

Furthermore, most delegates wished the Conference to work out decisions in such a form as to allow everyone to support them. A unanimous Conference would look more impressive to the rest of the world. And yet this was still hard to achieve. A further complication was that a letter had arrived from Karl Liebknecht. The contents called explicitly for civil war and urged socialists not to make a fetish out of party unity.[42] For Lenin, this was manna from heaven. Perhaps no event in the first two years of the First World War gave Lenin quite so much delight and reassurance that things would turn favourably in his direction sooner or later.

There followed a discussion of the German Social-Democratic Party's vote for war credits. The Zimmerwald Conference was not like Russian Social-Democratic Labour Party Congresses, with their debates on the grand theory. The discussion was severely practical. Lebedour tried to speak positively, calling for a joint anti-war declaration by German and French delegates. But Bertha Thalheimer came out strongly for Liebknecht.[43] This intra-German dispute persisted into the second day. Russians and other East Europeans became involved. Condemnation of the German Social-Democratic Party's ascendant party leadership in 1914 was common to all at Zimmerwald; but proposals for action were varied. Akselrod wanted the Germans to avoid a party split, whereas Zinoviev called precisely for that. On 7 September, Radek raised the temperature of the proceedings by presenting the Left's draft manifesto and draft resolution.[44] Lebedour opposed. In particular, he argued that Radek's talk of street demonstrations and political strikes would give advance warning of socialist intentions to the German government. Lenin at this point made his only lengthy contribution at the Conference table. Turning to Lebedour, he stated: 'The German movement is faced with a decision. If we are indeed on the threshhold of a revolutionary epoch in which the masses will go over to revolutionary struggle, we must also make mention of the means necessary for this struggle.' For good measure he added, 'you cannot make a revolution without explaining revolutionary tactics.'[45] Trotski too supported Radek in general terms, yet he retained doubts about Bolshevik attitudes to the peace movement and to Kautsky and the German centrists; he and Henrietta Roland-Holst from Holland put forward their own draft manifesto along such lines.[46]

Zinoviev disliked Trotski personally but did not share Lenin's automatic disdain, and beckoned him to come closer to the Radek–Lenin standpoint. He declared his pleasure that Trotski had taken 'a step towards' the Left.[47] But the rest of the Conference took little note of these amicable soundings since nothing would give victory to the Left in the proceedings; and Trotski in any case did not welcome Zinoviev's overture. The majority of the Conference, especially Lebedour and the French socialist Alfred Merrheim, felt that the Left underestimated the demoralisation of European working people.[48] The Left's plan for a detailed resolution was turned down. The Conference opted to publish only a short manifesto and a commission was created to elaborate it. But the Left's draft manifesto was doomed to failure; only Lenin, among its signatories, was included on the eight-person commission.[49]

Grimm announced an agreed Conference manifesto on 8 September. It defined the war as imperialist. It recalled the Second International's decisions on war before 1914 with approval, and stated that the official socialist leaderships had failed the European working class. It noted that ruling classes everywhere pleaded for civil peace for the duration of military hostilities. It called for 'irreconcilable proletarian class struggle'.[50] Had it not been for the Left, such phrases would have been weaker. Yet the manifesto was mainly a triumph for Grimm. He had stopped Lenin from specifying the need for party splits everywhere; he had kept the names of particular official leaders out of the limelight. He had also succeeded in avoiding mention of the practical steps needed to foster the cause of the anti-war movement. Lenin and Radek had expected this. And yet they insisted that the Left be allowed to register their objections in any future official Conference report. They were not too displeased. The Zimmerwald Left, a very assorted group, had attained a reasonable degree of co-ordination. The lines of disagreement had been drawn. Signs of the break-up of the German Social-Democratic Party had been glimpsed. Radek and Lenin were starting to emerge as European socialist leaders to whom it behoved the socialist parties of Central and Eestern as well as Eastern Europe to listen. Radek had made a stronger showing than Lenin. But Lenin was not a man to accept his secondary status permanently.

LENIN, BUKHARIN AND PYATAKOV

Not even Radek was perfectly *au fait* with the widening rift among the Bolsheviks. The problem was concealed at Zimmerwald since Lenin and Zinoviev were the only members of the Central Committee abroad and such disagreements as they had were kept secret. Lenin, while thinking Zinoviev was soft on Trotski, consoled himself that Zinoviev considered Trotski to be soft on Kautsky.[51] On the other hand, Zinoviev also differed from Lenin in refusing to blame the German Social-Democratic Party's behaviour overwhelmingly upon the party leadership.[52]

There were minor personal tiffs. Lenin was crotchety about Zinoviev's dilatoriness in exchanging books, while Zinoviev accused Lenin of 'egoism' in such matters.[53] The younger Bolshevik was wily. In summer 1915 Lenin moved from Bern to the mountainside village of Sörenberg above Lucerne. Zinoviev and his wife rented rooms in Hertenstein overlooking the Vierwaldstätter Lake. Unable to persuade Zinoviev to transfer to Sörenberg, Lenin urged him to bicycle over for the day to discuss party business. The route from

Hertenstein via Schupheim and Flühli would allow Zinoviev to ride downhill for the last twenty minutes.[54] Zinoviev declined. Lenin tried again by reminding his plump associate that the downhill stretch could be done 'without legs'.[55] Zinoviev, not a stupid man, refused again; he was well capable of calculating that, if there were twenty minutes of freewheeling down to Sörenberg, the return trip would involve a strenuous haul back up the same mountain. Nor was he likely to overlook the fact that the distance from Hertenstein to Sörenberg was over forty miles. A Swiss mountain, to Zinoviev's evident relief, continued to divide one half of the Bolshevik Central Committee in emigration from the other.

Krupskaya had remained with her husband. Regretting the growing fractiousness, she wrote to Karpinski in January 1915: 'These are difficult times, and the slightest clumsy expression or any tiny nuance [*sic*] gives grounds for opponents to "deepen" disagreements amongst Bolsheviks.'[56] At the time of writing, Lenin had not seriously fallen out with other Bolsheviks, but the tensions between him and Bukharin sharpened, and the fault lay with Lenin, not with Bukharin. Lenin was only biding his time for a confrontation. Krupskaya's comments were becoming eminently applicable to husband Volodya himself as 'full principled solidarity' gave way to polemics.[57]

Lenin communicated with Bukharin and the Baugy group confidentially, urging them to alter their stance on national self-determination. The urgency for victory over fellow Bolsheviks was increased, in Lenin's judgement, by the moves towards collaboration among the sympathisers of the Zimmerwald Left before and after the Conference. Among these sympathisers there were several, notably Luxemburg and Pannekoek as well as Radek, who opposed Lenin on the national question; and their hostility grew in wartime as far-left groups in socialist parties sensed that the war might well end with socialist seizures of power. They detested concessions to nationalism during a war which could not have occurred in the absence of aggressive nationalisms. Trotski proposed the slogan of United States of Europe, aiming at a post-war continental map without frontiers.[58] Neither Radek nor Luxemburg accepted the slogan since it was directed exclusively at Europe and failed to offer a global perspective.[59] Bukharin and Pyatakov, however, were attracted to Trotski's idea.[60] Lenin for a while vacillated. Initially he, too, was inclined to take up the 'United States of Europe' slogan; perhaps he thought that a continental socialist government, modelled on the structure of the capitalist USA or capitalist Switzerland, would allow sufficient self-expression to nationalities and ethnic groups for the national question to be resolved.[61] But he had second thoughts. Sensing that a chance to utilise repressed nationalisms might be lost, Lenin repeated that the right of secession from the European empires ought to be asserted. The Russian Social-Democratic Labour Party's programme and the pre-war decisions of the Bolsheviks were not to be abandoned.

He was right to take the national question so seriously and his annoyance with Bukharin's dismissal of his arguments is understandable: Lenin pointed out that 55 per cent of the population in Eastern Europe were national minorities in the various existing states.[62] But Bukharin was unpersuadable. Against Luxemburg, in addition, Lenin repeated that an independent Poland or Finland would suffer economically from being separated from the Russian empire. In a curious attempt to corroborate his arguments that the nation state was the normal vehicle of industrialisation, Lenin focused on the USA. Stressing that less than 11 per cent of its population were Negroes, he implied that ethnic homogeneity was an asset to economic advance.[63] This was a doubtful proposition, if only because the Whites in North America came from an even greater diversity of national backgrounds than did the peoples of Eastern Europe. Wisely, he omitted such contentions from his published material.

In opposing the United States of Europe slogan, the magpie-like Lenin also used arguments made against the slogan by the Bolshevik G. L. Shklovski when Lenin had advocated it.[64] He declared that the USA had the most advanced economy in the world. The establishment of a European state monolith would unite less-developed industrial countries whose interest would lie in obstructing the success of both North America and Japan. A United States of Europe would also, he asserted (in line with, but without acknowledgement to Rosa Luxemburg), oppress the non-European colonies more fiercely. There was in any case little chance that European capitalist states would bury their rivalries since the disjunctions of economic interest were too great among them.[65] Bukharin and Pyatakov retorted that Lenin had grasped the wrong end of the stick since the United States of Europe slogan was based on the assumption that socialists, not capitalists, would be in government. This only stimulated Lenin to pose a still larger question: was a complete European socialist revolution likely in the short term?

Lenin's answer was no. For him, such a revolution would probably require a whole epoch to come to completion. It would involve wars, and these would produce defeats as well as victories.[66] Political futurology has a giddying effect. But such talk was not peculiar to socialists in wartime. Let us remember, too, the German industrialists who dreamt up schemes for a new cartography of Russia and its periphery; or the Czech lobbyists who supplied the British Foreign Office with sketches of how to divide up the Habsburg domains into nation states at the war's end.

Lenin and Bukharin were even further from influence over general politics in their countries than German industrialists and Czech lobbyists in theirs; but the wartime disagreements of the two Bolsheviks would assume cardinal practical importance in 1917 when, as leaders of a Bolshevik party in power in Petrograd, they debated the strategy and time-scale for the introduction of socialism to Russia. Furthermore, their disputes were not only based upon political prognostication. They also revolved around questions about worldwide economic development. Bukharin, Pyatakov and the Baugy group believed that capitalism had more or less achieved global comprehensiveness. It had carved up the entire world. For Lenin, this was an empirical nonsense, ignoring the fact that China and many other semi-colonial countries had not yet been pulled fully into the imperialist thrall.[67]

Far from conceding ground, Bukharin pressed his analysis to another conclusion. The completion of the capitalist order had produced a hideously powerful innovation: 'the imperialist robber state'. Tossing aside *laissez-faire* economic objectives, it subvented the functions which had previously been carried out by private and semi-public capitalist associations. The state had begun not only to intervene directly in the economy but also to exert enormous ideological influence over the working 'masses', especially through the fostering of chauvinism. An all-powerful 'Leviathan' had been born. Bukharin looked back briefly to Marx's writings, and these appeared to confirm the orientation of Bukharin's thought: namely that the capitalist state could not simply be inherited by a socialist government and redeployed for socialist objectives. It had to be destroyed root and branch.[68] This fundamental revision of Russian Marxism's understanding of its tasks had echoes in the writings of other left-wing Marxists; in particular, Anton Pannekoek and Hermann Görter in Holland had similar ideas.[69] But it caused offence to Lenin. It seemed akin to anarchism; it was a break with the tradition of Russian social-democracy. Relations between Lenin and Bukharin worsened over 1915. The journal *Kommunist* began publication in Geneva in July 1915. It lasted for only two issues. In his subsequent account, Lenin claimed that the journal had served its purpose once it had printed *Socialism and the War* by Lenin and Zinoviev.[70] Thereafter, the gloves of ideological dispute were pulled off, and a struggle with no holds barred began.

The responsibility of Bukharin to act as a link between Shlyapnikov and Switzerland predictably became a bone of contention. In November 1915, a letter arrived from Stockholm requesting that Bukharin's group be sanctioned to act independently in the Central Committee's name in relations with Russia.[71] For Lenin, this was a thinly-disguised attempt to supplant the Central Committee, and some such thought surely must have been in Bukharin's mind. Lenin was outraged, and he announced his refusal to have any future connection with *Kommunist*.[72] Zinoviev was near to despair, discerning that Radek's description of the Bolshevik émigrés as a tiny group seemed about to become an overestimation of their strength.

Lenin came back to Zinoviev in 1916 and restated his self-justification. Zinoviev expressed boredom with the whole sorry mess.[73] A profession of almost any other emotion would have incited Lenin less. But boredom! Lenin administered a blistering dressing-down to Zinoviev.[74] Yet Zinoviev would not budge; and, moreover, Bukharin retained his sensitive position along the line of Bolshevik communications with Russia. Lenin wrote to Shlyapnikov explaining his stand.[75] Shlyapnikov remained unconvinced, regarding the scrap between the two Bolshevik writers as yet another unedifying émigré spectacle.[76]

Even Lenin contained his rage at Shlyapnikov; he recognised that otherwise he would have wrecked all chance of regular contact with and influence over Bolsheviks in Petrograd. Meanwhile he prevailed upon the long-suffering and reluctant Zinoviev to collaborate on the production of a rival journal to *Kommunist*, to be called *Digest of Social-Democrat*.[77] His letters to Bukharin became more abusive. Bukharin had heard that Lenin could not tolerate the other stars in his own galaxy; but he had rejected this as a slur on Bolshevism and its leader.[78] Suddenly he saw Lenin differently. He had thought that the disagreements could be kept within comradely bounds, and the eruption of conflict caught him wrongfooted. He wrote on 23 April 1916, to say that he bitterly resented Lenin's attacks, and adding that he continued to regard Lenin as his 'teacher'.[79] In midsummer he left unannounced for New York.[80] The émigré shenanigans in Europe had become altogether intolerable. Nothing could illustrate the contrast in styles better. It would be inconceivable for Lenin to have walked away from close political involvement at such a moment; and he would not have relinquished a position of such logistical importance as Bukharin occupied in Scandinavia. Feelings of a spoiled friendship would not have affected his decisions.

'IMPERIALISM AS THE HIGHEST STAGE OF CAPITALISM'

Both Lenin and Bukharin thought the war to be 'imperialist', and wanted to produce an explanation of imperialism. Both felt mutually-goaded into a bout of furious writing. First to complete a textbook was Bukharin, who completed *The World Economy and Imperialism* in 1915.[81] Lenin read it in draft and, despite his increasingly poor relations with Bukharin, composed an introduction. He basically approved of Bukharin's account, but phrased himself cautiously and offered no direct praise. There was also a section wherein Lenin tried to distance himself from Bukharin's chapters. Bukharin suggested that, if contemporary trends persisted, the economies would be directed by a 'world economic trust'. Lenin affirmed this to be an abstract extrapolation which would not become a reality, and implicitly criticised Bukharin's notion that capitalism was on the threshold of complete development around the earth.[82]

Lenin wanted to clarify his own thoughts on imperialism and connected subjects. He used not only Bukharin's but also many other books as his sources. The Austrian Marxist, Rudolf Hilferding's *Finance Capital* had a huge influence, which Lenin acknowledged. He also mentioned that the English radical liberal, J. A. Hobson, had been important to him (and indeed he had translated some of his work earlier in the century).[83] But this was not a job of simply elaborating an interpretation from other men's analyses. Lenin read a mountain of empirical literature: 148 books and 232 articles,[84] laboriously copying out excerpts which appear in his notebooks on imperialism – and the bulk of his reading was in German. He finished his own book in July 1916. His case studies came mainly from Germany and, to a lesser extent, Britain. This was not fortuitous since Lenin wished to secure publication in Petrograd, and a denunciation of Russian imperialism would not have helped. Even the notebooks have little on the Romanov lands, with a few sentences on cotton-growing in Turkestan constituting the lengthiest example.[85] Lenin was also careful about his title. His first idea was 'The Basic Characteristics of Contemporary Capitalism'. This was inoffensive but vague and unlikely to attract many readers. So instead he opted for 'Imperialism as the Latest Stage of Capitalism'.[86]

This is not the present title, which is 'Imperialism as the Highest Stage of Capitalism'; but terms like 'highest stage' signified that there might be a further non-capitalist stage (which, of course, was exactly what was in Lenin's mind). And so, like Hilferding and Radek before him, settled for 'latest stage'. The contents had also to be moderated. This in part involved self-restraint; Lenin stressed that his book did not deal with the 'non-economic side' of imperialism.[87] Political commentary would have annoyed the censor. Yet both the publishers and Lenin's sister Anna wanted further emendations, and unilaterally excised several abusive references to Kautsky.[88]

In fact, the February Revolution of 1917 took place before Lenin's book appeared in print (as was also true of Bukharin's). But the contents are a useful guide to his wartime thought. They are proposed as 'a popular sketch',[89] and Lenin included apt quotations from various tracts on the international economy. The style is punchy and simple, marking a resumption of the style of his *Iskra* days. Lenin – like Bukharin as well as Luxemburg, Radek and Skvortsov-Stepanov – started from Hilferding's arguments. All of them affirmed that the *laissez-faire* capitalist era had ended. Emphasis was laid upon the emergence of monopolies; on the growing impact of banks and 'finance capital' upon industrial decision-making; on the inadequacy of the domestic market for goods; on the increasing appeal to the state to intervene to protect each nation's industry; and the resort to foreign conquests in search of both cheap labour and controllable colonial markets. Thus modern imperialism was held to be the inevitable consequence of advanced capitalist development. Many scholars in subsequent generations have challenged aspects of Hilferding's brilliant analysis. It has been pointed out that banks did not have so important a role either in Britain, France or the USA as they did in Germany and Austria.[90] Secondly, he implied that a country's monopolies shared common interests. Yet clashes between them were endemic. Soviet historians, for example, have highlighted the rivalry among heavy industrial cartels in Russia before 1917.[91] The benefits of colonial expansion too have been challenged. Indeed Lenin's acknowledged influence, J. A. Hobson, had originated this view. Before the First World War, Britain was the world's greatest imperial power. Hobson claimed that the outflow of funds from the metropolitan country damaged industrial growth at home; and that the possession of an empire merely fostered militarist policies, causing wars which disrupted the economy as a whole. Imperialism has thereby been criticised as neither necessary nor rational for a country's material well-being.[92]

Lenin and Bukharin rejected such criticisms, including those by Hobson. They followed Luxemburg, Radek and Skvortsov-Stepanov in taking Hilferding's arguments to an extreme. The Austrian emphasised that a few banking magnates had come into possession of entire economies and that, once the banks were nationalised, socialism could quickly and easily be realised. Both Bolshevik writers agreed with him here. But Hilferding, in their view, had underplayed the political conflicts that would be entailed. He said little about the 'division of the world' by rival imperial powers. The transition towards socialism would therefore be accompanied by war and bloody revolution. In his notes, Lenin castigated Hilferding: 'It is necessary for us *ourselves* to seize *power* in the first place, and not chatter vainly about "power".'[93] Furthermore, Hilferding's policy on the war was close to Kautsky's. Bukharin and Lenin criticised him as a 'centrist'.[94]

Lenin had previously not offered an opinion on Kautsky's notion, which broke with the assumptions of Marx as well as of Second International leaders such as Rosa Luxemburg and Jean Jaurès, that war was not inevitable among the imperial powers. The First World War made up Lenin's mind for him that economic rivalry made inter-imperial wars unavoidable. But Kautsky pointed to data indicating that imperial expansion sometimes brought little economic advantage. In Egypt, Britain's semi-colony, German trade had increased while British trade declined.[95] So what were the benefits of empire? Lenin replied in *Imperialism*: highlighting imperialist clashes before 1914, he referred to wars in South America and China. Germany's economic barons, he affirmed, resented the tariff walls obstructing their penetration of foreign markets because of Germany's paucity of colonies. Nor, for Lenin, did the Egyptian case prove Kautsky's point. On the contrary, it only went to show that Germany's economic vigour was 'fresher, more organised, higher' than Britain's.[96] Lenin continued to assert that colonies were crucial for the sustaining of profits; and that economic motives therefore fuelled the eruption of the First World War. The balance of truth between Lenin and Kautsky remains controversial. Few historians, except those writing with official sanction in communist states, would extrude non-economic factors so sweepingly.[97] Kautsky's attentiveness to free will, to political contingency and to the variety of possible outcomes would now attract greater support than opposition. It is also true, at least since the Second World War, that direct colonial rule has been disbanded by the European powers. In addition, the rivalries of the advanced industrial countries have been conducted more or less peacefully.

On the other hand, Lenin's feeling that the First World War was scarcely avoidable has elements of cogency. The struggle by Germany for continental supremacy was powered by forces at home which were indeed hard to resist. The pressures on both Austria-Hungary and Russia not to flinch from war were strong. Both Britain and France had reasons to decide that Germany's continental and, possibly, global power endangered them. And the fact that a Second World War followed the First indicates that Kautsky was more optimistic than was justified.

If Lenin was a determinist against Kautsky, though, he remained a less than absolute one. Again, the contrast with Bukharin was perceptible. The map of the world was not simply a matter of a few imperial powers and their numerous direct colonies. 'China,' he asserted, 'has just begun to be divided up.' Argentina's position, moreover, was somewhere between an independent state and a colony.[98] Lenin also recognised, unlike Bukharin but like Maslov, the different qualities of the rival 'imperialisms'. The USA's economic progressiveness put it in the first rank. Germany and Japan were its near rivals. Britain and France came lower, and it was their aim to cripple the outpacing power of Germany that had led them into war. Near the bottom of the imperial heap lay Russia. Lenin noted that capitalist development in the Russian Far East was rudimentary. Portugal was at the nadir: formally speaking, it possessed colonies; but its empire was virtually a British protectorate.[99] Such differentiation appeared throughout *Imperialism*. Even subtler considerations were committed to his notebooks. It was a commonplace of many 'patriotic' Russian industrialists that Russia was a state debtor of France, and that this was reducing Russia to near-colonial status. Lenin guessed that the opposite was the case. So massive was the Russian debt, he wrote, that France was becoming dependent on Russia. French investors could not afford to threaten

Russia too blatantly for fear that the Russia might renege on the repayments.[100] So there were multiple potential consequences of such a global situation. Further divisions and redivisions of the world could be at hand. Bukharin's idea of a world economic trust was inappropriate; and sanguine thoughts of instant global socialism were misplaced.

According to Lenin, Bukharin had exaggerated the degree of 'planning' that had typified national industries.[101] Chaos and conflict remained intrinsic to capitalism even with the developments of cartels and monopolies. The disproportionality between investments in agriculture and in industry was unavoidable; and the fact that heavy industry became so efficient and attractive to investors harmed the development of light industries. Even this appeared to Lenin to constitute too light a verdict on capitalism. He added that firms, once placed in a monopolistic position, tended to become technologically conservative, and to buy up pioneering patents and allow them to gather dust on the shelves. Economic stagnation would, therefore, set in under capitalism.[102] Lenin was extrapolating from a small number of examples. His generalisations do not withstand scrutiny. For instance, the development of nuclear power, word-processing computers and genetic engineering have all been boosted by capitalist enterprise in the late twentieth century.

Nor did Lenin's sociological analysis of advanced capitalist societies display any greater sophistication than before 1914. The very word 'sociology' remained a term of contempt in his eyes; and, to the end of his life, he was annoyed at Bukharin for incorporating so much non-Marxist scholarship from this field in his own work.[103] Bukharin was unabashed by Lenin's criticism and pursued his interest in those social groups in capitalist society which seemed to show special favour to the politics of imperialism. Deepening insights derived from Hilferding, he described how industrial investment increasingly came from a mass of small investors, who had no direct part in production, rather than from self-financing industrialists. And these investors, or *rentiers*, vigorously backed imperial expansion.[104] Lenin knew of this trend, and jotted down material in his notebooks. He even suggested, like Bukharin, that the South of England might shortly become a region where an opulent, sizeable, indolent, parasitic class surrounded by servants would live out their lives on the basis of the exploitation of colonial countries.[105] But Lenin did not include these ideas in *Imperialism*. He preferred to rehearse the image of the tiny class of powerful, wealthy capitalists that needed to be overthrown. Banking magnates and industrial barons made for an easier target than the more pervasive but less easily caricatured middle classes. He wanted to keep his ideas on revolution simple and supple: targets had to be easily identified.

POLICIES FOR RUSSIA

Lenin resigned himself, in so far as this reflexive verb was ever applicable to so unbending a character, to the possibility that the European socialist revolution might be a decade or more ahead. But about its eventual occurrence he had no doubt; he was sure, too, that the current 'epoch' was revolutionary.[106] His comments upon Russia in particular contained nothing but optimism about the chances of pulling down the Romanov monarchy. It is widely believed that by the winter of 1916–17 he was virtually in despair about politics in his own country, but there is no evidence to support this. Throughout the war, as before, Lenin assumed Russia to be ripe for revolution;[107] and, as *Social-Democrat* announced in its January 1917 issue: 'The revolution is approaching, the government is preparing itself.'[108]

Bolsheviks did not underestimate the regime's resourcefulness. Lenin and Zinoviev, stressing the connections between foreign and domestic policies, suggested that the emperor might sign a separate peace with the Central Powers in order to prevent civil disorder at home.[109] Rumours about secret negotiations between the belligerent states on the Eastern front grew from 1915. Lenin thought Nikolai II to be cunning enough to carry off such a policy. He contended that no formal signature of a treaty might be required. All that would be necessary would be a secret gentlemen's agreement between Petrograd and Berlin that no more offensive would be undertaken. Everyone's prestige could thereby be preserved.[110] Lenin perceptively argued that such an arrangement might be seen as the only way of avoiding the autocracy's replacement by a coalition of the Kadet Pavel Milyukov and the moderate conservative Aleksandr Guchkov. Worse still for Nikolai II, he might otherwise be replaced by Milyukov and the right-wing Socialist Revolutionary Aleksandr Kerenski.[111] The events of spring 1917 were shortly to show how important these three opponents of the emperor would become. According to Lenin, a separate peace on the Eastern front might well result in Russia obtaining Galicia as war booty from an accommodating Kaiser Wilhelm II (who was quite capable of betraying his Austro-Hungarian ally).[112] Lenin also emphasised that the Anglo-Russian alliance was laden with tension. British and Russian interests were at variance in south-eastern Europe and the Near East, and there was no reason to suppose that Petrograd was meekly following everywhere in London's footsteps.[113]

Zinoviev went further. For him, the regime was gambling ferociously upon military victory in order to make annexations which would win domestic popularity.[114] His claim was that Russian foreign policy was not formed by the bourgeoisie. According to Zinoviev, 'tsarism' had decided upon expansionism and the industrialists had simply consented – and not *vice versa*. There was a natural corollary to this, and Zinoviev did not fail to articulate it. Russian imperialism was peculiar among the Great Powers. It was 'military, feudal'.[115] Indeed, it was not even 'an expression of the dominance of finance capital' since Russia was an importer rather than an exporter of capital.[116]

He was touching on the tricky area of inter-imperialist economic relations. Russian Marxists were debating this robustly. In the Petrograd legal press, the Menshevik Petr Maslov argued that Germany was hell-bent upon Russia's economic subjugation and the destruction of Russian industry (which was why Maslov supported the national war effort). He acknowledged that not all Germans wanted such a result; but argued that the most influential interest groups did, and that even the German social-democrats demanded specially favourable economic conditions for Germany as the price of peace.[117] Other Mensheviks felt unhappy with such an analysis. O. A. Ermanski maintained that German industrial interests were not uniform; and that the volume of Germany's exports to the Russian empire before 1914 would incline her eventually towards a policy of accommodation with Russia.[118] This controversy is yet another example of the subtlety of debates among contemporary Russian intellectuals. Only half a century later did historians evaluate the issues as clearly. No definitive answer has been given, but most work has supported Maslov's darker interpretation of Russo-German relations in the event of a German victory. Why Lenin so uncharacteristically did not join in the dispute among his own long-standing opponents is unclear. Later, in 1917, he was to judge Russian capitalism in the First World War to have fallen into dependence upon foreign capital.[119] He had always contended in any case that Russia's imperialism was inferior in quality to that of most other imperialist powers.[120] Perhaps he thought that Zinoviev, in drawing attention to the import of capital to Russia, was wrong in inferring that Russia thereby became economically dependent on her capital suppliers. This would tally with his notebook jottings of 1915–16.[121] Or had he changed his mind? Or simply not applied his mind to the problem until after the Romanov dynasty's overthrow? Or was there a calculation of convenience at work: namely that any such interpretation would rob him of his major political debating point that the Russian government was a major imperialist sinner which sinned independently and ought, for all Europe's sake, to be overthrown immediately?

It would have been harder to call for Russia's defeat if he had conceded that the Germans might try to crush Russian political and economic power. Freeing Russia from the Romanovs was his aim, and his expectation remained that the forthcoming revolution would be of the 'bourgeois-democratic' kind. Talk of the immediate inception of socialism repelled him. He took Bukharin to be advocating just such a deviation from Russian Marxist orthodoxy, and criticised him accordingly.[122] Lenin believed that only the end of 'the capitalist order' throughout Europe would prevent further wars; but, like members of the Central Committee's Russian Bureau, he did not expect the forthcoming revolution in Russia to be a socialist one.[123] The slogans of other Bolshevik groups, such as the Petersburg Committee, were similarly traditional.[124] They called for a democratic republic, the eight-hour day and the confiscation of gentry land.[125] Russia, he asserted, had not yet reached the level of 'the advanced countries of the West and North America'. She was not ready for socialism.[126]

But already in 1905 he had privately wondered whether to scrap the orthodox strategic schedule. His plan to establish a provisional revolutionary government of socialists was deprecated by Mensheviks as being essentially populistic; but Lenin had also asked himself, in his notebooks, whether there was any need to let the bourgeoisie come to power thereafter.[127] Russia in 1915–16 was not gripped by a revolutionary crisis as in 1905. But occasional remarks revealed where Lenin's instincts might lead him in the following year. Firstly, he castigated a seemingly totally innocuous call by Martov for social-democrats to demand the convention of a Constituent Assembly. He also took umbrage at a similar pre-war piece along the same lines by Rosa Luxemburg. Calls for a Constituent Assembly, according to Lenin, were not 'fighting' slogans.[128] This in itself did not signify a break with his idiosyncratic version of the two-stage theory of revolution. Lenin, after all, desired a temporary socialist dictatorship to initiate a fully democratic order in Russia. The Constituent Assembly would therefore not happen immediately after the monarchy's overthrow.[129] In the second place, he emphasised that the character of the war would remain the same even if the bourgeoisie came to power. Only the accession of 'the party of the proletariat' could change that.[130] Again, strictly speaking, this did not contradict the 1905 Leninist version of the two-stage revolutionary process. But a remark in an article published in October 1916 edged nearer to contradiction. He urged Bolsheviks to abandon 'the Menshevik theory of stages' whereby a democratic republic had to precede the inception of a socialist revolution.[131] The comment comes in connection with a discussion of Germany; but the phrasing does not explicitly exclude applicability to Russia. Moreover, the winter of 1916–17 was a period when Lenin began to believe that the most advanced phenomena of capitalist society were starting to characterise Russia.[132]

The temptation, then, to foreshorten the revolutionary schedule was again growing stronger. Lenin was returning closer to Trotski's demand for 'permanent revolution'; and on this occasion he had seen fit to air his views in a Bolshevik journal instead of at a closed Bolshevik Party Congress (or in his private notes).[133] These were straws in the wind. The views which caused Lenin to astonish his followers in March and April 1917 were already germinating in the previous year. They were as yet tentative; they were not the main theme of his discourse: and for that very reason they did not attract much attention either at the time or indeed among subsequent generations of scholars.[134]

The brunt of Lenin's writing about Russia in 1916 fell not so much upon anticipated stages as upon the significance of a Russian revolution for Europe as a whole. Before 1914 he had presented the Romanov autocracy's overthrow as a possible means of triggering off socialist revolutions elsewhere on the Continent. He had also highlighted the tendency for semi-colonial countries like Turkey after the Russian political upheaval of 1905–6 to experience an upsurge in the movement for democracy, and this continued to be a theme of his in the First World War.[135] Revolution, he repeated, could be an imitative experience. But he was also keen to stress a further development in his thinking in wartime. The emphasis of *Imperialism* had lain upon economic processes which had made the political world much smaller since the turn of the century: everything that happened in one major power had its impact on all the others. The continued existence of the Russian absolute monarchy was consequently a threat to the prospects of revolutions elsewhere. Lenin put it as follows: 'The bourgeois-democratic revolution in Russia is now already not only a prologue but an inalienable integral part of socialist revolution in the West.'[136] The phrasing is neither neat nor precise, but, if it means anything at all, it surely signifies Lenin's adoption of the opinion that an anti-autocratic revolution in Russia was not one of several possible detonators of 'the socialist transition' in the advanced industrial nations but rather a fuel whose absence would render ignition impossible.

LEADERSHIP AND THE RUSSIAN BOLSHEVIKS

Yet distance and war as well as the Okhrana, however, combined to minimise Lenin's impact on fellow members of the Bolshevik faction in the Russian empire. To an even greater extent than before 1914, Lenin depended upon communication by letter, yet the Eastern front prevented the mail reaching him in less than a month after dispatch.[137] An additional snag was that postal services to and from Russia in wartime passed through Petrograd, and the police had a greater chance to intercept subversive literature.

Nor did the Central Committee's Foreign Bureau recover fully from the effects of Roman Malinovski's treachery and exposure. Krupskaya's pre-war address book contained 287 names and locations for correspondence with the Russian empire, including most provinces.[138] The business of changing addresses had just begun when war broke out. In late 1916 it held the names of only 130 persons. The vast majority of these lived in central and western Europe: only twenty-six were political contacts in the Russian empire;[139] and, of the twenty six, sixteen had become inoperative before 1917.[140] Arrests of local Bolsheviks had a disruptive consequences. Consequently Petrograd, Moscow and far-eastern Siberia were the main holding points for mail. The statistics speak for themselves; only three other places in the empire figured in Krupskaya's book: Nizhni Novgorod, Simferopol and Vilno.[141] Krupskaya as Central Committee secretary issued an impassioned appeal to the Russian Bureau: 'We need direct relations with other towns.'[142] But the Petrograd-based Bolsheviks deemed it poor conspiratorial practice to put a highly sensitive list of addresses in the post. The impact on Lenin's activity was predictable. The official, and admittedly incomplete, chronicle of his life in 1916 records him as having dispatched only nineteen letters to the Russian empire in that year, and just four addressees seem to have been non-members of the Ulyanov family.[143]

Apparently whole months passed, furthermore, without his sending letters to non-relatives. The longest gap was from May through to August 1916, and another occurred from October to December[144] The passage of correspondence in the opposite direction, from the Russian empire to Switzerland, was equally weak and intermittent. Just seven Bolsheviks outside the Ulyanov family are known to have written to him in 1916. They included Shlyapnikov, on his various trips to Petrograd;[145] but others came from men like Kamenev and Stalin who were trapped in inactivity in Siberian exile.[146] Lenin, as ever, tried to cheer up his associates who had fallen into the hands of the Okhrana; he was a considerate party leader by any standards. But the fact that such letters bulk large in his correspondence is yet another sign that his links with the active party committee undergrounders was weak.

So, far from controlling the Bolshevik factional network in the Russian empire, Lenin could not expect to provide detailed advice on events as they developed. He hoped, of course, that some broad influence would be exerted by *Social-Democrat*. It continued to be issued approximately every month and to consist of a single sheet of closely-printed type; the only difference was that publishing costs forced up the price from ten to fifteen Swiss centimes.[147] Nevertheless the Okhrana rated it highly, reporting that 'guiding instructions' were reaching Russia-based Bolsheviks, 'even if with a large delay'.[148] Yet we must bear in mind the universal propensity of secret policemen to justify their functions and budgets by exaggerating the strength of the revolutionary movement; the Okhrana was no exception. Quite how many copies were successfully smuggled through customs is not known. In April 1915, Anna Elizarova-Ulyanova wrote that the newspaper was reaching Petrograd only in single copies.[149] In November she said that the first (and last) double issue of the journal *Kommunist* was in such short supply that she was holding on to it and charging Bolsheviks for reading her copy.[150] Outside Petrograd the situation must have been much worse; but, again, the figures are unavailable. Nor has any computation been made of the confiscations of Lenin's writings in wartime. Possibly this reflects a continuing official embarrassment that the number was small even at a time when the police were especially effective in their arrests of Bolsheviks.[151] Fellow members of his faction could not fairly hold Lenin responsible for the lapses in communications. As practical revolutionaries, they recognised that organisational co-ordination in Russia would have to remain largely a Russian affair. Local Bolshevik leaders had to get on with things in their own way and regard counsel from abroad as a boon which only occasionally might come their way. In the circumstances, it is surprising how much they achieved. In Saratov, moreover, they even managed to put out nine numbers of an officially-permitted newspaper before police intervened.[152] But this was an exceptional occurrence. Most Bolshevik activists who desired to publish their works in the First World War had to turn to the major Petrograd 'thick journals'; and it was typically the acknowledged theoreticians, including the émigré Lenin and the exiled Kamenev, who achieved this since non-Bolshevik editors chose what they took to be most interesting to their readerships. The alternative was to publish illegally; but the efficiency of the police, made this inordinately hard.[153]

Meanwhile the Russian Bureau of the Central Committee did its best. Lenin and Zinoviev did not rush to restore its membership after the arrests of 1912–14; no doubt they wanted to co-opt members only after reassuring themselves that the newcomers would follow their political line. At last, in September 1915, Aleksandr Shlyapnikov was rewarded with a place on the Russian Bureau; and he in turn drew G. I. Osipov, E. A. Dunaev and Anna Elizarova-Ulyanova into its membership.[154] But arrests began after Shlyapnikov departed for Scandinavia to pick up messages from Switzerland.[155] By 1916 the running of the Russian Bureau was in the hands of Anna Elizarova-Ulyanova with assistance from K. M. Shvedchikov.[156] But then Anna, too, was arrested. In autumn 1916 Shlyapnikov returned to reconstitute the Bureau, appointing V. M. Molotov and P. A. Zalutski as fellow members.[157] The Bureau's efforts were frenetic; but Molotov was later to recall how difficult it was even to know where the provincial Bolsheviks could be contacted. Turning up in Moscow, he searched for several fruitless days and then returned home.[158] Bolshevik illegal organisations had never been weaker. The Okhrana broke them up time and again. The Moscow City Committee, for example, was persistently smashed.[159] *Social-*

Democrat in 1916 announced the re-creation of groups in Samara and Nizhni Novgorod only to declare, in the same issue, that the police had re-intervened.[160]

The authorities had feared lest the link-up between the revolutionary social-democrats and the striking workers should become firm. Bolshevism was essentially the victim of the strike movement's success. The faction's active adherents must have amounted to no greater than a handful of thousands in wartime.[161] The Okhrana devastated the illegal committees. The only positive result, from Lenin's viewpoint, was that the arrests in Russia enhanced his position as Bolshevik leader. A harsh calculus was at work: the more enfeebled the faction's Russian committees, the greater the need for energetic, dedicated leaders based abroad.

Lenin was more than just an eminent leader among Bolsheviks. He was their 'Old Man'. He had acquired this nickname as a young activist in the St Petersburg Marxist movement of the early 1890s when his precocious *gravitas* impressed the fellow members of his group. In ensuing years the epithet steadily obtained a descriptive accuracy. Born in 1870, he was considerably older than any rival Bolshevik leader. Stalin was born in 1879, Zinoviev and Kamenev in 1883; the distance of a whole revolutionary generation separated them from Lenin – and they themselves were also senior figures among the faction's established figures. Most provincial committee members in the Russian empire were in their early twenties. Lenin's contemporaries from his St Petersburg days were no longer with him; they had either joined other factions after the turn of the century or, in one of other of the intra-Bolshevik struggles, were pushed out of Lenin's faction. Lenin was the great Bolshevik survivor: a real veteran. He was the sole member of his faction who had attended all Party Congresses since 1903. Security precautions disallowed the publication of full records of the faction's history, and long-serving participants had a distinct advantage over the younger leaders. They knew the careers of others and remembered past activities.

It must still be emphasised, however, that Lenin's impact on the faction in Russia was frail. *Social-Democrat* carried whatever news was forthcoming about the upsurge; but it was reporting and not directing actvity. In pre-war Bolshevik newspapers edited by Lenin there had always been regular features on developments in Russia. Difficulties in communications reduced this to a single and irregular section.[162] As in the *Iskra* days, the language and contents were aimed at the well-informed activist. *Social-Democrat* was not meant to be a popular workers' paper. Lenin had learnt over the years not to use too esoteric a terminology: he no longer used German-language phrases without translation, and he admonished Zinoviev for not following his example. 'Eh! eh!', he would scribble alongside the offending words.[163]

And yet the dwindling band of his correspondents in Russia did not give Lenin high marks in this regard either. His insistence on writing about abstract theory had irked activists before the war. After 1914, he was also criticised for his slogans. The call for 'European civil war' was extremely controversial. War-weary workers were hardly likely to be attracted to a party promising peace only through the eruption of yet another war. Sister Anna badgered him to compose a pamphlet, in a popular style, to put his case.[164] He ignored the request. Nor did he allow himself to be disturbed by complaints that he had attempted to fix party policy without prior consultation with Russia-based leaders. Kamenev was irritated that *Social-Democrat* had carried Lenin's theses on defeatism before the underground Bolsheviks in Petrograd and elsewhere had time to debate them.[165] *Social-Democrat* was quick to advertise any support for its policies. Its February 1916 issue reproduced an item from the Moscow Committee which incorporated a commitment to the slogan of 'civil war'; but the item also indicated continuing resistance to Lenin's idea that Bolsheviks should work for Russia's defeat.[166] An editorial comment somewhat lamely suggested that the subsequent modification of the defeatist policy (which had to be accepted by a reluctant Lenin) had cleared up such misunderstandings between Russia-based Bolsheviks and the faction's émigrés.[167]

Anna tried to handle her brother tactfully; but, while sympathising with his policies, she was annoyed by his spikiness and complained: 'You are terrorising me: I'm afraid of any incautious expression.'[168] Others went further. Shlyapnikov had always resented the émigré wrangling, and was 'embittered' by Lenin's treatment of Bukharin. In this instance Anna sided with Shlyapnikov,[169] but brother Volodya retorted that she 'had never made sense in politics'.[170] This was his mildest jibe at his critics. Just once Lenin acknowledged his wildness: 'I am now so badly disposed to Bukharin that I cannot write to him.'[171] This was not repentance but the bravado of a committed and conscious recidivist. In any case he seldom disguised his feelings, and now this most proper of middle-class Russians was starting to use foul language in his correspondence. 'Kautskyite shits' was a term deployed against non-Bolsheviks.[172]

It was indeed a heavy period for him. For distraction he turned to the published letters of Anton Chekhov and the Russian translation of Goethe's *Faust*.[173] Moreover, he suffered a family bereavement. His mother, whose health had been steadily deteriorating, died in July 1916.[174] No letter from him to his family about her death has yet come to light; but he was said by his brother Dmitri to be deeply upset. Perhaps he was assailed by feelings of guilt. His mother had been an inspiration to him since the days of childhood; she had sustained him morally and materially to the end of her life. Her financial assistance had often been crucial; she had never lost interest in his career; nor, it would seem, had she striven to dissuade him from the path of revolutionism. He had not seen her in her last few years, and often he had not written to her when she asked for letters.[175] His siblings, by contrast, had helped to sustain her. Dmitri had become a military doctor in wartime; his profession allowed him to keep a watch, if sometimes at a distance, upon his mother's condition.[176] Mariya, too, had taken up paramedical work, and both she and Anna kept in close contact with their mother.[177] Lenin in exile could do little but grieve after the event. Among the first things Vladimir did upon arriving back in Petrograd after the February Revolution was to visit her grave in the Volkovo cemetery to pay his last respects.[178]

He rationalised his career as a politician in a letter written to Inessa Armand in December 1916: 'This then is my fate. One campaign of combat after another – against political stupidities, vulgarities, opportunism, etc.'[179] The trace of self-pity was uncharacteristic of him. But the years of war took their emotional toll; and he probably found it easier to confide in Inessa than in most others: or possibly he felt, with a person who had been so close to him, a stronger need to justify his political behaviour. At any rate, he was right to suppose that his life was bound up inextricably with political struggle. The paradox was that, in the winter of 1916–17, the grandiosity of his ideas sprouted in inverse proportion to his immediate impact upon the politics of his native land.

5 Unsealed Messages: 1916 to April 1917

THE RUSSIAN EMPIRE ON THE BRINK

Popular uprisings are often described in volcanic imagery: the storming of the Bastille in 1789 grips the imagination two centuries later; the anti-Soviet revolt in Hungary in 1956 comes to us in pictures of uncontrolled mass fury on Budapest streets. The February Revolution of 1917 in Petrograd is no exception. The sudden outbreak of disturbances has been likened to the early stages of a hurricane. It happened so very quickly, and the crowds of workers and garrison soldiers constituted the force that brought it about. None the less, the notion that 'the masses' surged on to the Nevski Prospekt in spontaneous violence is at best a half-truth. The terms used betray the prejudices of the commentators (and these include Lenin and other leading Bolsheviks). 'The masses' and 'the crowd' are conventional terms for describing the participants in events in Petrograd. Yet the February Revolution was not just the outburst of some force of nature. Years of preparation had preceded it. Workers had turned against the monarchy in increasing numbers. They had not done this primarily under the influence of the political parties; but such parties also had for years been at work among them. Furthermore, although the party activists were few in Petrograd in February 1917, there were enough to give guidance to an uprising once the chance to overthrow the autocracy had become fully evident. Bolsheviks, Mensheviks and Socialist Revolutionaries were operating in the suburbs. Trade unionists were actively engaged in the struggle; and even the work-gangs in the factories provided a vehicle for organising the attack on the monarchy.[1]

Nevertheless there was no planning from on high for these events; and the surprise at the February Revolution was universal at Court, in the Duma, in the public organisations, among the revolutionary undergrounders and in the emigration. Vladimir Ilich Lenin, Marxist commentator and lifelong foe of the Romanov monarchy, has been mocked for not sensing that the dynasty's downfall was imminent despite having predicted it for years. But his forecasts had not pretended to strictly chronological exactitude: he had not set himself up as a day-by-day revolutionary astrologer. Writing about the wartime political situation, he stated: 'Will it lead to revolution? This we don't know, and no one can know this.'[2] Even so, he cannot be let entirely off the hook. It is a remarkable fact that in 1915–16, except for commentary on disputes among socialists in Petrograd, he wrote only one article specifically about general politics in the Russian empire – and a short article at that;[3] and he overlooked the provinces altogether. It was events in central Europe which grasped most of his attention. He kept a steady eye on Germany, observing every sign that the leftists were gaining in popularity in the German Social-Democratic Party.[4] He felt too that his own star was on the rise. Lenin jotted down in his notebooks that a German centrist had described Liebknecht as a follower of 'the Russian Lenin'.[5]

But life in Europe was not without its niggling worries on the domestic plane. Lenin's finances remained shaky; Nadezhda Krupskaya was distressed that her inability to get regular work as a part-time teacher compelled him to take on too much literary work for money.[6] His health, too, was unstable. In May 1916, he took to his bed for three days (although he typically added a postscript to a letter by Krupskaya to the effect that he only had 'a little influenza').[7] Periodically, the mental strain on him was also tremendous and Lenin sometimes refused invitations to speak in public. 'My nerves,' he explained, 'are no good. I'm scared of giving lectures.'[8] Work pressure was a factor. An additional irritant was the possibility that Switzerland might get drawn into the war. Russian émigrés might fall subject to deportation. Dire contingencies called for dire measures. Lenin contemplated a campaign to persuade Swiss socialists to press for all foreigners with six months' residence in Switzerland to have automatic right to Swiss citizenship. Rather that than exile from Europe.[9]

Lenin's absorption in mid-European affairs was not wholly voluntary. The war destroyed all but a few of his links with Russia, and he complained that he had 'incredibly little news'.[10] In September 1916 he moaned that he was 'sitting here without Russian newspapers'.[11] Swiss newspapers were no adequate substitute. At the very least he wanted to read the Petrograd liberal legal dailies regularly. When he obtained copies of these, however, the information was far from being exhaustive. Nor could the Foreign Bureau of the Central Committee obtain data through Bolsheviks arriving in Switzerland from Russia. Only in January 1917 did he finally meet anyone who had been in the Romanov empire since the war's outbreak. This, too, failed to provide a comprehensive report. The newcomers were not Bolsheviks but a pair of ordinary conscripts who had escaped from German captivity.[12]

So Russian political emigrants in Switzerland had greater excuse than most in failing to perceive in early 1917 that the ultimate crisis for the Romanov monarchy was maturing fast. The disaster at Tannenberg in the war's first months was followed by successful retrenchment. The Germans' advance was halted, and Russian forces intimidated the Austrian–Hungarian troops on the Eastern front's southern belt. On the Western front the British and French held the line after the loss of Belgium and northern France. The protraction of the fighting, involving vast expenditure of human and material resources, made necessary the total mobilisation of each combatant country's economy. The Germans, not being able to import by sea because of the British navy, had to do this most quickly. But even Britain, which had a traditionally low level of state intervention in economic affairs, was compelled to recast her arrangements. David Lloyd George, who became Prime Minister in 1916, had made his name by securing an increase in the munitions available to the British Expeditionary Force. The government's regulation of production and supplies in industry grew everywhere. Output, too, expanded; and the labour-forces of all countries were 'diluted' with unskilled workers, including women, who had no prior experience of factory or mining employment. Technological modernisation continued and was even speeded up in wartime.

Social pressures built up most dangerously in those countries where the economic and cultural transformation associated with industrialisation was least advanced. Of all major belligerent powers, this was most evident in Russia. The railway network was dense enough to handle passenger and freight traffic in peacetime, but not after 1914, when the army's requirements – which included hay for the horses as well as men and machines for the regiments – grew sharply.[13] The quality of rolling stock deteriorated. The transport of food supplies to the towns was bound to be affected and the harvests stay close to the pre-war level. The German naval blockade prevented the usual export of grain, but by 1916 the trains were no longer running as smoothly and the beginnings of a shortage of deliveries was becoming apparent.[14]

For an economic commentator like Lenin, this worsening situation would normally have called forth pages of analysis; and, as a revolutionary, he would normally have displayed an informed pleasure. But he was distracted by mid-European events. No Russian Marxist except Petr Maslov was better-noted for his attention to rural affairs. But Lenin ignored, or probably more accurately, was unaware of, the peasantry's problems. Inflation rocketed after 1914 as the state borrowed heavily and printed paper roubles frantically in order to finance armaments production. The incentive for peasant households to trade their grain with the towns decreased. Apart from the problem of a depreciating currency, the peasantry was annoyed at finding so few goods to purchase. Factories produced primarily for the army. In the crucial machine-tool sector, 78 per cent of business was directed at military purposes. Peasants preferred to keep their grain; they fed themselves and their animals better and also, when the government banned the sale of vodka for the war's duration, they distilled and drank their own spirits using their harvested grain. There was acquiescence in the conscription of millions of rural lads and few signs of revolt were noticed, yet the countryside's loyalty, after the troubles of 1905–6, was no longer to be taken for granted by the emperor and his government; and even the landlords, who had difficulty obtaining labourers as a result of mass conscription, were grumbling.[15]

Factory workers were openly discontented. The early rally to the government's cause faded. Strikes swept over Russia in the winter of 1915–16 and again in late 1916. The authorities blamed German *provocateurs* and pointed to the rise in real wages for skilled labourers in the armaments sector as a sign that things were not as bad as was claimed. But the food shortages of winter 1916–17 affected even the better-paid workers. The huge industrial expansion (and Lenin, when in 1917 he was to take a closer interest in wartime economic processes, was virtually alone in emphasising that an expansion of output in factories and mines had occurred)[16] was accompanied by problems. Funds were unavailable for an increase in housing stock and social and cultural amenities. Nor did the state enforce its own safety standards. In officially-monitored factories there were 3.5 million workers by January 1917. The cities and towns teemed with discontent.

The moderate conservatives and liberals in the Fourth State Duma saw the need to contact the working class through war-industry committees which were constituted by both industrialists and workers. The Octobrist leader Aleksandr Guchkov remained prominent among them. He used them astutely to confirm his case that the Duma leaders were more competent at the tasks of government than were the imperial Council of Ministers.[17] The court became a national laughing stock. Rasputin debauched himself until, after several attempts, he was assassinated in December 1916; and the German background of the empress Aleksandra formed the basis of popular allegations that she unpatriotically sought a separate peace with Germany and Austria-Hungary. Nikolai II, after the initial military set-backs, resolved to demonstrate his commitment to the struggle for victory by appointing himself as Commander-in-Chief in 1915. The Russian armies continued to acquit themselves well, and in 1916 General Brusilov succeeded in breaching the Austrian lines and, albeit only temporarily, forcing the enemy to retreat. The problem for the emperor was not military but political. His position at army headquarters in Mogilev, nearly 800 kilometres from Petrograd, left him almost as isolated from knowledge of current developments in Petrograd as were émigrés such as Lenin.

The regime's nerve had not cracked. Nikolai II and his ministers, who constituted an increasingly gerontocratic administration after 1914, doled out splendidly shabby treatment to the State Duma throughout the war. The Kadets and Octobrists who had formed a 'Progressive Bloc' in 1913 called in vain for a 'government of confidence', meaning principally the introduction of Duma politicians to the government. The incompetence of the administration was exaggerated by the Progressive Bloc, but the myth struck deep roots. In 1916, Kadet leader Pavel Milyukov, whose preference was for a constitutional monarchy, asked provocatively whether ministers were guilty of stupidity or treason. In the winter of 1916-1917 the equally exasperated Octobrist leader Guchkov took discreet soundings among the generals about their attitude to a potential coup against the emperor.[18]

The Minister of Internal Affairs strengthened its policy of clampdown: strikes were broken up and socialist activists were incarcerated. Yet the underlying threat to the dynasty remained, and the disorganisation of the indigenous socialist movement was never complete. Throughout the First World War, socialist journals continued publishing. Newspapers were persecuted severely, and direct discussions of the government's war aims and general competence were not tolerated. But a degree of public debate among the intellectuals persisted; even Swiss-based émigrés, such as Lenin himself, were not disbarred from publication so long as they employed the conventional Aesopian language. The war-industry committees, despite being shunned by Bolsheviks on the grounds that they were merely a means for prosecuting an imperialist war more successfully, allowed the Mensheviks to organise covert anti-regime propaganda. Bolsheviks no longer had seats in the Duma; all their deputies languished in Siberian exile. But the Menshevik N. S. Ckhkeidze and his colleagues maintained their carefully-phrased criticism of the government; and Chkheidze, after a period of vacillation, came down against any support for the regime against Germany and Austria-Hungary.[19] The Russian empire's stability was even more brittle than in the Russo-Japanese war of 1904–5; the internal fissures were widening. And the man who was wrestling with the intellectual dilemmas of Hegel and Aristotle in the Bern Public Library was about to enter the pages of world history.

THE KIENTHAL CONFERENCE

Lenin's considerations on Russia at war skirted developments on the Eastern front. Nearly all statements by him in 1915–16 referred to political rather than military aspects of the war; the contingencies of battles, troop transfers, sieges, strategical thrusts and diversions did not interest him. From late 1915 the Russian armed forces acquitted themselves adequately. Germany's armies had occupied all of Poland, and the Turks proved more troublesome in the south than had been expected. But the front held; shell-shortages began to be surmounted; and Russian generals recovered confidence. Austria-Hungary had experienced even greater difficulties and, with Italy's entry into the war in 1915, repeatedly needed German armies to rescue her.

On the Western front, the French and British had fought back strongly after the initial disasters of 1914 when the German lines came to within sixty miles of Paris. The Schlieffen plan of the German High Command had assumed that a rapid surge through Belgium would leave France at Germany's mercy and make victory on both Western and Eastern fronts inevitable. This had not occurred. Nevertheless, the German armies yielded little ground, and the Allied governments turned to other strategems. The British expedition to the Straits of the Dardanelles was an unmitigated disaster; Austria attacked and overran Serbia; and a joint Allied landing at Salonika failed to shake the pattern of the war. Both the Allies and the Central Powers, particularly Germany, judged that the Western front was the decisive military theatre. In February 1916, the Germans launched an enormous assault on the fortress of Verdun. Fierce resistance followed, as the French regarded the town's defence as a symbol of the national war-effort. Governments on both sides worried lest continued lack of success might breed popular disaffection. Mutinies took place in the French forces. Strikes broke out in all countries as working conditions worsened and bread rations were lowered. In order to undermine the Central Powers' war effort, the British imposed a naval blockade on Germany and tried to foment unrest among Austria-Hungary's minorities. Germany replied by opening a submarine offensive on Allied shipping.[20]

It took the Dublin Easter Rising of 1916 before Lenin began to pay close attention to the Irish factor in British politics, and a mini-polemic occurred with Radek (who, true to his anti-nationalist standpoint, refused to greet the insurrection with acclaim).[21] But Lenin's day-to-day preoccupation was not so much with general politics and social life as with the factional strife among Europe's socialists after the Zimmerwald Conference of September 1915. It was plain to him that Robert Grimm would do his utmost to prevent a further leftward shift among Zimmerwaldists. Lenin had never trusted him: this was Lenin's usual reaction to someone with whom he disagreed and who wielded influence. Zinoviev had to spend a lot of time reassuring Lenin that the Swiss socialist did not seek to exclude him from discussions.[22]

This boded ill for future relations. Zinoviev, the Bolshevik representative on the International Socialist Commission established at Zimmerwald, constantly expressed reservations about Grimm's centrist motivations. The Commission met on 3 February 1916 to plan a second 'Zimmerwald Conference'. Lenin, Radek and Zinoviev wanted one for its own sake, while Grimm supported the idea only because the International Socialist Bureau had remained inactive.[23] Two months were set aside to send out the invitations and allow the delegates to arrive. Much had happened since the previous Conference. Events in Germany in particular appeared to be moving in a direction favourable to Zimmerwaldists. The German Social-Democratic Party was beset by divisions as Haase and Kautsky revealed their objections to the official party's leadership's policy on the war. In December 1915, at last, Haase's group in the Reichstag took the plunge and voted against war credits. Even so, this did not bring about a *rapprochement* with the far-left faction: Kautsky and Haase called for peace without annexations, but gave little indication about how to achieve it. Liebknecht and Luxemburg, along with Lenin, called unequivocally for a campaign of opposition to the government. In Luxemburg's case, the anti-war propaganda had to be produced from a Berlin prison after her arrest in 1915; Liebknecht's immunity as a Reichstag deputy as yet protected him. The German Social-Democratic Party, renowned for its unity and discipline, moved towards schism.[24]

Grimm took pleasure from the shift in the tactics of Haase and Kautsky, which resembled his own. The strengthening of a 'left-centrist' bloc among Europe's socialists would, he hoped, marginalise those such as Lenin, Zinoviev and Radek whom he regarded as impulsive extremists. This was yet another reason why Lenin detested Kautsky. He feared that Kautsky might emerge as the leader of a mass German anti-war movement; and what happened in Germany, in the eyes of the Zimmerwald Left, was crucial to the prospects of European socialist revolution. Grimm keenly sent another invitation to the forthcoming Conference in Switzerland.[25]

Proceedings opened in the Volkshaus in Bern on 24 April 1916, and were transferred on the following day to the Bärenhotel in the nearby village of Kienthal. There were about forty delegates, who varied in number from day to day.[26] The Kienthal Conference, like its Zimmerwald predecessor, could have been placed in a handful of charabancs without undue discomfort. Grimm had a harder time than anticipated. Haase and Kautsky, denouncing the whole Conference as an infringement of the International Socialist Bureau's prerogatives, refused their invitation.[27] Lenin and Zinoviev, delighted by the snubbing of Grimm, aggravated the situation by introducing intra-Russian disputes on to the Conference floor. The mandate of Martov and Akselrod to represent any Russian group was, as usual, challenged by the Bolsheviks.[28] The objection was overruled, but then the Left won a further victory: the Swiss social-democrat, Hermann Greulich, who had met up with a German governmental emissary, had come to the Conference. After heated debate, he was compelled to leave.[29] Worse was to follow for Grimm:

the leading French delegate at Kienthal, Pierre Brizon, had voted in favour of war credits. The Left at Kienthal circulated a petition criticising Brizon, and collected nineteen signatories.[30] Only Grimm's intervention as chairman stopped Brizon from storming out in retort. Two precious days had already passed. Pressed for time, the Conference resolved to start discussions on 26 April at eight o'clock in the morning.[31]

They nearly succeeded: Grimm opened proceedings just a quarter of an hour late. Again the Left, though comprising a minority of the delegates, had been causing another upset: Zinoviev resumed the attack on Martov and Akselrod on the grounds that the group they claimed to represent, the Petrograd Mensheviks, were hostile to the Zimmerwald Manifesto. The objection was overruled.[32] Radek, too, made trouble. The Dutch socialists had been unable to send a contingent to Kienthal, and Radek claimed the right to sit as their representative. For Grimm, this was almost the last straw. Karl Radek, a Polish Jew, might well claim to have been Germanised by his lengthy sojourns in Germany and by his former membership of the German Social-Democratic Party; but no trace of a Dutch connection existed.[33]

All this, and Lenin had not yet opened his mouth. At last the Conference turned to its main business: the question of war and peace. Grimm read out his theses. Their content showed that he, too, had shifted leftwards since Zimmerwald. He castigated 'bourgeois-pacifist' schemes for the termination of the war. Only 'the revolutionary struggle of the proletarian class', he asserted, would bring about peace.[34] But the Left at the Conference were unsatisfied. Their pressure upon Grimm, as well as the upsurge of strikes in Europe, had still not brought him to specify a series of measures to bring about the war's end. C. Meyer called for an unequivocal ban on both voting war credits and paying taxes.[35] There was a brief relief for · Grimm. A telegram was read out from 'Robert and the Family Roland Holst' about the outbreak of street demonstrations in Holland. But this only served to stir the delegates of the Left to greater confidence. Radek stood up to present a rival project, cobbled together by Russian Bolsheviks, the Polish left socialists and the German social-democrats from Bremen. Radek urged that even 'democratised diplomacy' would never end the war; that peaceful capitalism was a 'utopia'; and that the German centrists, such as Kautsky, belonged to the category of 'the petit-bourgeois, the opportunists and the social-pacifists'.[36] Martov, too, offered a project. Vigorously hostile to every aspect of the war, it had the very pacifist undertones that Radek deprecated.[37] A clash was imminent; and all agreed that a compromise would be achieved only if the main groups were invited to join a Conference commission. The atmosphere remained highly charged. Brizon's presence at Kienthal still offended the Left. An ebullient figure, he scribbled a quick note to Lenin charging that his ideas were mere 'theory'. Lenin passed a note back to him stating yet again that only political revolution would suffice to terminate the war.[38] Brizon felt himself to be generally isolated and humiliated. He defended himself as 'a socialist and a Frenchman'; and, while admitting that he had not previously opposed war credits, he claimed that to have acted otherwise would have courted political suicide. He also gave his word not to vote for war credits in future.[39]

The session ended in tumult; the mutual wounds inflicted at Zimmerwald festered at Kienthal. But balm was applied overnight, and proceedings were resumed on 27 April. Still Lenin had hardly opened his mouth in the open sessions. But he had been a member of a second commission set up by the Conference to discuss what to do about the International Socialist Bureau, which had been relocated to The Hague after the German conquest of Belgium.[40] In the commission, he and his associates were again in a minority. The Italian delegate, C. Lazzari, giving the majority's report, was still willing to acknowledge the International Bureau's authority so long as it met without delay, rejected war credits and demanded peace without annexations and indemnities. Lenin intervened for the commission minority, stating that the Bureau had had more than enough time to convene. In reality, he insisted, a split in the international socialist movement had already occurred.[41] His speech brought all the private unhappiness with him into the open. Martov declared that, if there was a problem in inter-socialist relations, then the Bolsheviks had helped to cause it.[42] Akselrod spoke scathingly of 'Lenin and his friends'.[43] Grimm lost his customary poise, accusing the Left of not wanting to be practical.[44] Lenin retreated into the background, resuming an angelic silence. It was Radek who demanded, unsuccessfully, that Grimm retract his 'insinuation'.[45]

But the Left, too, did not want the Kienthal proceedings to end without an agreement on policy. After much haggling, Zinoviev produced a form of words acceptable to the delegates on both sides. The Conference roundly criticised the International Socialist Bureau and planned to substitute its own Commission for the Bureau; but it would meet again to reconsider its position in the event that a general meeting of the Bureau took place. This compromise obviously left the question open even though the Left had managed to harden the resolution.[46] The commission on 'the relationship of the proletariat to the peace question' had not yet completed its work, and the Conference went into recess on 28 April to allow a draft to be agreed. Proceedings recommenced next day, and Grimm's line was accepted. In particular, the Conference called for a ban on war indemnities and for 'compulsory arbitration courts' to decide territorial disputes among nations. The demand was made for an immediate truce on all fronts.[47]

The Left saw this as utopian thinking; but they had nevertheless inserted sections more to their liking. 'Socialist pacifism' was deprecated. The emphasis was also made that workers would influence the course of the war only by 'vigorous action directed towards the capitalist class's overthrow'.[48] The Left voted for the resolution, but made clear their reservations. In fact, the Left itself was divided. As at Zimmerwald, Radek usually had the edge over Lenin. It had been Lenin's intention to coax the Left into promulgating the principle of national self-determination; but Radek's influence forced him to back down.[49] Lenin could not afford to split the Left without risking making the already small group of far-left socialists still smaller and less authoritative, and even ridiculous. The Conference was not yet over, since a manifesto had not been produced. A third commission was created. Brizon protested about its leftist composition; Radek laughed that it would be 'idiocy' for him to sit on the same commission as Brizon.[50] A shambles loomed again, but Brizon was eventually calmed down. The commission sat for the rest of the day, presenting its work to the weary Conference at 1.15 in the morning of 30 April. Nearly three hours of debate ensued. The Left wanted the Manifesto to call for illegal political activity, political strikes and even civil war. This was totally unacceptable to Brizon. In the end, no agreement could be reached. Grimm's proposal was accepted to hand over the final drafting to the International Socialist Commission.[51] The Left had not won, but their ability to stop the Conference majority from getting its way had made the Kienthal Conference quite different from its predecessor at Zimmerwald. The exhausted delegates dispersed from the Bärenhotel at four o'clock on a beautiful spring morning in the second year of the bloodiest and largest war in history.

'MARXISM ON THE STATE'

Lenin was a serious thinker; but he was also in serious need of sustaining his confidence. He would turn anywhere in order to validate his strategical optimism. His predictions about political conturbation in Europe swung from one country to another. At one moment he was anticipating upheaval in Russia, at another in Switzerland,[52] but the country which he most usually expected to initiate the European socialist revolution was Germany. In 1915 he had denied 'that the victory of socialism in one country is impossible' (although he still assumed that the full achievement of socialism would require its dissemination to more countries than just one).[53] He did not nominate a country where socialism might first triumph, but he must have had Germany in mind. The passage continues as follows: 'The victorious proletariat of that country, having expropriated the capitalists and organised socialist production, would stand up against the capitalist remainder of the world, attracting to its cause the oppressed classes of other countries.'[54] There is no reason to suppose that he thought that Russia, whose industrial capacity and cultural level he judged to be immensely lower than Germany's, could have fulfilled such a role.[55]

Until January 1917, Lenin did not ponder exactly how the inception of socialism, wherever it took place, would be undertaken; the future dictatorship of the proletariat lay undefined.[56] But certain tangential statements give clues about his orientation as it developed. In 1915, he studied the nineteenth-century German military theorist Karl von Clausewitz, and the lessons he learnt were selective. Largely neglecting Clausewitz's discussion of the variegated aspects of warfare, Lenin underscored the sections deriding the pretensions of generals.[57] For the Bolshevik leader, it was Clausewitz's description of the organisational simplifications brought about by modern technology that were impressive (as well as his *sang froid* about war and death).[58] When he read Engels's military works, Lenin focused on the same theme and was convinced by the assertion that an army's need for lengthy, specialist training had been made obsolete by modern conditions.[59] Lenin also surveyed the changes in the wartime capitalist economies. Bukharin had postulated the emergence of 'state capitalism', meaning that the 'bourgeois state' no longer merely reflected capitalist interests. It had become a prime organiser of economic production; it was also fast accumulating capital. The system remained capitalist. Profits still accrued to large private enterprises in particular. But the state, as Bukharin emphasised, was acquiring greater autonomy in economic regulation.[60]

Until 1916, Lenin had baulked at accepting the term 'state capitalism', perhaps because it infringed the premise that capitalism by its nature was an anarchic mode of economy.[61] But the extension of planning inside the German and British economies was an irrefutable reality, and Lenin contended that the Russian economy too had the same features to an increasing degree.[62] He did not propose a theory of state capitalism, but scattered sentences displayed his feeling that such economic developments simplified the tasks of any forthcoming socialist administration. Centralisation and state control under capitalism had been augmented; and, according to Lenin, what 'the Junkers and petty gentry' were doing today could be done tomorrow by 'conscious workers'. Not only did a revolutionary situation exist in Europe but the revolution could swiftly and easily be carried through.[63] As Marxists, Lenin and Bukharin might have been expected to explore the technological changes that, in their view, had made 'the transition to socialism' an imminent possibility in advanced industrial countries. But it was the wartime changes in political and social organisation that mostly grasped their attention; in particular, they were mightily impressed by the militarisation of the German economy after 1914.

Lenin, furthermore, began to show an edginess in his rejection of Bukharin's claim that a future socialist government would have to destroy the old capitalist state and construct its own state from scratch. Lenin merely urged him to 'allow his views to mature' before publishing his ideas:[64] not a symptom of comprehensive criticism of Bukharin. In January and February 1917 Lenin took his own notes on Marxism and the state. Filling forty-eight closely-written pages, he examined what had been said by Marx and Engels on the subject. Bukharin had mentioned them only fleetingly; for him, the need to crush the bourgeois state was justifiable on intrinsic grounds.[65] Lenin desired the textual security of support from Marxism's co-founders. His notes give glimpses of his mind at work: early on, he becomes sure that Marx had somewhere talked of destroying the bourgeois state; but where? Lenin searched furiously, and decided that it was in *The Eighteenth Brumaire of Louis Napoleon*.[66] He was equally zealous to discover when Marx had first mentioned 'the dictatorship of the proletariat'. Surely it was before 1871? 'Apparently not', was Lenin's conclusion until his further research convinced him otherwise.[67] Then there were the tiny embarrassments. Of all people, what was Engels doing using a tautology like 'political state'?[68] Every state is by definition political. These, however, were minor frissons. An admiring excitement pervades the 'blue notebooks'. And Lenin's conclusions were a shock to him: Marx and Engels had indeed recommended a destruction of the old state machine; and, therefore, Kautsky's wish to inherit such a machine was thoroughly un-Marxist.[69]

Lenin correctly emphasised that Kautsky had put pressure on Engels himself to delete sentences from his commentary on Marx in 1895 which advocated the use of force as a means of bringing about the transition to socialism.[70] Marx in the 1870s, as Lenin knew, had granted the possibility of peaceful change.[71] Yet Lenin asserted that 'bureaucratism' had entered into all public and commercial life since then, including even socialist parties. The bulwarks of capitalist self-defence were growing stronger year by year, and violent revolutions would be necessary.[72]

But what about the dispositions to be made after power had been seized. Here Lenin, referring to Bukharin's call for the destruction of the old state, backtracked by proposing that 'in the essence of the matter Bukharin is nearer the truth than Kautsky',[73] but this was still only a qualified approval of Bukharin. Lenin continued to believe Bukharin to be misguided on a number of points, especially in his apparent conviction that there would be no need for a state at all once the socialist seizure of power had occurred.[74] Lenin, on his side, urged the need for proletarian dictatorship.[75] In addition, Bukharin as well as his fellow far-left Marxists in Europe such as Pannekoek and Görter failed to offer a practical plan for the dismantlement of the old state machine.[76] Lenin called for an innovation of cardinal strategical significance: that the dictatorship of the proletariat should be constructed on the institutional basis of the soviets.[77] In 1905 he had seen them as organs of insurrection against the absolute monarchy, and suggested that they could constitute the framework for the ensuing provisional revolutionary government. In January and February 1917 he went further: the workers' soviets were not merely to bring down the Russian monarchy and establish a democratic political framework for capitalism, they were also to initiate the entire transition to socialism. In addition, their importance would not be confined to Russia: they should be regarded as vehicles for revolution across Europe.[78]

As to the functions of such soviets, he was less concerned to investigate how they had actually operated in 1905 than to indicate how they might operate in the future. They would be able, according to Lenin, to eradicate all material privileges. Abuse of authority would cease. Deputies elected to the soviets could be recalled at the request of their constituents. There would be mass participation in the running of the state, and the majority of the population would be involved. Sounding a note that was novel for him, Lenin declared the desirability of the 'fullest local self-administration'.[79] A standing army and a professional police and civil service would be neither necessary nor desirable. He wanted to limit the bounds of authority exercised 'from above', declaring: 'On the basis of socialism "primitive" democracy will not be primitive.'[80]

It occurred to Lenin that such a system, being based upon social self-regulation, was hardly describable any longer as a 'state'. The dictatorship of the proletariat evoked images of ultra-centralism. Now Lenin readily cited Marx as treating it as merely a 'semi-state'.[81] Even this would not be the final stage. Under the dictatorship of the proletariat, which would introduce socialism, the principle would prevail that 'he that does not work neither shall he eat'. Pay would be given in accordance with the amount of work done. But the objective would be the ultimate stage: communism. Then and only then would social classes cease to exist. Then the state would have disappeared entirely. The previous division between mental and physical labour would have vanished. The society's productive resources would have attained a high level of development; work would have ceased being a burden and have been accepted as a 'primary necessity of life'; and the time devoted to work would have been drastically reduced. Then at last the principle would be secure: from each according to his talents, to each according to his needs.[82] Thus Lenin's notebooks, which he headed 'Marxism on the State', offered not only the most detailed but also one of the most elevated statements by a twentieth-century Marxist on the transition from capitalism; they undermine all those interpretations of him as a desolate, worried individual in 1916–17. Only the news of events back in Russia in February 1917 interrupted the writing up of his materials.

And yet, despite the assertions that the proletarian dictatorship would be so pleasant an affair, there were very grim sides to his thinking. The dictatorship would suspend the civic rights of the other classes. Lenin's notes, moreover, took it for granted that capitalist society is neatly divided into two contending classes, the proletariat and the bourgeoisie. They made no comment on the fate of intermediate groups; the peasantry and the town traders are not mentioned. A deep contempt for parliaments, which he regarded as mere talking shops, was also evident. The dictatorship, by contrast, was meant to be a 'workers' corporation'.[83] Uniting all legislative, executive and judicial powers, it would simply get on with 'the administration of things'. The dangers of abuse of power were brushed unreflectingly aside. Furthermore, Lenin began from the premise that the proletariat would be a monolithic whole. No differing interests would divide it. Hence there seemed no requirement to talk of competing parties – and this most party-minded of theorists did not once refer to parties in the course of his forty eight pages of notes. The combination of direct intention, naïve expectation and failure to think issues through boded ill for the chances of realising the freedoms that, in the first two months of 1917, he professed to desire.

THE FEBRUARY REVOLUTION

Abruptly, from the beginning of March 1917, Lenin was forced to take greater account of developments in current politics in Russia. On 23 February 1917, International Women's Day, women textile workers went on strike in Petrograd. They contravened advice from the local revolutionaries of all parties, who remained demoralised by the police arrests earlier in the winter. But the lengthening bread queues and the worsening factory conditions had snapped the women's patience. Streaming out on to the streets, they called on workers in other factories, men and women, to show solidarity. The strike movement grew fast. By 25 February, almost all Petrograd factories had been closed. The revolutionary activists gathered their nerve and began again to organise for the speedy overthrow of the government. Bolsheviks, Mensheviks and Socialist Revolutionaries were involved. The émigré leaders could play no part since they heard about what was happening only after the thrust towards revolution had occurred. Activists in Petrograd improvised as best they could, and calls for the re-establishment of soviets were already being heard. Demonstrations were arranged: the proximity of the Vyborg industrial quarter to the centre of the city increasingly worried the authorities. Yet the crucial unknown factor was the attitude of the troops garrisoned in Petrograd. The answer came on 27 February, when the Volynski Regiment mutinied. It was on the same day that the revolutionaries, mainly at Menshevik instigation, formed the Petrograd Soviet of Workers' Deputies.[84] The revolt was headed by workers and soldiers. The emperor prorogued the Duma on 26 February, but this was really a preventive measure: the Progressive Bloc did not try to lead the people on the streets. To the end of the old régime the emperor could count on the parlousness of the liberals and moderate conservatives in the Duma; and the Kadet leader Pavel Milyukov aspired to the dynasty's preservation as a constitutional monarchy. Lenin's contemptuous dismissal of Russian liberalism as the fifth wheel on the carriage of tsarism was harsh but, at such a time of crisis, not wide of the mark. The most that the liberals did in February 1917 was to form an unofficial Duma Committee to hold discussions until the Duma should be reconvened.[85]

On 28 February, Nikolai II belatedly recognised the emergency in Petrograd for what it was. He left general headquarters in Mogilev for his palace in Tsarskoe Selo outside the capital. All Petrograd was in ferment. The Petrograd Soviet had issued a proclamation demanding the dynasty's removal. Demonstrations filled the central thoroughfares. The Duma Committee, which had been acting like a government for some days, plucked up courage to demand a transfer of power. The next day, 1 March, found the emperor still en route to Tsarskoe Selo. He declared his willingness to form 'a responsible ministry', which would have included Duma Committee members. But the revolution was spreading elsewhere. Disturbances broke out in Moscow and the Kronstadt naval garrison. The Petrograd Soviet, moreover, had a Menshevik and Socialist-Revolutionary majority favouring the abolition of the monarchy and the installation of a 'bourgeois' government drawn from the Duma leadership. On 2 March the Soviet's representatives negotiated with the Duma Committee to this end, and Octobrist leader Aleksandr Guchkov met the emperor at Pskov to seek his abdication. In Petrograd, Pavel Milyukov announced the formation of a Provisional Government; and in Pskov, Nikolai II agreed to abdicate.[86] On 3 March Prince G. E. Lvov was proclaimed premier of the Provisional Government. Milyukov the Kadet became Foreign Minister, Octobrist Guchkov became Minister for Military and Naval Affairs, and the Socialist Revolutionary Aleksandr Kerenski, Minister of Justice. An absolutist dynasty which had ruled Russia since 1613 had been supplanted, in the space of little more than a week, by an administration led by its liberal opponents.

The émigré revolutionaries perforce relied mainly on non-Russian sources of information. Petrograd dailies arrived only after the February Revolution's occurrence. The Swiss newspapers *Zürcher Post* and *Neue ZürcherZeitung* appreciated the momentous political possibilities in Russia; but their Germanophile editorials made their reports suspect.[87] On 28 February, in his latest extant letter from the days before the emperor's abdication, Lenin wrote to Inessa Armand without mentioning events in the Russian capital. The Bolshevik leader's continuing preoccupation was with socialist polemics in Europe, and he noted trenchantly: 'There is nothing coming from Russia, not even letters!!'.[88] But at last, on 2 March, the *Zürcher Post* carried the announcement that the emperor had been overthrown and that Duma leaders had taken power.[89]

The Russian emigration was ecstatic. There were celebratory embraces and evening-parties, congratulatory messages to the newspapers; Bolsheviks, Mensheviks and Socialist Revolutionaries proclaimed that a millstone had been removed from the shoulders of the people of Russia and her subject territories. Lenin shared in the cheer without letting himself be carried away. On 2 March 1917 he was not ruling out that 'the Germans' had manufactured a story which the world's press had foolishly fallen for.[90] On 3 March, in a letter to Aleksandra Kollontai in Oslo, he could not resist patting himself on the back (and why should he not have done?) for having predicted, on New Year's Day 1917, that Milyukov, Guchkov and Kerenski might soon be forming a post-Romanov government.[91] To Kollontai, too, he repeated his opposition to policies involving 'defence of the fatherland'; and so deep was his mistrust of the Kadets that he proposed the retention of an underground central party apparatus in Petrograd. He called for 'international proletarian revolution', but offered no prescription as to what should be done in Russia.[92] By 4 March, he was writing to Kollontai that '*peace* would come only from an armed Soviet if it will seize power';[93] and on the same day he sketched a statement of policy.[94] This included a demand for a 'workers' government', effecting 'a union with the poorest mass of the rural population' as well as 'with the revolutionary workers of all belligerent countries'.[95] This constituted a rupture with the old Bolshevik programme. Bolsheviks in 1905 called for a coalition of socialist parties representing all the workers and all the peasants. Lenin now demanded a government representing the entire working class but only the most impoverished sections of the peasantry.

'A workers' government' had figured prominently as an objective in Trotski's writings, which Lenin had previously rejected.[96] Trotski was to make much of the similarity in his memoirs. But it has lain unobserved that Lenin's phraseology about the poorest peasants was like that of Leo Jogiches and Rosa Luxemburg. Lenin seldom collected his eggs from a single nest.[97] At any rate, he had severely distorted the conventional Russian Marxist two-stage revolutionary schedule. To this he did not own up, saying only that 'the revolutionary proletariat' could not help but 'set itself the task of continuing the struggle for the achievement of a democratic republic and of socialism'.[98] This was near to appealing for the inauguration of the transition to socialism. But he was not yet ready to commit himself totally to this. In a telegram to Bolsheviks leaving Scandinavia for Russia, also on 4 March, he restricted his recommendations: no support for the Provisional Government; suspicion of Kerenski; the arming of the proletariat; elections to the Petrograd municipal council; and no *rapprochement* with other parties.[99]

His reference to the Petrograd municipal council, whose importance was negligible, demonstrated how isolated he was from happenings in Russia; and he was equally out of touch in imagining that Nikolai II aimed at a return to power by means of a separate peace with the Germans.[100] Nothing was further from the former emperor's mind, and the pressures on the Provisional Government came from elsewhere. The Petrograd Soviet insisted that the cabinet should promulgate a full range of civic freedoms, hold elections to a Constituent Assembly, and fight only a defensive war against Germany and Austria-Hungary. The ministers in any case aimed to introduce a liberal constitution and to convoke a Constituent Assembly. Yet Milyukov and others shared Nikolai II's expansionist objectives, and the whole cabinet ruled legislation on fundamental social reform in advance of the Constituent Assembly. The land question in particular was held in abeyance. The Provisional Government had to act circumspectly since the Soviet's Menshevik and Socialist-Revolutionary leaders had been elected by workers and soldiers who had overthrown the monarchy. When the Soviet issued its Order No. 1 to garrison troops, relieving them of the harsher aspects of discipline and allowing them to set up their own soldiers' committees, the cabinet reluctantly gave its assent.[101]

The consolation for the Provisional Government was that the Mensheviks and Socialist Revolutionaries did not want to take power; and, not wishing to unsettle military defence, they advocated a compact with the middle class so that factory production might be maintained. A socialist assumption of power, in their view, would lead to civil war. Doctrinally too they were inhibited by the tenet that the country's cultural and economic level had to be raised before socialism could be contemplated. A 'bourgeois government' ought to carry through a 'bourgeois revolution'. Mensheviks and Socialist Revolutionaries aimed to influence policies by providing the Provisional Government with conditional support, and indicated that this support would be withdrawn if any deviation from democratic politics were to be observed. Only 'revolutionary defence' would be tolerated. Those Mensheviks such as Maslov who advocated a campaign for outright victory over Germany were in the minority; the 'centrists', under Irakli Tsereteli, who had just returned from Siberian exile, and N. S. Chkheidze, held sway among Mensheviks and were backed by prominent Socialist Revolutionaries such as Abram Gots.[102]

Lenin had long before made his mind up about Chkheidze as being an inveterate and untrustworthy compromiser, and ruled out unification with him and his adherents.[103] Bolsheviks in Petrograd at the time of the February Revolution independently felt a similar distaste. The Russian Bureau of the Central Committee, meeting on 28 February under Shlyapnikov's guidance, called for the formation of a provisional revolutionary government of socialists, in line with traditional Bolshevism.[104] The Bureau refused to offer any support to Lvov's cabinet. But the Menshevik and Socialist-Revolutionary acceptance of the Provisional Government prevented the Bureau's aims from being realised; and the Bolshevik City Committee, too, opposed the Bureau.[105] Shlyapnikov and his associates, being forced to reconsider tactics, edged towards advocating a role for the soviets as 'embryos of the new power'.[106] Allies for Lenin were coming into existence without either the allies or Lenin being conscious of such an alliance. Yet the Bureau faced difficulties from 12 March with the return from exile of Lev Kamenev, Iosif Stalin and M. K. Muranov. Kamenev and Stalin had been leaders in the pre-war illegal party machine; Muranov had been a Duma deputy: each wanted conditional support of the Lvov cabinet.[107] Kamenev's behaviour at his trial in 1915, when he had disowned Lenin's defeatist policy on the war, rankled with the Bureau; but Stalin was accepted as a co-editor of the revived *Pravda*.[108] Stalin proceeded to print an article by Kamenev articulating the policy of conditional support. Disputes between *Pravda* and the Russian Bureau persisted through March 1917.[109]

Lenin rued the absence of rapid communication between Petrograd and Switzerland. On 7 March he drafted the first of five 'Letters from Afar'. He repeated that the European 'imperialist war' would lead to a continental war between classes – and erroneously suggested that workers had overthrown the emperor in the interests of bringing about peace; he also still averred that the Provisional Government sought a deal with the dynasty.[110] A novel proposal was for the creation of 'soviets of agricultural workers'.[111] But his most significant request was for the Bolsheviks to move from 'the first to the second stage of the revolution'.[112] This phrase was even more ambiguous than his ideas as drafted on 4 March. Did he mean a socialist revolution or didn't he?

On 8 March, writing a second 'Letter from Afar', he left less room for doubt by calling for a workers' militia combining 'all-state functions with military functions and with control over social production and the distribution of products'.[113] He also shifted his analysis of foreign policy, now claiming that the Russian cabinet functioned merely as 'the agent of English capital'.[114] The third 'Letter from Afar', composed on 11 March, showed signs of awareness of the transformation wrought by such ideas in the generally accepted concept of Bolshevik strategy. Such a revolution, Lenin claimed, would not be decreeing socialism or even inaugurating the dictatorship of the proletariat. Instead, in backward Russia, it would establish 'the revolutionary-democratic dictatorship of the proletariat and the poor peasants'; and only time would tell whether the workers would show sufficient 'consciousness' to carry it through.[115] The next day, in the fourth 'Letter', Lenin stopped talking of the militia and said instead that 'an All-Russian Soviet (or a Petersburg Soviet temporarily acting as its substitute)' should take power.[116] But if the future socialist state was not the dictatorship of the proletariat but a peculiar Russian hybrid form, what were the measures to be enacted? In the fifth 'Letter', written but not finished on 26 March, he said that they would be only 'transitional measures' leading ultimately to socialism.[117]

It is not evident when most of his telegrams and articles reached Russia. Certainly *Pravda* carried only the first 'Letter from Afar', on 21 and 22 March, and the editors hacked off the more radical recommendations from its contents.[118] The last four 'Letters' remained unpublished until after Lenin's death. His own information, however, was gradually improving in quality. He combed the abundant foreign press which, after its early failures, was improving in quality and dependability; and he excerpted from not only Swiss newspapers but also *The Times*, *The Manchester Guardian* and the *Frankfurter Zeitung*.[119] And yet, while feeling impelled to offer a strategical analysis, Lenin cautiously refrained from presenting them as the formal policy of the Central Committee's Foreign Bureau even though Kollontai seems expressly to have requested 'directives'.[120] This showed a recognition that the Foreign Bureau, consisting of himself and Zinoviev, should not throw its weight about when it had neither the knowledge to impress the Russian Bureau and *Pravda* nor the formal right to instruct them. But Lenin's self-restraint did not signify a lack of confidence. His jauntiness was proved on 14 March when he gave a talk on his developing ideas, 'The Russian Revolution, its Significance and its Tasks', to a gathering of Russians in the Volkshaus on Helvetiaplatz in Zürich.[121] It is conventionally supposed that debate between Lenin and his opponents began in Petrograd, after his return to Russia in April. Not so: he reappeared at the Volkhaus on 16 March to hear the responses of others and to respond to them in his turn.[122] Menshevik and Bundist luminaries turned out in force. Lenin's perennial adversary, A. S. Martynov, deriding his recommendations as 'utopian' and 'over-simplified', urged trenchantly: 'Don't get in a hurry, comrade Lenin. We still don't have a republic, we still lack the eight-hour working day.' R. A. Abramovich accused him of an unthinking and dangerous inclination 'to pull leftwards' and thereby to ignore the 'correlation of forces'. He declared Lenin's ideas to be 'Blanquist', exhibiting an unbridled frustration with objective political circumstances and a will to deploy violence to attain socialist ends. S. Semovski, another old foe since their entanglement over the national question before the war, stated that the scheme for a workers-and-peasants dictatorship appeared to intimate a coalition of Kerenski and Lenin. Martov, too, joined the attack. There was wide agreement that Lenin had produced a woefully 'confused idea'.[123] The construction of the anti-Lenin Marxist case in 1917 had begun.[124]

RETURNING LEADER

For a while it was not these issues but the problems of organising the journey home which chiefly concerned the émigrés. The obvious first option, which was taken seriously by Lenin and all the Swiss emigration, was to take a North Sea steamer. Plekhanov, sailing to

Sweden, took a train through to Petrograd in the company of British socialist Will O'Grady and was fêted in a hero's welcome in Petrograd.[125] This was not the physically ideal route to take: there was the danger that German submarines were sinking Allied shipping; but at least such a trip had the advantage of not giving rise to the objection that it was undertaken under the auspices of the Central Powers.[126]

Yet the British and French authorities would not facilitate the passage of Russian politicians opposed to the Allied cause. Lev Trotski and Nikolai Bukharin, making their way back from New York, had little choice but to risk travelling via Britain.[127] They paid the price: both were held up by the British government and did not reach Russia until midsummer. That the majority of Russian socialists in Western and Central Europe could count on the same treatment was demonstrated by the failure of the Socialist-Revolutionary leader Viktor Chernov to obtain the necessary official documents of transit from France. Lenin, who had a declared preference for Germany to defeat Russia, was still less likely to be successful. He cursed his decision to sit out the war in Switzerland and not to join other Bolsheviks in Scandinavia.[128] But he determined not to temporise as in 1905, when it was nine months after Bloody Sunday before he returned. Any danger was worth running. Lenin fantasised about crossing Germany unrecognised by donning a wig and using V. A. Karpinski's passport.[129] (Karpinski's response to the proposal to deprive him of his passport is not known to posterity.). Another daydream, with even spindlier roots in reality, was to assume the identity of a deaf, dumb and blind Swede. Krupskaya, more amused than horrified, dissuaded Lenin by pointing out that he would give himself away by muttering complaints in his sleep about Mensheviks.[130] Lenin even considered chartering an aeroplane to fly him across the Eastern front; but the impracticality of the enterprise, in the era before planes had fuel tanks to last them hundreds of miles, put him off.[131]

Martov cooked up the most practical idea: an exchange of the Russian political emigrants in Switzerland for German citizens interned in Russia. This would require permission to traverse Germany from not only the German government but also the Russian Provisional Government, to arrive in Petrograd.[132] Lenin latched on to the plan, and Zinoviev attended an International Socialist Commission meeting on 6 March to discuss its handling. The Commission set up an inner body for negotiations with the relevant authorities. These were protracted. Russian Foreign Minister Pavel Milyukov did not yearn to greet politicians struggling against his government's policies and even, in Lenin's case, working for its overthrow. The negotiating body dispatched telegrams to the Petrograd Soviet requesting that pressure be put upon the Provisional Government. Still no satisfaction from Russia. On the other hand, the talks with the Germans proceeded wonderfully. Swiss socialists Robert Grimm and Fritz Platten had approached the Swiss Foreign Minister Hermann Hoffmann; Hoffmann had consulted with German diplomats, who obtained the consent of the German high command for the German consul in Bern, Gisbert von Romberg, to issue transit documents.[133]

Lenin, never having expected much good from Milyukov and suspecting that Grimm lacked singlemindedness as a negotiator, grabbed the initiative.[134] He gave the talks entirely into Platten's hands, and a deal was put together. The German authorities would allow sixty internationalist socialists to travel across Germany by train unimpeded by customs checks or any interference *en route*; there was not even to be an examination of the names of the travellers.[135] The journey was to begin on 27 March. Lenin sent invitations to fellow socialists to join him. He also obtained supportive statements from figures on the European socialist left, such as Paul Levi and Henri Guilbeaux.[136] There remained the fear lest he might be arrested in Russia. 'Your arrival is desirable, his sister telegraphed to him, but avoid taking a risk.'[137] Risk was inherent in the situation, and Lenin was ready to take his chances. Martov spurned Lenin's invitation and waited for the Provisional Government's sanction, condemning himself to starting out weeks after Lenin[138] Several Bundists and the Polish social-democrat Karl Radek, however, did consent. The final number of passengers was thirty-two, and twenty of them were Bolsheviks[139] Krupskaya talked of coming later so that she could wind up factional and personal business; but Lenin would not hear of this. They packed three large suitcases and a primus stove to cook for themselves on the train and the two of them bustled about so much in the last days[140] that Lenin had no time to finish the fifth and last of his 'Letters from Afar'.[141]

On 27 March the travellers assembled for lunch in Zürich's Zahringerhof. Lenin was mindful of the European political perspective and read out a 'Farewell Letter to Swiss Workers'. Polemical to the last, he excoriated the socialist centrists under Grimm and called for the victory of the leftists in Swiss socialism. He claimed that, despite having been mocked for his slogan of 'turning the imperialist war into a civil war' in 1914, the February Revolution's occurrence meant that 'only the blind cannot see that this slogan is correct'. Far-left socialists in Europe in general, and Germany and Switzerland in particular, should be steadfast and optimistic: 'Long live the proletarian revolution *which is beginning* in Europe.'[142] With a bluntness absent from his 'Letters from Afar', which were intended for Russian Bolshevik readers, he declared: 'Russia is a peasant country. It is one of the most backward of European countries. Socialism cannot triumph there immediately.'[143]

The difference between the 'Letters from Afar' and the 'Farewell Letter' is of slant and style rather than content; for the fifth 'Letter from Afar' had stated that Lenin's measures constituted only '*a transition to socialism*' and did not embody socialism.[144] Yet he had refrained from so bald a statement of the difficulties in Russia, and the contrast says much about his perceptions about how to encourage Russian and Swiss socialists respectively (as well as about our need to calibrate our assessment of Lenin's opinions to the specific political context woven around them). Needless to add, Lenin's mind after the reading out of his 'Farewell Letter' was fixed on the journey to Russia. At 3.10 pm the group left the hotel and, after walking through a crowd of malevolently raucous fellow Russian émigrés, crossed to Zürich central railway station to take the suburban train up to the Swiss border village of Gottmadingen. A certain Oscar Blum, who was a social-democrat suspected by Lenin of being a Russian spy, surreptitiously joined the party on the train. Lenin put his regular physical exercises to use and hauled him bodily out of the carriage.[145] The train departed to the hisses of bystanders. Drawing up to the border, the passengers were subjected to Swiss customs searches at Schaffhausen and Thayngen; but only their food was confiscated.[146] At Gottmadingen the two German army officers who were to accompany them across Germany ordered them, without warning, to form themselves into separate groups of men and women. Panic gripped the travellers, who felt they had walked into a trap. Lenin edged back towards a wall and the other Bolshevik men stood protectively in front of their leader. But the Germans merely wanted to complete formalities, and minutes later the party boarded the train.[147]

It was one carriage long, with eight compartments. Despite the limitation on space, Lenin and Krupskaya were given a compartment to themselves by their comrades. Lenin protested at the discrimination; but it was explained to him that the arrangement would allow him to work more conveniently. The catalyst for this generosity was his companions' knowledge of his fastidiousness. Karl Radek, Inessa Armand, Olga Ravich and Georgi and Valentina Safarov occupied the next-door compartment, and wished to enjoy themselves. The trip across Germany was to stretch over four days since the train would halt every night. The route from Gottmadingen was to take the Russians via Stuttgart, Frankfurt-on-Main and Berlin to the small ferry-port of Sassnitz. Lenin went on filling his notebooks. Yet he could not bear the noise made by the impish Radek and by Olga Ravich with her high-pitched laughter. On the first evening Lenin burst out of his compartment, banged on their door and pulled out a surprised Olga. Her companions, however, stood up for her; and Lenin released her to their continuing carousing.[148]

At Stuttgart, with the German government's co-operation, the German social-democrat and trade union leader W. Janson sought a meeting with Lenin. The request was turned down by Lenin, who threatened to beat him up if he came on board.[149] Tiffs among the Russians persisted. Lenin stipulated that all smoking should be confined to the lavatory. This quickly caused congestion as non-smokers were driven to waiting in a queue to answer calls of nature. As inventive as he was punctilious, Lenin introduced a priority system whereby those wishing to smoke were issued with a 'second-category' pass and had to give way to those with 'first-category' passes.[150] Radek poked fun at Lenin, declaring that his imperious dispositions in the carriage fitted him to 'assume the leadership of the revolutionary government'.[151] This was a joke whose acidity was to lose its bite later in the year; at the time it played upon the uncertainties of a trainload of Russian Marxists approaching their destination without guarantee that arrest did not await them in Petrograd. Sassnitz was reached on 30 March. Boarding the ferry *Queen Victoria* for the Swedish port of Trelleborg, Lenin, out of habit, gave an assumed name. Consternation resulted since his contact man in Sweden, Jan Hanecki, had telegraphed to enquire whether a Mr Ulyanov had arrived on ship; but the situation was clarified and Lenin owned up to his identity.[152] Trelleborg was reached, and the passengers boarded a train for Malmö. That night they caught another train for Stockholm, which they reached at ten o'clock on the morning of 31 March.

News of his trip was being picked up by Sweden's socialist newspapers. Lenin received an invitation from Alexander Parvus-

Helphand, a member of the German Social-Democratic Party who carried out missions for the German government with funds to disburse to Russian revolutionaries whose activity might destabilise the Russian government, to meet for discussions. Lenin declined.[153] He also tried to brush off Radek's call for him to go on a shopping spree, but in vain. Radek was disconcerted by the thought of the leader of émigré Bolsheviks returning to Petrograd in a pair of hobnailed mountain boots, so a reluctant Lenin agreed to buy new footwear. Radek also persuaded him that a new pair of trousers would not go amiss. Beyond that, however, Lenin would not budge, expostulating that he was not going back to Russia in order to set up an off-the-peg clothes stall.[154]

The Russian group took the train that evening for the Finnish frontier. Radek, who was an Austrian subject, had to be left behind as an enemy alien; he could, however, perform useful technical services for the Bolsheviks by basing himself in Stockholm.[155] A day later the passengers alighted at Haparanda and took a sleigh-ride over the border bridge into the town of Tornio. But several nasty surprises awaited them. Firstly, at the border post they were searched by British guards being used by the Russian customs authorities. Nothing incriminating was found, and Lenin telegraphed a message to his sisters that he would arrive in Petrograd on 3 April.[156] It was at Tornio, too, that he obtained copies of the new central Bolshevik newspaper *Pravda*;[157] and, in the dimly-lit customs hall, he found himself a quiet corner to read them while Zinoviev busied himself with practical arrangements for the journey. Two further surprises were contained in the newspapers. Flicking through the pages, Lenin suddenly turned pale: 'Malinovski,' he shouted over to Zinoviev, 'has turned out to be a *provocateur*!'[158] He also read the editorials by Kamenev and Stalin and discovered their policy of conditional support for the Provisional Government. Again he called over to Zinoviev: 'Look how they're muddling things!' This surprise, unpleasant as it was for him, caused him less worry than the news about Malinovski, however. 'Well,' he muttered confidently, 'we'll soon sort this out!'[159]

Boarding the train at Tornio on 2 April, the travelling revolutionaries had a further seven hundred miles to go. The carriages were halted at the Russian–Finnish border at Beloostrov. Central Committee member Kamenev and other Bolsheviks had journeyed out to meet them. Lenin curtailed the exchange of pleasantries, blurting out to Kamenev: 'What have you been writing in *Pravda*?

We've seen a few copies and have called you all kinds of names!'[160] But Kamenev took no offence; and he reassured a concerned Lenin that the Provisional Government did not plan to arrest him in the Russian capital. Shortly before midnight on 3 April they pulled into Petrograd's Finland station.

A massive crowd was waiting. This had already become the traditional experience for revolutionary leaders coming home from the emigration. Plekhanov had had a similar reception some days beforehand. Each party or faction tried to outdo the rest in turning out a large gathering of supporters; but the co-operation among the capital's socialists in March 1917 meant that most receptions became an opportunity for general festivities. Presumably Kamenev had forewarned him, and Lenin showed neither astonishment nor embarrassment. It was a high point in his career. The popular acclaim of a mass of ordinary people (who as yet, let us remember, knew next to nothing about Lenin except that he had suffered at the hands of the Romanovs and had refused to give up the revolutionary struggle) had not happened to him before. A month after the monarchy's collapse, he was being treated as a major figure in Russia's legal politics, but Lenin did not let the occasion go to his head. Chkheidze from the Petrograd Soviet greeted him with a speech calling for unity among all socialists. Lenin, with a deliberate snub, made no reply but announced the need for 'worldwide socialist revolution'. As he left the station waiting-room, he was pressed by his supporters to address the crowd. He did this from on top of an armoured car requisitioned by the Petrograd Bolsheviks. His tirade against the capitalist order in Russia and abroad was fiercer than minutes earlier. The challenge to the Provisional Government and to its conditional supporters among the ranks of socialism, including many Bolsheviks, was posed on the streets of the capital.[161]

'THE APRIL THESES'

On the trains across Germany, Sweden and Finland Lenin had worked on his ideas, and he made yet another and final draft of them just hours after leaving the Finland station. This had the title, 'On the Tasks of the Proletariat in the Present Revolution' and was presented in the shape of ten theses; it gained immediate fame as *The April Theses*. The text as a whole ran to 579 words. It was Lenin's shortest major work, by a margin of many thousand words. It was also the opus by him which had the greatest direct impact on the history of Russia; its significance is comparable both with Constantine's Edict of Milan in 313 and with the ninety-five theses pinned by Martin Luther to the doors of Wittenburg Cathedral in 1517.

Lenin's motives in March-April 1917 for breaking with the traditional Bolshevik strategy of revolution are obscure. He omitted to state what had changed between 1905–6 and 1917 to alter his mind, and he made a virtue out of this avoidance. As regards his proposals, he had declared in March that he did not intend to 'classify them theoretically' in Marxist terms. The priority was to deal with 'the complex, essential, fast-developing tasks of revolution'.[162] *The April Theses* abided by this theoretical self-abnegation (or self-liberation). It is noteworthy that neither 'the dictatorship of the proletariat' nor even 'the dictatorship of the proletariat and the poorest peasants' appeared in them. As an item of political propaganda they were masterly; as Marxology they were brazenly evasive. The kindest interpretation, never offered by Lenin, is that *The April Theses* were essentially a reproduction of the notebooks on 'Marxism on the State'.[163] Lenin had begun, in the winter of 1916–17, to perceive Russia as being characterised by aspects of 'state capitalism';[164] but these were preliminary musings. On the other hand, he still acknowledged that Russia was not in the front rank of the industrial powers, and in his 'Letters from Afar' urged the concept of a 'revolutionary–democratic dictatorship of the proletariat and the poorest peasants' for Russia.[165] The notebooks, then, influenced the theses but were not the exclusive factor.

Not having explained why the economic 'forces of production' had become adequate for the establishment of socialism in industrialised Europe, he now also avoided stating why a largely agrarian society like Russia could begin to undertake a similar enterprise. In fact the older Bolshevik strategy had never been a clear two-stage revolutionary strategy. Thus there was but a short step from the 'provisional revolutionary–democratic dictatorship of the proletariat and the peasantry' of 1905–6 to the 'revolutionary–democratic dictatorship of the proletariat and the poorest peasants' in 1917; and, regardless of Bolshevik intentions, the traditional strategy would always have hobbled a 'bourgeois revolution' in Russia.[166]

Moreover, the First World War and its political repercussions dominated Lenin's life after 1914, leading him to reject all persons and notions which appeared to him to fail to oppose imperialism in a fundamental fashion.[167] And Lenin in 1917 obviously sensed the existence of a crack in the dam, giving him an opportunity to unleash the flooding waters of history. To conceive him as having elaborated a theory in *The April Theses*, based on a discrete analysis of Russian circumstances, before recommending specific measures, is to fly in the face of the evidence.[168] In the main, he was announcing his measures in advance of his theory. This does not mean that theoretical understandings and inclinations did not condition his thinking; but it is ludicrous to pretend that theory preceded and predetermined everything. Another point has to remain speculative. But surely Lenin, being a politician competing with other politicians, experienced a temptation noted by political scientists with regard to most openly-competitive systems of politics: namely to mark out for himself an easily identifiable spot on the political spectrum; and, as an inveterate adherent of far-left socialist ideas, he felt himself at his most comfortable when criticising other socialist parties and groups for their insufficiency of radicalism.[169]

The April Theses's fundamental message, expressed and re-expressed in Theses One and Two, was a call for a second stage of the revolution to put power 'into the hands of the proletariat and the poorest strata of the peasantry'.[170] There were definite shifts away from the 'Letters from Afar'. For example, the fourth thesis conceded that 'revolutionary defencism' was sincerely advocated by a vast number of elected popular representatives in the soviets, and that the Bolsheviks constituted merely a 'pale minority'.[171] Lenin also admitted: 'Russia *at the moment* is the freest country in the world of all the belligerent countries.' The Bolsheviks should concentrate upon using the new political liberties.[172] Lenin's finessing probably resulted from conversations in Sweden with Bolsheviks in closer contact with Russian conditions than the correspondent of *Zürcher Post*, or from his exchanges with Kamenev at the Finnish frontier. Or perhaps his own few hours' experience of the freedoms of Petrograd induced the fresh nuances.

At any rate, Lenin contended flatly that the workers' soviets were *the sole possible* form of revolutionary government.[173] In line with his last 'Letter from Afar', he argued that the establishment of a parliamentary republic would be a retrograde step. The old state machine ought to be superseded by a 'republic of soviets of workers', farm-labourers' and peasants' deputies'; and payment of officials, all of whom should be elected to office and subject to instant recall by their electorate, should be at a rate no higher than the wage of a 'good worker'.[174] Thesis Nine called for alterations in the party programme so as to incorporate ideas about imperialism and the 'imperialist war' and to put forward *'our* demand for a "commune-state"'.[175] In economic policy Lenin had a couple of proposals. In Thesis Six, he advocated land nationalisation (which he had failed to have officially accepted by Bolsheviks in the past).[176] In contrast with 1905–6, however, he looked more to the farm labourers than to the peasantry as a whole as the reservoir of rural political support. He wished such labourers to establish their own separate soviets and to set up 'model farms' on the larger agricultural estates. In Thesis Seven he recommended that the country's banking should be centralised and brought under the control of the soviets.[177] This, according to Lenin's eighth thesis, signified not a scheme for instant socialism but 'a transition immediately only to the *control* by the workers' soviets over social production and the distribution of products'.[178]

A sense of urgency was fostered by the style of the ten theses. They varied a great deal in length. The first was the longest, running to 142 words. But a thumping brevity was typical, and the tenth thesis was rapped out in twelve Russian words: 'Renovation of the International. Initiative to create a revolutionary International, an International against *social-chauvinists* against *the centre.*'[179] Snappy, truculent phrases abounded, often without being incorporated in full sentences; and ideas were reiterated, despite Lenin's self-imposed confines of space, to drive home the message. Italics and exclamation marks accentuated the abruptness, conveying his clenched-teethed determination.[180] At one point, in the first thesis, he simply urged: 'Fraternisation'. His invocation in Thesis Five dispensed with the word 'and' from a list of nouns: 'The elimination of police, army, bureaucracy.'[181] All of this enhanced the effect of the drumbeat rhythms. Despite the inelegance and the hurried composition, the rhetorical subtleties of Lenin's writing were arresting.[182]

Curtness of style, furthermore, was balanced by a degree of political tact. In regard to adherents of 'revolutionary defencism', the party's task was 'to explain their mistake to them especially circumstantially, insistently, patiently'.[183] (Now there's a typical adverbial triptych for connoisseurs of Lenin's prose!) In his second thesis he admitted that this would require intensive effort. Propaganda would have to be undertaken 'in the milieu of the incredibly broad masses of the proletariat which had recently awoken to political life'.[184] (It may be thought that the phrasing betrays a certain intellectualist condescension; but Lenin wrote *The April Theses* mainly for the party's leaders, central and local, who used such terminology regardless as to whether they were of middle-class or working-class background.) But the question arose: how was power to be taken from the Provisional Government? The third thesis came nearest to addressing this ticklish subject by stipulating that 'no support' be given to the Lvov cabinet.[185] This was scarcely a plan of detailed guidance for Bolshevik organisers, but at least it advised what was not to be done. Lenin knew that the *April Theses* were merely a preliminary sketch. Only his thesis on land nationalisation, demanding that 'model farms' should be formed from expropriated estates of 'around 100 desyatinas to 300 desyatinas [270 to 810 acres] depending on local and other conditions',[186] achieved a slight measure of specificity – and even this wording left much unclear.

Most surprisingly, Lenin made no mention of the organisation of industry under the proposed socialist regime. There was nothing about the level and nature of governmental intervention. Not a word about nationalising factories and mines. Nothing about central planning, except for a very general plea for soviet control 'over social production and exchange of products'.[187] Nor do the theses say anything on the growing food-supplies crisis. Equally striking was Lenin's silence on the economic and social rights and duties of workers, peasants and soldiers. He focused on politics and on the soviets as the centre of political life; he made no mention of possible reforms in the running of factories; and the influence of workers over industrial management was ignored. Nor did Lenin confront the problems of relations between peasants in the rural economy once the gentry had been removed: there was nothing in the theses on the hiring of labour or the renting of land.

Lenin's technique was to deliver assertions and demands, not explanatory analysis. Kamenev, his main rival in Bolshevik theory in the post-February days, issued only *Pravda* articles; no straightforward summons to action came from him. Lenin was emerging as a master of the channels of debate in his party, and a principal aspect of that mastery was his ability to give a wide berth to uncongenial issues. The theses were not a comprehensive sketch of future politics even though political issues constituted the bulk of the contents. The relations among the respective soviets of the workers, peasants, farmworkers and soldiers were left unclear. It was also unclear whether the workers' soviets would have powers superior to the soviets of the other social groups.[188] Furthermore, the rural network of soviets was only patchily described; and Lenin, using a variety of formulations, gave scant guidance as how to settle relationships among the farmworkers, the poorest peasants and the peasantry as a whole.[189] But the skimpiness of theory in *The April Theses* caused Lenin himself no embarrassment. He dealt with the doubters by claiming that 'the art of administrating cannot be learned from books' and that the Paris Commune of 1871 provided an excellent precedent. He urged, 'Try it out, make mistakes, learn how to administrate.'[190]

These were the early days of a revolutionary era and these were revolutionary politics. *The April Theses* were the first broad-ranging statement of a fundamental Bolshevik alternative to the policies of Kamenev and Stalin. Many Bolsheviks agreed on the desirability of another revolution in Russia in the near future; but neither Shlyapnikov nor any other Bolshevik radical had come forward with quite so broad-ranging a schema. The theses instigated a bitter dispute among Bolsheviks, and Lenin had made striking contribution to the politics of Bolshevism after the February Revolution.

6 There Is Such a Party! April to July 1917

FIGHTING FOR BOLSHEVISM

The February Revolution span the kaleidoscope of Russia's politics, jolting the alliances and rivalries among the parties, and politicians gained a freedom of choice unrestricted by the Romanov monarchy. Lenin's *April Theses* were the acme of free will. Yet no political leader, not even Lenin, could escape the constraints of circumstance in their entirety. Each had to take the measure of terrifyingly exigent pressures: the Eastern front, economic dislocation, and popular discontent. Parties coped by modifying their physiognomies, and the changes were by no means random occurrences. Monarchism for a time was defunct as a political force.[1] The possibilities for a right-wing military dictatorship were as yet limited by the destruction of the old order in the armed forces. So it came about that the Kadets, who had traditionally advocated parliamentary democracy and universal civic liberties, were the nearest party to the righthand pole of the political spectrum with the slightest chance of holding power.

The situation was daunting. A centralised state structure was retained by the Provisional Government; but its authority was fragile from the start. The commissars and other newly-appointed functionaries in the provinces of the old empire had to consult in reality with local elective bodies. Many of these were sectional mass organisations, especially the soviets, which quickly set up agencies in every town and city. In Petrograd there was said to be 'dual power', shared by the Provisional Government and the City Soviet. Aleksandr Guchkov took a gloomier view, claiming that the Soviet had all the ultimate power. Other organisations, too, had influence in both the capital and the localities; trade unions and factory-work-shop committees in the urban areas, and peasant communes in the countryside impeded the implementing of the Provisional Government's policies. Sanctions of coercion available to the Lvov cabinet were frail. The police had fled, and the garrison soldiers regarded their loyalty to their soviets as being primary; troops on the Eastern front increasingly exhibited the same attitude. The 'lower social classes' everywhere flexed their collective muscles. Rates of pay were renegotiated: workers in both private factories and government-owned plants, such as the Putilov works in Petrograd, secured wage rises. Foremen who had behaved unpleasantly were humiliated by the workforce; some were tied up in sacks and pushed around the factory premises in wheelbarrows. Soldiers demanded a relaxation of discipline and the permission to elect their own committees to represent their interests; and the Petrograd Soviet issued its 'Order No. 1' to encourage them. Occasional lynchings took place. Tensions among the nationalities were also noted: requests for limited rights of autonomy were voiced in Finland and the Ukraine. The peasantry in certain regions refused to await the Constituent Assembly's resolution of the land question and several gentry estates were seized in Penza province in March 1917.[2]

The Kadets in the Provisional Government tried to tame rather than to ride the tiger. Their ideas and rhetoric were similar to liberalism elsewhere in Europe; but, sensing the weakness of their popular support, they favoured the closest collaboration with the industrialists, bankers and the landed gentry. This signalled a retreat from their earlier social radicalism (which in 1905 had involved the promise to hand over the agricultural land to the peasantry, albeit with compensation to the landlords). In 1917 they argued that the land could not be handed over to the peasants without disrupting agriculture in the short term, diminishing the supply of food to the towns and tempting soldiers to desert and return to their native villages. Kadets claimed, too, that workers who went on strike or demanded steep wage rises damaged the national war effort. The Provisional Government never failed to stress the catastrophic consequences for Russia if Germany won the war.[3] Without planning it, the Kadets became a catch-all party for large and medium-sized proprietorial interests.[4]

They were not alone in bowing to circumstantial pressures and in shifting their previous stance. The same was done by both the Mensheviks and the Socialist Revolutionaries, who had traditionally expected that the overthrow of the Romanov monarchy would inaugurate the rule of the bourgeoisie. Yet they declined to move into outright opposition when the Provisional Government's fragility became evident. Thus they had come to offer their 'conditional support' to Lvov's cabinet; and, as the difficulties of ministers became acute, their assistance was crucial to the regime's survival. Continuing to think that socialism in backward Russia was a premature project and that national unity was essential in wartime, they hoped to constrain the Provisional Government to act within the limits of policies based on democratic political liberties and territorial defence; and, immediately after the February Revolution, most workers, peasants and soldiers felt likewise. Their votes provided the Mensheviks and the Socialist Revolutionaries with majorities in the soviets.[5] Furthermore, the left wings of the Mensheviks and Socialist Revolutionaries proved to be indecisive and ill-led; and few of their representatives held the objective of forming an all-socialist coalition. Martov, the leading left-wing Menshevik, advocated such a goal only from July onwards.[6]

Nevertheless the problems of war and economy and politics would predictably worsen greatly before they got better, and the appeal of a radical programmatic alternative to Menshevism would grow. The stimulus for the Bolsheviks, who before 1917 had attacked the liberals more aggressively than had the Mensheviks, to fight to replace the Provisional Government with a socialist regime would increase. *The April Theses* may have shown intellectual disjointedness and question-begging assertiveness; they may also have been based on false and over-confident guesswork. Yet in general they were working with the grain of the popular grievances in 1917.[7] Returning to Petrograd, Lenin was adept in expressing popular attitudes which had not yet fully developed. His opponents reacted to him with horror, not least because the more astute among them recognised the potentiality of the theses to attract support.[8]

His task was facilitated by the often-overlooked fact that even the principal leaders of the Bolshevik right, Kamenev and Stalin, had already distanced themselves from the policies of contemporary Menshevism.[9] At the beginning of April, this pair acted as major Bolshevik spokesmen. It was they who were chosen by the Russian Bureau of the Central Committee to put the Bolshevik case at the assembly of soviet deputies, drawn from all over the country, which met in Petrograd from 29 March. Kamenev and Stalin argued for organisational links with the Mensheviks (who supplied most representatives to the gathering of deputies); they also won over the Bolshevik fraction (or caucus) to the policy of conditional support for the Provisional Government 'insofar as it follows the path of satisfying the demands of the working class and the revolutionary peasantry'.[10] Negotiations between the Bolshevik and

Menshevik fractions proceeded on this basis. Later accounts have portrayed these negotiations as yet another case of Kamenev and Stalin behaving cravenly in Lenin's absence.[11] Obviously, Stalin and Kamenev were not following Lenin's line. Yet they were not cringing before Menshevism either: Stalin made clear his belief that the Provisional Government's days were numbered and that sooner or later, after 'a break with the bourgeoisie', the soviets would assume power;[12] and Kamenev persuaded the Menshevik negotiators to criticise even the Petrograd Soviet's foreign policy, to call for a publication of secret treaties and to repudiate the principle of 'civil peace'.[13] Furthermore, other Bolshevik speakers emphasised the necessity for a radical series of direct-action measures.[14]

The tentative agreements between the Bolshevik and Menshevik fractions did not hold. On 30 March, the Mensheviks and Bundists retracted their support from the motion criticising the Petrograd Soviet.[15] Kamenev in turn announced the deal with Irakli Tsereteli to have been rendered obsolete, and declared: 'Our task is to show that the only organ deserving our support is the Soviet of workers' deputies.'[16] Hardly a declaration likely to endear himself to most Mensheviks. Similarly, Stalin on 1 April stated that he favoured unity only with those Mensheviks who accepted the Zimmerwald and Kienthal Conference decisions.[17] This would have excluded Menshevik right-wingers; and, as Stalin must have realised, neither the Menshevik centrists nor the Menshevik leftists would have linked up with the Bolsheviks on such terms.

For a few days, Tsereteli's ascendancy over Russian socialists seemed unshakeable. Tsereteli carried a motion of support for the Petrograd Soviet by 325 votes against 57 when the Bolsheviks and the Mensheviks emerged from their respective fractions to debate at the national conference of soviets; he even persuaded several Bolsheviks to the right of Kamenev, such as V. S. Voitinski, to support him.[18] Yet Bolshevism itself, as a whole and in its constituent proto-factional parts, was in flux. Lenin returned home at the moment when all Bolsheviks recognised the need for a wide-ranging discussion to formulate the general line of Bolshevik strategy and to put an end to all this fluidity. The idea that Kamenev and Stalin would have co-operated, or would even have been permitted to co-operate contentedly, with the Mensheviks without extracting large concessions on policy if only Lenin had not taken his 'sealed train' through Germany is implausible. Kamenev's sympathisers, while not agreeing with Lenin, distrusted the Mensheviks; and the position of the

Bolshevik right was anyway under persistent challenge. The radicals in the Russian Bureau of the Central Committee did not cease to press for overt opposition to the Provisional Government. Russian Bureau member V. M. Molotov and the City Committee member N. A. Skrypnik declared that Stalin's hard bargaining with the Menshevik faction was nowhere near hard enough.[19]

It was in this unstable situation that Lenin, arriving on 3 April, talked into the night with Bolshevik leaders in the party's head-quarters in the Kshesinskaya Palace (which had simply been sequestred by force).[20] At noon next day he was accompanied by them to the Tauride Palace where he spoke to about seventy Bolsheviks and read out his *April Theses*. He stunned his audience with the audacity of his proposed strategy. Voitinski, disturbed by what he had heard, suggested that the debate should be postponed and that the audience should adjourn to a joint meeting of Bolsheviks and Mensheviks scheduled for the afternoon.[21]

N. S. Chkheidze, as chairman of the afternoon meeting, gave the platform to Lenin to expatiate on his theses. He was listened to in silence; and his faction's unity lay sundered by the end of his speech. V. S. Voitinski and I. P. Goldenberg, despite being Bolsheviks, spoke strongly against him. Goldenberg, a Bolshevik who was moving over to Menshevism, shouted: 'Lenin has now made himself candidate for one European throne vacant for thirty years: the throne of Bakunin!'[22] Mikhail Bakunin had not only been a founding father of anarchism in Russia and Europe in the nineteenth century but had also been engaged in virulent disputes with Marx and Engels. Lenin was not amused. Aleksandr Bogdanov, still more bluntly, called Lenin's theses 'the ravings of a madman'; and Fyodor Dan called them 'the party's funeral', adding that the 'bourgeois revolution' was incomplete. Y. M. Steklov argued that Lenin underestimated the concessions wrung from the Provisional Government. Yet it was Tsereteli, the Petrograd Soviet's dominant figure, who offered the most sustained criticism. He accused Lenin of overlooking a Marxist 'class analysis' and of failing to see that not every section of the Russian bourgeoisie had an interest in a war for territorial gain. Tsereteli repeated Engels's warning about the dangers of a class taking power prematurely. The Mensheviks, according to Tsereteli, provided practicality while Lenin put up only 'naked slogans'.[23]

Even the Bolsheviks at both meetings were stupefied and remained as yet unconvinced; apparently, only Aleksandra Kollontai spoke on Lenin's behalf. He was unabashed. Tsereteli asserted: 'However irreconcilable Vladimir Ilich may be, I am convinced we'll be reconciled.' Such sentiments were immediately brushed aside by Lenin, who had by then repaired to a seat in the journalists' box. Unable to restrain himself, he rose to his feat and, leaning over the balustrade, shouted to a shocked Tsereteli: 'Never!'.[24]

On 6 April, Kamenev attacked Lenin's views at the Russian Bureau of the Central Committee.[25] Further debate was called for, and Lenin's theses appeared in *Pravda* on 7 April.[26] Kamenev replied in *Pravda* on 8 April, declaring that Lenin's theses lacked concreteness and failed to specify whether the Provisional Government should be overthrown. Kamenev also asked how it was possible to talk of a completed bourgeois revolution when land reform had not even begun; and he complained about the absence of any reference to the Constituent Assembly.[27] Initially, Kamenev, using arguments deployed by Mensheviks in the Zürich Volkhaus and in Petrograd's Tauride Palace, had the upper hand. The Petersburg City Committee rejected Lenin's *April Theses* by thirteen votes to two on 8 April.[28] Nor, seemingly, did any major local committee immediately come over to Lenin's support.[29] Lenin had no choice but to meet and talk to as many Bolsheviks as possible.[30] But his words were not automatically accepted by Bolsheviks; the history of Bolshevism showed this, and Lenin himself knew it. Initially, he gambled on making his audacious ideas more audacious. In so far as he responded to Kamenev it was to accentuate the differences between them. *Pravda* on 9 April carried Lenin's article 'On Dual Power', which addressed the question about the Provisional Government's fate: 'It must be overthrown since it is oligarchical, bourgeois and not a government of the whole people; it *cannot* give peace or bread or full freedom.'[31] Not even *The April Theses* had been so explicit or combative. Lenin could not have made it clearer that he was calling for a second revolution.

Several factors were in his favour. Voitinski and those Bolsheviks who opposed Kamenev's stand against Tsereteli quickly abandoned the Bolsheviks altogether.[32] The Bolshevik right wing was severely weakened. Furthermore, the Kamenevites who had manipulated *Pravda* and buffeted the Russian Bureau in March did not reflect the opinions of all Bolsheviks among lower committees, especially at the district level, in Petrograd. The Vyborg District Committee's hostility to Kamenev was intense; and other lower party bodies in dozens of other towns and cities were equally annoyed.[33] The anti-Kamenevism was, however, muted and removed from public attention so long as the existing town committees remained in existence. The scheduling of an All-Russian Bolshevik Conference for late April opened windows of opportunity for Lenin. Local Bolshevik conferences had to be called and party policies had to be openly debated. These were attended by elected representatives; and the local conferences in turn elected representatives to the All-Russian Conference. Only 15 per cent of Bolshevik delegates to the national soviet conference in Petrograd from 29 March to 2 April were re-elected to the Conference which opened three weeks later.[34] Many reasons explain this turnabout. Some participants in the early gathering were pushed aside by the more prestigious leaders, who by then had returned from Siberian exile or, like Lenin, from emigration. The national soviet conference, moreover, had not included representatives from all local committees. Not even the Moscow Bolsheviks had dispatched representatives.[35] Almost certainly the change of composition as between the national gathering on 29 March and the Bolshevik April Conference also reflected the fact that rank-and-file Bolsheviks, when their opinion was consulted, chose leaders who approved of radical alternatives to Kamenev's policies. This occurred, moreover, before Lenin had a chance to contact Conference delegates except through the medium of his brief and patchily-argued articles in *Pravda*. The balance of opinion among the Bolsheviks was swinging his way, and *The April Theses* accelerated the process.[36]

Lenin in person, meanwhile, had success at one local conference, and it was the most influential local conference at that. The Petrograd Bolsheviks met on 14 April. Lenin addressed its delegates, making his fullest oral advocacy of *The April Theses*. By then, however, shifts of emphasis were noticeable in his presentation. To a still greater extent than in his theses, he highlighted the need to win a majority of opinion in the soviets. By implication, this would take time. He had said this in his *Pravda* article on 9 April; but now it was heavily stressed. Thus his final motion spoke of the need for '*lengthy* work' in propaganda.[37]

This won over Bolsheviks like Prisedko who, in their own account, had originally been frightened off by his ultra-radical talk.[38] Lenin also modified his presentation at the Petrograd City Conference itself. His original intention had been to specify that, if a general peace without annexations and indemnities could not be brought about, a new socialist administration should fight a 'revolutionary war' against imperialism. This did not find favour with a gathering which wanted to stress the party's ability to bring about peace rather than to intensify war; and Lenin, however reluctantly, agreed to omit the slogan from the final resolution. Kamenev and his supporters were evidently not without impact.[39] In addition, certain other participants who did not accept all of *The April Theses* still welcomed many of them. Specific objections were voiced, for example, to the notion of a commune-state; evidently not all Bolsheviks agreed with Lenin's critique of Kautsky's views on the state. Doubts were predictably raised also about land nationalisation and its likely reception among the peasantry.[40] Still other participants, while not being convinced of the Marxist authenticity of Lenin's definition of the current stage of the revolutionary process, endorsed his practical policies.[41] Moreover, it actually helped Lenin that his *April Theses* were not a finished product and left much to be decided. F. I. Goloshchekin, with a touch of exaggeration, declared: 'You can sketch in whatever pattern for practical steps you like on comrade Lenin's theses.'[42] He was at least right that Lenin's policies left many options open. Consequently, there was a variety of reasons why the City Conference supported the final resolution proposed by Lenin, by thirty-three votes to six, with two abstentions.[43] The ground was being scooped from beneath the feet of Kamenev, beaten but not dispirited, whose amendments were rejected overwhelmingly by the Conference.[44]

How representative were the Petrograd Bolsheviks in their movement towards *The April Theses* is not yet known with precision; but, very probably, party committees elsewhere in the country inclined in Lenin's favour for similarly mixed motives, and not all of these implied total submission to Lenin's will.[45] Nor, of course, did the Bolsheviks debate strategy in a political vacuum. Events occurred at dizzying speed in spring 1917. At the Petrograd City Conference, Y. A. Yakovlev noted that the peasants were already taking radical direct-action measures without waiting for any political party to instigate them to do so.[46] Workers and soldiers, as all Bolsheviks were aware, were still busily extending their rights; and already there were signs that wage settlements would not keep pace with inflation. Meanwhile, food supplies declined.[47] In such circumstances it was hard for Kamenev to win over the Bolsheviks with ideas of even conditional support for the Provisional Government.

And yet it was probably a certain development in international relations which improved Lenin's chances most of all. On 19 April it became public knowledge that Foreign Minister Pavel Milyukov had secretly notified the Allies of his government's desire to implement the treaties signed by Nikolai II. The Menshevik and Socialist-Revolutionary policy of 'conditional support' for the Provisional Government had failed its first test. Mensheviks, Socialist Revolutionaries and Bolsheviks took to the streets in protest on 20 April; and, in view of the precedent whereby the monarchy had been brought low by largely peaceful crowds of demonstrators, the Lvov cabinet was severely shaken.[48] The Bolshevik Central Committee, at Lenin's instigation, had encouraged the protest demonstration and suggested that only a seizure of power by 'the revolutionary proletariat together with the revolutionary soldiers' could bring about 'a truly democratic peace'.[49] This was not exactly a summons to immediate insurrection. Not exactly; but it did not preclude it, and S. Y. Bagdatev and several other leaders of the Petrograd City Organisation on 21 April issued a leaflet urging the immediate overthrow of the Provisional Government.[50] The cabinet appreciated the gravity of its position. It was forced to affirm a policy of national defence and non-expansionist war aims, and Milyukov and Guchkov were obliged to resign.[51] The crowds of demonstrators left the streets. For the Bolsheviks, the 'April crisis' had profound consequences. Those Bolshevik activists who had wavered between Lenin and Kamenev were having their minds made up by the proof that the Provisional Government was to be given neither conditional support nor even conditional trust. Little could now save Kamenev from defeat at the All-Russian Bolshevik Conference.

THE SEVENTH ALL-RUSSIAN CONFERENCE

Yet no victory was going to fall into Lenin's lap unless he handled his Conference imaginatively. The proceedings, which began on 24 April in the main hall of the Kseshinskaya Palace, were a landmark in Bolshevism's history. Previous Conferences of Bolsheviks were held in Finland or in the emigration. The April Conference was the first such Conference held in Russia. It was also the first Conference which no one was prevented from attending because of imprisonment or exile. But the April Conference's prime importance lay in its ploughing up of the virgin soil of the politics of Russia. From April

1917 the Bolsheviks followed a clear (if not totally straight) line of opposition to the Provisional Government, and sowed and cultivated the seeds of a further revolution. One hundred and fifty-two delegates attended, from nearly all major organisations associated with the Bolsheviks.[52] The hall was draped with red and green banners, and the mood was excited. The elections to the Conference presidium intimated what lay in store. Both Lenin and Zinoviev, but not Kamenev, were selected for the five-man body; and, for good measure, the Conference extended its greeting to 'the first internationalists Karl Liebknecht and Vladimir Lenin' (even though Liebknecht was still in a Berlin prison).[53] Such a step confirmed that the party had a European viewpoint on the scope of its tasks and that Lenin was regarded as inferior in status to no European socialist leader. His esteem among Bolsheviks had reached its highest point yet. It was natural for him to be chosen by the Central Committee to deliver a report on its behalf 'on the current moment'. His stance was criticised by A. S. Bubnov from the Bolsheviks' Moscow Regional Bureau, who wanted clauses inserted on the need to 'control' the Provisional Government since it had become 'counterrevolutionary'.[54] Bubnov was on the party's left; and he, no less than Lenin, sought the overthrow of the Provisional Government. But Lenin argued that all talk of 'controlling' the Kadet ministers in advance of seizing power was 'a most empty phrase'. He also declared that Bubnov underestimated the extent of the reforms already promulgated since the February events. Lenin maintained, in disregard of Kamenev's earlier arguments, that 'the bourgeois revolution' had been completed.[55]

His own proposed administration would be a socialist 'state of the Paris Commune type'; but it would also be a 'dictatorship' which did not rely on 'the formal will of the majority'.[56] The soviets would embody the new state power. There would be nationalisation of the land, the banks and large industrial syndicates.[57]. This was as far as he was ready to go with legislative details. Lenin reaffirmed that 'lengthy work' was needed to persuade workers and peasants to follow the Bolsheviks; and he acknowledged that it was still unclear how successful the party would be with the peasantry.[58] But he agreed that, so long as the existing civic freedoms remained, it was essential to rely on propaganda rather than force. Talk of civil war must be abandoned.[59]

Lenin sat down; he had shown, as at the Petrograd City Conference just days before, that he could adjust his public posture to the requirement of obtaining a mass political following outside the party. So he was not averse to compromise after all! At least, not averse to certain sorts of compromise. With this in mind, the delegates waited to hear what Kamenev would say in his co-report. Kamenev, with impeccable Marxist logic, asked yet again how on earth could the bourgeois revolution be said to have ended while the landed gentry retained their estates. He queried, too, the basis in Marxist thought for a socialist administration involving not only 'the proletariat' but also the peasantry. What had happened to Marx's simple and unadorned dictatorship of the proletariat?[60] And what, enquired Kamenev, did Lenin offer to the party to fight for in the period before the transfer of power to socialists? By scrapping the two-stage revolutionary schedule, Lenin had left no short-term reforms to be aimed at.[61] Several influential speakers – V. P. Milyutin, P. G. Smidovich, V. P. Nogin, A. I. Rykov and S. Y. Bagdatev – took Kamenev's side. Bagdatev was especially mordant, stating that it was difficult to discern a completed bourgeois revolution when the gentry retained their land and neither a system of progressive taxation nor the eight-hour working day had been promulgated.[62] Even V. V. Kuraev, a sympathiser with Lenin, complained about the absence of a sketch of the steps to be taken towards socialist revolution in *The April Theses*.[63]

Yet there was less disunity than there appeared to be.[64] Like Stalin in March, Kamenev argued that a clash between the soviets and the Provisional Government was inevitable and vouched that eventually 'power must belong to the soviets'.[65] Bolsheviks since 1905 had urged that only mass socialist organisations could ensure the establishment of a truly democratic order in Russia, so that Kamenev's call for a transfer of governmental authority was not entirely unexpected.[66] But Kamenev also made an announcement on Lenin's motion on the war: 'In general I agree with it.' The war, he added, was imperialistic and could be ended 'only by worldwide revolution'.[67] In conclusion he even described Lenin's ideas as 'a magnificent programme of development of the revolution'.[68]

Kamenev was also cheered by Lenin's discomfiture at the insurrectionary appeal made on 21 April by Bolshevik activists in Petrograd: Lenin was forced to disown and criticise it (even though his own Central Committee resolution had helped to contribute to its composition).[69] Perhaps Kamenev thought that Lenin might be pulled even closer to his policies in the near future. Kamenev almost theatrically welcomed the Central Committee's ban on insurrectionary slogans.[70] Lenin and he could at any rate agree on several practicalities while clashing over underlying strategy and Marxist definitions. Bubnov stirred things up again by asserting that it was inept to squabble over whether the revolution was bourgeois or socialist; for him, the situation was more complex, and elements of both types of revolution were present.[71] Lenin, while in Switzerland, had affirmed the pointlessness of attempts at theoretical classification; but he now implicitly rejected such agnosticism. Perhaps he found Bubnov's formulation to be too reminiscent of Trotski (who as yet remained a figure of suspicion among Bolsheviks).[72] Or perhaps Lenin had invested so much intellectual capital in the concept of an already completed bourgeois revolution that he could not quickly withdraw. The disputants, however, were already becoming exhausted and peace began to settle upon them. A seven-person drafting commission was elected. It neatly balanced Lenin and Zinoviev on one side with Kamenev and Nogin on the other; Bubnov had earned a place by his interventions; and Stalin (who had edged away from Kamenev to occupy an intermediate position in the debate) and I. G. Pravdin, were also included.[73]

Nogin then reported on a peace conference of European socialists being arranged by the Danish social-democrat F. Borbjerg with the German Social-Democratic Party's encouragement. On balance, Nogin wanted Bolshevik representatives to attend, if only to contact and co-ordinate activities among the European socialist left.[74] Lenin and F. E. Dzierzynski, the Polish social-democratic leftist who had now joined the Bolsheviks, argued against Nogin that the peace conference would be a sham since British and French socialists would not be participating.[75] Kamenev also spoke against Nogin, urging the party to confine its dealings with foreign groups to those which were in favour of 'civil war'. The Lenin–Kamenev line carried the day.[76] The defeated Nogin proceeded to introduce a debate on the party's relation to the soviets. His call for greater participation was welcomed by a series of speakers who told the Conference about the growing power of mass organisations in their respective areas. This provoked Lenin to remark that Petrograd and Moscow were now lagging behind the provinces in revolutionary achievement. 'The dictatorship of the proletariat,' he declared, 'is being realised in the small localities.'[77]

At the sixth session of the Conference, on 27 April, Lenin introduced a motion on the war. The crux of his remarks was that the Bolsheviks, on coming to power, should 'openly propose a democratic peace to all peoples on the basis of a complete renunciation of any annexations whatever'.[78] He asserted that this would 'inevitably lead to insurrections of the proletariat'. He conceded that others had challenged the validity of his prediction but maintained that, if insurrections failed to occur, the party's duty would be 'to support those parties and groups abroad which really conduct a revolutionary struggle in wartime against their imperialist governments and their bourgeoisie.'[79] It deserves emphasis here, in the light of what was to become Soviet policy in 1918, that this policy was far short of advocacy of 'revolutionary war'.[80] Be that as it may, Lenin's motion was passed *nem. con.* and with only seven abstentions.[81] His place on the platform was taken by Zinoviev, who introduced a debate on the Provisional Government. His proposed clauses were basically the same as those of the Petrograd City Conference: he saw the soviets and other mass organisations as the likely organs of revolutionary governmental authority. Yet he nodded gently in the direction of the Bolshevik right wing, saying that the Constituent Assembly might embody the new power.[82] Smidovich urged the restitution of the Assembly as an unconditional objective. But this was too much for Lenin and Zinoviev, and Zinoviev spoke against. His motion was accepted against only three opposition votes, with eight abstentions.[83]

In the evening session, Lenin initiated a brief debate on the agrarian question. A section of the Conference had already met to formulate a motion, and no substantial disagreement had emerged. Lenin had successfully revived his land nationalisation scheme of 1905. As before, he defended it as being 'necessary from a bourgeois-democratic viewpoint'.[84] He did not present it as a socialist measure but as a means for removing the feudal obstacles to agricultural modernisation within a capitalist economic framework. State ownership of land would not preclude land use for private profit, and the exclusion of the gentry would facilitate an enormous rise in productivity. For the first time he admitted that this would require 'a gigantic bureaucratic apparatus'; but he countered that the democratic structure of the revolutionary state would prevent dangers of abuse.[85]

All this was old hat for those who had listened to Lenin's agrarian ideas of the previous decade. Only two aspects were in any fashion startling. The first was that nowhere in his speech did he expressly contend that an epoch of rural capitalist development lay ahead; he merely implied it. The second was that he commented that land nationalisation would 'ineluctably give a push towards wider measures'.[86] This strangely indefinite wording surely signifies that Lenin was contemplating a faster movement towards the setting up of collective farming than he had previously envisaged; and this must have been sweet music to the ears of those on the Bolshevik left who dreamed that the collectivisation of agriculture could quickly be decreed and imposed by a forthcoming socialist administration.[87] In any event, Lenin's speech was well received. Only one delegate, N. Angarski from Moscow, questioned Lenin's arguments at all. Angarski's critical point was that the notion of nationalisation would offend the peasantry's wish to own property. At least two other Bolshevik leaders, Iosif Stalin and M. I. Kalinin had made the same case in *Pravda*;[88] but neither was willing to help Angarski at the Conference. In fact, Angarski was right in his judgement; but the Conference, by a majority, did not think so and Lenin's ideas became official party policy.[89]

This drastic reversal of the defeats sustained at the hands of his own Bolsheviks in 1905–7 was accomplished with little discussion. Nearly all the Conference delegates operated in towns and cities. Possibly most of them did not take the agrarian question very seriously even though it involved the vast majority of the country's inhabitants. It was only after the Conference that wiser heads prevailed in relation to Angarski's arguments about nationalisation.

Yet the deliberations were even briefer on other policies, so one imagines that the restricted time available for discussion must have been another factor.[90] Zinoviev's motion to oppose the entry of socialists into coalition with Kadets was swiftly accepted. So was Lenin's on the need to start work on the writing of a new party programme. All delegates, particularly those who were only visiting Petrograd, wanted to know more about events in the capital. The daily press was avidly scanned; and G. F. Fedorov, member of the Petersburg City Committee (which refused to change its name to the Petrograd Committee as a protest against the government's 'chauvinism' in renaming the capital), reported on the progress of the Petrograd Soviet debate on the acceptability of a government coalition of liberals and socialists. On the Conference's last day, 29 April, V. V. Shmidt reported on the activities of the Petersburg City Party Committee. The proceedings continued with Zinoviev's report on the need for the Bolsheviks to unite with all social-democrats regarded by them as truly internationalist in orientation. He picked out the Interdistricters (*Mezhraiontsy*) as a prime example. The

Interdistricters were close in strategy to Trotski; and Zinoviev, deliberately or not, was initiating a process which culminated in Trotski's entry to the Bolshevik party in July. The quiet approval for his suggestion made it seem that the Conference was gently drawing to a close. Far from it: the very last session produced the stormiest debate. Stalin gave a report on the national question, proposing that all peoples oppressed under the Romanovs should be given the right of secession. In accordance with the pre-war writings of Lenin and Stalin, the report stressed the desirability of dissuading non-Russian nationalities from exercising that right. He hoped that, for example, the Ukrainians and the Transcaucasian peoples would content themselves with 'regional autonomy', since the party would guarantee national freedom 'in schooling, religious and other questions'.[91]

But the Central Committee had chanced its arm by choosing Stalin. Unhappiness with Lenin's attitude to the national question had long been widespread among Bolsheviks, and the section established by the Conference to formulate a motion refused to give approval to Stalin's viewpoint. Instead the section had voted for the motion of G. L. Pyatakov;[92] and Pyatakov, Lenin's opponent on the national question, was not minded to give way to Stalin. He repeated his belief that, in a world where national economies had become deeply interconnected under capitalism, the demand for national independence was 'reactionary'; and he asked what would happen if most Poles desired secession while the Polish working class wanted to belong to 'a general socialist' state.[93] Lenin's ripost was his most passionate contribution to the Conference: 'There's no people which could be so pervaded by hatred to Russia, there's no people which could so terribly not love Russia as the Poles.' Pyatakov, he suggested, had woefully underestimated the significance of national consciousness. Lenin professed a readiness to contemplate the secession of the Ukrainians as well as the Poles and the Finns; but he predicted that the Ukraine would in the event be content with a 'fraternal union' with Russia. Even Lenin, furthermore, added a qualification: 'We absolutely do not want the Khivan peasant to live under the Khan of Khiva.'[94]

He left unsaid both how he would prevent such an outcome if Khiva's peasantry wanted a khanate, and what criterion for approval of secession he would use. Filip Makharadze leaped on this uncertainty, asking why the Tartars should not gain independence if the Finns were to obtain it.[95] Stalin's final speech dwelt on the usefulness of the national liberation movement as a 'bridge' between East and West. Every movement directed against imperialism, he concluded, should be supported. Stalin's motion won by 56 votes to 16 on the Conference floor.[96]

The results of the ballot for the new Central Committee were announced. A hundred and nine delegates had stayed to vote. Lenin came top of the poll with 104 votes, followed by Zinoviev with 101 and Stalin with 97. Next came Kamenev with 95.[97] There had been resistance to Kamenev's standing when the candidatures had been discussed in closed session because of his behaviour in the Bolshevik court case of 1915, but Lenin came to his rescue, arguing the need to let bygones be bygones[98]. Evidently he felt that there was enough common ground between himself and the leader of the Bolshevik right to keep him in the Central Committee; and perhaps he already valued him as a potential counterweight to leftists who might want to force the revolutionary pace even faster than Lenin himself wanted. Similar reasons presumably underlay Zinoviev's successful support for the election of Milyutin and Nogin (who came in fourth and fifth with 82 and 76 votes).[99] But Lenin and Zinoviev did not get things all their own way. Krupskaya's candidacy failed. So, too, did that of E. D. Stasova, whom Lenin wanted to run the Central Committee Secretariat; she was dropped in favour of Y. M. Sverdlov, whom Lenin neither knew much about nor wanted in the Central Committee.[100] In addition, I. D. Teodorovich failed to be elected despite a supportive speech from Zinoviev. The two remaining members of the nine-person Central Committee were I. T. Smilga and G. F. Fedorov.[101]

None of Lenin's colleagues were his stooges, and several were hostile to his general strategy. Furthermore, virtually the entire Central Committee would be based in Petrograd. Only Nogin would be hundreds of miles away, in Moscow. Smilga could shuttle freely between Petrograd and nearby Finland. So Lenin would not be able to push through his decisions because his colleagues were under arrest or dispersed in various countries. Even Zinoviev was willing to take him on, urging the Conference to dispatch a representative to the socialist peace conference in Stockholm in order to increase Bolshevik influence over the European socialist left. Lenin disagreed; but the Conference backed Zinoviev.[102] Lenin, however, could feel satisfied. As the Conference came to an end, he knew he had won most of the policy discussions. Fittingly he gave the closing speech. His difficulties were in any case those which anyone would have had with a dynamic political organism such as the Bolshevik party. Ahead lay the problems of putting the official policies into practice.

AGAINST DUAL POWER

The Bolshevik All-Russian Conference's resolution forbidding socialists to enter the Provisional Government was passed in a week when Lvov was negotiating for Menshevik and Socialist Revolutionaries to join his cabinet. Mensheviks and Socialist Revolutionaries, remembering that the Bolshevik prohibition was in line with the Second International's policy,[103] regarded the invitation with distaste; and Kerenski had had to seek special permission from the Petrograd Soviet before becoming Minister of Justice in March.[104] But the April crisis over foreign policy showed that the Provisional Government would be impotent unless individuals from the Petrograd Soviet's leadership were included. Ministers had not been elected and lacked legitimacy; and the official local organs of authority remained chaotic. Trouble had flared up in April when the Finnish Sejm, the regional government, gave official expression to a popular demand for greater autonomy. Independence was not the objective, but the Provisional Government insisted that only the Constituent Assembly could decide the matter. The unofficial organisations throughout the rest of the old empire were even more irksome: soviets, trade unions and other mass organisations acted practically as they wished. The Provisional Government was at loggerheads with the Kronstadt Soviet, constituted by the sailors of the Kronstadt island's naval base; and delegations from the cabinet travelled out there to mollify anti-governmental sentiments.[105] In Petrograd, the Vyborg District Soviet was solidly hostile to the cabinet after the February Revolution. Most soviets, especially at the city level, remained in the hands of the Mensheviks and Socialist Revolutionaries. But the lower the level, the stronger the representation of the Bolsheviks. The worst omen for the Provisional Government was the Bolshevik majority at the First City Conference of Factory-Workshop Committees in May 1917, and its acceptance of Lenin's motion on measures to deal with 'economic ruin'.[106]

Bolsheviks concluded that it was only a matter of time and political effort, before the Petrograd Soviet fell to them, and those among them who still hankered after a united Russian Social-

Democratic Labour Party with the Mensheviks diminished. The liaison between the Kadet party and the Mensheviks and the Socialist Revolutionaries strengthened Bolshevik intransigence. Aleksandr Kerenski was promoted to Guchkov's vital post in the Ministry of Army and Navy Affairs. Irakli Tsereteli and M.I. Skobelev, both Mensheviks, became respectively Minister of Posts and Telegraphs, and Minister of Labour; Viktor Chernov, from the Socialist Revolutionaries, took charge of the Ministry of Agriculture. This first coalition government was not totally without prospects of survival. It was left-of-centre and aimed to defend the country and rally support across classes. It spoke the language of democracy; it contained many who had suffered for their opinions under the Romanovs. Yet no minister felt very optimistic. Tsereteli was aware that his duties as Minister of Post and Telegraphs prevented him from giving due attention to the affairs of the Petrograd Soviet.[107] The Menshevik and Socialist-Revolutionary ministers set about extracting the maximum of concessions from the Kadets short of driving them from the Provisional Government. Skobelev insisted on measures to protect workers at the site of work, and on taxes to curb excesses of war-profiteering among industrialists. Regulations on prices of raw materials for manufacturing enterprises were introduced despite the objection of Progressist leader and Minister of Trade and Industry, A.I. Konovalov.[108] Chernov was given to understand that no agrarian reform would be permitted until the Constituent Assembly's convocation. But he, too, managed to snatch concessions from his Kadet colleagues. The conscription of millions of able-bodied young males to the armed forces had reduced the number of mouths to feed in peasant communes and had diminished the pressure on peasant families to seek work on the landed gentry's estates. Chernov secured assent for such land to be put at the disposition of elective rural committees. Kadets thought this to be tantamount to offering a cover for peasant land seizures.[109]

But the liberals had the consolation that the Mensheviks and Socialist Revolutionaries still wanted them to govern, and that Kerenski in particular, as Minister of Army and Navy Affairs, had moved closer to their viewpoint; they also retained, in the person of M.I. Tereshchenko, control of the Foreign Ministry. This was also, however, a source of delight for the Bolsheviks, who could stand up at open public meetings and denounce the Mensheviks and Socialist Revolutionaries for conniving in the 'bourgeois rule' and the prolongation of a worldwide imperialist war. Propaganda and organisation were a Bolshevik party priority, and the party activists benefited from the spare time unavailable to their rivals who carried the burdens of central and local governmental office. For Lenin, it was the heyday of his public appearances. He spoke at the First All-Russian Congress of Peasants' Deputies and the First Petrograd City Conference of Factory-Workshop Committees in May, and at the First All-Russian Congress of Soviets of Workers' and Soldiers' Deputies in June.[110]

Bolshevik Central Committee policies were modified for popular consumption. Less was said at open mass meetings, in soviet sessions or in *Pravda* about aspects of their plans which jarred against the inclinations of workers, peasants and soldiers. The Central Committee simplified the April Party Conference's resolutions, which were phrased in terms impervious to most non-Marxists, and indeed many Bolsheviks. The incentive came with the need to set out a list of the party's demands and slogans for the forthcoming election of deputies to the Petrograd Soviet. Lenin sketched a draft calling for 'no support' for the Provisional Government and for an end to the war without annexations and indemnities and with full self-determination for all peoples.[111] The draft was unfinished, and the proposal published in *Pravda* on 7 May was issued in the Central Committee's name. Lenin's popular style had been rendered more popular, his ideas more accessible and electorally-appealing. The *Pravda* proposal asserted that the war had been started by kings and capitalists and that only a government of workers, peasants and soldiers could bring about 'a just peace'.[112] Both Lenin and the Central Committee, moreover, avoided mention of the possibility of 'revolutionary war' or 'European civil war'. These topics continued to be addressed among Bolshevik leaders through 1917; but there was a recognition that such talk would not gain universal approval on the streets.[113]

How much pressure was exerted on Lenin by Central Committee colleagues to mollify and fudge his policies is not known. That pressure *was* exerted is scarcely disputable. Certain of his key slogans, such as 'land nationalisation' and 'model farms', failed to be mentioned in the Central Committee proposal, which simply stated that the land should be transferred 'without compensation to the peasants'. Nor did the proposal as published in *Pravda* refer to the nationalisation of banks and large-scale industry. Instead, the demand was made, more vaguely, for a transfer of power to the soviets, which would exert 'control' over production and distribution.[114] Lenin's incomplete draft did not state how the party should campaign at the local level. Evidently, however, he himself was already backing away from too emphatic or too frequent a commitment to 'revolutionary war', 'European civil war' or even that cornerstone of his Marxism: 'dictatorship'. The manicuring of policies did not always occur against his wishes or without his instigation.[115] Before 1917 his policies had been aimed more at getting support in his party than at communicating with Russian society; he had seldom worried lest his provocative declarations might prove unacceptable to workers and peasants. He did not entirely change his ways even after the April Conference, but a distinct shift towards taking known popular attitudes into account certainly occurred.

The gain in political appeal was not yet matched by clarity about the methods whereby the Provisional Government was to be removed. Bolsheviks did not believe that a socialist revolution would occur by spontaneous self-generation. Political demonstrations had brought down the Romanovs, and it was natural that further demonstrations, against Lvov's cabinet and the system of 'dual power', should have appealed to the activists of the party. Lenin failed to offer an opinion: Kamenev's jibe in April that Lenin supplied a strategic destination without the route map was more than a little apposite. The scheme for an armed march of protest against the Provisional Government, coinciding with the convocation of the First Congress of Soviets of Workers' and Soldiers' Deputies, was instigated by members of the Bolshevik Military Organisation. Lenin, without being in constant touch with the Military Organisation, had a host of admirers among its leading cadre.[116] The Military Organisation was formally subject to the Central Committee and was empowered to co-ordinate party activity and party groups through the Russian armed forces. Its radicalism and willingness to take the initiative were already well known, and several of its members felt that the Central Committee's response to the April crisis over Milyukov had been insufficiently revolutionary. Thus their radicalism overspilled the bounds respected by Lenin himself since the All-Russian April Conference of the Bolshevik party. A mass display of strength at the First All-Russian Congress of Soviets of Workers' and Soldiers' Deputies, in their view, would gain further support for the party and possibly shake the position of the government itself; it might even prevent the expected resumption of an offensive on the Eastern front.[117]

This was the nearest any Bolshevik had come since the February Revolution to stating how the Provisional Government might be overthrown. The arguments for and against a demonstration were still being debated in the various party committees in the capital when the Congress of Soviets began on 3 June. The Mensheviks and Socialist Revolutionaries held their expected majority; only 105 out of 777 were Bolsheviks.[118] Tsereteli gave a ringing defence of the coalition government's policies. It was the high point of the anti-Bolshevik socialist movement in Russia; and the alliance of Mensheviks and Socialist Revolutionaries easily dominated the Central Executive Committee of the Congress of Soviets which was elected to assume the functions of national soviet leadership.

On the second day, 4 June, Lenin was given the chance to reply on behalf of the Bolsheviks. His speech, which was limited to fifteen minutes by the rules of the Congress, restated his party's well-known line on the Provisional Government and on the transfer of power to the soviets. Among the stabbing comments he directed at Tsereteli was one which has entered every history book. He sneered that 'the citizen Minister of Posts and Telegraphs' had declared there was no political party in Russia which would express its readiness to take power entirely into its own hands. Lenin exclaimed: 'I reply: "There is! Not a single party can refuse this, and our party does not refuse this: at any minute it is ready to take power entirely."'[119] Most delegates, being supporters of the Mensheviks and Socialist Revolutionaries, laughed him down for the remark – the last recorded occasion in his life when he suffered such treatment. But it was apparent that the Bolsheviks lacked the support in the country for any attempt at the formation of a government. The seriousness of the Bolshevik party's intentions about an anti-governmental demonstration were not yet public knowledge. Not even many Bolshevik delegates to the Congress knew.[120] A joint meeting of the Central Committee, Military Organisation and the Petersburg Committee's Executive Commission took place on 6 June while the Congress was in session; and, behind closed doors, the case for a demonstration was offered by Military Organisation leader N. I. Podvoiski.[121]

Lenin concurred, but the right-wingers in the Central Committee spoke against. Kamenev saw the proposal as another example of radicalism for its own sake without any specification of attainable aims. Not only Nogin but also Zinoviev, in his harshest rupture with Lenin to that date, agreed with Kamenev. A clash between Lenin and Nogin ensued; and Nogin vehemently expostulated: 'Lenin is proposing a revolution. Can we do this? We are a minority in the country.'[122] But Lenin ignored Nogin's interpretation of his intentions. It would indeed seem that Lenin was aspiring not to the installation of a Bolshevik government but rather a transfer of power to the soviets, which would have resulted in a government of Mensheviks and Socialist Revolutionaries. He also thought that such a cabinet would be in a position to propose conditions for a general peace in Europe.[123]

Lenin had most members of the Central Committee with him, and nearly all leaders of the Military Organisation and the Petersburg Committee also opposed Kamenev over the next few days.[124] At the next joint meeting, on 8 June, the Central Committee resolved firmly in favour of a demonstration, on 10 June, to be planned by the Military Organisation and the Petersburg Committee.[125] Kamenev extracted only a single concession, but a potentially significant one: the Central Committee was to stipulate that the demonstrators should march unarmed. No overt provocation to the Provisional Government was to be given. In practice, however, the organisers let the marchers come as they pleased, with or without arms.[126] No one knows whether Lenin approved of this infringement of the Central Committee's orders. A canny politician, he may even have deliberately steered the Central Committee away from detailed oversight of the demonstration precisely so that such an infringement might more easily occur; but no decisive evidence is available. The Menshevik and Socialist-Revolutionary leaderships were worried by the posters pinned up around Petrograd by Bolshevik activists. The First All-Russian Congress of Workers' and Soldiers' Deputies as a precaution banned the holding of any armed demonstration without the permission of the Petrograd Soviet. The scene was set for the first test of strength between the Bolsheviks and the Provisional Government.[127]

Lenin panicked. The problem was that he had originally underestimated the will of the Mensheviks and Socialist Revolutionaries to call his bluff. The banning of a demonstration by the Petrograd Soviet had not entered his calculations. He had proved more adept at manipulating the levers of the Central Committee than in steering the engine of national politics. The Central Committee met in the early hours of 10 June. Five members were able to attend despite the short notice: Kamenev, Lenin, Nogin, Sverdlov and Zinoviev. Kamenev and Nogin had always perceived the dangers of an armed clash; and Zinoviev, who had edged towards Kamenev since the April Party

Conference, supported their proposal to cancel the demonstration. Outvoted, Lenin and Sverdlov abstained.[128] Lenin salved his revolutionary conscience; but he would have been forced to cancel the demonstration if Kamenev had not done it for him. Party comrades were dispatched to give instructions to the Military Organisation and the Petersburg Committee. *Pravda*, too, had to be warned. Posters had to be torn down and replaced.[129]

The worry for Lenin was the attitude which might be taken by the First Congress of Soviets of Workers' and Soldiers' Deputies. Tsereteli objected to Lenin's casual temerity in initiating the demonstration and treated his activity as part of a conspiracy to set up a Bolshevik government.[130] The Central Committee had, in fact, wanted power transferred to 'the soviets'; and, if this had occurred, Tsereteli would have been a strong candidate for the premiership. The minutes of the Central Committee's discussion were in any case unavailable to Tsereteli: he was guessing. His vehemence, moreover, was opposed even by several non-Bolsheviks. Martov spoke against the proposal for the Bolsheviks to be physically disarmed. Trotski, not yet a Bolshevik but showing sympathy with Lenin, blisteringly denounced the Provisional Government and its socialist ministers.[131] The result, on 12 June, was that the Bolsheviks were merely censured for recklessness.[132] Not even Tsereteli had much stomach for the repressive measures that Lenin and Trotski would have applied to them in similar circumstances. The Congress also decided to hold its own peaceful demonstration on 18 June to display support for its policies on the coalition cabinet and on the war. The crisis went off the boil. The Bolsheviks participated in the demonstration with the Mensheviks and the Socialist Revolutionaries even though there were frictions over the Bolshevik party's insistence on marching under its own slogans, including 'All Power To The Soviets'.[133]

A LEADER ON CAMPAIGN

Doubts about Lenin's mettle as a revolutionary leader were surfacing. The Petersburg Committee, convening on 11 June, was irritated by the fumbling and bungling of the Central Committee. The displeasure was intense since it was the Petersburg Committee's activists and not Lenin who had the uncongenial task of dissuading agitated crowds of anti-governmental workers, soldiers and sailors from undertaking a demonstration which the Central Committee had encouraged. Nearly all participants in the debate in the Petersburg Committee criticised Lenin's leadership directly or by implication.[134] He survived their anger mainly because no Bolshevik figure on the party's left offered himself as an alternative leader and because he handled his defence with firmness and discretion. While not pretending that all had gone well with the Central Committee's plans for a demonstration, he did not apologise.[135]

He was helped by his status as the whipping boy of the anti-Bolshevik press. Lenin had become one of a handful of politicians known by name to everyone in the country interested in politics. This was inevitable once he had declared his policies and had tightened his grip on the sole major party unequivocally hostile to the Provisional Government. He appeared as the personification of the project for socialist revolution. Most onlookers found the similarities rather than the differences between the Kadets and the non-Bolshevik socialists most impressive. Lenin and his party, by contrast, opposed the entire historic compromise between Russian liberalism and Russian 'moderate' socialism; and the barrage of invective fired at him in national newspapers served to enhance his eminence. The less delicate conservative organs portrayed him as an unbridled sexual hedonist, and rumours were spread about his supposed affections for Aleksandra Kollontai.[136] 'Respectable' liberal newspapers confined themselves to reviling him as a German agent. Neither the Mensheviks nor the Socialist Revolutionaries were as scurrilous, but they castigated him relentlessly as a dangerous fanatic.[137] The net effect of the vilification, at least until early July, was to disseminate the proposals of the Bolsheviks more widely. It is said that mud sticks; but mud also has its uses.[138]

Lenin and his associates, however, were perturbed by the smear campaign. The party in the provinces expressed its concern, and requests were made to the Central Committee to counter the anti-Bolshevik tirades by publishing information on the real Lenin, his background and personality. Lenin began a sketch of his life. He did this as if he were filling in a particularly tedious bureaucratic form, and never completed the task.[139] But he saw the need for its accomplishment; his own diffidence as an autobiographer did not prevent him from allowing Krupskaya to prepare a biographical article on him and supervising and correcting its contents.[140]

And yet the effort to cleanse the bespattered image of their leader was not a true priority for the party. Krupskaya's piece was printed

not in *Pravda* but in a Kronstadt newspaper;[141] and another sketch
by M. S. Olminski, published in *Social-Democrat* in Moscow, failed
to be reproduced elsewhere.[142] Bolsheviks were evidently not
intending to establish a 'cult' around him. They recognised Lenin
as their party chief with fewer reservations than the Socialist
Revolutionaries had about Viktor Chernov or even the Kadets
about Pavel Milyukov;[143] but they held back from adulation. The
'heartfelt greetings' sent by a 7000-strong meeting of workers in
Bogorodsko-Glukhovo to 'the respected fighter and leader of the
working class, comrade Lenin' was more the exception than the
norm,[144] and Lenin did not pursue exceptional treatment for himself.
Neither in speeches nor in articles did he try to draw attention to
himself at the expense of his colleagues or the party as a whole. He
had often expressed dislike of the term 'Leninist' on the grounds that
it implied an overestimation of the personal factor in politics.[145] This
attitude is not incompatible with a tendency to 'back into the
limelight'; the loud disclaiming of personal merit or influence can
be an indirect way of inviting praise. But even if this is what he was
doing, it may well have stemmed from Lenin's instincts rather than
his conscious choice: his was not a self-inquiring mind.

And so, whereas the rest of the press presented him as an
individual politician capable of bringing down the Provisional
Government, Lenin as ever did not emphasise the word 'I' and
preferred phrases like 'we, the workers'. This inaccurate self-
description had appeared in his intra-party writings in the past
and had looked odd to those who knew his background. But it was
not so embarrassing in the 'mass politics' of 1917. There was also a
sartorial aspect to his carefully-cultivated political image. He gave
up his homburg, the conventional headgear of émigré Russian
revolutionaries, for a workman's peaked cap (which is now so
much associated with him that it is often called a Lenin cap). Ex-
undergrounders such as Stalin, who had come from humble social
origins, had always dressed in such a style; but former emigrants like
Kamenev kept to their previous mode of dress, so Lenin no longer
looked like most leading politicians of his vintage and background.
Before his return to Russia he had been likened in appearance to 'a
schoolteacher from Smaland about to lay into the priest with whom
he had fallen out'![146] He did not lose this combativeness, but
increasingly he looked more like a working-class Bolshevik than a
middle-class pedagogue; he obviously found the revolutionary
environment congenial.

He proved adept too at mass oratory. Speaking at public meetings was among his principal duties on the party's behalf. Photographers caught him in characteristic pose, leaning out over the balcony on a raised platform, fist raised high and face straining to convey the party's programme. May and June 1917 were busy months for him. Besides Central Committee sessions and local party occasions in Petrograd, Lenin had to address eleven large gatherings. These included not only formal speeches to the Petrograd Conference of Factory-Workshop Committees, the All Russian Congress of Peasants' Deputies and the All-Russian Congress of Soviets of Workers' and Soldiers' Deputies but also five open-air speeches at the gates of Petrograd factories.[147] At the Putilov works he was confronted by an audience of thousands of labourers, and eyewitnesses concur that he was a rousing figure who could improvise brilliantly.[148] Yet his words lacked the emotional range of several other orators such as Trotski or Zinoviev: he avoided their use of pathos, and rarely mentioned the concrete conditions of life and toil of the working class; he neither showed pity for workers nor encouraged them to pity themselves. The socialist revolution, he implied, would not demand material self sacrifice of them. Lenin suggested that whatever deprivations needed to be made would be paid for by the enemies of the working class. Socialist policies would supposedly have been painless for the mass of the population.[149]

This message, with its combination of invocation and reassurance, must have contributed to Lenin's advance on power. And yet his success came only slowly. After his spectacular and rapturous reception at the Finland station on 3 April, he found non-Bolshevik audiences less enthusiastic for several weeks. A speech to a massed workers' meeting in a factory yard on 21 May was heard 'in the silence of a graveyard' and 'there was no stormy applause'.[150] His proposals were not yet familiar and acceptable to most factory workers. On returning to Russia, furthermore, he had no illusions about his inexperience and often fidgeted nervously as he waited his turn to speak. Aleksandra Kollontai, who admired him and thought him to be as confident as he was competent, was taken aback on one occasion when he suggested that she should take the platform in his place. She refused to comply. And he, once he had started speaking, was calmed by the positive response of listeners; and he soon lost all his fear.[151]

None the less, a proper assessment of his influence has to take account that only persons who were in his audiences at those eleven meetings in May and June 1917 caught sight or sound of him. Such people were countable in tens of thousands: a tiny fragment of the population. Petrograd was a base from where he ventured only rarely. Not once in 1917 did he set foot in Moscow, the country's second capital, or in any urban provincial centre. Apart from a weekend summerhouse jaunt to the countryside outside Petrograd, he had no acquaintance with rural Russia in the first three months after his arrival at the Finland Station.[152] He did not visit the Eastern front. He did not journey to any of the non-Russian regions of the country. For all his down-to-earth reputation among his followers as being quite unlike the other 'politickers', he was very much the metropolitan leader. It pleased him to comment that the provinces were supplying examples of greater radicalism than the capital, and that 'the revolution' was welling up 'from below', 'from the depths'.[153] But nothing would have induced him to shift his focus of work from Petrograd. He knew about the provincial political processes only from newspapers and from Bolshevik activists coming to Petrograd for meetings, conferences and congresses

This also meant that direct knowledge of Lenin the man was thinly-spread in the rest of the country. Such newsreel film as was produced was devoted to ministers of the Provisional Government; recordings of Lenin's speeches were not made. Not even his physical image, moreover, was widely disseminated. *Pravda* contained no photographs. Kerenski, on entering the Lvov cabinet, had thousands of postcards made which portrayed his bust, surrounded by a glowing aureole and against a background of the magnificent state buildings of Petrograd. This was not, at least not yet, the Bolshevik party's style. Bolsheviks printed most pictures of their leaders later in the year, after they had seized power. The contemporary anti-Bolshevik press saw no advantage in publishing photos of Lenin; cartoonists had sport with him, but usually provided a *passe-partout* drawing of evil and made no attempt at realistic portraiture.

Consequently Lenin's impact upon general politics in Russia stemmed in large measure from his newspaper articles. The year 1917 was the golden age of Russian print journalism, and Lenin devoted more hours per day to writing for *Pravda* – he wrote little for other Bolshevik outlets – than to any other political function. In May 1917, he had a total of thirty pieces published in the newspaper's twenty-four issues.[154] The print-run was around 85,000–90,000 copies,[155] and distribution was made to virtually all towns and cities. Only the villages, which had hardly any Bolshevik party groups, were left outside the normal distribution network. Thus Lenin's opinions were communicated directly to a vastly greater number of people outside Petrograd than the few hundred provincial activists who heard him speak. Even so, it must be added that nearly half the copies were sold in Petrograd and that therefore not even all literate Bolshevik rank-and-filers can have read the words of their party leader).[156] Most of his *Pravda* articles, furthermore, were pitched below the altitude of abstraction typical of his earlier writings in the war. His vocabulary became simpler, his style more direct. Everyday contact with workers no doubt attuned him to the newspaper's needs. To be sure, he was still not writing in expectation of being read by the entire literate working class; but he did at least hope to reach out to all members of his party: and three fifths of these in 1917, it is reckoned, were labourers of some sort.[157]

Lenin was *Pravda*'s regular columnist on current political issues; and in this role he especially aimed to acquire the support of Bolshevik committee-men in Petrograd and the localities for his strategy. Marxological polemics were not put aside. Certainly, he did not cease to attack Kautsky, but no longer did he do this regardless of circumstance. He had learned enough about Russian working-class opinion to confine his assault on 'Kautskyism' to pamphlets unintended for mass consumption.[158] In his more popular articles he had a quick eye for denigration. Each fresh turn of policy or even phrase of Lvov, Kerenski, Tsereteli or Chernov was scanned for its worst possible meaning then denounced with relish. He loved to group together the Mensheviks, Socialist Revolutionaries and Bundists as an undifferentiated, counter-revolutionary mass. Using a term invented by the Bolshevik versifier Demyan Bedny, he called them 'Liberdans'.[159] This was a play on words, referring to the Menshevik leader Fyodor Dan and the Bundist leader Mark Liber. Sarcasm was the hallmark of his prose.

And Lenin, like his Central Committee colleagues, carried a heavy load of responsibilities on the Bolshevik party's behalf. No single leader could do everything, and a degree of functional specialisation made practical sense. Lenin and Krupskaya were relieved of the business of correspondence with local party committees.[160] Nor did he have to greet many activists on their visits to the Central Committee.[161] He was not charged with the technical oversight of the production of party newspapers. Moreover, it was Kamenev's main job to direct the Bolshevik fraction in the Petrograd Soviet (whereas Lenin, the great advocate of 'all power to the soviets' in the

spring, was not elected to the Soviet). Zinoviev was an indefatigable
speaker dispatchable to any large gathering. Nogin, at his own
insistence, worked in the Moscow Soviet.[162] Stalin helped with the
editing of *Pravda* and took on further tasks as the changing situation
required. Sverdlov ran the Central Committee Secretariat with a
small but efficient staff and, like Stalin, was among the less 'visible'
figures in the Bolshevik leadership.[163] Despite Lenin's doubts about
him at the April Bolshevik Conference, Sverdlov could hardly have
been closer to Lenin's policies, and his indefatigable service to the
Central Committee and its Secretariat freed Lenin to focus on his
chosen activities.[164]

Nevertheless, Lenin was bothered by Kamenev's persistent sniping
at his strategy. Zinoviev, too, was emerging as a figure of substance
on the Bolshevik right. In order to strengthen his hand, Lenin looked
outside the party in search of prominent Marxists opposed to the
Provisional Government. He would have liked to work inside the
same party as Martov if only Martov could have broken with the
Menshevik leadership, which supported the Lvov cabinet.[165] He was
ever ready to forgive and forget, especially when it was his own sins
which were being forgiven and forgotten. Suspicion of him, however,
remained strong; and the Menshevik leftist leaders in any case
refused to split from their party. A similar mixture of rancour and
political calculation held back leading anti-Lenin Bolsheviks from
the pre-war period, such as Aleksandr Bogdanov. They repudiated
Lenin's case that the transition to socialism could be begun in
backward and war-torn Russia.[166]

The one major group to join were the so-called Interdistricters.
Lenin apparently did not have all the Central Committee on his side
in opening negotiations even though the April Party Conference had
given its approval. A *Pravda* editorial, in a curious hint about his
problem, reported that the invitation had been made 'in the name of
comrade Lenin and several Central Committee members'.[167] Trotski,
too, was approached. He reached Petrograd from the emigration
only in May 1917. Even before the February Revolution, as Lenin
and Zinoviev noted, he had denounced Chkheidze and the Menshevik Duma deputies;[168] and, upon his return to Russia, he agreed
with the Bolsheviks that a rupture was desirable with the Menshevik
leaders who condoned the coalition with the Kadets. He felt that
Lenin, whether he said so or not, had embraced the Trotskyist theory
of 'permanent revolution' in place of the traditional two-stage
revolutionary schedule; and indeed, after joining the Bolsheviks,

Trotski defended his strategy of 1905–6 with enthusiasm in Bolshevik publications.[169] He was not constrained to defer to Lenin, who welcomed Trotski's adhesion to the Bolsheviks not only since he was an increasingly needed advocate of radicalism but also because of his technical and oratorical skills; and he was asked to help with the editing of 'a popular organ';[170] No Bolshevik leader could match his record in this respect. The two old adversaries tacitly agreed to forget past differences. The development of Lenin as a chairman of Bolshevik opinion and as a leader who could coax unlikely partners to co-operate had begun.

THE JULY DAYS

The First All-Russian Congress of Soviets of Workers' and Soldiers' Deputies elected a permanent body to co-ordinate soviet affairs across the country. This was the All-Russian Central Executive Committee (or VTsIK), and its leading members were Mensheviks and Socialist Revolutionaries as well as some Bundists. Its business was transacted by an inner group of politicians: Tsereteli, Chkheidze, Gots, Dan, Liber and others. All were members of the Petrograd Soviet, whose importance declined at the national level. Bolsheviks, under Kamenev's leadership, constituted a minority on the All-Russian Central Executive Committee.

These Bolsheviks could barely believe that the All-Russian Central Executive Committee, which had relations with virtually all soviets in cities and on the Eastern front, refused to take power from the Kadets. The need for strong government and strong solutions was acute. The economy was swiftly collapsing. The labour-force in a few enterprises in Petrograd, despairing of a fair deal with the employers, established 'workers' control' over management.[171] Closures of factories became frequent, and the scourge of unemployment started to lacerate workers. Even so, strikes and other conflicts in factories which stayed in operation disrupted production. Employers were determined to quell opposition; P. P. Ryabushinski suggested that only 'the bony hand of hunger' would constrain the workers to moderate their demands. Industrial production faltered, and shortages of coal and other raw materials grew. Finance tightened; foreign investment largely ceased.[172] Peasants were meanwhile becoming more restless. Illegal felling of timber and illegal pasturing of animal occurred widely. Land hunger persisted. Direct seizures of landed estates rose in number from June 1917. The economic ties between town and village broke down. Food supplies dwindled as peasants, faced with inadequate state-fixed prices and a shortage of marketed industrial goods, hoarded their grain.[173] War-weariness was also growing, especially among the troops. Desertions from the front were still only a trickle, but the trend was growing.

Yet premier Lvov and his Minister of War, Kerenski, believed that the war could be won and that an offensive had to be launched if the Provisional Government was to retain credibility in the councils of the Allies.[174] The military advice was that the Austro-Hungarian sector of the Eastern front, in Galicia, afforded the best chance. The attack was initiated on 18 June. An early powerful advance was halted when German forces were transferred south to stiffen the Austrian defence, and Russian armies were soon pushed back further into the Ukraine than before. The Provisional Government was humiliated, and the Mensheviks and Socialist Revolutionaries incurred criticism for acceding to Kadet militarism.

An abundance of combustible political material existed to be lit. The material was self-igniting because the mass organisations elected by the workers, soldiers and peasants were not completely controllable by the political élites. The cabinet; the high command; the party leaderships: all these were important to prevent 'mass action' on the streets. Not surprisingly, Lenin found it difficult to strike the balance between enunciating a radical strategy and restraining his adherents from its premature application. Addressing a conference of the party's bodies in the armed forces from all over the country on 20 June, he stressed the need to secure fresh victories in the elections to the soviets and other mass organisations.[175] Kamenev was well pleased. Earlier in the month, Lenin had been able to hide his own last-minute uncertainty about holding a demonstration behind the cloak of the Central Committee decision, inspired by Kamenev, to call off the demonstration. This time, however, such a manoeuvre was impossible; Lenin himself had to administer 'a cold shower' of discouragement to activists who thought they were pursuing his line of action. His agitation was obvious to his audience as he warned them against being 'drawn into a provocation'. He added, for the benefit of anyone who had not understood his message: 'If we were now able to seize power, it is naïve to think that having taken it we should be able to hold on to it'.[176] The conference fell into heated debate, and only with difficulty did the demand of Lenin and the Central Committee prevail.[177]

The Petersburg Committee was also in session on 20 June. A resolution was passed condemning isolated revolutionary actions; but the Central Committee was disconcerted by an amendment, which was successfully proposed by Military Organisation leader, M. Y. Latsis, to the effect that 'if it proved impossible to hold back the masses, the party should take the movement into its own hands'.[178] Radicals felt that they had obtained a sanction to continue to do as they had always wanted, and the Military Organisation's newspaper published inflammatory material despite the Central Committee's desire to avoid immediate trouble with the Provisional Government.[179]

The political atmosphere was volatile. And yet it was precisely now, on 29 June, that Lenin felt able to take a rest for a few days in Neivola, a village in the Finnish countryside some four or five hours distant from Petrograd by local train. He had been complaining of overwork and headaches in April. Perhaps this was an early symptom of the cerebral arteriosclerosis which killed him in 1924, or possibly he had simply been overworking. In any case he noted jocularly that, even when he withdrew from speaking engagements in order to recuperate, the enemies of the Bolsheviks nevertheless claimed he had turned up and demagogically roused the crowds to fury.[180] (Who needs to construct a 'cult' for himself when others will do it so much better?). Lenin was always aware that he needed to look after himself physically. His instinct for self-care was one of the few cracks in his armour as a politician. In 1904 he had gone off on an Alpine jaunt, laying himself open to intra-factional attack by V. A. Noskov.[181] In midsummer 1917 the political stakes were much higher, and yet Lenin unconcernedly departed to stay in Vladimir Bonch-Bruevich's rural dacha.[182] Unintentionally, this leader, who thought no one equalled his competence in dealing with affairs at the apex of the Bolshevik party, was leaving the Central Committee to face alone the party's most fiendishly difficult test since the February Revolution.

Among the garrison soldiers, no group was more discontented than the First Machine Gun Regiment. Its support for the abortive demonstration made it suspect to the Provisional Government; and, when orders were issued for the transfer of units and guns to the front, the natural assumption was made that an attempt was being made to root out anti-governmental trouble-makers. The machine-gunners reacted by planning a further demonstration against the Lvov cabinet. Low-level Bolshevik activists were involved. The All-

Russian Bureau of the Military Organisations had apparently learnt of this development by 1 July. The Central Committee was alerted next day, and its instructions were short and sharp: the Bureau was told to prevent violence and to have nothing to do with the demonstration.[183] The crisis for the Bolshevik Central Committee coincided with a crisis in the Provisional Government. After the February Revolution, Ukrainians had formed a Central Rada (or Council) in Kiev and, demanding greater national autonomy, convoked a Ukrainian National Congress. The Provisional Government, apart from granting permission for the formation of Ukrainian regiments at the front, asserted the need to respect the prerogatives of the Constituent Assembly. Negotiations followed. On 2 July, Tsereteli proposed that the Rada be recognised as a regional government so long as the Provisional Government's supreme authority was recognised. Most Kadet ministers, having already become disenchanted by the coalition with the Mensheviks and the Socialist Revolutionaries, rejected the compromise and resigned from the Cabinet.[184] This crisis failed to become public knowledge immediately because events on the streets suddenly ran out of the control of the authorities. The First Machine Gun Regiment met to finalise plans. The postal workers went on strike on 3 July. The machine gunners toured the capital, calling on other regiments to join them. Workers downed tools at the Putilov factory and other enterprises, and sailors from the Kronstadt naval garrison began to arrive in Petrograd.[185] Bolsheviks in the party's lower echelons did little to restrain the crowds; some of them actively fomented trouble. When the news reached the Petrograd Bolshevik City Conference, the delegates ignored the Central Committee's prohibition and offered to lead the demonstration 'if this proved necessary'.[186]

Kamenev, Tomski and Zinoviev tried to restrain the local activists from such a course of action.[187] Yet the party was not a machine to be stopped and started at will, and the crowds on the streets were not instruments at the party's disposal either. At the Kshesinskaya Palace, Sverdlov harangued the gathering crowds into going home. But they would not budge, to the delight of a Bolshevik All-Russian Bureau of Military Organisations which announced its readiness to guide the demonstration. The affair had its own momentum. But the Bolshevik leadership, in the Petersburg Committee and in the All-Russian Bureau of Military Organisations, were following rather than guiding events; and, although most participants hoped that the turmoil would somehow result in the overthrow of the Provisional Government, they had no definite set of tactics.[188] Clashes between demonstrators and pro-government troops occurred before midnight on 3–4 July. The crowds swelled around the Tauride Palace where the Petrograd Soviet and the Provisional Government were based.[189] Zinoviev too was at the Palace; and, yielding to the atmosphere, he appeared alongside Trotski commending the demands for the transfer of power to the soviets.[190] On 4 July the Central Committee's members accepted that the demonstration would take place regardless of the party's official recommendation. The All-Russian Bureau of Military Organisations took operational command. Kamenev still refused to believe that events could not be turned back; but his colleagues rejected his advice.[191] The Central Committee 'authorised' only a peaceful demonstration. The worry persisted that the outcome would not be happy, and the Bolshevik central leaders wanted to take as few obviously incriminating steps as possible. On the other hand, it was to be a peaceful demonstration which also removed the government. Stalin was instructed to draft a leaflet in the early hours of the morning of 4 July calling for a transfer of power to the soviets. In essence this was Bolshevism demanding that the 'Liberdans' should rule.[192]

At last it crossed the minds of the Central Committee's members that their convalescent leader might with profit be informed about the developing situation, and asked to disrupt his rustic holiday. M. A. Savelev was sent out to the dacha in Neivola. He arrived, unannounced, at 6 am on 4 July.[193] Lenin and his companions, Bonch-Bruevich and his sister Mariya dressed hurriedly. In less than three quarters of an hour they had caught the morning train for Petrograd, pulling into the Finland station at eleven o'clock. As when he had travelled there in April, he was buried in thought the whole journey;[194] but this time no crowd awaited him. This must have brought him some relief, since a huge agglomeration of people would have signified that things had run into even greater trouble than he had been led to believe.

Elsewhere in the capital there were signs of the demonstration in the making. Kronstadt's sailors were on their way. They made for the Kshesinskaya palace to seek out the Bolshevik leaders. Sverdlov and Anatoli Lunacharski addressed them from the balcony; and Lenin, who had in the meantime arrived, was asked to come out to say a few words. At first he refused, signalling his unhappiness with the march. The incongruity continued when he stepped out: a massive ovation awaited him. He repeated his slogan of 'all power to the soviets', but accompanied this with a plea for self-restraint.[195] M. I. Kalinin, who had no warmer desire than Lenin for a demonstration, was to recall that Lenin nevertheless spoke with his fellow leaders as if he was still not completely convinced that the march would be a fiasco and that the Provisional Government would not fail.[196] The sailors moved on towards the Tauride Palace, and machine-gunners and striking workers converged with them. Clashes in the streets were frequent with pro-government troops. At the Tauride Palace, Viktor Chernov emerged to address the crowd; he was nearly lynched when he affirmed that the Mensheviks and Socialist Revolutionaries were standing by the government coalition. A voice from the mob was heard: 'Take power, you scoundrel, when it's being given to you!'[197] The Provisional Government sent for reinforcements to its loyal forces at the front; and the Minister of Justice, P. N. Pereverzev, contacting troops in the capital who had not declared support for either side, released the bits of circumstantial information in the hands of the authorities which purported to show that Lenin was a German spy.[198]

The Menshevik and Socialist-Revolutionary leadership of the Petrograd Soviet, stiffened by Tsereteli's resolve, resisted the pressure to take power. Tsereteli was lucky that few people outside the Provisional Government knew of the Kadets' resignation. The left wing of the Menshevik party was led by Martov, who had returned in May but who until early July was not willing to endorse a transfer of power to the soviets. But Tsereteli's line held the day.[199] Towards nightfall, moreover, troops began to arrive outside the Tauride Palace who were loyal to Lvov, Kerenski and Tsereteli.

Military dispositions were made, and the demonstrators started to disperse to their garrisons and to their homes. By the early hours of 5 July, it was clear that the demonstration had been a failure. The Bolshevik Central Committee called on the crowds to leave the streets. *Pravda* announced the turnabout in policy on a back page.[200] When Lenin was faced with the angry disappointment of the All-Russian Bureau of Military Organisation's leaders, he responded with a barrage of detailed, operational questions as to what forces could be deployed if the demonstration was to be revived. The answers failed to satisfy him, exactly as he had expected.[201] The Bureau's newspaper did not announce its withdrawal; but no action on the streets was recommended.[202] By noon on 5 July, the troops of the disorganised Provisional Government held sway in the capital.

The Bolshevik Central Committee was disrupted and demoralised and _Pravda_'s printing press was seized.[203] On 6 July, a handful of Central Committee members met in a flat in the Vyborg district. Lenin declared that the revolutionary process was entering a critical phase. The progress of previous months had ended. Political 'reaction' had set in. Counter-revolution was on the offensive. No one could tell, he emphasised, how long it might last. The Bolshevik party needed to make tactical adjustments to survive and flourish again.[204]

ESCAPE TO THE LAKES

Anti-Bolshevik repression had ensued in Petrograd. The deaths of demonstrators ran into the hundreds, and there were many reports of violence being meted out to known or suspected Bolsheviks encountered on the streets. The expression of anti-semitic sentiments was rife. On 6 July, warrants were issued for the arrest of several prominent party leaders. Lenin, Kamenev and Zinoviev headed the list of those hunted by the authorities. Kollontai's name was added. Trotski and Lunacharski, despite not belonging to the Bolshevik party, had been involved in negotiations about the demonstration; they too were sought by troops loyal to the Provisional Government.[205]

Nearly all of them surrendered to the authorities and were imprisoned. The exceptions were Lenin and Zinoviev. This was odd in its way since Lenin was guiltless, unless it was a crime to take a holiday when great events were in the making. As regards Zinoviev, he retained a reputation as a radical Bolshevik but was by now closer to Kamenev than to Lenin, and had opposed the demonstration from its conception. The underlying problem for them was the recurrent charge that they were German agents. They had consistently repudiated the accusation, taking space in Bolshevik newspapers to explain their story and to stress that they would have returned via France and the North Sea if only the Allied authorities had given permission.[206] But Pereverzev's official investigations were intensified in the period before and after the July demonstration; and, even before the enquiry was complete, preliminary indications of its findings were being 'leaked' to the press. The principal journalists to pick up the story were Vladimir Burtsev and Grigori Aleksinski.

Burtsev had spent a career exposing police agents in the Russian revolutionary movement; Aleksinski was a former Bolshevik whose hostility to Lenin had induced him to found a newspaper, *Without Superfluous Words*, dedicated wholly to the exposure of Bolshevik misdeeds.[207]

Even so, Lenin and Zinoviev initially thought to deliver themselves up to the authorities on condition that the Petrograd Soviet would guarantee physical protection and a fair trial.[208] Several Bolsheviks advised this. The risk was obvious, but there was a tradition among socialists of using trials to denounce the authorities and proclaim revolutionary objectives to the widest readership. This had been done by Lenin's brother, Aleksandr Ulyanov, at the trial of populist-terrorists in 1887.[209] It was Kamenev's less than totally defiant comportment at his trial in 1915 that continued to earn him contempt among fellow Bolsheviks after the February Revolution.[210] And yet even Kamenev allowed himself to be imprisoned after the July Days although he, together with Trotski, was intimidated by the vehemently anti-semitic hysteria being whipped up. The additional consideration was that all revolutionary parties, including the Bolsheviks, assumed that no single leader's fate should be put before the good of the party and the Revolution.

Abruptly, on 8 July, Lenin and Zinoviev had second thoughts and decided to avoid arrest. They resisted pressure from several leading figures in the party who argued that their absconding would make it harder to make a case in their favour and would bring the party as a whole into disrepute. Such leaders included V. Volodarski and D. Z. Manuilski, who had contacts with factory workers in Petrograd.[211] By then, however, several newspapers were baying for Lenin's blood. Gruesome cartoons depicted Lenin on a scaffold.[212] But Bolshevik calls for him to surrender himself to the authorities subsided, and Lenin and Zinoviev went into hiding in the capital.[213] The next twenty-four hours convinced them that Petrograd was too dangerous for them. It was the one city in the world where tens of thousands of people could recognise their faces. On 9 July the two fugitives travelled at night the twenty miles north west of Petrograd to Razliv, a village outside Sestroretsk on the Gulf of Finland.[214] For the next month they stayed with the Bolshevik and factory worker Nikolai Emelyanov, who had, like many Russian workers, retained a house and some land in the countryside. Lenin and Zinoviev slept in the barn-loft. Sestroretsk was a resort town, and summer was a period when town-dwellers would swarm out to coastal residences.

The two men felt able to stroll around so long as they took reasonable care, but scares sometimes happened. On one occasion the sight of approaching armed men caused Lenin and Zinoviev to dive into a haystack. Lenin whispered to his companion: 'The only thing left now is to die decently!'[215] The strangers with the rifles were, in fact, out for a day's duck-shooting; and the site itself has become a shrine of the Soviet state, containing the world's only haystack which is also a national monument.[216]

But time passed, in the main, slowly and tranquilly. Lenin and Zinoviev swam; they went on walks, plagued only by the mosquitoes that ravage the summers of people seeking repose by the lakes of those parts. The Provisional Government's repressive zeal was fading somewhat, and Lenin and Zinoviev received secret visits from Bolshevik Central Committee members.[217] From 23 July 1917 *Pravda*'s position as the central party organ was transferred by the Central Committee to the Military Organisation's *Worker and Soldier* (which was the new name for *Soldier's Pravda*).[218] By 26 July, Lenin's articles were appearing in it.[219] His flight from Petrograd gave him a sabbatical for his writing. Retrieving his notes on 'Marxism and the State', he resumed the work commenced in Switzerland on the 'dictatorship of the proletariat'. The fruit of this labour was to be his masterpiece in political theory: *The State and Revolution*. Lenin remarked to Kamenev: '*Entre nous*, if they do me in, please publish my notebook 'Marxism and the State'.'[220]

Yet Lenin and Zinoviev felt insecure even near Sestroretsk. Politics in Petrograd remained unstable. The collective resignation of the Kadet leaders in the July governmental crisis had thrown the coalition into chaos. Frantic discussions ensued, and a leftward shift in the Provisional Government's composition was inevitable. Prince Lvov stepped down and Aleksandr Kerenski, the right-wing Socialist Revolutionary and Minister of Army and Navy Affairs, was appointed as premier on 7 July. Tsereteli also resigned, deciding to concentrate on the business of the All-Russian Central Executive Committee of the Congress of Soviets. A Socialist Revolutionary, N. D. Avksentev, became Minister of Internal Affairs, and the liberal M. I. Tereshchenko remained as Foreign Minister. The Mensheviks and Socialist Revolutionaries were the majority in the cabinet, but the policies remained largely unchanged except that nobody any longer contemplated the resumption of an offensive of the Eastern front. The idea that no further alienation of Kadet support should take place was emphasised. For Kerenski, Lenin was only the tip of the iceberg of his problems. The question of law and order in Petrograd and other cities lay under the surface; and frequent discussions were held between the new premier and General Lavr Kornilov, the Commander-in-Chief of Russian armed forces, in pursuit of a solution.[221]

Lenin desired to put greater distance between Petrograd and himself. The Bolshevik party had a warm relationship with Finnish social-democrats, even receiving financial assistance from them. Successful overtures were made on Lenin's behalf to obtain sanctuary in Finland proper. Finland by then, and much to the Provisional Government's annoyance, was practically an independent state even though Finnish politicians, however nationalist they were, seldom demanded outright independence; and the proximity of the Russian naval garrison in Helsingfors (as the Russians called Helsinki) ensured that Bolsheviks had ready support among armed troops.

Lenin prepared himself for the journey to Finland with his customary attention to detail. He jotted down (for he was a compulsive jotter) a list of things he would require. The toothpaste had to be white, the sewing-thread black; and he asked for two pencils, one red and the other blue, to mark the passages in newspapers he wished to use in his writing. A Finnish-and-Swedish phrase book also seemed a good idea, and Lenin asked for a do-it-yourself hairdresser's clipper in case he needed to disguise his appearance.[222] Around the first week of August he set off. He was dressed as a worker and had documents identifying him as a Mr Konstantin Petrovich Ivanov.[223] He had shaved off his beard and wore a wig. This was sensible since the contemporary newspaper cartoons portrayed him as bald and bearded. Lenin had a photograph taken of his self-transformation. This was a rare manifestation of vanity, which was all the more remarkable since the photo could have fallen into hostile hands.[224] Accompanied by Nikolai Emelyanov, E. Rahja and A. V. Shotman he made his way to the Russo-Finnish border railway station of Dubina. They stayed there overnight, departing next day by train into Finland. This time Lenin masqueraded as an engine stoker.[225] He arrived in Helsingfors on 10 August and stayed at various addresses arranged for him by Finnish social-democratic leaders G. Rovio and K. Wiik.[226] Lenin pressed on with his research for *The State and Revolution*, and continued to submit articles to the Bolshevik central newspapers and to write to the Bolshevik Central Committee.[227]

The Finns made Lenin's contacts with the Bolshevik Central Committee easier than they had been in Razliv. Krupskaya, taking on the appearance of a Sestroretsk woman worker, managed to visit him. She, too, had her photograph taken: hardly an indication that the whole business was regarded as acutely dangerous. Such was Lenin's nonchalance that he accompanied her back nearly as far as the railway station itself.[228] Understandably, he would vastly have preferred to resume his public career in Petrograd. His previous sojourn in Finland, in 1906–7, had been followed by a decade in emigration in Central and Western Europe. He did not expect the same to happen again. Nor did he expect the existing chance of a Bolshevik assumption of power to recur: it was now or never!

7 The Fire Next Time: July to September 1917

CONSIDERATIONS ON PARTY STRATEGY

The internal life of parties in revolutionary Russia ran on the basis of persuasion and consent. The Bolsheviks were feared for their discipline and hierarchy; and yet their party was, by the standards of its own rulebook, highly ill-disciplined. Not even the Central Committee could enforce its policies on local party bodies if these objected. Communications were faulty; administrative staff and finances were not plentiful. Indeed, tensions affected relations at all levels of the Bolshevik party's formal hierarchy. Thus the Bolsheviks were not so unlike the Mensheviks and Socialist Revolutionaries as later mythology contended;[1] and the fact that the Bolshevik party was ill co-ordinated allowed its local activists to react dynamically to the particularity of local events. The Bolsheviks, furthermore, had the inestimable advantage of agreement on certain key ideas: that the Provisional Government should be overthrown and a socialist administration of some sort established; that urgent moves be made to end the war; that the peasants should get the land and that the economic rights of the bourgeoisie should be curtailed. Being innocent of the co-responsibility for the Provisional Government which affected their rivals, Bolsheviks could organise their political campaign unfettered. Such disputes as they had did not affect their practical activity. The disagreements among the Mensheviks and Socialist Revolutionaries led instead to factionalism; both had left wings which wanted to break with the Kadets entirely: and the Socialist Revolutionaries were to split into two separate parties in November 1917. In these conditions it was natural for dissentient leftists at lower levels to leave and join the Bolsheviks.[2]

Despite the finessing of policy which had occurred after the Seventh Party Conference in April, however, the July Days left the party's strategy for taking power uncertain. Lenin aimed to introduce both clarity and determination. On 10 July 1917, already on the run, he penned, 'The Political Situation (Four Theses)' for submission to the Central Committee. Kerenski's cabinet, he declared, constituted 'a military dictatorship'; and the Menshevik and Socialist-Revolutionary leadership had become 'the fig-leaf of the counter-revolution'.[3] Lenin concluded: 'All hopes of a peaceful development of the Russian revolution have disappeared definitively.' Now that the Menshevik-led soviets had supported the persecution of Bolsheviks it was vital to withdraw the slogan 'All Power to the Soviets!'. The need, according to Lenin, was for nothing less than 'armed insurrection'.[4]

His new theses massively overstated the repressive capacity and intentions of the Kerenski cabinet: most Bolshevik party organisations encountered little harassment. The Central Committee met on 13–14 July, in the absence of Lenin and Zinoviev (as well as the imprisoned Kamenev),[5] to consider strategy. Representatives of the party's local leaderships of Moscow and Petrograd as well as Central Bureau of the Military Organisation also attended. In demanding the abandonment of 'All Power to the Soviets!', according to Ordzhonikidze's later account, Lenin let it be known that the factory-workshop committees could provide the institutional base for the forthcoming socialist administration.[6] Even the April Party Conference had given no absolute commitment to rule by soviets;[7] and in *The State and Revolution*, written in the months after the July Days, Lenin had barely mentioned the soviets.[8] Even so, the Central Committee was aghast. Only Sverdlov fully accepted Lenin's viewpoint immediately after the July Days.[9] The idea that the soviets should be the institutions to deploy revolutionary power had taken a hold on the Bolshevik imagination. In addition, the party had invested its energies in persuading workers that 'soviet power' was the noblest objective; and the practical difficulties of justifying Lenin's proposed change of slogans, when Bolshevik activists spoke at open mass meetings, would be considerable. The Central Committee meeting rejected Lenin's invocation by ten votes out of fifteen.[10]

Lenin wrote a short article, 'On Slogans', in reply and condemned the Central Committee for what he saw as a lack of tactical flexibility. With a dismissiveness extraordinary even among Bolsheviks, he mocked the existing soviets as being 'like sheep brought to the abattoir'.[11] 'On Slogans' was published by the Kronstadt Bolsheviks, and reached a number of activists in the provinces.[12] Lenin's efforts did not go unrewarded; and a shift towards his stance had in any case been occurring in the Central Committee even before

'On Slogans' became widely known. Stalin was nominated to speak on the Central Committee's behalf at the Second City Party Conference in Petrograd on 16 July. Stalin concurred with Lenin that Kerenski had presided over 'the triumph of the counter-revolution'.[13] When pressed in debate, furthermore, Stalin conceded that the 'All Power to the Soviets!' slogan had lost its appropriateness.[14] Yet he affirmed that the ultimate objective remained the same: namely to establish a socialist administration of soviets. Stalin added: 'We are unequivocally in favour of those soviets where we have a majority, and we shall try to set up such soviets.'[15] The Central Committee's motion still stopped short of calling for the old slogan's abandonment and was approved by the City Conference by twenty-eight votes to three.[16]

Yet Lenin's fortunes were not as bad as they seemed. Twenty-eight delegates to the City Conference refused to take sides and abstained, but he could reasonably hope to win them over. Furthermore, he was willing to move a little towards the Central Committee. 'On Slogans' contained the following pronouncement on the post-Kerenski era: 'The soviets can and must emerge in this new revolution, but not the soviets of *today*, not the organs of collaboration with the bourgeoisie but the organs of revolutionary struggle with it. It is indeed true that we would then be in favour of the construction of the whole state on the soviet model.'[17] Thus he made clear that his rejection of the soviets was not to be regarded as permanent. Perhaps this clarification (or modification, if Ordzhonikidze's statement in his memoirs about the factory-workshop committees is to be believed)[18] nudged Stalin and the Central Committee majority towards accepting that Lenin's hostility to the 'All Power to the Soviets!' might not be as impolitic as they had thought. Lenin's Bolshevik critics may also have been reassured to note that he acknowledged that an immediate insurrection was impracticable.[19] A further factor assisting his case was the continued harassment of the Bolsheviks in the capital and the complicity of the Menshevik and Socialist-Revolutionary leaderships.

Such a situation must have convinced at least many wavering Bolsheviks that Lenin's demand for 'All Power to the Soviets!' to be abandoned was reasonable. Discussions were turning in his favour and, as the date of the Sixth Party Congress's convocation approached, a definitive decision was in prospect. The Central Committee pressed ahead with the Congress despite the difficulties in Petrograd. On 26 July 1917, the 157 voting and 107 non-voting delegates convened.[20] Lenin and Zinoviev could not risk the journey;

and Trotski, Lunacharski and Kamenev were in prison. Precautions were taken to avoid alerting the Provisional Government. Halfway through the proceedings, the venue was changed from an assembly hall in the Vyborg district to a workers' club in the Narva district. Tension was increased by a governmental decree, announced on 28 July, enabling ministers to ban any gathering deemed to threaten state security.[21]

The decree was not unwelcome to Lenin inasmuch as it dissuaded Bolshevik critics from continuing to demand that he should deliver himself up to the authorities.[22] He also kept in contact with the Central Committee in order to influence the Congress discussions. Apparently, a secret meeting between him and Stalin took place shortly before the proceedings commenced.[23] There is a strong possibility that the Central Committee's motion on the political situation, as presented to the Congress by Stalin, was based on a draft handed over by Lenin.[24] Lenin's physical absence did not preclude his political semi-presence. Even so, he influenced the Party Congress to a much smaller degree than he had the April Party Conference. The haste of the Congress's convocation meant that the Central Committee, too, had to entrust its representatives with considerable initiative. Close vetting of official reports did not occur. Central Committee spokesmen often had to write their speeches on their laps just before delivering them.[25] This may well have resulted in a freer expression of opinions than was usual. And the anti-Bolshevik campaign of the Provisional Government after the July Days compelled the promotion of less famous members of the Central Committee to greater prominence. A troika of leaders guided the debates at the Congress: Sverdlov, Stalin and Bukharin.

At the first session, Sverdlov obtained agreement on the Congress agenda. The next day, 27 July, Stalin delivered the Central Committee's report on its activities since the April Conference. His main aim was to show that the Bolshevik leadership had not provoked the clashes on the streets of the capital in early July.[26] Clamour ensued when E. A. Preobrazhenski impugned Stalin for his preoccupation with metropolitan politics. But the Moscow-based Central Committee member V. P. Nogin leapt to Stalin's defence.[27]

Sverdlov's organisational report in the third session claimed a rise in the number of party members to 200,000.[28] But the proceedings continued to be troublesome for the Central Committee. Y. Larin, a Menshevik-Internationalist visitor to the Congress, produced a flurry of excitement on 28 July when he objected to the abandonment of the slogan of 'All Power to the Soviets!'.[29] Stalin's report had avoided the topic, but Congress delegates knew that the Central Committee was proposing to debate the wording of a new slogan. Larin's intervention was a sign of uneasiness among several delegates about any change. Another voice of protest was heard when M. I. Vasilev complained that the party's agrarian policy was still so vague that the Bolsheviks were failing to win support among peasants.[30] On 30 July, Bukharin delivered the report 'on the current moment'. He asserted that the June offensive was made on the orders of 'Allied capital'; and that support for the Provisional Government's aggressive foreign policy was forthcoming from the peasantry[31] But he added that the workers could nevertheless effect an alliance with the peasants by offering them the land. He looked forward also to socialist revolution in the West. Yet Bukharin acknowledged that, if such a revolution did not break out immediately after the Bolsheviks had taken power in Russia, the Russian armed forces might well be incapable of triggering it off by an offensive revolutionary war. In such a contingency, according to Bukharin, the Bolsheviks would have to fight a defensive revolutionary war against the Germans.[32]

M. M. Kharitonov objected to the tendency in Bukharin's draft resolution to treat the European political situation as a uniform whole and to play down the peculiar opportunities afforded in Russia; he also pointed out that, so far from there being certainty that socialist governments would be established in the West, the war might end with 'an imperialist peace'.[33] N. Osinski, like Bukharin on the left of the party, nevertheless objected to Bukharin's refusal to differentiate the respective interests of the richer and the poorer peasants.[34] Lenin, while sharing Osinski's concern intellectually, would surely have approved of Bukharin's tactful reticence. Bukharin, in fact, agreed that 'an imperialist peace' was possible, and sarcastically added that 'our peasant isn't becoming a Left Zimmerwaldist'.[35]

Stalin intervened to defend the Central Committee against more basic opposition. He mentioned that 'certain comrades' still believed it to be 'utopian to raise the question of socialist revolution' in Russia. His reply shows a willingness to confront a problem evaded by Lenin. Why had the strategy of the Bolsheviks changed after the February Revolution? Whereas Lenin had held forth about the era of imperialism and the imminence of European socialist revolution, Stalin addressed the specificity of Russia. A socialist administration, he declared, had been made necessary by the wartime devastation and by the refusal of the Russian bourgeoisie, unlike the bourgeoisie elsewhere, to accept the desirability of state economic regulation; and the high degree of organisation and morale among Russian workers made such an administration feasible at last.[36] In retrospect, this appears a much less light-headed justification for Bolshevism in 1917 than the Europe-centred Marxologisms of Lenin. Stalin stated, more simply, that the country faced ruin; that its present rulers had no solutions; and that the only group with the capacity to do anything was the working class together with other sympathetic groups. Stalin's viewpoint, moreover, was not radically different from the standpoint being supported by increasing numbers of leaders such as Martov on the left of the Menshevik party. Martov, too, could see no salvation coming from further collaboration with the Russian bourgeoisie.[37] On the other hand, Stalin as a Bolshevik did not agree with Martov that there was any point in expending much energy in persuading the centrist and right-wing Mensheviks that an all-socialist government coalition should be formed.

Even Stalin's cautious arguments for a socialist take-over were resisted by N. Angarski, a delegate from Moscow province, who had criticised Lenin at the April Party Conference and who still advocated a return to pre-1917 Bolshevik tenets.[38] The other critics accepted *The April Theses*, but concentrated on the persistent evasiveness of official spokesmen about the party's slogans. Stalin read out the Central Committee's motion 'on the political situation', which called for the abandoning of 'All Power to the Soviets!'. In his accompanying comments, interestingly enough, he still omitted to mention this abandonment – possibly a manifestation of lingering personal doubts. In any event he placed emphasis on the desirability of an alliance between the proletariat and the poorest peasantry.

This vagueness was castigated by Preobrazhenski, who enquired what he meant by 'poor peasants'; and K. K. Yurenev said that Stalin had offered no sensible slogan to replace the previous one.[39] Trying to rescue Stalin, Milyutin suggested a new slogan: 'All power to the proletariat supported by the poorest peasantry and the revolutionary democracy organised into soviets of workers', soldiers' and peasants' deputies'. This was less a slogan than a mini-treatise, and the Congress adjourned until the following morning, 31 July.[40] Stalin reopened the debate in his own right: 'Now we are putting forward the slogan of the transfer of power into the hands of the proletariat and the poorest peasantry.'[41] He was attacked immediately by P. A. Dzhaparidze for ignoring the prospect of socialist revolution in the

1. Lenin in January 1910.

2. Lenin, after release from prison in Poland, August 1914.

3. Aged-looking Lenin goes mountain walking in Galicia, Summer 1914.

4. A rejuvenated Lenin not long before leaving Switzerland for the last time.

5. (*above*) Lenin and his fellow travellers reach Stockholm, April 1917.

6. (*below*) Lenin delivers 'The April Theses', 4 April 1917.

7. Lenin in disguise, July 1917.

8. The Central Committee elected at the Sixth Party Congress.

9. The Military-Revolutionary Committee of the Petrograd Soviet after the October seizure of power.

Отъ Военно - Революціоннаго Комитета при Петроградскомъ Совѣтѣ Рабочихъ и Солдатскихъ Депутатовъ.

Къ Гражданамъ Россіи.

Временное Правительство низложено. Государственная власть перешла въ руки органа Петроградскаго Совѣта Рабочихъ и Солдатскихъ Депутатовъ Военно-Революціоннаго Комитета, стоящаго во главѣ Петроградскаго пролетаріата и гарнизона.

Дѣло, за которое боролся народъ: немедленное предложеніе демократическаго мира, отмѣна помѣщичьей собственности на землю, рабочій контроль надъ производствомъ, созданіе Совѣтскаго Правительства — это дѣло обезпечено.

ДА ЗДРАВСТВУЕТЪ РЕВОЛЮЦІЯ РАБОЧИХЪ, СОЛДАТЪ И КРЕСТЬЯНЪ!

Военно-Революціонный Комитетъ
при Петроградскомъ Совѣтѣ
Рабочихъ и Солдатскихъ Депутатовъ.

25 октября 1917 г. 10 ч. утра.

10. Proclamation of the Provisional Government's overthrow, 25 October 1917.

11. (*left*) Lenin: official portrait, January 1918.

12. (*below*) Lenin and members of the Sovnarkom Coalition.

13. (*above*) Poster including both Lenin and the Mayor of Cork among the seven greatest men in the world.

14. (*left*) Anti-Bolshevik poster saying that 'The Federal Soviet Monarchy' had promised 'Bread, Peace, Freedom' but had given 'Famine, War, The Cheka'.

15. (*left*) The magazine *Punch* considers the Treaty of Brest-Litovsk.

16. (*above*) Lenin goes for a stroll in Moscow, Spring 1918.

A WALK-OVER?

West, and by D. Z. Manuilski for undermining faith in the soviets.[42] V. M. Molotov got to the root of the matter with a statement that was vintage Lenin: 'It is necessary to point out the path for the taking of power into our hands: that is the basic problem.'[43] But no agreed slogan emerged. The Central Committee, for all its confidence, had not come properly prepared to the Congress. Its own members engaged in controversy, with an exasperated Stalin castigating Bukharin for asserting that the peasantry as a whole was in league with the bourgeoisie.[44] The only answer was to choose a commission to compose an acceptable resolution' on the political situation'.[45]

Then came Milyutin's report on the economic situation. It was very pessimistic: 'It is often said to us that we and our slogans are promising to avoid a crisis. That is untrue. We cannot avoid a crisis.'[46] He itemised the problems: food-supplies shortages, transport breakdowns, a lack of regulation of industry, and inflation. Milyutin's measures included action from above and below. A socialist administration would nationalise large-scale enterprises and push other enterprises into forming trusts and syndicates; it would control production and distribution of goods, including foodstuffs. A stronger system of fixed prices would be introduced and profiteering would be eradicated. Power would be given to workforces to supervise the work of their managements. The Provisional Government's method of bargaining with the industrialists and the bankers had not worked. The time had come to give the workers their chance.[47]

Milyutin was convinced that the basic solution to the country's problems lay with the ending of the war and the reorientation of industry to civilian production so as to draw the peasantry back into the marketplace.[48] In the meantime Russia was 'on the eve of famine'.[49] D. P. Bogolepov agreed, but concluded that sterner measures were therefore required 'right through to the introduction of famine communism'.[50] He failed to specify what such measures might involve. Osinski wanted more fundamental reforms; and yet he also objected to the slogan of governmental control over production since such control would be dangerous if exercised not by the Bolsheviks but by Kerenski.[51] Other speakers too thought that the severity of the economic crisis called for an expansion of the party's objectives. Milyutin defended himself: 'So has our slogan "Land to the peasantry" become outmoded? Of course not. In just the same way many of our economic measures have not become outmoded.'[52]

But he agreed that a greater specificity about Bolshevik economic projects was essential.[53] The debate ended with Milyutin's motion being taken as the basis for the Congress resolution. It had been notable for Milyutin's difficulties with the left wing of the party, difficulties which would become acute in the winter ahead. It was also remarkable for its tacit confirmation that Lenin's land nationalisation proposal, which had been accepted by the Seventh Party Congress in April, should be dropped. No delegate even mentioned it. The Central Committee, as Stalin and Milyutin had intimated, had for months been using slogans which simply urged the transfer of the land to the peasantry.[54]

After a day's break, the proceedings were resumed on 2 August to discuss the party rules.[55] Time was running out and the delegates agreed that the revision of the party programme would have to be postponed until the Seventh Party Congress.[56] Bukharin presented the motion on 'the current moment and the war' which had been agreed by a Congress commission. He had been forced to make concessions. Originally, he had said that the entire petit bourgeoisie had supported Kerenski's aggressive foreign and military policy; now he stated (but did he really agree?) that only 'the upper layers of the petite bourgeoisie and the peasantry' gave that support. He had also been persuaded to introduce a more cautious formulation on revolutionary war: the first version had proposed a defensive revolutionary war if a war of attack proved impossible; the second declared merely that a socialist administration would confront 'the task of rendering every kind of support, including armed support, for the militant proletariat of other countries'.[57]

The Central Committee debate in January 1918 was to show that Bukharin was stepping on the throat of his opinions at the Congress.[58] But the remaining discussions were swiftly expedited. Milyutin's economic resolution was accepted, and Glebov-Avilov delivered a report on the trade unions. A feeling of expectancy grew as Stalin rose to present the Congress commission's resolution 'on the political situation'. Its main interest was the choice of a new official slogan for the party: 'the complete liquidation of the dictatorship of the counter-revolutionary bourgeoisie'.[59] While most delegates concurred with the dropping of the slogan of 'All Power to the Soviets', I. T. Smilga thought Stalin's proposed replacement was too negative and vague; and the Congress passed his amendment which added a phrase declaring that only a revolution of the proletariat with the support of poor peasants was capable of accomplishing the removal of the so-called bourgeois 'dictatorship'.[60] Stalin's last point emphasised the need for 'a seizure of state power'. But this, too, drew criticism. Preobrazhenski wanted to specify that the movement towards socialism in Russia was dependent on 'proletarian revolution in the West'. Stalin, with the Congress behind him, retorted that such an idea underestimated what could be achieved in Russia on the country's own resources.[61] Here Lenin would probably have sympathised with Preobrazhenski's basic point. Stalin's later advocacy of 'socialism in one country' was being broached in a sketchy manner even before the October Revolution.

The Congress elected a Central Committee. Only four of the twenty names were made public; concern about security remained and the party reverted to pre-1917 conspiratorial precautions. All these four were in hiding or in prison: Lenin, Zinoviev, Kamenev and Trotski.[62] The election of leaders who perforce could not attend meetings was not only a break with convention but also a sign of their prestige in the party. Trotski, who had only recently become a Bolshevik, now joined the central party leadership. Yet the most vital change in the Central Committee's composition went unnoticed at the time. The Bolshevik right, which had been strongly represented in the central party body after the Seventh Conference in April, had lost ground.[63] Only five Central Committee members were definitely rightists: L. B. Kamenev, V. P. Milyutin, V. P. Nogin, A. I. Rykov and G. E. Zinoviev. As Lenin put his thoughts in order for a seizure of power and for a programme of social and economic reforms, he could look to a more receptive set of colleagues than he had possessed since entering the politics of Russian Marxism.

KERENSKI AND KORNILOV

Despite the dispute over slogans, no Bolshevik at the Congress gave the impression of expecting to take power in the immediate future. If Lenin had been there, things might have been different. Possibly; but delegates were more fearful about the party's prospects of survival than intent on planning Kerenski's overthrow. This situation changed later in August 1917. Kerenski had put together a second coalition cabinet on 25 July, containing a majority of socialist ministers for the first time. For Lenin, this proved conclusively that the Mensheviks and Socialist Revolutionaries were collaborating with the forces of counter-revolution.[64] Kerenski's policies, even though Lenin exaggerated, undoubtedly moved rightwards. The peasants, while being appeased by a doubling of state-imposed grain prices in August, were warned that no solution to the 'land question' would be permitted until the Constituent Assembly's convocation. Groups of gentry landowners, moreover, had been formed to preempt the popular challenge to the existing agrarian order.[65] Kerenski refused to promise autonomy to non-Russian areas of the old empire and spared no effort to convince the urban middle and upper classes that the Provisional Government intended to quell unrest among the working class. In foreign policy, the Allies were told that the Russian commitment to winning the War was undiminished. The policies of the Lvov cabinet survived under Kerenski. Chernov, the Socialist-Revolutionary leader, was finally disillusioned and resigned as Minister of Agriculture in late August. With his departure there vanished any slight evidence of the Provisional Government accommodating itself to the aspirations of workers, peasants and soldiers; the field of political agitation was cleared for the Bolsheviks.[66]

Kerenski, as Lenin continually asserted, relied on military support to reimpose the cabinet's will in Petrograd. There were risks in following this course. Hoping to terminate the Provisional Government's isolation, Kerenski convoked a 'State Conference' in Moscow on 12 August. The Conference was attended by an array of public groups: the cabinet; the political parties; the army high command; deputies of the pre-revolutionary Dumas; the soviets, trade unions and co-operatives. The sole major omission from the list of participants was the Bolshevik party.[67].

This was an appalling time for Kerenski. On 21 August, the city of Riga fell to the Germans, pushing the Eastern front to within six hundred kilometres of the Russian capital. No positive consequence, furthermore, flowed from the State Conference; and, from Kerenski's standpoint, much harm ensued. The problem was the truculent posture of Commander-in-Chief, Lavr Kornilov. His presence in Moscow was accompanied by right-wing demands that Kerenski should take a hard line with the soviets; rumours grew that army officers were planning to place Kornilov in power.[68] Discussions were held between Kerenski and Kornilov about Petrograd. With Kerenski's consent, Kornilov began to move regiments from the Eastern front to the capital; but confusion thereupon intervened between Kerenski and Kornilov, being aggravated by the mischief of their aides. On 28 August Kerenski panicked, fearing that Kornilov might be plotting a *coup d'état*. There is no proof that this was true. And yet Kornilov's demeanour had constituted a menace to any government failing to do what he thought was patriotically necessary. At any rate Kornilov disobeyed Kerenski's order which countermanded the transfer of troops to Petrograd. Rebellion had broken out, and Kornilov continued to move on the capital. The fate of both the cabinet and the soviets hung in the balance.[69] The immediate effect was to compel Kerenski to muster support not only from Mensheviks and Socialist Revolutionaries but also from Bolsheviks. The military forces available to the Provisional Government could not halt Kornilov. Only agitators despatched to mingle with Kornilov's troops were able to prevent a coup. By 2 September, to the capital's relief, Kornilov was under house arrest. The Bolshevik Central Committee was cock-a-hoop. A counter-revolutionary mutiny had restored them to free activity in the capital; the sole major Bolshevik who could not afford to appear in the open was Lenin. In fact, the obstacles to the party's activities had never been so great elsewhere as in Petrograd. But the relief that the struggle for power in Petrograd could occur without harassment was cause for celebration.[70]

Lenin, analysing the events as reported in the press, swung between interpretations. Sometimes he described Kerenski as the puppet of the counter-revolution; but he also occasionally portrayed him as a putative Russian Bonaparte who had succeeded in strengthening his personal rule while politics in the capital remained tensely balanced among the various political and military groups.[71] Both versions had an element of truth, but an even larger element of inaccuracy. The authority of Kerenski and his cabinet never recovered from the Kornilov revolt. The detestation of Kadet leaders for the Kerenski cabinet had been obvious throughout the summer. Lenin's claim that Milyukov colluded with the Kornilov revolt has not been corroborated;[72] but it was widely believed that he expected a coup and would give it his approval. Kerenski's relations with the Kadet party deteriorated sharply in September. Accordingly, Kerenski badly needed to mend his fences with the Mensheviks and Socialist Revolutionaries in the soviets. The Provisional Government's desire to legitimate its position was intense. Remembering the fiasco of the State Conference, Kerenski announced the calling of a Democratic Conference which would include all parties and mass organisations to the left of the Kadets. The rising influence of the Mensheviks and the Socialist Revolutionaries induced even Lenin to raise, on 1

September, the question of whether a peaceful development of the revolution was possible. In an article, 'On Compromises', he suggested that the Bolsheviks might drop their ideas about a violent seizure of power if the Mensheviks and Socialist Revolutionaries would agree to take power for themselves in the name of the soviets. The Bolsheviks would then promise to avoid violence and try to obtain power from their rivals by the strength of their persuasion.[73] Lenin noted that peaceful revolutions, while being rare, were not inconceivable.[74] It was an intriguing phase in Lenin's career. Was he sincere in offering a truce to his fellow socialists? It is possible, but not certain, that his reconsiderations reflected his true feelings. Nevertheless, the feelings were insecure. 'On Compromises' contained a long post-script, written on 3 September, which contended that 'the offer of a compromise had already been outdated' by events.[75] Even so, he still toyed for a few more days with the feasibility of a peaceful political development of the revolution. Other articles written in the first two weeks of September gave no definitive indication for or against.[76]

Lenin, in short, was wavering. But not for long. By 12 September he was writing 'The Bolsheviks Must Seize Power' and demanded an immediate uprising; and, on 14 September, he repeated this call in 'Marxism and Insurrection';[77] both documents were letters addressed to the Central Committee. The 'compromise' offered by him had never been innocent of violent implications. If the Mensheviks and Socialist Revolutionaries were going to take power, they could hardly expect Kerenski to withdraw without a fight. Thus the 'peaceful development' of the revolution sketched by Lenin would have started only after a violent phase had been endured. But now he shrugged off restraint. He had tacitly abandoned his previous denial that he would take power without having secured majorities in revolutionary mass organisations. From mid-September he urged his party to seize power and acquire formal popular sanction only afterwards. His first justification was that both the Petrograd and Moscow Soviets had acquired Bolshevik working majorities earlier in the month.[78] He also asserted that Kerenski was planning to surrender Petrograd to the Germans and would hold negotiations with them for a separate peace on the Eastern front. Above all, he maintained: 'On our side is the majority of *the class* – the vanguard of the revolution, the vanguard of the people – which is capable of attracting the masses. On our side is the *majority* of the people since Chernov's departure is far from being the only sign but is rather the most obvious and glaring sign that the peasantry won't receive the land from the Socialist-Revolutionary bloc (or from the Socialist Revolutionaries).'[79] This last point was unbuttressed by factual references. He did not pause to examine the Central Committee's likely reaction. The two letters were literary steamrollers. The Central Committee, in any case, did not receive them until 15 September.[80] Meanwhile, on 13 September, the central party newspaper (which had been renamed *Worker's Path*) continued to call for an agreement between the Bolsheviks and the Mensheviks and Socialist Revolutionaries.[81] The Central Committee met on the same day to consider the party's tactics for the opening session of the Democratic Conference the following day.[82] Kamenev and Trotski, who had both been released from prison, were nominated as Bolshevik spokesmen and required to demand the removal of Kerenski and the installation of a government composed entirely of socialists.[83]

Lenin, however, now demanded a Bolshevik-led insurrection and no longer contemplated an interim period of government by the Mensheviks and the Socialist Revolutionaries. Trotski, too, was moving towards such a standpoint and earned a plaudit from Lenin for the taunts he flung at the non-Bolshevik socialists at the Democratic Conference: 'Bravo, comrade Trotski!'[84] But even Trotski believed that insurrection could not immediately be undertaken, and the Central Committee as a whole resisted Lenin's proposal. On 15 September, its members met to consider his two letters. Both were treated as documents which might endanger the party's very existence if they fell into the hands of the authorities. It was as if Lenin had been the boss of a gang intent on robbing a bank who had incautiously confided his intentions to paper – his fellow gang-members wished to destroy the incriminating evidence. Efforts were undertaken to discover and obliterate all but the copies in the hands of the Central Committee Secretariat.[85] Lenin's discomfiture was emphasised on 16 September by the publication of an article in *Worker's Path*, 'The Russian Revolution and Civil War', which had been written in the brief phase of his support for inter-party compromise.[86] Thus the Central Committee deftly used the prestige and authority of 'Lenin' to oppose Lenin. Its members rejected as sheer madness his notion that Bolshevik delegates to the Democratic Conference should walk out, travel to the gates of factories and barracks in the capital and organise an uprising without delay.[87]

Lenin's tactical acumen waxed and waned in 1917; it was eclipsed for a time in late September. It was great good fortune for the party that their leader and his acknowledged powers of cajolement were safely removed to Finland. A September Revolution, taking place before the party held many soviets in Russia, would have been a disaster for Bolshevism.[88] A successful revolutionary needs to be impatient and demanding; but a certain self-control is also required. Time was really on the Bolshevik party's side. Martov and the Menshevik-Internationalists and the Left Socialist Revolutionaries had already moved towards accepting the need for an exclusively socialist government to be formed.[89] Having been annoyed with Kerenski in July for his repressiveness, they had become even more enraged since the Kornilov revolt and the Democratic Conference with his powerlessness. Their own parties had helped to create problems for him. The Democratic Conference, meeting between 14 and 20 September, had been unable to agree whether the Kadets should be invited to join the Mensheviks and Socialist Revolutionaries in the next coalition government.[90]

Ostensibly this indecisiveness gave Kerenski free rein; and on 27 September he introduced a new cabinet including representatives from all those parties. But his practical authority was reduced. The Democratic Conference had established from its own midst a Council of the Republic (or 'Pre-Parliament'). Its powers in relation to the Provisional Government were to be solely advisory, but Kerenski could not feel able to act independently of its wishes in October. Such institutional factors none the less counted for less in the Provisional Government's decline than the general erosion of its authority in the country as a whole. The Cabinet's ability to call in the assistance from the generals on the Eastern front had been damaged by Kerenski's behaviour towards Kornilov; and it was scarcely wise to transfer soldiers from the trenches when the German troops had so recently rampaged along the Baltic littoral. In addition, Kerenski knew that his reputation with the conscripts at the front was as low as it had long been with the Petrograd garrison.[91] Nor were expeditionary units available from the Allies. Local government in many towns and cities, moreover, was already in the hands of the soviets even where a formal declaration of 'soviet power' had not occurred. Through the first weeks of October there was a series of victories for the Bolsheviks in elections to the various mass organisations. Soviets, trade unions and factory-workshop committees were falling into their control. This was especially obvious in northern and central Russia; but the pattern was also beginning to be observable elsewhere.[92]

To be sure, these pro-Bolshevik voters were not wholly conscious of the nature of Bolshevism; and, outside Russia and the Russian-dominated cities in the peripheral regions of the old empire, direct support for the party was minuscule. Lenin's affirmation that 'the majority of the people' favoured the Bolsheviks lacked cogency. And yet the majority was indubitably antagonistic to the Provisional Government. The Bolsheviks were continuing to work with the grain of popular grievances, and Lenin correctly discerned that the opposition to the installation of a socialist government would not be robust.

This perception drew strength from developments in society and the economy. Inflation mounted. Foreign loans were unobtainable; Russia's Allies thought their money was best put to use in financing their own armies. Transport difficulties grew more serious. Supplies of raw material to factories shrank fast: coal output fell by 27 per cent between January and August 1917; and factories received less than two-fifths of their needs in pig-iron as early as April.[93] Manufacturing industry collapsed. Profits were tightly squeezed, bankruptcies were frequent. Workers used their freedom to strike; but the danger of forced redundancy was driving them to other forms of struggle. In Petrograd there were a few takeovers of enterprises by their workforces to pre-empt attempts by owners to closedown operations. This saved jobs, but did not halt the decline in real wages. Moreover, the poor in the towns faced a winter of starvation. Food supplies in the eight months of the Provisional Government were only 48 per cent of the country's officially-calculated requirements.[94] The Menshevik and Socialist Revolutionaries in the provinces still held most soviets. Workers and soldiers turned to other mass organisations for more radical solutions. Hostility to the Kerenski cabinet was focused on trade unions and factory-workshop committees (as well as suburb soviets). Nor were the peasants quiescent. Land seizures had occurred as early as March 1917, and the number rose steadily through to July.[95] There was then a decline in such expropriations; but the government's writ was never the less ignored as the village land communes exerted their influence: it was a rare landlord who stayed behind on his estate to risk the wrath of his peasants.

Lenin's insistence that time was not on the side of the Bolshevik party is therefore hard to explain. Kerenski's days were numbered.

Lenin suggested that a further Kornilovite coup attempt could be in the offing; he also maintained that Kerenski would deliberately hand the country over to the Germans. These allegations remained unsubstantiated. Why, then, the urgency of the call to insurrection? We can only guess about Lenin's motives. He was probably showing the effects of having been in hiding for several months. He was frustrated: he wanted to be centrally involved, he wanted to do something. Lenin wanted a revolution and, surely, he wanted it on his own terms. He knew that the idea of a post-Kerenski socialist coalition was gaining in popularity among Mensheviks and Socialist-Revolutionaries. He had already mentally rejected all but the left wings of these two rival parties as potential collaborators; and he did not want to moderate his policies in the compromises needed inside a coalition with Tsereteli and Chernov. He needed 'his' revolution to take place before the Mensheviks and Socialist Revolutionaries officially advocated the formation of a socialist coalition ministry. If he was to succeed, he had to act fast.

'THE STATE AND REVOLUTION'

Lenin's hardheaded campaign for what he saw as his party's interests was one aspect of a multifaceted political personality. He was also a theorist, and wanted to put down a general statement on the nature of socialist revolution. The result was his treatise on *The State and Revolution*. Since it remained unpublished until 1918, the book did not and could not have shaped events before the October Revolution; but its ideas reveal the contours of mind of the man who helped to instigate the seizure of power. On every page his sincere disgust with the nature of capitalism was abundantly evident. *The State and Revolution* was the most refined embodiment of Lenin's strategy for the carrying through of a socialist transformation in modern industrial societies.

Written in the weeks of hiding in Finland, the book was planned to have seven brief chapters. It contained somewhat fewer than thirty thousand words and was a feat of rapid literary labour. The contents amounted to a co-ordination and explication of the textual data collected in the notes on Marxism and the state taken before the February Revolution. He had continued with the research after the July Days, requesting copies of Marx and Engels's *Communist Manifesto* and Marx's *The Poverty of Philosophy* to be sent out to him.[96] His basic thinking had largely been done in Switzerland. The novelty was to have been constituted by chapter seven, dealing with the Russian revolutionary process in 1917. But only six chapters were written. As the author festively explained in his postscript, he had been weighed down by 'the encumbrance' of assisting with the October Revolution.[97] Lenin had always intended to present himself as a mere re-teller of the original Marxian story, and the absence of the projected last chapter reinforced the work's exegetical character. Thus the first chapter resumed the writings of Marx and Engels on the nature of the state. As Lenin pointed out, Marxism's co-founders believed that every society since the ending of ancient communism had been divided into rival classes. Harmony among them had never been possible, and the structure of economic power had always led to the emergence of a ruling class (or classes). This power required political self-expression. The ruling class consolidated its position by creating and controlling its own state apparatus, and deployed it against all internal and external threats. Revolutionaries could not expect to come to power peacefully. Violent overthrows, as Engels had written in his *Anti-Dühring*, would be the norm.[98]

Lenin's second chapter discussed the viewpoint of Marx and Engels on the revolutionary upsurge across Europe in 1848–51. Their *Communist Manifesto* contained a summons to the proletariat to turn itself into 'a ruling class'. Marx's *The Eighteenth Brumaire of Louis Bonaparte* emphasised the need to smash the existing state 'machine'.[99] Lenin tossed these citations in the face of Karl Kautsky. How on earth could a Marxist, he asked, believe that the civil service and the standing army under the capitalist order was politically neutral? Would they not associate themselves with the status quo? Had not Kautsky exaggerated the tension between 'the bourgeois state' and the middle classes?[100]

The third chapter focused on Marx's writings on the Paris Commune of 1871. Marx had stated in *The Civil War In France* that 'the working class cannot simply take charge of the state machine ready-made and set it in motion for its own particular objectives'; and, in a letter to L. Kugelmann at the time of the Commune, he had stressed the need 'to smash' the existing 'bureaucratic-military machine'.[101] The Paris Commune, for Marx, embodied the political framework required 'to eliminate not only the monarchical form of class domination but even class domination as such'. Lenin retailed the characteristics approved by Marx. These included the abolition of a standing army and its replacement by the people under arms; the disbandment of the police; the introduction of the elective principle to the civil service and the right of electors to insist on the immediate recall of officials and representatives. No official, moreover, would be paid more than the average worker's wage.[102] Marx, as Lenin explained, did not intend the new institutions to work like parliaments with their lengthy gaps between elections and their separation of legislative from executive organs. Instead, he wanted a 'working corporation', and Lenin perceived this fundamentally as a plea for mass participation in public life.[103]

How had such a proposal become realistic? Lenin's answer was that modern capitalism had simplified the functions of administration. Large-scale factories, railways, postal services and telephones had put the running of the state within the range of the abilities of 'all literate people' (or to 'townspeople in general'). The need for a specialised and privileged bureaucracy had disappeared. State functions were now reducible to 'the simplest operations of registration, recording and checking'.[104] It would be a retrograde action to place the new structure on federal foundations. Centralism, as Marx had repeatedly stated in criticism of the French socialist P. J. Proudhon, was more efficient.[105]

The result of the establishment of the dictatorship of the proletariat would be the beginning of the movement towards the end of the need for a state at all. As every citizen became involved in public affairs, so the dawn of communism would draw nearer.[106] By any standard this was hyper-confidence; the return to Russia in 1917 had reinforced his sanguine earlier hopes as articulated in 'Marxism on the State'. The fourth chapter dealt with Engels's elaboration of such ideas. Lenin noted the *Anti-Dühring*'s notion that the state would eventually 'wither away'.[107] This, however, was not a relapse into anarchism. Lenin reproduced the arguments of Marx and Engels in the 1870s against contemporary anarchists. The ultimate Marxist objective was a state-free society; but Lenin maintained that the transition from capitalism to communism required an intermediate stage of socialism which would be inaugurated by the formation of a socialist state: the dictatorship of the proletariat.[108] Marx's attacks on anarchism had led Karl Kautsky and others to treat the state as a permanent feature of human society. Lenin repudiated this, drawing attention to Engels's letter to the German social-democratic leader August Bebel in March 1875. Engels had argued that the Paris Commune constituted a form of rule which lacked qualities characteristic of previous states; and that it was better described as a *Gemeinwesen* (which was the German equivalent of the French *commune*).[109] Thus Engels admired the Paris Commune partly because of its statelike features and partly because it appeared as a possible mode for the eventual 'withering away' of the state as such.[110]

As a Marxist, Lenin wanted to examine 'the economic foundations' for this withering away. His fifth chapter castigated 'capitalist democracy' as 'truncated, squalid, false' on the grounds that it was 'democracy only for the insignificant minority, for the rich'.[111] His supportive points were few; but he mentioned both the various limitations on parliamentary suffrage, especially the non-enfranchisement of women, and 'the purely capitalist organisation of the daily press'.[112] This was argumentative brevity taken to an extreme. Lenin's allegations of financial corruption and political manipulativeness were cogent; and an ampler indication of the collusion between governmental ministers, industrial magnates and press barons would have bolstered his case considerably. But Lenin was writing for Marxists, who needed no persuasion on such issues. He flatly declared that the dictatorship of the proletariat would rid the great mass of the population of exploitation and oppression. Complete freedom would not exist until communism itself had been attained; but the dictatorship would not last forever, and eventually the state itself would disappear and a communist society would emerge: from each according to his talents, to each according to his needs.[113]

In the sixth chapter Lenin turned to the reasons why, in his view, Marxian ideas on state and revolution had previously been misunderstood by Marxists. He was offering his book as a work of explication, not of theoretical inventiveness. Among his main purposes was a desire to demonstrate his own ideological authenticity as a Marxist. Reviewing the controversies between Karl Kautsky and Eduard Bernstein in the 1890s, Lenin pointed out that Kautsky had expressly refused to engage in debate about 'the problem of the proletarian dictatorship'. Again in 1902, in *The Social Revolution*, Kautsky had avoided the topic.[114] According to Lenin, Kautsky had perennially overlooked the crucial aim of destroying the state. This naturally raised the question of why Lenin had not criticised such alleged neglect before 1914. Lenin replied that Kautsky had at least adhered to basic Marxist standpoints until 1914, particularly the idea that 'the revolutionary era was beginning' (which appeared in *The Path To Power* in 1909).[115] On the other hand, Lenin recognised that Anton Pannekoek, Rosa Luxemburg and Karl Radek had convincingly exposed Kautsky's 'passive radicalism' before the war.[116] Kautsky had objected to Pannekoek's call for the elimination of a professional civil service. For Lenin, this had come to demonstrate Kautsky's lack of understanding that a socialist political order would be based on the model of the Paris Commune and would dispense altogether with the need for a 'bureaucracy'.[117]

At this point Lenin stressed his own theme, stating that Pannekoek's writings suffered 'from imprecision and insufficient concreteness'.[118] This was a reference to the absence of a description of the 'dictatorship of the proletariat' in general and the soviets in particular. It also made Lenin's *State and Revolution* seem more original than it was. Bukharin's name was not mentioned even though his wartime reconsiderations of Marxism had been influential in leading Lenin to the basis of his new contentions.[119]

Lenin and Bukharin continued to have their disagreements about revolutionary strategy, but no direct discussion of *The State and Revolution* ensued between them.[120] Non-Bolsheviks felt no such inhibition. Kautsky and Martov attacked the book robustly; their remarks were all the more interesting inasmuch as both were Marxists and shared many of Lenin's intellectual premises. They rejected *The State and Revolution*'s claim to orthodoxy.[121] Kautsky questioned whether Marx, when he mentioned 'the dictatorship of the proletariat', was referring to a specific form of rule. Did Marx aim at the suspension of universal civic freedoms? Did he oppose a general suffrage? Kautsky's answer was a resounding no. He asserted that Marx conceived of the dictatorship as a general political 'condition' rather than a specific political technique, and that a Marxian dictatorship would simply allow the proletariat to pursue its interests without impediment. It would not involve the disenfranchisement of other social groups. On the contrary, since the proletariat and the rest of the exploited population would be a massive majority there could be no excuse for fearing the electoral menace posed by the middle classes.[122] Martov, agreeing with Kautsky's basic analysis of the attitudes of Marx and Engels, supplied a close examination of their texts. He emphasised that Marx's *Civil War In France* involved approval of the universal-suffrage arrangements of the Paris Commune;[123] and that Engels's introduction to the 1891 edition of the same work had described these arrangements as being among the Commune's 'infallible methods'.[124]

Martov's examination of such texts matched Lenin in exegetical skill. This was an important accomplishment since *The State and*

Revolution was aimed at arrogating exclusive Marxist orthodoxy for its author. Martov delighted in exposing Lenin's sleights of hand. A crucial example was Lenin's suggestion that Engels had endorsed a democratic republic as an objective solely on the grounds that it provided 'the shortest way which leads to the dictatorship of the proletariat'.[125] Engels, as Martov's lengthy quotation indicated, indicated no such thing. The passage contained no reference to an ensuing dictatorship.[126] Martov and Kautsky had proved that Lenin's interpretation of Marx was not watertight. This is not to say that their own interpretations were correct. Kautsky, bending over in the opposite direction, overstated the commitment of Marxism's co-founders to democratic procedures.[127] Martov's treatment was more complex since he was more willing to discern changes in Marx's thought (whereas Lenin, devoted disciple of Marx, took it as axiomatic that his master's thought exhibited undeviating, progressive development). For example, Martov stressed that Marx's advocacy of locally-based communes in 1871 was aberrant from his normal standpoint, and that it contradicted his more typical ridiculing of such opinions as mere anarchism of the type propounded by Proudhon.[128] No doubt Martov underplayed Marx's long-standing interest in popular and local self-emancipation (as opposed to emancipation through a centralist state); but it is equally arguable that Lenin overestimated the continuity between the 'statism' of *The Communist Manifesto* with the anti-statism of *The Civil War In France*.[129] Above all, Martov and Kautsky were right that Marx did not state that the proletarian 'dictatorship' would typically involve disenfranchisement of non-proletarians.[130] Both felt that Lenin's raucous claims to 'orthodoxy' were therefore illegitimate. The reverential tone of his references to Marx and Engels did not prevent them from affirming that the true precedents for his attitude were non-Marxist. Wilhelm Weitling in Germany and Louis-Auguste Blanqui in France were picked out for their dictatorial inclinations.[131]

They might also have mentioned the Russian agrarian socialist Petr Tkachev.[132] But Martov and Kautsky were fair-minded pole-micists and presumably they recognised that *The State and Revolution*, unlike anything composed by Tkachev, at least empha-sised the need for mass political support and participation in the making of revolutions. His book was far from being a summons to conspiracy and élitism. Indeed, Lenin saw himself as offering a vision of a totally harmonious and self-regulating society which was realisable within a not too lengthy period; and he anticipated a more or less easy, trouble-free socialist revolution.[133]

His non-Bolshevik critics, however, did not limit themselves to Marxology. Kautsky drew attention to the large proportion of the population even in an advanced capitalist country such as Germany which would lose civic rights under the dispensation of Lenin's recommendations; he questioned whether the level of repression could ever be as low, under such circumstances, as Lenin claimed.[134] Martov took another approach. Starting from Lenin's assumption that the proletariat would constitute the immense majority in a society undergoing a socialist revolution, he asked what there would be to fear from allowing the supposedly tiny middle-class minority to continue to vote (especially if Lenin was sincere in saying that such a revolution was inconceivable unless mass popular support already existed).[135] Martov and Kautsky saw the protection of the rights of minorities as a vital safeguard against abuses of power.[136] As practical political analysts, history has shown them to have been true prophets in this regard. Moreover, Lenin's two antagonists did not share the unargued premise of his book that each class would gravitate permanently towards support for a single party. The State and Revolution did not mention parties at all; and Kautsky and Martov were introducing data from 1918, when a one-party state became an enduring phenomenon in Russia.[137] But Kautsky was justified in saying that the existence of a plurality of parties permits a diversity of opinion and interests to be represented more easily and that suppression of competing parties is bound to diffuse authoritarian abuses throughout the political and social order.[138] Furthermore, Martov had a sound point when he stated that no working class is devoid of differentiated immediate interests.[139]

Lenin very probably had no conscious intention that a socialist dictatorship should undertake a large-scale and bloody repression; but this only serves to demonstrate the facile quality of his thinking: the objective likelihood of such a dictatorship having to turn to terrorist methods in order to sustain its power was strong. The State and Revolution was reticent on the point. But his other writings in 1917, especially as regards the future governance of Russia, revealed an abiding fascination with terror as a technique of rule.

Other gaps in the book's argumentation existed. Lenin failed, for example, to explain how the local soviets would interact with central soviet organs after the revolution. He simply asserted that harmony would prevail.[140] Nor did he give his reasons for supposing that the fusion of legislative, executive and judicial institutions in the new socialist state would be more just and efficient than the separate institutions were in democratic capitalist states. He merely scoffed at the very idea that parliaments could be 'working' organs and moved on to other topics.[141] This is not to claim that Western parliamentary democracies always embody a just and efficient system of rule in every way; but the point at issue is that Lenin's alternative does not seem inherently more just or more efficient even from a theoretical standpoint. Nowhere was his naïveté more obvious than in his treatment of administration. He argued that the tasks of running a modern capitalist society were becoming ever simpler. Professional experts would need to be retained only temporarily. Literate ordinary workers, Lenin maintained, could take over these tasks with ease. In fact, the need for experts, as contemporary sociologists such as Max Weber and Roberto Michels affirmed, does not diminish with the onset of industrialisation. Rather, it increases.[142] If anything, the administrators of yesteryear were amateurs in comparison with the professionals of today. The days are gone when British under-graduates with an ability to translate Shakespeare into Greek iambics were expected to have all the necessary skills to administer a modern state. Technological inventions expand the number of fulfillable tasks and the speed of their fulfilment: they do not dispense with the necessity for specialisation.

It is not sensible to assume, as Lenin did, that administrators can be prevented from forming themselves into a corporate group (or into groups) simply by insisting on electivity, on the right of instant recall and on payment at a worker's rate. Administrators, by virtue of their job and training, tend to comprehend and manipulate political systems better than 'ordinary' people'; and the scarcity-value of their skills usually enables them to obtain a level of remuneration higher than that enjoyed by the mass of waged people. Kautsky put it in a nutshell when he retorted to Lenin that classes can rule but cannot govern; and that mass participatory democracy is utopian.[143]

POLITICAL PROJECTS

The State and Revolution was an attempt at grand theory. Yet what was the relationship between such theory and subsequent Russian history? Many have argued that Lenin's book was a calculated deception inasmuch as he had no intention of trying to establish mass participatory democracy: he was not so huge a hypocrite. Several political leaders who knew him intimately, including Yuli Martov, implied that the first person he deceived was Vladimir Ilich Ulyanov-Lenin. Some writers have argued that *The State and Revolution* is therefore best regarded as a libertarian tract. In their opinion, the repression and civil war after 1917 constituted a clean break by Lenin with the tenets of his book; and it is often stressed that Lenin the libertarian in any case was a temporary aberration from a pattern of thinking that was characteristically authoritarian. Yet Kautsky and Martov pointed out that many aspects of *The State and Revolution* were bound to lead to violent conflict if implemented.[144]

Even they presented too straightforward a picture. For they overlooked another side of *The State and Revolution*: its many internal contradictions. Lenin dreamed about locally-based mass self-emancipation while also anticipating a future socialist economy which would be 'organised like a postal service', such as he had witnessed in Switzerland.[145] He did not see that the vision of mass initiative and discussion and the vision of rigid hierarchy and order were at variance with one another. Lenin's offering was a strange concoction. It was the utopian expression of a utopian mind, and its results were likely to involve large-scale bloodshed even though its author probably did not consciously intend this. It was also a half-baked intellectual product. The cook had yet to decide which ingredients were to be given the greatest weight and importance in the final dish.[146] A further complication is that the book had all industrialised countries as its subject. Russia was not the exclusive focus; and, when he started taking notes on socialist revolution in January 1917, Lenin must have had Germany more firmly in mind than his native land. *The State and Revolution* was meant to be about an entire epoch in future world history. Lenin did not specifically state that his book was intended as a blueprint for the immediate future of Russian politics (even though many scholars have treated it simply as such).[147] But he did not specifically dissociate it from Russia's future either. As is true of many other areas of this thought in 1917, he left no very clear opinion to posterity.[148]

Even so, there was an obvious need for him to say to his followers what kind of state he wanted to establish at home once he came to power. In *The State and Revolution* he had referred repeatedly to 'the dictatorship of the proletariat'. All therefore knew of Lenin's intentions with the utmost clarity. Or did they? In the first place, of course, *The State and Revolution* appeared only in 1918.[149] Secondly, Lenin's other writings in 1917 usually avoided suggesting that 'the proletariat' should hold exclusive power.

He knew only too well that the old Russian empire's population was constituted predominantly by peasants, and wished as a Marxist theorist to take account of the fact. Already, in mid-March 1917, Lenin had been urging that 'power in the state should belong not to the gentry and the capitalists but to *the workers and the poorest peasants*'.[150] By April he was demanding government by 'the proletarians and the semi-proletarians';[151] and in May he rephrased this as 'the proletariat supported by the semi-proletarians'.[152] In July he called for power to be transferred 'into the hands of the proletariat supported by the poorest peasantry'.[153] But there was no fixed terminological pattern, and Lenin sometimes reverted to the formulas he had evolved in the spring.[154] He also occasionally employed, even for Russia, the fundamental notion of 'the dictatorship of the revolutionary proletariat'.[155] But from September 1917 he tended to enunciate a demand for 'the dictatorship of the proletariat and the poorest peasants', and it was mainly variations on this gruesome and cumbersome formula which were used by him through to the October Revolution.[156] Consequently, the proposition that Lenin throughout 1917 starkly and regularly advocated 'a dictatorship of the proletariat' to his party and its supporters is incorrect.[157]

This topic would have little more than a Marxological antiquarian interest if it were not for the curious chronology of his statements. For he barely ever used the term 'dictatorship' in public from the end of April until the end of August.[158] It was probably Kornilov's revolt that made him less restrained. The threat of a right-wing military dictatorship may well have made him feel that the concept of a socialist dictatorship, which would impose 'order' and 'control' over the middle classes, might have become more respectable amidst Bolshevik activists; and possibly Kornilovism convinced even him more strongly that dictatorial methods would be needed. The second point is that Lenin apparently made only eight explicit references to dictatorship from the start of September through to 25 October[159] – not a enormous number in view of the topic's importance.

In addition, all those references occurred in the carefully-composed prose of Bolshevik newspaper articles and pamphlets.[160] Fair enough: what other options of communication were open to a Lenin in hiding? Yet the result was that the great mass of workers and peasants outside the Bolshevik party can scarcely have known about his full range of plans. This can hardly have been fortuitous; Lenin cannot have wanted to upset popular sensibilities unnecessarily, and the virtues of dictatorship would not automatically have commended themselves to the Russian working class. Not only Lenin but also the other Bolshevik leaders in the central (and presumably also local) newspapers seldom described their prospective administration as a 'dictatorship'. The Central Committee's advice to Bolsheviks campaigning for election to the soviets, published in *Pravda* on 7 May 1917, was simply to call for 'all power to the soviets'.[161] Stalin's writings do not mention dictatorship.[162] Nor do those of Trotski or Bukharin or Zinoviev.[163] And Lenin himself, on the few occasions when he advocated socialist dictatorship, framed his arguments very carefully. Typically, he would assert a desire to emulate and surpass the democratic achievements of the Paris Commune.[164] His demands for power to be transferred to the working people, for mass participation, for an expansion of the rights of workers, peasants and soldiers: these were the demands that were most prominent and frequent in his writings and speeches in the months before October.[165]

On the other hand, notions about dictatorship undoubtedly held Lenin within a powerful magnetic field even though he mentioned them comparatively rarely. A link therefore exists between his pre-October thought and his post-October actions. The concept of an administration unencumbered by legal restraints was neither random nor temporary. And so, whereas the general population – probably including most rank-and-file Bolsheviks – was unaware of his fiercer intentions, careful and regular readers should have picked up the message.[166]

Lenin, indeed, did not stop short of anticipating the use of 'terror' in Russia. In June 1917 he expressed unstinted admiration for the French Jacobin law of 1793 on 'enemies of the people': 'The example of the Jacobins is instructive. Even today it has not become outmoded; but we have to apply it to the revolutionary class of the twentieth century, to the workers and the semi-proletarians. The enemies of the people for this class in the twentieth century are not monarchs but landlords and capitalists as a class.'[167] This wide definition of enemies of the Russian people was attenuated a little by his contention that the guillotine would not be needed. So overwhelming would be the popular majority in favour of socialism that the terror would need only to involve the imprisonment of '50–100 magnates and big-shots of banking capital, principal knights of public embezzlement and bank theft'. These prisoners would be released within weeks, as soon as their financial dealings had been investigated and ascertained.[168] This was Lenin the authoritarian in whimsical mood. He was less endearing about capital punishment, which was reintroduced by Kerenski in July 1917. Lenin wanted the law changed so that '*the exploiters* (i.e. the gentry and the capitalists)' might be shot 'for concealment from and deception of the people'.[169]

Such a desire gave fresh meaning to the proverb: 'One law for the rich, another for the poor.' Strictly speaking, Lenin's plan for differential legislation on capital punishment did not involve arbitrary violence; he wanted capitalists executed for specific offences, not just because they were capitalists. Whenever he spoke expressly of terror before October, he glossed over the various issues by asserting that little terror would be necessary under socialism. The projected arrest of merely a few dozen capitalist 'magnates' is an example. For most of the year, however, he preferred to avoid the topic altogether or to concentrate on what he described as the terror being perpetrated against the Bolsheviks by the Provisional Government.[170]

His statements on the Constituent Assembly too made him appear more 'democratic' than he really was. Before returning to Russia in 1917, he had scorned those Marxists who called for its convocation as a major party goal; but after the February Revolution he persistently demanded the Assembly's convocation.[171] He accused the Provisional Government both of delaying the Assembly and of fiddling the arrangements in favour of Kerenski's supporters.[172] In Lenin's prognosis, the peasants electing deputies to the Constituent Assembly (and who would be the majority of the electorate) would be to the left of the Socialist Revolutionaries.[173] He owned to great optimism: 'Is it really hard to grasp that *with power* in the hands of the Soviets the Constituent Assembly is *assured* and its success is assured.'[174] Yet this fell short of predicting a victory for the Bolsheviks as such. In addition, he stated: 'The question of the Constituent Assembly is *subordinate* to the question about the course and outcome of the class struggle between the bourgeoisie and the proletariat.'[175] This statement, which appeared in an article significantly entitled 'About Constitutional Illusions', showed that Lenin's commitment to abiding by the results of the Assembly elections was far from being absolute. The 'course and outcome of class struggle', along with his party's victorious role in that struggle, counted for more.[176] Bolshevik-led mass organisations would therefore constitute the new government whatever the result of the Constituent Assembly poll. But, again, only careful readers of his articles would have appreciated the nuances of his intentions.

Nor was Lenin's willingness to ignore the formally-registered will of the majority confined to his ideas about the Assembly: he was no more solicitous as regards the mass organisations. In *The State and Revolution* he had referred to the soviets only six times, mainly to assert how badly the Mensheviks and Socialist Revolutionaries had behaved at the helm.[177] Admittedly, he wrote most of the book in the period when he was campaigning against the 'All Power to the Soviets' slogan.[178] And yet even from September, when he ceased to demand the slogan's withdrawal, he offered no depiction of the future institutional framework of governance by soviets. His attitude to the alliance between workers and peasants in the soviets displayed a particularly weak belief in democratic procedures. He frequently omitted to refer to the peasants' soviets at all in describing the future framework, and his party's opponents noted that this implicit downgrading of the peasantry's significance and rights cannot have been an accident.[179] Being a Marxist rather than a populist, Lenin had a firmer trust in the capacities of the workers and was not going to hand over the forthcoming socialist revolution to the peasants. The working class was to be the revolutionary vanguard. He omitted to say what he would do if this vanguard were to turn against the Bolsheviks and favour other parties; he had developed no ideas of multi-party competition.

NATIONALITY PROJECTS

Lenin beat the drum about the struggle for political revolution, summoning workers, peasants and soldiers to overthrow the Provisional Government; but the rhythms of the national question were not forgotten by him. Before and during the war, he had offended many colleagues by tapping out the theme that national self-determination should be the party's slogan and that the right of secession should be advocated; and he had carried the Seventh Conference with him in April 1917. The Provisional Government and its Menshevik and Socialist-Revolutionary supporters were fearful lest the Bolsheviks should take advantage of its difficulties with some of the non-Russian nationalities. The troubles between the cabinet and the Finnish Sejm, which had broken out soon after the February Revolution, continued to give cause for concern through the summer, and the Ukrainian problem grew more acute even after the resignation of the Kadet ministers in early July and the assumption of the premiership by Aleksandr Kerenski. Such conflict was grist in Lenin's mill, and after the Seventh Bolshevik Party Conference he continued to demand that all nations in the old Russian empire should be accorded the right of secession.[180] It remained his argument that socialists, by advocating the right of secession, would earn the trust of the non-Russians and thereby persuade them to stay within or to rejoin a multinational state which included the Russian people.[181]

A fraternal 'union' of peoples was accordingly required.[182] The fact that neither Finns nor Ukrainians were currently striving for complete independence bolstered Lenin's case against his party's left wing, that his talk of the right of secession was a danger to the formation of a large socialist state in the old Russian empire.[183] In the main, however, he avoided reference to disputes among Bolsheviks on the national question. Having won the fiery debate at the April Conference, he did not want to rekindle the embers. His aggressiveness was directed at the Provisional Government, and he insisted that, if Lvov had imitated Nikolai II, the Mensheviks and the Socialist Revolutionaries sought to ape Lvov.[184]

This was scarcely fair. It was the insistence of Tsereteli and Chernov on effecting a *rapprochement* with the Ukrainian Rada that had helped to provoke the collapse of the Lvov coalition Cabinet in July when the Kadet ministers resigned. The Mensheviks had debated the national question at their All-Russian Conference in May 1917. They had laid down that 'broad political autonomy' should be granted to regions where a large non-Russian population existed; and that 'guarantees of cultural development' in schooling and in the use of languages should be given.[185] Both the Menshevik party and the Jewish Bund at the First Congress of Soviets of Workers' and Soldiers' Deputies in June had affirmed that the right of national self-determination, even if it led to secession, should be promulgated. Subsequently, however, the national question faded from prominence among the anti-Bolshevik socialists;[186] and the Menshevik Congress in August did not have it on their agenda.[187] S. Semkovski, the Menshevik Organisational Committee member who had disputed the national question with Lenin before 1914, was the only Petrograd-based Menshevik to write extensively on it in 1917. His views were consistent: he continued to call for territorially-based national autonomy within the existing centralised state.[188] He also repeated his pre-war contention, which was welcomed by Mensheviks generally, that ethnic intermingling in the Russian empire was so complex that internal territorial partitions could not be devised to protect the conditions of all non-Russians. He called for the enactment of measures to ensure that, in areas like the Ukraine, Jews and Poles did not suffer at the hands of Ukrainians.[189]

Mark Liber, the prominent Bundist, had repeated Semkovski's arguments in his report on behalf of the Mensheviks, the Socialist Revolutionaries and the Bund at the First Congress of Soviets;[190] but Lenin treated both Liber and Semkovski with silent contempt throughout the year.[191] Admittedly, the Mensheviks and Socialist Revolutionaries, even when they had greater opportunity to influence the Cabinet after Kerenski's elevation to the premiership, did little to demonstrate their commitment to national autonomy in practice. But account should also be taken that, in terms of ideas, Lenin's proposed solution of the national question within a unitary state had much in common with Semkovski's. Lenin too called for 'broad regional autonomy' in areas populated by a large non-Russian nation and for schooling to take place in the native language.[192] The crucial difference was that Lenin entirely refused to consider Semkovski's arguments on ethnic intermingling (and it was only after the October Revolution that he began to face up to the problem).[193]

In addition, Lenin in 1917 could no longer claim to show much greater concern than the Mensheviks lest the non-Russians should be held in a multinational state against their will and be refused the right of secession. The Mensheviks also acknowledged that a post-war diplomatic settlement might involve Polish and even Armenian independence.[194] But they did not often mention the topic, and it was evidently not a primary worry for them. For Lenin it mattered more. In particular, he objected to the Menshevik notion that only the Constituent Assembly ought to resolve the national question. Nor was his thinking confined predominantly to issues arising from the old Romanov empire. Indicating that the Provisional Government's engagement in the war was determined by global factors, he asserted that national self-determination be enshrined as a universal basic principle as the means for bringing about a general 'democratic peace'. The war, in his estimation, was imperialist, and socialists should aim not only to prevent further annexations at the end of the war but also to reverse the annexationist results of past wars. Each empire, including Russia's, ought to proffer the right of national self-determination.[195] He often mentioned Poland, Finland and the Ukraine as possible secessionist states.[196] And yet we should be wary of assuming that even Lenin made national self-determination into a prominently visible plank in his platform. What he said and wrote deserves attention. But how often he did so, and when, is also significant. In his pre-October publications of 1917, he composed only three short articles on future national and ethnic policy. All of them, moreover, were composed between May and mid-June. Although thereafter he commented *en passant* on the national question, he obviously no longer thought it deserved vociferous, sustained commentary.[197] The reason for this decline in attention is a matter of guesswork. Perhaps he was too busy with other questions; but this can hardly have been the main reason inasmuch as, until April 1917, he had made so much fuss about national self-determination. Possibly he recognised that the future boundaries of the old imperial state were beyond prediction and that emphatic talk by Bolsheviks about the right of secession might induce more secessions than would otherwise occur: he explicitly avoided offering a set of 'demands' on behalf of specific nationalities. Leading Bolsheviks privately asked him to clarify his policy; but he argued that it was more advisable to limit the party's pronouncements to a simple 'declaration of principles' (and even then he published this prevaricatory remark not in a mass-circulation newspaper or at an open mass meeting but in the low-circulation 'thick journal' *Enlightenment*, which was read mainly by Bolshevik intellectuals).[198] Simultaneously he repeated his wish for as large a state as possible.[199] Moreover, he rarely suggested that the most recently conquered areas of the empire should be allowed to secede. He mentioned Turkestan in this connection in only one article;[200] and all the while he stressed that similar dispersals of colonial empires would serve the greater goal of strengthening the authority of socialist states in Europe.[201] In summary, neither Lenin nor anyone else in the Bolshevik Central Committee – contrary to the conventional wisdom in Soviet and Western accounts – played 'the national card' for all it might be worth in 1917.[202]

Lenin probably considered the matter as being less immediately critical than he had earlier imagined. The outbursts of fury which had shaken the Romanov imperial administration in 1905 did not recur in 1917. Nationalist hostility was at its strongest in Finland and the Ukraine. Poland was no longer an internal problem since it was occupied by German forces and the Baltic provinces were also under Germany's control. And, even where the Provisional Government faced troubles in non-Russian areas, the underlying problems were characteristically economic and social in nature. Nationalism in the Ukraine, for example, was a vehicle for peasant disgust with existing land legislation.[203] There were also regions where national sentiment barely existed. Not only central Asia but even Belorussia constituted an example. To have devoted the party's main efforts to the national question would have been a pointless diversion.[204] It was wiser to leave the non-Russian areas to stoke up their own anger against the Provisional Government and to await further developments. Lenin did precisely that.

ECONOMIC AND SOCIAL PROJECTS

He discerned a much more urgent need to state and restate his intention in economic and social policy. All Bolsheviks saw that the economy's rapid deterioration was a crucial issue in the struggle among the political parties, and Lenin was his party's major economic spokesman. He got down to elaborating his ideas from early summer 1917. Newspapers across the spectrum of Russian public opinion were talking of an inevitable catastrophe. Economic ruin was the common currency of editorials. Lenin did not share this apocalyptic viewpoint. The troubles afflicting industry, agriculture, trade and finance were blamed by him on the continuing and preventable activities of capitalists.[205] His pre-revolutionary writings had been focused upon the inherent economic logic of capitalist enterprise which imposed itself willy-nilly upon capitalists. He did not abandon this approach in 1917, at least not entirely; but he shifted his emphasis towards moral condemnation (even though, since the 1890s, he had identified such condemnations as being the defect of Russian agrarian-socialist thought).[206] Lenin railed against the greed and selfishness of businessmen. Industrialists in particular, he declared in a *Pravda* article of 20 May, were directly responsible for 'the disorganisation of production'.[207] Such 'moralism' and 'subjectivism' were unusual for him, but obviously they were likely to attract a great deal of support from a hard-pressed working class. Lenin even asserted that the economic crisis was quickly soluble. His writings contrasted with those of Bolshevik economists such as V. P. Milyutin on the right of his party. Milyutin stated that a definitive solution was impossible in the short term.[208] Lenin retorted that the country abounded in food, coal, oil and metal and confronted fewer objective difficulties than did Germany.[209] His recognition that Milyutin was right came only after the October Revolution.[210] For the moment he continued to highlight the expansion undergone by national economies in wartime. In fairness to him, it must be said that his criticism of Russian contemporary commentators who had ignored this phenomenon had had a great deal of cogency in 1915–16; but the crippling strains on industry and commerce in 1917, especially from mid-summer, were unmistakable to all who experienced them. Perhaps his removal from Russia from early July affected his perception. Another impediment may have been the feeling that, as a party leader, he needed to imply that a socialist administration would have no difficulties. It is also possible that this underestimation was a genuine mistake; but a strong suspicion must persist that he deliberately exaggerated his optimism for public consumption.

The panacea, in Lenin's judgement, was to release the capacities of 'the people'. Mass participation was vital. Popular 'energy, initiative and decisiveness' would triumph where the middle classes had already failed;[211] and the 'proletariat', guiding the movement, would be able to perform 'miracles of organisation'.[212] Lenin and the Central Committee observed the campaign among workers in Petrograd for what he called 'workers' supervision (control)'.[213] Workplace democracy had hitherto not been the party's demand and had seemed more like anarchism or, at best, syndicalism to several leading theorists of Bolshevism; but the popularity of the basic idea was discerned and incorporated into the Bolshevik party's list of slogans. Lenin urged the idea's dissemination and implementation across the country and throughout all major industrial syndicates and banking institutions.[214] Lenin's intention was for wage-earners to supervise owners and managers. They were to have access to accounts and to planning decisions; they were to hear reports on the progress of business. He did not suggest that existing managements should be supplanted by workers' representatives, but rather that they should be placed under supervision.[215] He rejected as 'humorous' the notion that, for example, the railways should pass 'into the hands of the railwaymen'.[216] The organisational framework was left imprecise. The basic rôle would be performed by the factory-workshop committees elected by the workforce. Yet he added that 'all authoritative workers' organisations' should play a part, including both trade unions and soviets. A multi-organisational control, enthusiastically but vaguely articulated, was Lenin's keynote.[217]

Many leftist Bolsheviks wanted to go further than Lenin. Bukharin, returning to Russia in May, counselled the inception of a 'workers' control' which expelled the existing managers and replaced them with a collective board elected by the workforce.[218] This concorded with his more optimistic views on the extent of global capitalist development already achieved and on the speed which could characterise the inception of socialism in Russia as well as in Europe in general. Bukharin and his sympathisers also tended to support wholesale nationalisation of industry, finance and urban trade.[219]

Lenin was more cautious. In May 1917 he wrote about the desirability of governmental control 'over the trusts, over the banks, over trade, over the "parasites" . . . over food supplies.[220] But already he was contemplating something greater than control. In a pamphlet drafted in April and May, and printed in early June, he called for the passing of both industrial syndicates and banks into governmental ownership.[221] It needs emphasising that his proposal is drawn up well short of nationalising all large-scale factories and mines: he aimed to include only such enterprises of that size which had been grouped into some even larger conglomerate. Furthermore, he did not contemplate the nationalisation of medium-sized and small-scale enterprises; and he repeatedly stated that such measures did not amount to an introduction of socialism, and that control and regulation of the remaining private industrial sector would be the government's objective.[222] He refrained from defining the nature of the resultant economic system. In 1918 he was to dub it 'state capitalism'; but before the October Revolution he balked at such a term.[223] No doubt he sensed that it would hardly rouse his fellow Bolsheviks to a socialist seizure of power. Lenin seldom forgot his duties as chief of a political party. Possibly another reason was that his own thinking became less cautious over the summer months. In *The Imminent Catastrophe and How To Combat It*, a pamphlet written in mid-September, he claimed that his economic project would at least be 'a step towards socialism'. For he wanted industrial syndicates to be formed, under governmental compulsion, from not only large but even medium-size enterprises not already belonging to them.[224]

Other proposals put forward by Lenin included progressive taxation on incomes and property; compulsory publication of shareholdings of over 5000 roubles; universal labour duty, which would mean that those who did not work would not eat either.[225] The 'leftward' movement in his thinking was palpable here. In late June 1917 he had made play of his economic caution, noting that he was very far from proposing the confiscation of all industrial profits as did the Menshevik minister M. I. Skobelev.[226] Since then he had become less restrained. Lenin may have been cautious by Bukharin's standards, if not by Milyutin's, and even stood towards the right of Bolshevik economic thought in 1917; but he still occupied a spot on the extreme left of the spectrum of Russian economic proposals outside his party.

By and large, he treated the economy's industrial and financial sectors separately from its agricultural sector. Occasionally, however, he analysed the connections. In May 1917 he mentioned that, with the anticipated rapid ending of the war, there would be a demilitarisation of industrial production. The state would ensure that the factories were encouraged to boost the output of 'agricultural implements, clothes, footwear'.[227] This would be done in order to regenerate trade between town and countryside. Industrial products would be exchanged for grain, and the use of the co-operative movement as a channel for such dealing would be essential.[228] An extra incentive to the peasantry to look kindly on the urban authorities, he thought, would be the low level of taxation on peasant households.[229] It ought to be added none the less that such remarks were few before October. We should not allow this to pass unnoticed; for young 'V. Ilin' (Lenin's pseudonym as author of *The Development of Capitalism in Russia* in 1899) had focused on the intimate relationship between the respective advances of agriculture and industry.[230] His casualness in 1917 makes a sharp contrast. Furthermore, there was no originality in Lenin's points about demilitarisation. Not only were they central to his Central Committee colleague V. P. Milyutin's economic analysis, but they were also official Menshevik policy.[231]

As regards the land question, Lenin for months added little to what he had said at the Seventh Party Conference in April. His major contribution came in a speech to the All-Russian Congress of Peasants' Deputies in May. There he had repeated his argument that a simple transfer of the land into the hands of the peasantry as a whole would not help the village poor, who lacked the equipment, livestock and finances to farm independently: he was continuing to appeal mainly to the poorest section of the peasantry.[232]

Yet political considerations were already driving him away from enunciating land nationalisation as Bolshevik policy. The Central Committee, despite the April Conference's resolution, had never drawn attention to nationalisation; in its mid-May electoral advice to party activists it had proposed a demand that all lands should 'pass without compensation to the peasants'.[233] This was in keeping with Stalin's long held inclinations, which he repeated after the April Conference.[234] Even Lenin, at the Congress of Peasants' Deputies in June, avoided mentioning nationalisation explicitly; he was turning to more ambiguous formulas than before, urging that the land become 'the property of the whole people'.[235] This reticence about nationalisation cannot have been any more coincidental than his coyness about revolutionary war. Through the rest of the summer months, until the end of August, he continued to avoid the topic of land nationalisation.[236] It is likely that Stalin and his friends had obtained a reversal of the April Conference resolution at least for the purpose of public presentation. Not enough is known about the debates behind closed doors to allow us to say why Lenin altered his stance; but probably either the Central Committee forced him or he independently took cognisance that nationalisation would not prove attractive to the peasants. In any case, it is likely that pressure of some sort was brought to bear.

Be that as it may, most party members would have been unaware that nationalisation was party policy unless they happened to have joined before May 1917; and when, on 29 August, Lenin finally addressed the topic it was in order to confirm that the Bolsheviks no longer advocated land nationalisation.[237] A survey of peasant opinion, which had been undertaken by the Socialist Revolutionaries and published in mid-August, produced evidence that governmental ownership of land was not in line with the peasantry's demands. Two hundred and forty-two 'peasant instructions' had been collated, and Lenin urged that the party accept them as the basis of the Bolshevik party's policy. This was essentially a call for 'land socialisation'; it meant handing over the land to the peasants to do with as they saw fit while hoping that they would agree to desist from breaking up the large capitalist estates and to turn them into 'model farms'.[238] On 31 August, no doubt to Stalin's delight, the Central Committee ratified this decision.[239]

Lenin for a while ceased recommending the establishment of separate soviets for agricultural labourers. At last he had become the prophet for a general peasant revolution. No more, at least until after the October Revolution, did he fulminate against the rich peasants or extol the village poor.[240] Lenin's change of policy meant that he was taking up the Socialist-Revolutionary agrarian programme. He did so out of pragmatism, not from belief that 'land socialisation' would be realised in every detail. For he continued to contend that any attempt at restricting a peasant household's right to hire labour (as the 242 'instructions' proposed) would be circumvented in practice.[241] Nor did he think that the programme would bring about socialism. On the contrary, he thought that, despite what the Socialist Revolutionaries expected, their policy would in effect preside over capitalism in the countryside.[242] Lenin in any case concentrated on encouraging his party to get his new views through to the peasants. He emphasised that, although the Socialist Revolutionaries supported the 242 peasant instructions in principle, they refused to act on them until the Constituent Assembly. He noted as late as 24 October that S. L. Maslov, the agrarian spokesman of the Socialist Revolutionaries, was arguing against immediate peasant land seizures.[243] As it happened, the Mensheviks very belatedly came round to support the transfer of gentry-owned land to locally-elected land committees.[244] But this was still not an advocacy of peasant direct action, and left the Bolsheviks an open arena for agitation.[245]

Lenin enjoyed the discomfiture of his opponents, and was not at all disconcerted by the accusation that he had stolen another party's policy. He wanted power for himself and his party, and he wanted this power to be directed at the eventual attainment of socialism in Russia and Europe. The result was not intellectual coherence; indeed, the switch from policies aimed at workers and the poorest peasants to policies aimed at workers and the entire peasantry destroyed a pillar in the edifice of his strategy as announced in April 1917. But he was a revolutionary. He desired theoretical consistency and Marxist justification if he could obtain it; but it was not his absolute priority. He had a revolutionary's urgent sense that something needed to be done and that mistakes and uncertainties had to be accepted as an unavoidable cost.

This was an engaging and even endearing characteristic; but it also showed a casualness and, for a theoretician who had castigated all and sundry for their weaknesses of analysis and anticipation, an

8 To All the Peoples: September to October 1917

INTERNATIONAL PROJECTS

The evaluation of Lenin as a party leader and national politician also entails consideration of factors of general significance. The specific characteristics of Bolshevik party life in 1917 must not be ignored, but certain phenomena are common to nearly all modern political parties operating in multi-party systems. Few parties have central decision-making bodies possessing complete harmony among their members. Nor do all committee members and activists at lower levels always agree with their central bodies. Local committees may well agree on a range of policies (and this is far from being a universal phenomenon) while giving an idiosyncratic twist to particular policies. No central leadership, even if disciplinary sanctions are employable, is wise to alienate perpetually most of its activists. Prudence calls for some ambiguity in pronouncements on policy. Parties which seriously seek popular support, moreover, have to develop an attractive political programme. Ordinary party members are seldom acquainted with the details of their respective party's policies as closely as are party officials, and the mass of the electorate characteristically has even smaller knowledge. Hence there arises a stimulus to simplify the contents of policy, to accentuate those ideas with the greatest appeal to supporters, and to play down ideas which might alienate them. Fudging is not the whole of politics; but there are not many episodes in the history of modern political parties when, to a greater or lesser extent, it has not been in evidence.

Thus the principal leader of any party faces daunting tasks of elaboration and communication. Policies have to be crafted in such a fashion as to gain the sympathy of various groups inside and outside the party. The language has to suit the wishes of each group without excessively offending the sensibilities of the other groups. If these difficulties are large in the late twentieth century, when the instruments of the mass media are profusely available to political leaders, they were still larger in earlier decades.

Lenin's opponents, at the time and afterwards, focused upon his delight in manipulative politics.[1] Manipulator he certainly was, and he massively outmatched his Menshevik and Socialist-Revolutionary rivals in underhandedness. Yet we should also recognise that all effective politicians calibrate their statements to their perceptions of the character of their political support. Not only most workers, soldiers and peasants but also even most rank-and-file Bolsheviks in 1917 had barely heard of Karl Marx and knew little of the complexities of Russian and global politics. Furthermore, most Bolsheviks had only recently become Bolsheviks.[2] This does not signify that 'the masses' were irrational. But it does mean that, after years of limitations on free political discussion in the Romanov imperial state, there was a considerable lack of information and understanding about issues which did not directly impinge upon the lives of most subjects of the old empire. In the committees of the party there was greater awareness, and Lenin needed to express himself more sophisticatedly among activists and leaders in Petrograd. And yet greater subtlety did not always involve greater openness. Lenin sometimes had to modify his ideas or push some of them into the background in order to maintain his support; he did not rule the Central Committee. But he appeared to be content so long as he had his way on the few policies he thought crucial.

While he did not always achieve complete self-control, he was not a politician who always spoke his mind. No statement can automatically be taken at its face value. Whether in a treatise like *The State and Revolution*, or in a mass-circulation newspaper article, or at an open-air workers' gathering, or in a Central Committee closed session, or even merely in a jotted note which remained unpublished until after his death (and such notes elucidate vital aspects of his career): all his pronouncements must be analysed in the light of the prevailing circumstances and of the specific objectives pursued by Lenin at the time.[3]

Even so, it is a widely-held but erroneous assumption that the policies of a man whose collected works run to dozens of volumes are easy to ascertain. The difficulties are exemplified by his speeches, articles and letters about international relations. Ambiguity and inchoateness proliferated, but this partly derived from the reluctance of Lenin and other Bolsheviks to analyse developments in other countries in much detail. Strictly speaking, Lenin had no 'foreign policy'. The Bolshevik party's concern with countries to the West rested with the project of European revolution. As an internationalist, Lenin in spring and summer 1917 recognised no overt obligation to any single country, not even his own.[4] His perspective was global, and he saw himself as having an international rather than a foreign policy. In addition, the Bolshevik outlook was orientated upon classes rather than upon political élites.[5] Lenin had asserted that class-based struggle across Europe was desirable. For him, modern capitalism had given birth to imperialism and all the belligerent states in the war were either the perpetrators or victims of imperialist aggrandisement. Without explicitly saying so, he thought it a waste of time to analyse the distinctions of political stance within states. Liberals and conservatives were barely different shades of the same phenomenon; and such socialists as entered governmental coalitions with them or even just failed to oppose them were crypto-imperialists, or 'social-chauvinists' in Lenin's phrase.[6]

Hence the astounding neglectfulness of Lenin and most other Bolsheviks for the vicissitudes of high politics in Germany, Britain, France and the USA. No doubt too, such factors explain why he did not show much interest in changes in diplomatic or even military relations between states.[7] Lenin regarded them as topics of distractingly trivial importance beside the objective of international socialist revolution. Zinoviev and Radek wrote more about them, but even their articles were thin in substance.[8]

Lenin was preoccupied by the search for signs of discontent in factories and barracks in Germany. He stressed the problem of Berlin's bread shortages, going so far as to assert: 'In Russia it is possible to obtain bread, in Germany it is impossible to obtain it.'[9] This assertion exaggerated Germany's plight even after the 'turnip winter' of 1916–17, and failed to mention its source. Lenin as a party boss aimed to convince his colleagues and rank-and-file Bolsheviks, if they harboured doubts, that a seizure of power in Petrograd would quickly be followed by a fraternal revolution in Berlin. He was guessing and, as often, overstating. If he himself had doubts, he kept quiet about them. In any case he himself surely believed in his own contention that the epoch of European socialist revolution was at hand, and that the Bolsheviks would be prominent in ushering in the new age. He was excited by the strikes in German cities in April 1917 and by the mutiny in the Kiel naval garrison in August.[10] The Bolshevik central newspaper kept a steady eye on such events as they became public news.[11] Its editors, as well as Lenin from his Finnish hiding place, frequently claimed that there was evidence of a 'growing revolution' in Germany.[12] Other countries also exhibited unrest: Lenin was cheered by reports that governments in both Italy and Austria-Hungary were experiencing troubles similar to those reported in Germany.[13] Europe-wide revolution seemed imminent at last.

But events were to prove him wrong. Lenin was mistaking war-weariness and political discontent for a pan-European revolutionary situation. He was not, however, alone. Not only far-left socialists but even many conservative and liberal politicians, in the rest of Europe as well as in Russia, considered the disturbances to be signalling the possible outbreak of 'Red revolution': Bavaria and Hungary did, in fact, acquire revolutionary socialist administrations in 1919. Moreover, Lenin no longer had access to the accurate and up-to-date reportage about central Europe from Switzerland's newspapers, and his communication with Karl Radek and other associates in Scandinavia was apparently not detailed enough to be an adequate substitute.[14]

Unavoidably, he relied heavily on the Russian press, which did not supply comprehensive information. The French government successfully kept secret the mutiny in the French army in summer 1917 involving tens of thousands of troops. Only severe punishment by General Pétain prevented the dissolution of his forces. Lenin can scarcely be faulted for acting on the premise that the public record understated the continental tumult.[15] On the other hand, it remains remarkable that he offered only a few brief sentences on events which had a great impact upon the military and political conflicts of 1917. Neither he nor his Bolshevik colleagues provided serious commentary upon the German submarine attacks on American shipping, or the ensuing entry of the USA into the war on the side of the Allies. Lenin barely bothered to follow the changing fortunes of the armies locked in battle on the Eastern and Western fronts.[16] He and his associates were uninterested even by crucial re-appointments of personnel in Berlin. The German Chancellor, Bethmann Hollweg, resigned in July 1917. He had been harassed both by those who wanted him to make stronger overtures for peace and those who thought him hostile to an all-or-nothing military campaign. The German High Command, under P. von Hindenburg and Erich Ludendorff, pressed for his replacement by a chancellor more pliable to their demands. Their nominee, Georg Michaelis, was duly sworn in and an ultra-militarist government, shorn of the previous inhibitions, was installed.

Writers in the non-Bolshevik Russian press perceived these events as having a cardinal significance.[17] And yet not once did Lenin mention Michaelis by name.[18] His attention to developments in the British and French Cabinets was no more assiduous, nor did he reflect on the foreign policy of the American President, Woodrow Wilson, who was already declaring his hostility to a punitive peace treaty in Europe in the event of military victory for the Allies.[19] Menshevik, Socialist-Revolutionary and Kadet commentators interpreted Lenin's attitude in two ways: either Lenin lacked all trace of military and political realism, or else his zeal to pull Russia out of the War was so overpowering that he would sign a separate treaty with the Germans.[20] He appeared as either a simpleton or a deceiver. Calls by him and other Bolshevik Central Committee members for 'fraternisation' between Russian and German soldiers corroborated this dual conclusion among his enemies.[21]

And so Lenin was obliged to enunciate what he would do if, should he come to power, a European socialist revolution failed to ensue. His usual gambit was to brush the matter aside by contending that the Bolsheviks, simply by proposing a 'democratic peace' and publishing the secret treaties, would stimulate popular insurrections in Europe. Lenin proclaimed that the chances of success were '99 to 100'.[22] His confidence was enhanced by the precedent of the Russian near-revolution of 1905–6, when rebels in Asia and Europe had been inspired to demand democratic reforms. Lenin frequently called Turkey and Persia to mind,[23] and in 1917 predicted that the European imperial powers would face colonial revolts around the world once a socialist government had announced its existence in Russia.[24] References by him and by Stalin to the importance of non-European nationalism marked them off from several other leading Bolshevik strategists. Trotski, while not ignoring political possibilities in Asia, gave greater emphasis to Europe.[25] Bukharin and Pyatakov continued to regard the idea of encouraging nationalist movements with distaste.[26] Yet these differences shrank into insignificance alongside the agreement of Lenin and nearly all his colleagues that a series of socialist insurrections in Europe was on the immediate agenda and that capitalism's day was nearly over; they took it as axiomatic that an administration of revolutionary socialists would very soon be set up in Berlin. Even Bukharin and other Bolsheviks who, unlike Lenin, had always recognised the deeply-felt patriotism of the German working class in 1914, concurred. It was an article of Bolshevik faith.[27]

Opponents nagged away that the Bolsheviks needed a policy for
the contingency that the European socialist revolution might not
occur. In mid-May 1917, Lenin gave them his old answer in *Pravda*:
'Then we should have to complete preparations for and wage a
revolutionary war.'[28] At the first all-Russian Congress of Soviets of
Workers' and Soldiers' Deputies, he replied in like manner. In his
first speech, on 4 June, he suggested that, 'if circumstances . . .
were to place us in the situation of a revolutionary war', the Bolsheviks
would not refuse the challenge;[29] and in his second speech five days
later he announced that 'in certain circumstances we cannot get by
without revolutionary war'.[30]

His words clash with what was to become Bolshevik policy in
March 1918; there is an obvious contradiction between the Lenin of
1917 who fulminated against any notion of a separate peace with
Germany and Austria-Hungary, and the Lenin of 1918 who insisted
on the signature of exactly such a peace.[31] The contrast has
sometimes been interpreted as proof of his blatant disregard for his
own commitments.[32] But care should be exercised in drawing
conclusions from these pre-October declarations. Firstly, it must be
noted that none displays the enthusiasm for revolutionary war which
he had shown before the February Revolution. Lenin's statements
implied that the Bolsheviks would fight only if circumstances forced
their hand; and he eschewed any indication about the timing of such
a war.[33] In the second place, the circumstances of Lenin's remarks
deserve scrutiny. His *Pravda* articles and his speeches to the First
Soviet Congress were framed as a response to the allegations that the
Bolsheviks would sign a separate treaty with Germany.[34] He had to
propose his contingency plan for war if he was to rebut this charge.
Thirdly, and most importantly, his public statements from mid-June
right through to the October Revolution entirely ceased to commit
his party to war in the event that the continental socialist revolution
did not take place.[35] This cannot have been accidental or insignificant; his previous talk about revolutionary war had been too strong
for his silence to have been an aberration.

Consequently, most Bolsheviks did not know that 'revolutionary
war' had ever been among Lenin's proposals. Only party members,
not to mention people outside the party, who had followed debates
with more than ordinary attentiveness were acquainted with what he
had said in emigration or shortly after his return from Switzerland.
Such rank-and-filers were a tiny proportion of the fast-growing mass
party of midsummer and autumn 1917.[36] Lenin's journalism and

open speech-making gave an ever-diminishing impression of a man who contemplated the renewal of the war even as a contingency plan. His reluctance to call publicly for a war, on the other hand, fitted badly with his attitude in behind-the-scenes discussions among his close colleagues.[37] On 30 August, he wrote to the Central Committee reindicating his adherence to a policy of revolutionary war if the European socialist revolution did not occur.[38] The discrepancy is puzzling. Possibly Lenin recognised that his party's popularity lay in its promise to end the war, and that even a conditional prospect of continuing with the fighting would be unattractive. Other far-left socialists had been reticent about war talk for much longer than Lenin. Before 1917, Bukharin and Trotski objected to Lenin's dismissiveness towards the European peace movement.[39] The inclination to talk about peace and play down the theme of a possible revolutionary war grew stronger after the February Revolution, and Lenin followed rather than led his colleagues in this.[40] The Central Committee's official statements after April 1917 ceased to mention a contingency plan for war and accentuated the need to terminate military hostilities and compose a 'just peace'.[41] In June, July and August there was barely a mention of 'revolutionary war', and the few examples by individual leading Bolsheviks were typically tied to denials of the intention to sign a separate peace.[42] Even so, most leading Bolsheviks privately remained committed to revolutionary war if no European revolution occurred.[43]

Thus not only Lenin but also his Central Committee associates largely avoided a topic that would have damaged the party's popularity. Again, the avoidance was surely not fortuitous. But did Lenin, even in 1917, really have the same approach as the majority of his associates? There can be no definitive answer; but it is not inconceivable that, when writing privately in favour of revolutionary war, he was not revealing his genuine intentions but felt that the time had not yet arrived to convince his colleagues, especially those on the left wing of the Bolshevik party, of the impracticability of prolonging military engagement. Furthermore, even his private statements on revolutionary war from May through to October were rare, occurring in largely parenthetical remarks. Lenin did not inflate the balloon unnecessarily.

Indeed, it may be wrong to assume that Lenin really had a firm and considered attitude to 'revolutionary war' in these months. Perhaps, since he genuinely believed in the imminence of European socialist revolution, he felt no need to work out a detailed contingency policy. Such an elaboration, from this viewpoint, would muddy the waters of the party's propaganda with the public and stir up trouble in the Central Committee; it would also distract an already overworked man from other political business. Not that Lenin's thinking on international relations became stagnant before October 1917. Retaliating against the Provisional Government's accusation that he was pro-German, he chose to highlight the military danger posed to Russia by her own Allies. He wrote of the British (or English, as he put it) army as a potential future invader. This reflected his insistence on seeing the Allies and the Central Powers as equally imperialistic; and perhaps it also shows that he never seriously envisaged a protracted war with Germany because he took it for granted that the German working class would soon rise up and establish its own socialist government.[44] A second development in his thought, after April 1917, took place in his analysis of the Provisional Government. He stopped describing ministers as mere errand-boys of British and French capitalists, and stressed their autonomy in foreign policy.[45] Zinoviev and others had taken this line earlier in the war.[46]

Lenin's reasons for changing his emphasis are unclear. Subsequent economic or political research has demonstrated that the cabinets of Lvov and Kerenski did not act in direct subordination to Allied interests;[47] and Lenin may simply have been taking belated cognisance of the real situation.[48] He may also have sensed that his polemics against the Provisional Government would be more biting if the specifically Russian dimensions of governmental problems were pin-pointed by the Bolsheviks. Needless to say, this did not stop him from affirming that ministers were subject to the whims of capitalists. The Provisional Government, for Lenin, remained a capitalist government. But he saw not only British and French capital but rather 'Anglo-French and Russian capital' as being involved in a condominium over Russian state policy.[49] Again he exaggerated; but not totally unfairly. He was right to declare that the controls over capitalism introduced by Menshevik ministers in summer 1917 were ineffectual, and that the concessions on the land question extracted from the Cabinet by the Socialist Revolutionaries did not radically alter the rural economic order.[50]

None the less Lenin's thinking had its incoherences as well as its exaggerations. When it pleased him, he reverted to his description of the other Allies as the genuine masters of the Russian state's actions. Kerenski, according to Lenin, was a puppet of London and Paris and was merely acceding to direct external pressure in instigating the June offensive on the Eastern front.[51] Obviously, this was a guess; it was also untrue: the Provisional Government sensed the desirability of impressing its Allies with a resumed offensive but did not receive orders to fight.[52] But Lenin would beat Kerenski with any stick that lay to hand. And he could perceive that it would do the Bolsheviks no harm if they put themselves forward as better protectors of the national interest than were the Kadets, the Mensheviks and the Socialist Revolutionaries. Lenin started to sound an almost patriotic note, especially after the German advance along the Baltic coast in August, and the capture of Riga. He claimed, erroneously once more, that Kerenski was so scared about Bolshevism that he was planning to surrender Petrograd to the Germans without resistance.[53] At any rate Lenin disowned the aim of seeking the dissolution of the Russian armed forces.[54] It was an extraordinary outcome. Lenin, the unbending internationalist and harrier of all professed patriots, was simultaneously standing forward as the only sure defender of Mother Russia.[55]

THE GERMAN CONNECTION

Lenin disclosed no reasons for this modified stance on international relations. He had seldom commented on such modifications in the past, and saw no reason to break the habits of a political lifetime. He may also have decided that the cards of national defence were too high-scoring to be left unused. He could also have had a more personal motive. The German military danger, Kerenski's alleged treason and the need to keep the Russian army in operational order were themes helping to repudiate the accusation that Lenin and other Bolshevik leaders were German agents. The fabrication of the counter-charge that the Provisional Government was aiding the German war effort put his attackers on the back foot.

Most non-Bolshevik socialist commentators did not credit the Bolshevik central leadership with a genuine wish to inaugurate a pan-European socialist revolution. It would have been illogical to portray Lenin as a devoted underling of Kaiser Wilhelm II while suggesting that Lenin was aiming at the dissolution of the German Reich. Their charges laid emphasis on the presence in Stockholm of known German governmental agents such as the social-democrat and millionaire Alexander Parvus. The main accusers in the press,

Vladimir Burtsev and Grigori Aleksinski, stated that Lenin had met up with Parvus on his trip back from Switzerland. Without a German subsidy, they claimed, the Bolsheviks would not have been in a position to acquire their various printing presses and other facilities in the early days of the February Revolution: *Pravda* had appeared from early March 1917. Aleksinski published a recorded list of telegrams which had passed between Lenin (or other members of the Ulyanov family in Petrograd) and Bolshevik representatives such as Hanecki, Radek and M. Kozlovski in Sweden. These representatives, according to Aleksinski, were in collusion with German purseholders and spymasters.[56] German gold, German gold! Here we arrive at the source of the legend that the Bolsheviks would never have come to power in Petrograd without having been funded by the German foreign ministry.[57]

Certainly, German diplomacy had an interest in looking favourably upon the party of Lenin. Bolshevik propaganda about peace assisted in increasing Russian weariness with the war; and politicians in Berlin knew that if the Bolsheviks came to power in Russia, at the very least a truce could be arranged on the Eastern front. The advantage to the German government would be that its armies could concentrate their efforts on the Western front against Britain and France before the American units started to arrive in Europe.[58]

Lenin and Zinoviev maintained that their various accusers were motivated by political spite. Their contention, expressed in a series of formal statements from April to July, was that personal defamation was being used as a means of achieving the annihilation of the Bolshevik party.[59] Thus, in the 1890s, had French ultra-nationalists trumped up a case of treason against Alfred Dreyfus, a Jewish army officer, to fan the flames of anti-semitism and to shift the centre of gravity of French politics to the right. A Russian *Dreyfusiade* was supposedly in the making.[60] Most socialists in Petrograd, with the exception of Burtsev and Aleksinski, recognised the fatuousness of the claim of espionage. Even Plekhanov held back from such an accusation. Yet the allegation of some financial-cum-political connection remained in the air. Lenin's training in jurisprudence made him reply to it cautiously. He and Zinoviev denied both having met Parvus *en route* from Switzerland and having received funds from either Hanecki or Kozlovski.[61] This was probably true in a strict sense. And yet it does not amount to a refutation of the charge that the Bolshevik Central Committee frequently and knowingly received donations from the German government. The verbal parsimony of Lenin and Zinoviev was almost certainly a sign of economy with the truth. Ways can always be found by cunning leaders to ensure that potentially compromising transactions are dealt with by trusted intermediaries. Karl Radek has been suggested as the person who negotiated the cash transfers.[62]

That some cash was conveyed from Berlin to Petrograd is very likely, since the German official archives prove that German diplomats requested and obtained millions of Deutschmarks for subversive political purposes in Russia in spring 1917.[63] What is missing is incontrovertible proof that the money was aimed specifically at the Bolsheviks in the months between the February and October Revolutions, and that it reached them. But it is probable that at least some funds got through. Possibly Kozlovski sent a cheque through to Petrograd;[64] but the extent of forgery of documents by officials of the Provisional Government has yet to be ascertained. The German archives are more reliable: they indicate that money was given to the Soviet government after October 1917,[65] and there is little reason to disbelieve that such transfers had not happened before.

No moral considerations inhibited the Bolshevik Central Committee from receiving a subsidy from anyone at all. The Devil himself could be supped with, and his money taken. Lenin took Plekhanov's remark at the Second Party Congress as his guideline that the only question to be asked about any policy was whether it helped the prospects of revolution.[66] Every revolutionary party needed money. In 1900 the Russian Marxists had received funds from Russian liberal figures even though Lenin and his friends thought liberals to be likely, in a future political crisis, to make a deal with the absolute monarchy.[67] Lenin's principles allowed him to receive subventions from a 'bourgeois government' with equanimity. The fact that the government offering the funds in 1917 was at war with the government of one's own country was a matter of indifference for him. His self-justification would have been, if he had been able to announce it, that his party's strategy envisaged the speedy overthrow of both the Russian and German governments; and that the German authorities' recklessness in assisting the Bolsheviks financially would not alter his commitment to the strategy.[68] The only inhibition was a sense of prudence. Kerenski would treat the receipt of such monies by the Bolsheviks as high treason, and most Russian citizens would have sympathised with Kerenski's assessment. Trial and even execution of Lenin might easily follow. Not even all Bolsheviks would necessarily approve of the German connection. The new rank-and-filers, and even many central and local leaders, might well have been offended by it.[69] Lenin consequently had every stimulus to keep quiet about the financial arrangements. How many members of the party's leadership were initiated into the secret is not known. But presumably the number was small. This may explain why Volodarski and Manuilski, in the July Days, initially insisted that Lenin and Zinoviev should give themselves up to police custody instead of going into hiding. Such Bolsheviks were almost certainly unaware that much dirt might have come out in the wash of a public trial.[70]

Yet account needs to be taken that German financial subventions were not unique to the Bolsheviks. Berlin engaged in political warfare in the First World War: arms and money were passed to Irish nationalists, who attempted to overthrow the British authorities in Dublin in 1916 – and no one portrays such nationalists as mere agents of Germany.[71] In addition, the German archives show that funds had also been available for transfer to Russia's Socialist Revolutionaries before the February Revolution (even though their Central Committee does not seem to have been involved). Attempts were apparently made to do the same with non-Russian nationalists in the Russian empire.[72] The British and French governments, too, attempted to undermine the military capacity of Germany and the Austro-Hungarian empire by means of subsidies to political groups working for the destruction of the territorial status quo. The possibility of supporting anti-war German groups was limited, since few of them existed and these had no émigré bases to act as contact points. But the Habsburg lands were a different matter. Czech nationalists, in particular, aspired to grasp their independence at the moment of Vienna's distraction by the war.[73] Nor is it a uniquely twentieth-century idea that a state should aid the enemy of the state's enemy. Herodotus and Thucydides, the fathers of historiography, recorded an abundance of such tactics in ancient times.

And yet Aleksinski and his friends, as well as their successors since the Second World War, did not merely state that the Bolshevik Central Committee received 'German gold'; they asserted that the funds from Berlin were indispensable for the Bolshevik political advance in 1917. Seldom have so many non-Marxists proposed so extreme a variant of economic determinism for so important an historical conjuncture. No German subsidy, no October Revolution.[74]

Aleksinski, however, could not supply all the monetary details; and we still do not know how much money arrived in the Bolshevik exchequer.[75] The finances of political warfare were necessarily clandestine, with officials avoiding committing many details to paper. Characters such as Alexander Parvus, moreover, had a well-attested liking for money, young women and the high life;[76] it is by no means certain that all the funds at their disposal were handled scrupulously. Finances were in any case not the greatest difficulty for Russian parties in the months from March 1917. Not everything had to be paid for. The Bolshevik Central Committee obtained its premises in the Kshesinskaya Palace, but paid nothing for it and ejected the owner, the ex-ballerina and court favourite M. Kshesinskaya, from her property.[77] Nor did it have to pay for the sites of the various mass meetings through the year. The pavements outside factory gates were free of charge. Also, the 200–300,000 people who joined the Bolshevik party were expected to contribute to party funds,[78] and *Pravda*, after its first issue, was not given away but sold. Bolshevik officials, as the party gathered political backing, were able to get paid jobs in the soviets, the trade unions and the factory-workshop committees. And the material conditions and political worries affecting workers, soldiers and sailors and disposing them to look for a radical socialist party to solve their problems existed independently of Bolshevik instigation. A German governmental subsidy may have helped the Bolsheviks, but it cannot have been 'the key' to the party's political success in 1917.

THE BOLSHEVIK CENTRAL COMMITTEE

Lenin would have been the last person to think that money was more important than party organisation in making revolutions. In the summer he remained under Central Committee instructions to stay in hiding, and until the Central Committee's repudiation of his ideas on 15 September he had contentedly (nay, keenly) complied. But on 23 or 24 September, he left Helsinki for the town of Vyborg, eighty miles from the Russian frontier.[79] In the following discussions with Central Committee emissaries, Lenin insisted on returning to put his case. Even so, weeks passed. Only on 10 October was his request granted, and a Central Committee session was held in the flat of Galina Flakserman, an assistant in the Secretariat, in a district to the north of the centre of Petrograd. She was married to the left-wing

Menshevik Nikolai Sukhanov, whom she craftily persuaded not to come home that night because the weather was so 'wretched'.[80] Lenin arrived bewigged and beardless. Having fled to Finland dressed as a footplateman, he reappeared in the guise of a Lutheran pastor.[81]

Twelve Central Committee members attended. The proceedings were opened at 10 pm by Sverdlov, who passed on information about the party's difficulties in various zones and asserted that 'dirty business' was being planned by counter-revolutionary officers in Minsk, near the Northern front.[82] Then Lenin spoke for an hour. His theme was 'the current moment'. For conspiratorial reasons, the detailed minutes of the meeting were not written down; Trotski, Stalin, Zinoviev and Kamenev attended, but their speeches are lost to us.[83] The gist of Lenin's words, however, has survived. Again, he contrasted mid-October with early July, arguing that 'the majority' was behind the Bolsheviks.[84] He even acknowledged that the party would not win the Constituent Assembly ballot since the peasants were by far the largest section of the population and could not be expected to vote Bolshevik;[85] but he repeated that this did not matter since 'the agrarian movement' could no longer be suppressed by the Provisional Government, and that both the Bolshevik party and the peasantry agreed on the necessity of 'a transfer of power'.[86] Lenin did not deny that 'the masses' had lately exhibited a certain 'indifference' to high politics. But he contended that the cause was a dissatisfaction with mere 'words and resolutions'. Lenin's final and underlying argument was that the international situation was highly propitious, especially after the mutiny in the Kiel naval garrison in northern Germany.[87]

Before such an audience, which was in closer touch than he with current political developments, Lenin sought to argue that insurrection was urgently required. But his case was sketchily-constructed, resting heavily on the blunt allegation that the Provisional Government had decided to abandon Petrograd to the Central Powers. Hence, according to Lenin, the need for a pre-emptive uprising. Thus he tried to turn his only defensive point into grounds for an aggressive political strategy. He unequivocally urged that the regional congress of soviets from north Russia, due to meet in Minsk in a few hours' time on 11 October, should be the occasion for the announcement of Kerenski's downfall and the transfer of authority to the soviets.[88]

Heated, though necessarily quiet, debate ensued in the softly-lit apartment. M. S. Uritski, while being on the left of the Bolshevik spectrum, asserted that the military force available for an insurrection was insubstantial; but he took this as a reason for conducting strenuous propaganda among the Petrograd garrison soldiers.[89] Neither Kamenev nor Zinoviev, however, pulled their punches in attacking Lenin. After the Central Committee meeting they were to compose a letter to various leading Bolshevik bodies; and its contents presumably give an indication of the arguments used by them at the meeting itself.[90] They did not claim that a socialist government should not soon be formed; the Menshevik left wingers, after all, already advocated such a move. And Kamenev and Zinoviev agreed with Lenin that the Bolsheviks would not win the Constituent Assembly elections; but they concluded that popular opinion would compel the so-called 'petit-bourgeois parties' (as the Bolsheviks described the Mensheviks and the Socialist Revolutionaries) to 'seek out a union with the proletarian party against the gentry landlords and the capitalists'. This scheme for a socialist coalition Cabinet could be implemented with minimal force; and the Bolsheviks would either belong to such a coalition or, by virtue of being a large minority fraction in the Assembly, be able to influence the new Cabinet's policies. Kamenev and Zinoviev also reminded the Central Committee that the soldiers presently voting for the Bolsheviks would withdraw support if the party, in the absence of a European socialist revolution, engaged in a revolutionary war; and that the evidence that such a revolution was imminent was lacking. The clinching argument for Kamenev and Zinoviev was the uncontested information that few workers in Petrograd were willing to get out on to the streets and take part in an armed action.[91]

Yet the Central Committee solidly took Lenin's side, by a margin of ten to two.[92] Early on 11 October, as dawn broke, the members of the party's supreme body tucked into breakfast. Too tired to ponder the historic nature of their decision, they diverted themselves with a gentle teasing of Kamenev and Zinoviev.[93] None the less, Lenin had not got quite everything his way: the suggestion that the transfer of power should take place at the northern regional soviet gathering was rejected.[94] Trotski and others perceived that immediate action was impossible. Lenin, who preached that insurrection was 'an art', was thought to be inviting the party to commit political suicide. His colleagues also felt that, even if an uprising in Minsk were to succeed (which was unlikely), a damaging impression would be given that power was passing not to the soviets in general but to a splinter group of soviets dominated by Bolsheviks.[95]

So Lenin had carried off a crushing strategical victory. None the less, the question of timing and tactics was still not settled. It also remained to be discovered how the rest of the Bolshevik party would take to the Central Committee's line. Kamenev and Zinoviev dispatched their critical letter to the Petersburg and Moscow City Committees as well as to other influential party bodies and fractions inside the soviets;[96] they knew that other right-wing members of the Central Committee – notably Milyutin, Nogin and Rykov – had not attended on 10 October: the hope was nurtured that a further debate might pull Lenin back from the brink. Yet Sverdlov was also hard at work, sending out letters which propagated the official line. The party's local leaderships in cities as distant as Saratov were informed.[97] By its nature this could not be an open debate lest the Provisional Government might be alerted. Nor do all the major city committees of the Bolshevik party seem to have been initiated into the decision of 10 October. This possibly suited Lenin, since he knew he had a strong chance of support from the Petrograd and Moscow leaderships. But there is small reason to assume that Kamenev and Zinoviev would have succeeded if a greater number of committees had been drawn into the Central Committee's confidence. Throughout the Bolshevik party there was a growing sense that the time for the installation of a socialist administration had arrived; and even Kamenev and Zinoviev concurred that a socialist regime should quickly be established.[98]

Lenin's two critics in the Central Committee, however, were readying themselves for a last attempt to change the decision on the seizure of power. Another meeting of the Central Committee was planned for 16 October. Representatives from Bolshevik party committees and soviet and trade union organs in Petrograd were to be present; Kamenev and Zinoviev (who felt buoyed up this time by the presence of Milyutin, Nogin and Rykov) hoped to win them over to a more cautious strategy for the advance to socialism.[99]

Sverdlov took the chair. Lenin, the key speaker, arrived late. He was still beardless and wore a wig; and Ioffe was to recall that he seemed to be in a bad mood.[100] Casually snatching off his wig and placing it on the table in front of him, Lenin repeated the arguments in favour of speedy insurrection.[101] He rejected all compromise with the Mensheviks and the Socialist Revolutionaries and claimed that the country faced a stark choice: 'either a Kornilovite dictatorship or the dictatorship of the proletariat and the poorest strata of the peasantry'. He also asserted: 'It is impossible to be guided by the mood of the masses, since it is changeable and is not susceptible to calculation; we must be led by an objective analysis and evaluation of the revolution.'[102] If he offered such an analysis, it does not appear in the minutes. His recorded words indicate a still stronger restriction on his ideas as expressed in *The State and Revolution* than in his mid-September letters to the Central Committee.[103] Lenin's commitment to mass political participation and to respect for the popular will had not been absolute even before the July Days. But the commitment had not been insignificant, and did not cease to exist after the October Revolution (although it became increasingly attenuated). But the scathing reference to 'the mood of the masses', with all the implicit condescension of a middle-class intellectual politician, constituted a throw-back to the strategical and organisational authoritarianism of *What is to be Done?*. The 'masses' could not be entrusted with their own revolution. If their wishes accorded with those of the party, they were displaying mature 'consciousness'; if not, their 'mood' should be ignored.[104]

There followed several reports from Petrograd representatives. Sverdlov stated, with characteristic numerical inflation, that the number of party members had risen to 400,000.[105] On behalf of the City Committee, G. I. Boki said that active support for an insurrection was patchy in the metropolis. N. V. Krylenko, for the Military Bureau, stated that its members were divided on this question.[106] S. F. Stepanov from the Provincial Committee asserted that attitudes were favourable to the Central Committee's line in the environs of the capital; but he was accused by Boki, himself a leftist, of exaggeration.[107] V. Volodarski from the Petrograd Soviet maintained that workers would answer a summons from the Soviet to take to the streets. Shmidt and Shlyapnikov rallied to him. Only Ravich claimed that the workers would obey a call simply from the party.[108]

And yet Kamenev and Zinoviev were isolated. Every other speaker, including the Bolshevik rightist V. P. Milyutin, took it for granted that an armed clash was imminent and inevitable.[109] The failure of Milyutin, Nogin and Rykov to take a stand unequivocally against the Central Committee decision of 10 October was emblematic of a shift in opinion among Bolsheviks. It also displayed a feeling throughout Russian politics that Kerenski's government had lost its way; that Kerenski would not go quietly and would try to disarm the soviets; that the Bolsheviks should not flinch in the coming trial of strength. And so discussion shifted towards the question whether the Bolsheviks should initiate the clash. Milyutin thought not, and argued against insurrection.[110] This was not surprising in view of Milyutin's long-known viewpoint. But then Shotman, a leftist, announced agreement with Milyutin. Lenin castigated both of them for ignoring 'objective conditions'.[111] He was enraged that Kamenevism was being sneaked in by the back door; his opponents were suggesting that Kerenski should be allowed the opportunity to undertake counter-revolution before a revolutionary uprising should be attempted. Lenin's sharp words did not have an immediate effect. N. V. Krylenko, a leftist Bolshevik, argued that the party should support any insurrection but not organise one in the first instance: a curious standpoint for a Military Bureau member.[112]

It was beginning to look as if the meeting regarded defence as the best form of attack; and Zinoviev and Kamenev, sensing that their position was not in fact irretrievable, restated their objection to Lenin.[113] Zinoviev discerned that a purely negative attitude to the 10 October decision would not carry a majority. He had to supply an positive alternative policy. His solution was to suggest that the forthcoming All-Russian Congress of Soviets of Workers' and Soldiers' Deputies be kept in permanent session until the Constituent Assembly so as to pressurise the Assembly to carry out the appropriate decisions. Kamenev charged Lenin with forcing the political pace. 'I,' he declared, 'have a greater faith in the Russian revolution.'[114]

But several advocates of insurrection then took the floor: Fenigstein, Stalin, Kalinin, Skrypnik, Dzierzynki, Ravich, Sokolnikov, Skalov, Ioffe, Shmidt, Latsis, S. F. Stepanov.[115] No one offered succour to Kamenev and Zinoviev.[116] Probably the other Central Committee members felt that Zinoviev's scheme erred too much on the side of caution and indeed inaction. There was no guarantee that the Constituent Assembly would be held quickly. Lenin had for months declared that only the Bolsheviks would dare to convoke the Assembly. Zinoviev had fumbled tactically. Even so, only Ravich and Skrypnik took Lenin's ultra-impatient approach. Stalin, while hearkening to the insurrectionary summons, added the reservation: 'The day of the uprising must be convenient.'[117] A specific timetable was still avoided. Yet disquiet was expressed that nothing had yet been done to carry out the 10 October decision; the majority of the Central Committee concurred that insurrection would very soon have to be organised. Lenin's motion reaffirmed the 10 October decision and expressed 'complete confidence that the Central Committee and the Soviet would at the right time indicate the propitious moment and the appropriate methods of the offensive'.[118] Nineteen voted in favour and two against with four abstentions.[119] The two against were Kamenev and Zinoviev; and, although a vagueness about timing persisted, they perceived that only a few days remained before the uprising which they wanted to prevent would be attempted.

THE OVERTHROW OF THE GOVERNMENT

The same organisational looseness permitting local party committees to act independently of the Central Committee had allowed the Central Committee to take measures with little chance for the local committees to influence or repeal them. The Central Committee appointed a Military-Revolutionary Centre consisting of Sverdlov, Stalin, Bubnov, M. S. Uritski and Dzierzynski; all were instructed to 'enter the membership of the revolutionary Soviet committee'.[120] It is likely that the reference was to the Military-Revolutionary Committee of the Petrograd Soviet, and that this was its preferred instrument for the government's overthrow.

The idea of a Military-Revolutionary Committee had been debated by the Petrograd Soviet on 9 October. The Soviet sanctioned its formation on 16 October, empowering it to co-ordinate the garrisons for the capital's defence;[121] and the importance of the matter may explain why Trotski, who had been chosen as Soviet chairman, was absent from the Central Committee. In fact, the Military-Revolutionary Centre did not participate in the Petrograd Soviet's Military-Revolutionary Committee. When this Committee was selected on 20 October, its five-man Bureau included three Bolsheviks: Antonov-Ovseenko, Podvoiski and Sadovski. The remaining two members, Laasimer and Sukharkov, were left-wing Socialist Revolutionaries. Lenin approved the Central Committee's choice of the Military-Revolutionary Committee as the organ of insurrection and wished to keep its activities under review. After 16 October he had taken himself to the first-floor flat of M. V. Fofanova, who worked for the Bolshevik Central Committee, in the Vyborg district. Sverdlov maintained contact with Podvoiski, whom he sent to Lenin – probably on some date between 20 and 23 October.[122] Lenin conducted a gruelling interview since Podvoiski wanted the Bolshevik Military Organisation to head the uprising. Lenin supported the Central Committee in insisting that a non-party organ, the Petrograd Soviet's Military-Revolutionary Committee, should have charge.[123] This made practical sense. For the purposes of political presentation it was vital that 'the Soviet' and not 'the party' was seen to be seizing power. Others had said this in the Central Committee.[124] Lenin was merely accentuating their point (and at last displaying the tactical subtlety which was to win him such renown); but his intervention put a useful check on Podvoiski.[125] He wanted no repetition of the trouble caused by the Bureau of the Bolshevik Military Organisation in the July Days. Podvoiski got his own back by enquiring about Lenin's progress with 'the decrees on the land, on peace, on workers' control over production and on the organisation of the Soviet republic'. But Lenin laughed off Podvoiski's implied reproach: 'First it's necessary to seize power and then set about printing the decrees!'[126]

He was confident in his capacity to turn out any such decrees on the day (or night, as it turned out with the Decree on Land) of the uprising.[127] His own hotheadedness, furthermore, had not vanished. He was infuriated by the persistent struggle of Kamenev and Zinoviev to derail the Central Committee from its insurrectionary line. Kamenev and Zinoviev had dispatched an anti-Lenin letter to Bolshevik party organisations; and, on 18 October, Kamenev published a declaration against a seizure of power in the far-left socialist but non-Bolshevik newspaper *Novaya Zhizn* (or 'New Life').[128] Kamenev did not specifically divulge the Central Committee's decisions of 10 and 16 October. Even so, Lenin condemned this as 'strike-breaking' and urged the Central Committee to expel Kamenev and Zinoviev from the party.[129] His appeal was brushed aside by the Central Committee, and *Workers' Path* published an editorial comment playing down the differences between Lenin and his two adversaries.[130] Zinoviev himself wrote in the same issue and announced his solidarity with the position taken by Trotski in the Petrograd Soviet.[131] Trotski had taken to suggesting that, if the Bolsheviks took to the streets, it would happen only in reaction to an attack by the Provisional Government;[132] and Zinoviev was attracted to such a proposition even though he knew that Trotski was using it merely as a subterfuge.

The Central Committee acted carefully. The expulsion of Kamenev and Zinoviev would have ruined the chances of lulling Kerenski into delusions of safety until the last possible moment. It would also have lost the service of two talented leaders; Kamenev and Zinoviev were willing to stand by the party during an insurrection which they had deplored. Stalin, *Workers' Path* editor, probably calculated also that Zinoviev and Kamenev would help in restraining Lenin from too reckless a strategy in the days ahead. The Bolshevik Central Committee needed to stay in touch with movements of opinion in the garrison and the industrial suburbs and to monitor the Provisional Government's security measures. Lenin's incaution had acquired deserved notoriety in August and September; his harangues in favour of action at any price could have cost the party dearly in October.

Trotski manoeuvred astutely in the public arena and his oratorical mastery was put to the party's use. The Petrograd Soviet's Military-Revolutionary Committee continued preparations for an uprising whenever the moment seemed ripe. The Red Guards were readied for action and messages reached the Kronstadt naval garrison and various leading party centres in the country. The Bolshevik press in Petrograd warned constantly of the dangers posed by a resuscitation of Kornilovite conspiracies. A Bolshevik-led coup was the daily speculative fare of the other newspapers; the main substance of their guess-work was not whether the Bolsheviks would revolt but whether their power would last for very long after their rebellion. Delegates to the Second All-Russian Congress of Soviets of Workers' and Soldiers' Deputies were arriving in Petrograd; the Bolsheviks were already sure that a majority would be held by those socialists who opposed coalition with the Kadets and wanted a solidly socialist administration. On 22 October, Trotski broke cover by advocating that the forthcoming Congress of Soviets should select a new government for the country. Such a step, he affirmed, would halt the alleged moves to surrender to the Germans and to facilitate the solution of the problems of peace, land and industry. He asked a Petrograd Soviet crowd to pledge support to him and his endeavours. A resounding cry came back at him: 'We swear it!'[133]

There remained several Bolsheviks, not only in the Military-Revolutionary Committee but also in the party's City Committee, who demanded an immediate seizure of power: Lenin was not the only Leninist. But he was the only one holding Central Committee membership. The Central Committee leaned in favour of Trotski's solution; and Stalin wrote in *Workers' Path* on 24 October about the need for the Congress of Soviets to appoint a new government. Thus it would be hard for the anti-Bolshevik groups to claim that the military action was merely a Bolshevik coup.[134] Lenin lived on in M. V. Fofanova's flat. He acted circumspectly as the city's militia commander had put out an order for searches to be made for him,[135] and the newspapers reported that the Minister of Justice had become directly engaged in the hunt.[136] Fofanova, who worked in the Bolshevik Central Committee Secretariat, implored him not to venture out of doors.[137] He had plenty to do. The Central Committee had obliged him to prepare 'theses' for the Congress 'on the land, on the war, on power'. Milyutin was to do the same on workers' control; Stalin on the national question; and the 'report on the current moment' was entrusted to Trotski.[138] Events were hurtling to their conclusion. On 24 October, Kerenski tried to suppress Bolshevik newspapers in the capital; police raids were frequent. His obvious intention was to render it difficult for the Military-Revolutionary Committee to carry out an insurrection. Early in the day he appeared to have the support of the Pre-Parliament; but its evening meeting was a different affair: a majority of Mensheviks and Socialist Revolutionaries advocated the formation of a new government which would immediately inaugurate land reform and peace negotiations, and the proposal was accepted in the Pre-Parliament. Kerenski's last political prop had been kicked away; an all-socialist coalition Cabinet was demanded.[139]

Trotski, encouraged by the left-wing Socialist Revolutionaries in the Military-Revolutionary Committee, wished to avoid seizing power until the opening of the Congress of Soviets. To the Central Committee's delight, Kerenski's repressive *démarche* was widely taken to authenticate the Bolshevik claim that they were simply defending themselves when making their military dispositions. The Military-Revolutionary Committee had appointed its commissars to various regiments and units and arranged for the neutralising of hostile forces. Plans were in hand for the taking of post and telegraph offices, and the siege of the Winter Palace was being projected. Assistance from the Kronstadt naval garrison was requested.

And yet the proffered help of one central figure, Lenin, was shrugged aside. Lenin sent out Fofanova several times to the Central Committee in the Smolny Institute on 24 October with his pleas to be allowed out of hiding. Each request was denied. 'I do not understand them!' he exploded: 'What is it that scares them?'[140] Towards early evening, at six o'clock, he wrote his last letter to the Central Committee. By then he was frantic with suspicion that his colleagues were shirking their obligations. He wondered even whether the Congress of Soviets could be relied on: 'It would be a disaster, or just a formality, to wait for the vacillating vote on 25 October; the people have the right and duty to decide such questions not by votes but by force. The people have the right and duty at critical moments of the revolution to direct its representatives, even its best representatives, and not to wait for them.'[141] Delay, he maintained, was 'a crime'. He no longer minded which organisation assumed power: 'That's unimportant now: let the Military-Revolutionary Committee "or some other institution" seize it'.[142] He left a note behind for the peripatetic Fofanova: 'I have gone where you did not want me to go'.[143] He could no longer contain himself in the Vyborg apartment. He covered part of his face with a bandage, positioned his trusty wig on his head, grabbed his cap and went with Eino Rahja towards Bolshevik headquarters in the Smolny Institute.[144] On the way, he engaged in political conversation with the conductress of the tramcar: his conspiratorial instincts flew to the wind. Lenin and Rahja arrived at the Smolny Institute, after a narrowly-avoided encounter with a cavalry patrol, towards midnight.[145]

As yet the Military-Revolutionary Committee had limited itself to reacting to the Provisional Government's measures designed to prevent an uprising, but within a couple of hours of Lenin's arrival a more aggressive demeanour was displayed. The central electrical-generating station was occupied. Bridges over the Neva were lowered. The cruiser *Aurora* was moved to within firing range of the Winter Palace. In the early light of 25 October, the State Bank and the telephone offices were taken, and by 8 am the Warsaw Station, which was the terminal of the rail link with army head-quarters and the northern sector of the Eastern front, was in the Military-Revolutionary Committee's hands. As the Bolsheviks and their supporters in the armed forces and the Red Guard spread their power through the capital, a surprised and dejected Kerenski made his plans for escape from the cordon around the Winter Palace.[146]

The October Revolution in Petrograd on 25 October 1917 was violent, but, by the standards of revolutions, fairly bloodless. Lenin's impact was considerable, but not as great on the day of the uprising or on the preparatory tactics as it had been on the Central Committee's original decisions of 10 and 16 October. The crucial figures were Trotski in the Petrograd Soviet, Sverdlov in the Central Committee and Dzierzynski and Antonov-Ovseenko and their colleagues in the Military-Revolutionary Committee – not to mention those hundreds of local Bolsheviks and their sympathisers in Petrograd who used their initiative and took decisions in their own districts. The switch from pseudo-defensive to outwardly aggressive tactics was likely to occur at some point on 25 October, and probably before the opening of the Congress of Soviets. The Bolsheviks at the Smolny Institute, moreover, were aware that power was more or less already theirs. As G. I. Bokii put it: 'At night, at around 3 o'clock in the morning, the situation was clarified: power was in fact in our hands'.[147] Lenin's tactical recommendations were therefore little distinguishable from the Central Committee's current practice. There is one exception to this generalisation, and the exception is important. Whereas the Central Committee's activity might have led to a total overthrow of Kerenski before the Congress, there does not appear to have been a deliberate policy about such timing. Lenin sought to change this. The Congress was meant to meet on 25 October. It was Lenin's will to ensure that, when the delegates assembled, power would already have been grasped from the Provisional Government; and, as soon as he reached the Institute, he imparted this idea to his colleagues with characteristic insistence.

It is therefore entirely credible that his presence made a few hours' difference to the precise moment when the Kerenski cabinet was demonstrably incapable of further rule.[148] Lenin demanded, inspired, energised. He had attended the dawn meeting of the Central Committee. Not only Trotski but also Lenin's opponents Kamenev and Zinoviev were present.[149] Members crowded round the table in Room 36, with several participants and onlookers sitting on the floor.[150]

Lenin, usually a punctiliously efficient person, still had not prepared the various 'theses' asked for by the Central Committee on 21 October.[151] Milyutin and Larin had drafted a Decree on the Land, for presentation to the Congress of Soviets. Its contents are unknown;[152] but Lenin took over the final elaboration.[153] There was discussion, too, about the name for the new administration and its officials. 'Ministers' seemed too bourgeois a nomenclature. Trotski, to general acclaim, suggested 'people's commissars'; and Lenin added that the government could be called the 'Council of People's Commissars'.[154] A list of potential commissars was compiled.[155] By mid-morning on 25 October, the Winter Palace was the only major building not yet in the possession of the insurrectionaries. Most ministers of the Provisional Government remained there at their posts even though the cabinet knew that the chances of a successful defence of the palace were slim. At 10 am Lenin decided that the moment was appropriate to announce the regime's removal. Composing a manifesto 'to the citizens of Russia', he declared: 'The Provisional Government has been overthrown. State power had passed into the hands of the organ of the Petrograd Soviet of Workers' and Soldiers' Deputies: the Military-Revolutionary Soviet, which stands at the head of the Petrograd proletariat and garrison'.[156]

THE SECOND CONGRESS OF SOVIETS

The manifesto carefully mentioned the time of its publication. Lenin presumably wanted to have it recorded that the insurrection had been undertaken before the Congress met. He would have damaged his party's interests if several days had intervened between insurrection and Congress; but the interim of a few hours was short enough for the action still to appear as a true transfer of power to the soviets rather than to a single party. This interim, on the other hand, prevented any possible vacillation by the non-Bolshevik delegates to the Congress about Kerenski's overthrow; they would meet with a *fait accompli*.

Lenin's case for urgent measures was not entirely a figment of his fevered brain. The Bolsheviks, while knowing that they would constitute by far the largest party at the Congress with around 300 out of 670 delegates, knew they would lack a clear majority.[157] He wanted to leave nothing to chance. Kerenski took leave of his ministers in the Winter Palace and took a limousine through the ill-guarded cordon at 11 am to seek military support outside Petrograd. Lenin redoubled his demands for a storming of the palace, but the besiegers were reluctant to spill blood. A Petrograd Soviet session opened at 2.35 pm under the chairmanship of Trotski. His statement that Lenin was to address the Petrograd Soviet drew 'unremitting applause'. Trotski gave him a suitable introduction: 'Long live comrade Lenin, who has now returned to us!'[158] Lenin, hardly identifiable without his moustache, spoke briefly on the programme of the as yet unformed Soviet government. His voice was loud and hoarse, but every word was enunciated with clarity; a Menshevik participant noted how he stressed the ends of his sentences: obviously he wanted his policies to be clearly understood.[159] He was followed by Zinoviev, who made an equally rousing contribution. For the while, the appearance of Bolshevik political unity was maintained. There was no debate on the speeches. An unnamed member of the audience interjected that the Bolshevik party had improperly arrogated the rights of the Congress of Soviets. But Trotski firmly closed the meeting and the leaders rushed away to their other duties.[160]

Still the Winter Palace had not fallen. The Congress's opening, scheduled for 2 pm, was several times postponed; the fractions of the various socialist parties prepared themselves all day for a confrontation. The Left Socialist Revolutionaries and the Menshevik Internationalists decided to convene separately from their respective parties; both these leftist groups of anti-Bolsheviks felt it would be counter-productive to abandon the Congress of Soviets to the Bolsheviks. Yet Dan and Chernov, guiding the majority of Socialist Revolutionaries and Mensheviks, disagreed. They were infuriated by the pre-Congress overthrow, and planned to demonstrate their annoyance by walking out from the Congress.[161]

Neither then nor later did Lenin indicate whether his tactics had been deliberately geared towards this very result. But there can be no doubt that the reaction of Dan and Chernov played into his hands. Martov, himself no great tactician, could scarcely believe that Dan and Chernov, who twenty four hours previously had endorsed policies designed to bring about an immediate peace and an immediate confiscation of gentry-owned land, would walk out of a Congress which was about to announce exactly such policies, and that they would toss aside the opportunity to bargain with the Bolsheviks about the composition of an all-socialist coalition government.[162] Dan opened the proceedings on behalf of the Central Executive Committee from the previous Congress at 10.40 pm in the Smolny Institute. The incongruities of the occasion were sensed by everyone. A building which once had served as a private school for privileged metropolitan girls and whose ceilings were hung with delicate candelabras, was seething with hundreds of representatives of the working class and soldiery of all Russia. Many were armed. The crowd was packed so tightly that some deputies had to perch precariously on the window ledges. The air was fuggy with smoke; protests were made by non-smokers, and it was agreed that cigarettes should be stubbed out – but the smokers kept on smoking.[163] Dan, in almost a caricature of Menshevik diffidence, announced on this most political occasion that he would avoid making a political speech on the grounds that his friends were under fire in the Winter Palace. His statement evoked little sympathy.[164] Elections were held for the Congress's presidium. Fourteen Bolsheviks, led by Trotski, and seven Left Socialist Revolutionaries took the platform. A place was also reserved for a Menshevik Internationalist; but Martov refused to let his group become identified with the day's violence, and the place remained unfilled.[165] Martov rose, on the Congress floor, to call for a peaceful resolution to the conflict on Petrograd's streets, and for negotiations to produce a government consisting of all the parties represented in the soviets. Most delegates to the Congress, including many Bolsheviks, had come to the capital with the intention of creating just such a coalition government.[166]

And Martov's speech, according to the Socialist-Revolutionary newspaper, drew warm applause from a majority in the hall.[167] The Left Socialist Revolutionary, S. D. Mtsislavski announced approval; and A. V. Lunacharski, a member of the *Novaya Zhizn* group, who had rejoined the Bolsheviks with the Interdistricters, declared that he had 'absolutely no objection' to Martov's suggestion. The mainstream leaderships of the Mensheviks and the Socialist Revolutionaries, however, held to their plan; they castigated the Bolshevik-led violence, demanded further negotiations with Kerenski and walked out. Their departure at last left the Bolsheviks with an absolute majority at the Congress and with a freer hand to influence the makeup of the next government.[168] The ineptitude, while understandable in the circumstances, was stunning. Martov stood up again to plead for a general coalition of socialists in government. But this time Trotski was the master of the situation. Tersely he exclaimed: 'No, here no compromise is possible. To those who have left and to those who tell us to do this we must say: you are miserable bankrupts, your role is played out; go where you ought to go: into the dustbin of history!' Martov was provoked beyond endurance, and he too led his group from the hall. Trotski was unrepentant, claiming that the walkouts had served to purge 'the workers' and peasants' revolution of counter-revolutionary influences'.[169]

Earlier in the year, there had been vituperative claims that Lenin had returned to Russia to claim the long-vacant throne of the anarchist Bakunin. Such claims misread Lenin's intentions; for the stateless communities of anarchism were no part of the Bolshevik leader's intentions for the 'dictatorship of the proletariat and the poorest peasants'. Even those who had made the claims, however, must have been surprised by the lack of ceremony attendant upon Lenin's 'coronation'. The first full day of the Congress of Soviets proceeded without him. He continued to try to precipitate the Military-Revolutionary Committee into action. Midnight passed and still no action, but the Winter Palace's defenders steadily diminished in number. At around 2 am on 26 October the troops of the Military-Revolutionary Committee burst in. Resistance was minimal. The ministers of the Provisional Government were placed under arrest and the completion of the insurrection was announced to the Second Congress of Soviets by the insurrection's earliest critic, Lev Kamenev. Lenin remained in Smolny for a while, but had not yet visited the Congress. The task of writing and editing decrees and public announcements demanded his close attention. It was he who composed the proclamation, 'To The Workers, Soldiers and Peasants!', which announced the assumption of power by the Congress of Soviets. But he consigned the job of reading it out to Lunacharski.[170] The Congress ratified the proclamation at 5 am, and Lenin left the Smolny Institute to take a few hours' rest in the nearby flat of V. D. Bonch-Bruevich.[171] Busy discussions followed through the day. The Bolshevik fraction of the Congress of Soviets met to co-ordinate tactics. The Military-Revolutionary Committee met and then the Bolshevik fraction met with the Left Socialist-Revolutionary fraction in a vain effort to bring about a two-party soviet government. The Bolshevik Central Committee met. Lenin was busy in all of them: he had returned to the centre of action. Decrees and resolutions on the government, on the land and on peace were hastily negotiated – and Lenin, having sent his sister Mariya back to Fofanova's flat for material, undertook most of the composition.[172] The Second Congress of Soviets reconvened at 9 pm on 26 October. Trotski and Lenin, joint architects of the October Revolution, shared the stage; and Lenin, to tumultuous applause, introduced the proceedings and laid the 'Decree on Peace' and the 'Decree on Land' before the Congress.[173]

FIRST WEEK, FIRST DECREES

The various pronouncements made by the Bolshevik leadership in the week after the October seizure in Petrograd were of momentous significance in modern Russian history; and they also deserve scrutiny inasmuch as their wording reveals much about the worries which the Bolshevik party leadership had about the political situation. Lenin had previously been arguing that the party's supporters would appreciate action better than words. The seizure of power placed an extra premium on words. In a country where power had become locally-based there was a corresponding increase in the effort needed for communication and persuasion. An outline of the hopes and intentions of the revolutionary socialist administration was urgently required for both Russia and the world, and Lenin's literary fluency was put to intensive use.

The proclamation written by him for the Congress of Soviets on 25 October[174] had justified the 'victorious uprising' in Petrograd by reference to the 'will of the huge majority of workers, soldiers and peasants'. Lenin stressed that several peasant delegates had been present at the Congress.[175] This revealed a nervous recognition that the gathering had been drawn overwhelmingly from elections by workers and soldiers in a country with a demographic preponderance of peasants. These were early days, and the Bolsheviks and their supporters watched warily how the countryside would react to them. The proclamation described the intentions of 'soviet power'. 'An immediate democratic peace to all peoples' would be proposed. Land owned by the gentry, the crown and the monasteries would pass 'to the disposal of peasant committees'. 'Workers' control' would be introduced 'over production'.[176]. The Constituent Assembly would be convoked in a timely fashion. Care would be taken about the acquisition of bread for the towns and essential products for the villages. 'Soviet power' would also guarantee the right of self-determination for 'all nations inhabiting Russia'.[177] Emphasis was also placed upon the armed forces. There would be a 'democratisation of the army'; and a promise was made to tax 'the property-owning classes' heavily and to requisition their property in order to secure the well-being of soldiers and their families. Soldiers, for their part, were asked to 'render active resistance to the Kornilovite Kerenski'.[178]

The Decree on Peace, issued by the Congress on 26 October, had equally portentous significance.[179] For the first time in the First World War a major belligerent country's government called for a speedy and omnilateral end to the fighting. The most important aspect was the aim of 'a democratic or just peace'. Military victory by any nation; territorial annexations; post-war financial indemnities: all these possibilities were expressly repudiated. The forcible incorporation of 'small nationalities' was explicitly rejected.[180] The Soviet authorities declared a wish to abandon secret diplomacy forever. The treaties concluded by Nikolai II with the Allies would shortly be published, and the revolutionary administration in Petrograd promised to deal 'entirely openly' with the outside world.[181] This last commitment was unprecedented in world history. Yet Lenin was not quite as incautious and lacking in guile as might appear. Throughout the previous months he had spoken unremittingly about the achievement of a democratic peace in Europe through European socialist revolution. The overthrow of existing belligerent governments had been a basic demand. The Decree on Peace made a proposal 'to all warring peoples and their governments quickly to begin negotiations about a just, democratic peace'.[182] It contained no call for revolution, no direct threat to the governments of either side in the conflict, no mention of imperialism.[183]. The reasons were not explained by Lenin. The claim has sometimes been made that he was already backing away from his earlier commitment to international revolution, or at least that he was placing the interests of the Soviet state's survival above those of potential revolutions elsewhere.[184] This seems far-fetched. A more likely explanation that he was playing on American President Woodrow Wilson's known wishes to see the war terminated speedily and a peace composed on the basis of national self-determination. Lenin consequently employed uncharacteristic vocabulary, describing the continuation of the War as 'the greatest crime against humanity'.[185] Evidently he calculated that such wording would make it harder for the British and French governments, in the event of an Allied victory, to impose an annexationist peace.

In addition, the fact that he expressed an appeal to 'peoples and their governments' indicated a break with the diplomatic practice which recognised only relations between governments or states; and a section of the decree was devoted to a denunciation of secret diplomacy and secret treaties. From then onward only open and reported negotiations would be entertained.[186] The last paragraph addressed itself 'especially to the conscious workers' of 'England [sic], France and Germany', declaring that they had supplied 'models of proletarian heroism and historical creativity' and expressing confidence that they 'would understand the tasks resting on them for the liberation of mankind from the horrors of the war and its consequences'. The decree ended with a summons for workers to bring about a peace which would involve 'the emancipation of the labouring and exploited masses of the population from all slavery and all exploitation'.[187] This was as near as Lenin could go towards a call for international socialist revolution without aggravating the already great risk that his decree would not be published outside Russia.[188] He had no similar problem with the Decree on Land. It contained five brief clauses.

The landed property of the gentry, the imperial family and the church was 'abolished without compensation' and placed 'at the disposal' of local land committees and peasant soviets until a definitive ruling on the land question was given by the Constituent Assembly. A warning was given against wastage of confiscated soil and equipment, which 'now belonged to the entire people': a strict inventory was to be kept. The decree also stipulated that 'the lands of rank-and-file peasants and rank-and-file cossacks' were not subject to confiscation.[189] These generalisations were accompanied by a word-by-word reproduction of the 242 'peasant instructions' collated by the Socialist Revolutionaries. The absolute and final end of 'the right to private landed property' was asserted. Land could no longer be bought, sold, rented or mortgaged; it was to become an 'all-people legacy'.[190] Only estates engaged in specialised forms of farming, such as stud farms or orange groves, were to become the property of the state. The vast remainder was to stay with 'the people'. Even resources, such as woods, small lakes and farm equipment were to be used by peasant communes as they saw fit; and every citizen was accorded 'the right of use of the land'. Distribution of the land was to be egalitarian, with local factors determining whether equality was to be assessed by the number of mouths to be fed in a family or the number of hours of labour expendable by a family on the land alloted to it. Peasants were also allowed to separate from the commune if they desired.[191]

There were gross uncertainties in the decree. Not the least was the confusion about the division of responsibility among land committees, peasant communes and peasant soviets. Furthermore, Lenin asserted that the land of 'rank-and-file peasants' was not subject to confiscation. He omitted to define such peasants; and it may be that he allowed his inveterate anti-kulak attitude to creep into the decree here (or at least suggested that he would not be aghast if the poor peasants expropriated their richer brethren).[192] Such vagueness cannot have been simply the result of hasty composition. On the other hand, the decree's central thrust was plain. The new government wanted the peasants to get on with their own revolution with the minimum of interference from the towns. A party resting its main hopes upon the support of the urban working class was directing its first major social reform, not to the workers but to the peasants: it is yet another indication of the worries of the Bolsheviks in the first weeks of their power.

Also on 26 October, an enactment[193] was made affirming that 'a workers' and peasants' government' would rule until the convocation of the Constituent Assembly. Its name would be the Council of People's Commissars and 'Vladimir Ulyanov (Lenin)' was announced as its 'chairman'.[194] The new government would follow 'the programme proclaimed' by the Second Congress of Soviets.[195] The emphasis was on liberation and mass participation. The principal measure signalling the other side of Bolshevik intentions was the Decree on the Press which was published on 27 October. This allowed for the closure of newspapers deemed to be producing material inimical to the new political order.[196] It marked a contrast with the early activities of the Provisional Government when virtually unlimited civic freedoms were implemented. The Decree on the Press made plain that the Soviet authorities under the Bolsheviks would brook no fundamental opposition (and the contemporaneous searches of houses and printing enterprises by the Military-Revolutionary Committee enforced the decree immediately). Bolshevik spokesmen argued, as had Lenin in *The State and Revolution* that the propertied classes had always had an unfair advantage in setting up newspapers, and that the use of the press should not be confined mainly to the rich. Yet the basic intention to close down anti-Bolshevik newspapers was only lightly veiled. Themes of repression figured less in the output of decrees and instructions than themes of liberation; but this did not signify that Lenin came to government with gentle aims. The absence of terms such as 'dictatorship of the proletariat and the poorest peasants' from his formulations was cosmetic and temporary.

One other crucial decree, on the eight-hour working day, was passed in the first week. This included several limitations not only on the length of each working day but also on night work and on work by women and minors.[197] It was an important reform. Yet it hardly amounted to the radical transformation in human relationships represented by the Decree on Land. Laws to nationalise banks and industrial syndicates, which Lenin had talked of before the October seizure of power, had yet to be formulated.[198]

Thus the urban working class was not informed about what was to happen to finance and industry. The party and government of the workers gave greater attention in its public pronouncements to defusing potential hostility from the peasants and the soldiers. This made political sense, since working-class support for the removal of Kerenski's administration, if not monolithic, was strong. And yet it is hard to suppress the suspicion that the slowness of legislative movement in the sector of the economy affecting the working class was an involuntary, preliminary sign of the inherent intractability of the problems of industrial recovery and expansion. Eventually, on 5 November, twelve days after the Petrograd uprising, Lenin released a statement calling on workers to 'introduce the strictest control over production and accounts' and to arrest anyone found committing sabotage.[199] It was, again, vague and incomplete as a declaration of policy. Instead, the new authorities laid their stress on the rupture with the politics of Russia and Europe constituted by the October seizure of power. And a truly historic rupture it was. Workers, along with soldiers and peasants, were being encouraged to 'take all power in the localities into the hands of their soviets'.[200] No such summons had been issued by a government before; and Lenin and his associates were convinced that the dawn of a new era would soon shine upon them.

9 The View from Petrograd: November to December 1917

NEGOTIATIONS ON POWER

The 'October Revolution' was not a single act which titanically prescribed the entire political process for the rest of the country. Russia and its subject regions in 1917 experienced myriads of further revolutions after the fall of the Romanov dynasty, in cities, in the armed forces, and in the villages. Some preceded, others followed the Military-Revolutionary Committee's seizure of power in Petrograd. Some of these felt the initial impact of events in the capital more than did others; and, indeed, some of them also influenced the Petrograd uprising itself. Consequently, the Bolshevik Central Committee, with much skill and not a little luck, linked its political revolution in Petrograd to the revolutions elsewhere. There was a parallelism of intent: the various revolutions shared an antipathy to the policies of the Provisional Government and a belief that a radical alternative should be sought. Yet the Bolshevik Central Committee appreciated that, in the disintegrated and localised condition of politics at the time, the Petrograd seizure remained as yet a local revolution. Obviously, it was the crucial local revolution; but its impact had yet to be realised. 'Soviet power' under the Bolshevik aegis had to be disseminated across the country. This undertaking would put the strategy of Lenin to its greatest test. The parallel movement of the myriads of anti-Kerenski revolutions would inevitably be disrupted by an involuted and multilateral geometry of antagonisms among the classes and groups whose original commonalty of purpose had been the campaign to overturn the policies of the Provisional Government.

In those first weeks it was unclear whether the Bolshevik-led revolution in Petrograd would prove adequate to guide and dominate the others. Nor was it even settled that Lenin and Trotski would succeed in imposing their own particular vision on their Central Committee colleagues. The great question of coalition with competing socialist parties was unanswered. Russian politics were in a state of flux. Such had been the impotence of the Provisional Government and the hostility towards it that a socialist government of some sort would probably have emerged in late 1917 even if Lenin had not returned to Russia across Germany in his sealed train. But any socialist government, with or without him, would have confronted similar immense problems in trying to control, reconcile and co-ordinate the parallel revolutions of 1917.

And yet both Lenin and Trotski had returned from emigration, and their activity in late October gave them a directing influence over the design of the government and its policies which emerged from the uprising in Petrograd. With an impudent astuteness, which has been largely overlooked by historians, Lenin had succeeded in persuading the Bolshevik Central Committee to steer a course towards establishing a government without debating the same government's personal composition. This was like the stereotypical second-hand car dealer selling a vehicle without inviting the customer to look under the bonnet. In reality, neither Lenin nor Trotski had the slightest intention of sharing power with the Mensheviks and the Socialist Revolutionaries. The title of Lenin's letter to the Central Committee, 'The Bolsheviks Must Seize Power', gave an enormous hint about his aims; and his endless criticism and ridiculing of the Mensheviks as being a 'petit-bourgeois party' in pursuit of 'social-chauvinism' was scarcely an attitude conducive to co-operation with them.[1] Lenin and Trotski did not make their opinion totally clear-cut until after 25 October: namely that they would countenance coalition only with the more radical members of the Party of Socialist Revolutionaries who had remained at the Second Congress of Soviets when their centrist and right-wing fellow members had walked out.[2]

Even so, it is mysterious why so many leading Bolsheviks stayed blissfully unable to recognise the extent of Lenin's intransigence. Otherwise they might have hearkened more readily to Kamenev's and Zinoviev's arguments. But apparently even Kamenev, usually a perceptive assessor of Lenin's tactics, failed to discern the restrictive basis of his planned future government.[3] It took the October Revolution to expose the fact that Lenin and Trotski were political literalists. Their unconditional verbal assaults on Menshevism and Socialist-Revolutionism were not mere rhetorical gestures.[4]

Lenin and Trotski were not alone in impeding the moves towards a wider all-socialist coalition. Dan and Chernov detested Lenin and Trotski both politically and personally and the October Revolution merely sealed the lid of their hatred. Clashes would have been inevitable over policies on the middle classes and their parties; on food supplies; on the rights of workers; and, ultimately, on the war. Lenin found it hard enough to keep his own Bolsheviks united in the winter of 1917–18, and the dispute over the signature of a separate peace in March 1918 was to come near to breaking up his party. In a governmental coalition with Mensheviks and Socialist Revolutionaries the roles would have been different: he would have been the disunifier and the source of disruption. In such a role he had no equal in Russian politics. He had also acquired a co-leader in the person of Trotski who had the determination to strengthen his case in the Bolshevik Central Committee. The same Trotski who had once depicted Lenin as an incorrigible non-compromiser had emerged as the leader second only to Lenin in his opposition to compromise. Nevertheless, Lenin and Trotski had to face certain unpleasant realities. Firstly, the Bolsheviks were isolated from every other political force in the country; even the Left Socialist Revolutionaries refused to join the Council of People's Commissars (or Sovnarkom). Secondly, several members of the Bolshevik Central Committee had made the October Revolution on the assumption that 'soviet power' would be shared among all the various socialist parties and would not be a Bolshevik party monopoly. Out of 366 soviets and army committees represented at the Second Congress of Soviets, according to an incomplete but believable questionnaire, 255 had sent delegates to Petrograd on this basis; and no delegate had been dispatched with a mandate to seek the extrusion of non-Bolsheviks from the new government.[5]

The exodus of the Mensheviks and Socialist Revolutionaries from the Congress had eased Lenin's position by permitting the claim that they had implicitly repudiated the objective of a general socialist coalition. But talk about such a coalition was quickly resumed, not only by Mensheviks and Socialist Revolutionaries but also by other Bolshevik leaders. Negotiations among all socialist parties were inevitable. Lenin's tactics had to be those of a spoiler; he could not countermand the inter-party discussions. In addition, it was not yet clear that the efforts of ex-premier Kerenski and General Krasnov to eject the Bolsheviks from power would prove fruitless. Lenin might yet need the help of the Mensheviks and the Socialist Revolutionaries even as they in their past had needed the Bolsheviks to suppress the Kornilov mutiny in August 1917.

The Military-Revolutionary Committee felt a growing lack of confidence in the defensive capacity of the garrison troops. Worse still for Lenin was the announcement from the All-Russian Executive Committee of the Railwaymen's Union (Vikzhel) that, unless the Bolsheviks agreed to negotiations with other socialists, a rail strike would commence on 29 October. This encouraged the Menshevik Internationalists and leftists in the Jewish Bund to canvass more strongly in their parties for the inception of talks designed to produce a compromise with the Bolsheviks and an all-socialist coalition government.[6] The Bolshevik Central Committee convened on 29 October. Lenin and Trotski did not attend, and their absence remains unexplained. They had duties in Sovnarkom; but this was also true of others who none the less attended the Central Committee on that occasion.[7] Perhaps Lenin and Trotski were engaged in arrangements for the defence of the capital against the anticipated return of Kerenski in full force. But it is also possible that neither Lenin nor Trotski yet wanted to be seen as obvious road blocks in the way of inter-socialist harmony; or that they had already determined on coalition talks as a delaying tactic until such time as the Bolsheviks were in a stronger position. Certainly Lenin, by 1 November, was describing the negotiations as merely 'a diplomatic cover for military actions'.[8]

He was still taking a risk here. Kamenev was present at the Bolshevik Central Committee session on 29 October; and he and G. E. Sokolnikov were empowered to attend the talks presided over by the Railwaymen's Union.[9] Kamenev seized his chance, just as Lenin would have done in his place: he participated vigorously in the talks and, by the late evening of 30 October, was consenting to the replacement of Sovnarkom with a so-called People's Council, with no places being kept for Lenin and Trotski.[10]

By then Lenin was feeling less constrained. Kerenski's counter-coup had collapsed earlier the same day when Krasnov's Cossacks were routed by troops and Red Guards loyal to the Soviet authorities; and the likelihood of a national rail strike steadily receded.[11] Lenin could also complain that Kamenev as a negotiator had vastly exceeded his remit from the Central Committee, especially when ignoring the injunction that any coalition should be subject exclusively to the All-Russian Central Executive Committee of the Congress of Soviets.[12] Kamenev had conceded that not only soviets but also city councils and trade unions, including the Menshevik-led railwaymen, should control the government.[13] Trotski resumed the political offensive in the Bolshevik Central Committee on 1 November, opposing the exclusion of Lenin from any coalition. Obviously, he was not keen to see himself dismissed from the government either. The Bolsheviks, he exclaimed, had not made a revolution merely to negotiate it away.[14] Kamenev, Rykov and Zinoviev wanted the coalition negotiations to be pursued to a successful conclusion,[15] but Lenin and Trotski would tolerate them only as a delaying tactic. The Central Committee, siding with Lenin, called for talks to be resumed, but for Bolshevik representatives to deliver the ultimatum that the other parties accept the Bolshevik party line on peace, land, workers' control, food supplies and the struggle with Kaledin and Kerenski.[16] A further resolution made plain that the purpose of resuming talks was essentially to bring about 'a final cessation of further talks about coalitional power'.[17]

Meanwhile, the Menshevik central leaders were toughening their stance. The Decree on the Press led to raids on non-Bolshevik newspapers such as the liberal-owned *Rech* and even *Den*, which was run by the right-wing Menshevik (and one-time collaborator of Lenin's) A. N. Potresov. Politicians taken captive by the Military-Revolutionary Committee had not been released, and fears increased for their ultimate safety. The Mensheviks, under Martov's influence, demanded on 2 November the liberation of all political prisoners along with an end to military actions and to what they referred to as the Bolshevik 'terror'.[18]

The terroristic aspects of the new government's rule were still in a perinatal condition: no one had presentiments about the scale of the Red (or indeed the White) Terror which was to develop when civil war raged in full flood. But ominous thresholds were being crossed in the first days of the October Revolution, and with reckless abandon. The Menshevik negotiating requests were the very least that a self-respecting Menshevism could have made; but they were also enough to smash the hopes of any reconciliation with Bolshevism. By ten votes to five, the Bolshevik Central Committee condemned the 'opposition' within its own midst as being intimidated by the bourgeoisie and supported only by 'the tired (and not revolutionary) part of the population'.[19] Lenin had outmanoeuvred Kamenev, pushing home his advantage with customary impassive ruthlessness. The next day, Lenin, while chairing Sovnarkom, announced his total opposition to the Vikzhel negotiations. Bolshevik power in Moscow had been secured; Vikzhel's authority over its own railwaymen was successfully challenged by the creation of a new union under Bolshevik direction; and food supplies were at last reaching central Russia from the Volga.[20] The necessity of further pretence, in the eyes of Lenin and Trotski, had evaporated. Mensheviks and Socialist Revolutionaries could now be faced down, and the discussions with them aborted. Kamenev, Zinoviev, Rykov, Nogin and Milyutin had to face the consequences. Lenin drew up an ultimatum: either they obtained the party's approval to form a coalition government, and Lenin would feel free to campaign against such a government; or else Lenin would obtain the party's sanction and the opposition itself would campaign against Sovnarkom. Better an 'honourable and open split' than the existing messy unity.[21]

No one with the merest acquaintance with Bolshevik history could think that Lenin was bluffing; he seemed to live by the motto: 'If in doubt, split.' Kamenev and his supporters none the less resolved to dig in their heels. They felt that, while Lenin's position had strengthened somewhat, their own was far from being hopeless. An already isolated Bolshevik government was getting ready to isolate itself further from several of the most prominent Bolshevik leaders. Kamenev thought that Lenin could not hold out for ever, however hard he tried; and Kamenev and his four colleagues resigned their places in the Central Committee on 4 November. They reserved the right to fight for their ideas in the party at large.[22] Sovnarkom, too, was affected: Nogin, Rykov and Milyutin simultaneously gave up their places in the Council of People's Commissars.[23] Kamenev withdrew from the All-Russian Central Executive Committee of the Second Congress of Soviets. In total, five out of fifteen People's Commissars refused to continue to work in Sovnarkom because of opposition to Lenin's and Trotski's intransigence. These included some of the party's most expert politicians. And there were others like Aleksandr Shlyapnikov, People's Commissar for Labour, who agreed not to leave their posts but made public their disgust with the role of Lenin and Trotski in the collapse of coalition talks.[24]

Yet Lenin's nerve held; and Trotski, far from apologising for the restrictions on press freedom, gloried in the arguments for repression.[25] Lenin was not so abrasive in public. He also remained imperturbable in tackling issues of broader politics. The Council of People's Commissars aspired to rule a country with a majority of peasants, and it was vital to reassure the peasantry that Bolshevik intentions were pure. Mariya Spiridonova and the other Left Socialist Revolutionaries could not be treated dismissively, even though they had refused to join the Soviet government at the Congress of Soviets of Workers' and Soldiers' Deputies. The Left Socialist Revolutionaries themselves were beginning to recognise that the Soviet government might not prove to be so ephemeral as once seemed likely. Consequently, contacts between Bolsheviks and Left Socialist Revolutionaries were never entirely cut. Left Socialist Revolutionaries continued to attend the sessions of the All-Russian Central Executive Committee of the Congress of Soviets, badgering the Council of People's Commissars with criticisms of its officials' conduct.[26] In another political context they might have appeared to be intent on taking on the role of loyal opposition. The temptation to join the Bolsheviks in coalition increased. It galled the Left Socialist Revolutionaries that Lenin and not Spiridonova had signed the Decree on Land, which Lenin unembarrassedly admitted was a decree purloined from Socialist Revolutionaries. With further agrarian legislation in prospect, Spiridonova and her associates would be in a much stronger position to influence its wording from within rather than from outside the Council of People's Commissars. For some days after the termination of coalition talks involving the Mensheviks and the Socialist Revolutionaries, Spiridonova continued to hold back. The Left Socialist Revolutionaries retained an all-socialist coalition as their ideal objective.[27] But opinion was gradually shifting. Left Socialist Revolutionaries tended to lay a lesser blame on the Bolsheviks than on the anti-Bolsheviks for the breakdown of talks. They formed their own separate party in November 1917 and openly opposed Chernov at the Second All-Russian Congress of Soviets of Peasants' Deputies.[28]

This Congress, which convened in Petrograd from 26 November to 10 December, had a majority of Left Socialist Revolutionary delegates.[29] Chernov's centrist group was eclipsed by the dazzle of Spiridonova. With this mandate from peasant Russia in their pockets, the Left Socialist Revolutionaries felt able to re-enter negotiations with the Bolsheviks. Lenin was a willing interlocutor, and on 10 December seven Left Socialist Revolutionaries joined Sovnarkom as new People's Commissars. They had a minority of the places, and most key Commissariats were withheld from them, apart from those of Justice and of Agriculture. Bolsheviks argued that the Bolshevik party was entitled to this superiority since the Left

Socialist Revolutionaries had delayed their entrance into government until the going was safer. But both parties, for the time being, were satisfied by the deal.[30]

THE SPREAD OF SOVIET POWER

Lenin's energies were large but not infinite. They were consumed by the problems of setting up Sovnarkom; of brow-beating his party's Central Committee; of cajoling the Left Socialist Revolutionaries into office; of overseeing the disposition of military and political forces in Petrograd to ensure the final removal of Kerenski and his diminishing band of supporters; of writing and elaborating the legislation which poured forth from the government's chaotic offices in the Smolny Institute. These were responsibilities enough for a whole Cabinet.

He was not a good delegator of duties and functions unless he could keep a close eye on those to whom he was delegating. In other words, he was adept only at semi-delegation; and this was why his working relationship with Krupskaya had operated efficiently. However, in November 1917 he had no choice but to entrust provincial contacts to Yakov Sverdlov. Lenin's disrespect for him had long disappeared. Sverdlov was a brilliant and hard-working organiser (even though he suffered even more direly from an inability to delegate to others);[31] and, as leader of the Central Committee Secretariat and chairman of the All-Russian Central Executive Committee of the Congress of Soviets, he sent off telegrams in all directions. His main difficulty consisted in fending off requests for assistance. Shortages of personnel, funds and propaganda material were more severe in the provinces than in Petrograd.[32] Lenin, Trotski and Sverdlov knew that they barely had the capital under control, and that Kerenski's defeat might merely be the prelude to a grimmer civil war. If they agreed to distribute the Red Guards, Kronstadt sailors and Latvian riflemen throughout Russia, the result would be a dissipation of the party's metropolitan strength. Lenin repeatedly urged the need for local initiative and local efforts and achievements.[33] Elites could seize power; but the support and participation of 'the masses' was assumed to be vital if that power was to be maintained. Lenin in his writings continued to speak of the need for popular creativity. The ideas of *The State and Revolution* remained dear to him. The workers, soldiers and peasants had nothing to fear except fear itself: the lower social orders of Russia, he declared, had to make their own revolution.[34]

The language of his articles remained lofty and abstract. The Smolny Institute teemed with people who had come off Petrograd's streets and brought news of the dislocation produced by the October Revolution; but Lenin, who had had much success in identifying himself with the cause of the working class, gave little evidence of acquaintance with the concrete circumstances produced by the seizure of power. Violent incidents recurred in the capital; and administrative confusion abounded as the new structures of authority were constructed and challenged, sometimes by the Bolsheviks themselves. There were occasional riots and not a few outbursts of drunkenness when wine-cellars were ransacked. While being warm and inspiring in face-to-face meetings in the Institute, Lenin continued to write the austere prose of the theorist of socialist revolution. He had insisted that insurrection was an art and not a science; but he left it to others to learn the artistic competence for themselves.

Sverdlov was more down-to-earth but hardly exhaustive in his instructions. Asked for advice and assistance by the Berdyansk Bolshevik Committee, he responded: 'You understand, comrade, that it is difficult to give you instructions any more concrete than "All Power To The Soviets". This is apparently all that can be said, except to add that it is of supreme importance to take charge of the post and telegraph offices and also the railways.'[35] Local Bolsheviks were simply implored to make their own political arrangements and keep an eye on the central party newspaper for general guidance. The Central Committee was acting in accordance with the stated Bolshevik philosophy of a dual revolution from above and from below; but it was equally a reflection of practical possibilities. And least of all did Lenin, the father of Bolshevik centralism, believe in principle in non-intervention in local affairs. On the contrary, he committed loyal forces to crucial armed struggles so long as Petrograd's defence was thereby not unduly weakened. Moscow was a case in point. The resistance to Bolshevism there was greater than in Petrograd. Fighting lasted for several days.[36] Nevertheless, the records of Sovnarkom reveal the overwhelming nature of the requirements involved in the establishment of a state machine at the centre. Not only Moscow but also the town of Vladimir and the Donbass region were discussed, but the topics related to nationalisation and financial assignations rather than to detailed political guidance and military support; and it had been local Bolshevik and soviet organs which had put them on to the agenda.[37] The flimsy messages and even flimsier guidance issuing forth from Sovnarkom and the Bolshevik Central Committee in Petrograd left most soviets to their own devices. The transfer of authority was in any case easier in most other cities and towns of central Russia than in Moscow. A peaceful process was reported in Ivanovo-Voznesensk after the arrival of news about the Petrograd insurrection on 27 October.[38] Urban soviets in the region either were already under Bolshevik influence or else had a large and growing contingent of Bolshevik deputies.

To the north-west, around Petrograd, it was the same story. Some soviets had for months been in the hands of socialists seeking the Provisional Government's overthrow. The Petrograd Soviet, despite a certain finessing of its relations with Kerenski in order to avoid the accusation of overt disobedience, had set such an example. The Kronstadt Soviet had been notorious for its virtual independence from Kerenski's control since early summer; and there were other such rebel soviets elsewhere: Ivanovo-Voznesensk in central Russia and the Volga town of Tsaritsyn in the south-east.[39] The Urals, too, had soviets willing to recognise Sovnarkom.[40] Even in the south-east, in the old heartland of the Socialist Revolutionaries by the Volga, the Bolsheviks and other left-wing socialists secured their successes. In Tambov it took some days of violence before the transfer of power was effected, but in Nizhni Novgorod, there was little armed conflict;[41] and the soldiers in the Kazan garrison were so pro-Bolshevik that other groups in the population offered no resistance. In Simbirsk, the native town of Vladimir Ilich Ulyanov-Lenin, fighting broke out but the rapid victory of the pro-Bolshevik forces was never in serious doubt. Overall, the process was uneven and protracted. What became known as the triumphal march of soviet power stretched over the last months of 1917 and into 1918.[42]

Lenin, Sverdlov and the various leaders of the Military-Revolutionary Committee were jubilant, but they could still not observe the march at first hand; and the reports received by them were frequently delayed and inaccurate. Conversations by telephone or by the cumbersome Hughes apparatus provided only fitful linkage with the provinces.[43] Lenin's decrees and proclamations had had an undoubted impact. They were characteristically formulated for their inspirational effectiveness. This concern to rouse the local soviets, trade unions and factory-workshop committees to revolutionary action helps to explain why Lenin, a trained jurist, was vague to the point of remissness in framing the legislation. The laws were instruments of agitation and propaganda; they displayed a commitment to revolution at all costs which spilled over into legal nihilism.[44] Lenin was accustomed to explaining party policies in greater detail through the Bolshevik press, but this was no longer physically possible for an overworked politician. He published just one brief letter in the central party newspaper in November and December 1917.[45] Visits from provincial Bolsheviks were another channel of contact, but neither Lenin nor his visitors could expend many hours in verbal exchanges. Sovnarkom's chairman is recorded as having received a few dozen visitations from outside Petrograd in November and December 1917. Only one activist arrived from the Ukraine, and not all towns in Russia were successful in getting anyone through to him.[46] Nevertheless, even this situation had its bright side for him. A large influx of party activists from the provinces could only have meant that the Bolsheviks were being forced to flee. In fact they were exercised by the tasks of taking and retaining power. And, when reportage on local developments reached Petrograd (and it must be borne in mind that Sverdlov was meeting more people),[47] Sovnarkom and the Bolshevik Central Committee were confirmed in their optimism. The greatest gap in the daily news, unavoidably, related to the countryside. Sovnarkom and the People's Commissariat of Agriculture sent 50,000 agitators into the villages in the first six months;[48] and Lenin, like the Romanov emperors before him, began to give personal audiences to peasants travelling to the capital. He knew that, unless the villages sided with or at least failed to oppose the Bolsheviks, all the political progress in the towns might be reversed.

The news from the front was encouraging. Bolshevik party activists had won notable victories in elections to soldiers' committees on the northern sector of the Eastern front in the autumn; and the transfer of power in Petrograd left few generals with the illusion that the moment was yet propitious for a counter-revolutionary strike at Sovnarkom. Despite Bolshevik fears, there was a widespread distaste in the officer corps at all levels for intervening in politics. It is true that the Socialist Revolutionaries retained much sympathy among soldiers on the southern sector. And yet the chances of mobilising regiments against the Bolsheviks were as slim as in the north. On both northern and southern sectors, moreover, the Decree on Peace and the consequent negotiations for a truce with Germany and Austria-Germany were taken as a sanction for collective self-demobilisation. The human material for a right-wing military coup was exiguous.[49]

The soldiers streamed back in their millions to their villages. Many carried with them the first information that an October Revolution had occurred and that a leader called Lenin had issued a Decree on Land. The expropriation of the gentry's fields, equipment and buildings increased in pace and scope. Lenin lent his support in the Smolny Institute, listening to peasant complaints and encouraging them to push forward with revolutionary measures.[50] But the process also had its own dynamic; peasant soviets were increasingly being set up in Russia in late 1917.[51] Their impact on the rural scene was not as substantial as that of their urban counterparts on the towns. The peasant land commune emerged ever more prominently as the instrument to implement peasant aspirations. The Decree on Land's injunction to maintain the larger capitalist estates intact was seldom accepted. Peasants who had left the commune under the Stolypin reforms of the pre-war period were obliged to rejoin if they wished to obtain a portion of the redistributed land.[52] From the Bolshevik party's viewpoint, it was irritating that communes became so important. Lenin had made his name as an economist in the 1890s by trying to demonstrate that the communal arrangements of the Russian peasantry were a vehicle of rural capitalism. But the peasants' surge to take the solution of the agrarian question into their own hands pleased a Sovnarkom which depended on their acquiescence in the October Revolution.

SECESSION AND FEDERATION

The Bolsheviks could not afford to be satisfied with their successes in the Russian heartland, and aspired to spreading 'soviet power' to the non-Russian segments of the old empire; and Lenin was especially keen to embark upon a process of what we nowadays would call 'de-colonisation'. This has become so widespread a phenomenon since the Second World War that it is important to recognise how extraordinary it was in 1917. The 'nationalities' were to be courted, Russian chauvinism disavowed. Yet Lenin, unlike the members of British and French cabinets in the 1950s, did not expect the result to be a large number of new nation-states. In Finland's case, to be sure, he encouraged secession. But his prognostication was that the granting of Finnish independence would act as a model for other subject peoples in Europe to emulate and would hasten the inauguration of a pan-European socialist order; he did not seek to establish Finland as a permanent nation-state on Russia's borders. But, as regards most other peoples of the empire of the Romanovs, he supposed that his offer of national self-determination would lead them to trust Sovnarkom and welcome a voluntary and non-imperial union with Russia.

The shape of such a union was not defined. Stalin had been asked by the Central Committee on 21 October to produce 'theses' on the national question for submission to the Congress of Soviets,[53] but, distracted by his other commitments, Stalin failed to supply these. Only the broadest assumptions of policy were announced, and, in fact, these came mainly from the hand of Lenin. The appeal issued to 'workers, soldiers and peasants' from the Second Congress of Soviets on 25 October offered a guarantee of 'the authentic right of self-determination to all nations inhabiting Russia'.[54] Lenin's Decree on Peace, on 26 October, repeated the idea that no nation in Europe should be forcibly retained within the confines of a state against its will. Such retentions were to be regarded as annexationist.[55] Stalin was appointed as People's Commissar for Nationality Affairs and instructed to establish practical links and to elaborate policies. This, too, could not be effected overnight. In the meantime, on 2 November, a Declaration of the Rights of the Peoples of Russia was accepted by Sovnarkom and issued next day under the signature of Stalin and Lenin; it called for 'a *voluntary and honourable* union of the peoples of Russia', abolishing all previous national privileges and other discriminations and confirming the right of each nation to secession.[56]

Lenin and Stalin remained allies on the national question; and, since principal opponents such as Bukharin and Pyatakov were outside Petrograd (in Moscow and Kiev), and others such as Dzierzynski were busy in the Military-Revolutionary Committee, they pushed forward with the official policy as formulated by the April Party Conference. Much heat had disappeared from intra-Bolshevik discussions about the non-Russian nationalities by summer 1917,[57] and Lenin acted with a stealthy purposiveness. Secession was quickly offered to the Finns. By October, Finland was in reality self-governing; Kerenski had no more been able to rule its people than he could impose his authority in Russia. Lenin hoped that Finnish independence would be secured by a revolutionary socialist administration of Finns.[58]

The policy was fraught with an unanticipated difficulty: the Finnish social-democrats, whose left wing under Karl Wiik had been expected by Lenin to install a socialist government, failed to come to power. Lenin's letters to Finnish social-democrats before the October Revolution reveal how badly he misjudged the socialists of Finland even though he had spent the summer among them.[59] The Finnish social-democrats were reluctant to budge even after the October events in Petrograd. Offers of direct military assistance from the Bolshevik commanders of the Russian naval garrisons in Finland did not dispel Wiik's caution.[60] He and his colleagues organised a general strike in Finland's cities; but they resisted the Bolshevik plea to make a revolution because they neither wanted civil war nor were convinced that the Soviet government would long survive in Russia.[61] Without becoming the party of government, moreover, the Finnish social-democrats were in no position to declare their country's independence: the summer's elections had produced a conservative administration in Helsinki under P. Svinhufvud. The Bolsheviks made clear that they would grant independence even to Svinhufvud's cabinet. But again they had no success. Svinhufvud did not want to offend the Allies and wanted to obtain independence from the Constituent Assembly in Petrograd. Only gradually were his doubts about the practical benefits of secession and about Lenin's sincerity dispelled. At last, on 18 December 1917, a bemused official delegation from Helsinki to Petrograd obtained on request a document confirming the secession of Finland from ties of state with Russia.[62]

The fiasco of forcing independence down the throats of Finnish politicians proved that those contemporaries who felt that Lenin had no ideological beliefs and was exclusively an unprincipled power-seeker had misunderstood him. While he changed some policies, he stuck to others. No black-and-white depiction can be accurate for so complex a figure; and the diplomatic traffic between Petrograd and Helsinki testifies to a substantial initial commitment to his pre-October policy on the 'national question'. Nevertheless, those Bolsheviks who had argued against Lenin's line on secession were buoyed up by the fiasco. European socialist revolution was not to be the consequence of Finnish independence, and Svinhufvud rather than Wiik held sway in Helsinki.

The only other subject nation to be guaranteed sovereignty over its affairs was Poland. This did not need to come in an official declaration by Sovnarkom since the Provisional Government had already granted independence to the Poles.[63] The German armies had overrun all the Polish territory of the Russian empire and prevented a Russo-Polish exchange of formal documents. And yet this also made it easier for the Bolshevik negotiators to gain support throughout the party for the tactic of embarrassing the German and Austrian delegations at the peace talks in Brest-Litovsk by affirming the need for all peoples to be accorded the right of national self-determination. Russians were no longer oppressing Poles; it was German military might that governed Poland.[64] Lenin and Stalin co-operated closely in elaborating policy towards the rest of the former empire. Finland and Poland had always been recognised as special cases by Lenin; but he had specified that the Ukraine might be the next most likely nation to want to secede.[65] Neither Finland nor Poland were crucial to Russia's internal economic and political well-being in 1917, but the same was not true of the Ukraine. Lenin and Stalin continued to goad the Finnish social-democrats into a seizure of power after December. They had an even stronger wish to have a socialist administration in Kiev. They began carefully, relying both on the attractiveness of their Decrees on Peace and on Land, and on the ability of Ukrainian Bolsheviks to seize power for the soviets in Kiev, Kharkov and Ekaterinoslav.

The Ukrainian Rada shared the same reluctance as Svinhufvud's Finnish cabinet to declare independence. But on 3 November 1917 it announced that, in the absence of a legitimate and effective power for the Ukraine, it was assuming power. The prospect of conflict with the Soviet authorities in Petrograd was increased by the Rada's demand that any future state settlement should involve a federal union between Russia and the Ukraine. No Bolshevik leader yet approved the principles of federalism.[66]

The Bolsheviks in Kiev avoided a clash with the Rada, but prepared for the forthcoming Congress of Soviets in the Ukraine. But the Rada steadfastly opposed Sovnarkom and linked up with the anti-Bolshevik force among the Don Cossacks. A clash in Kiev was inevitable, especially after the arrest of Bolshevik leaders in Kiev in late November. Until then the Sovnarkom had declined to intervene actively. Apart from disseminating copies of its legislation of 25–26 October, it had contented itself with appeals to the brotherhood of nations and with the restoration of Ukrainian treasures and national symbols to Kiev as proofs of good intent.[67] On 4 December a formal ultimatum was delivered to Kiev.[68] Further discussions followed. A difficulty for the Bolsheviks was that the Ukrainian Congress of Soviets in Kiev found them in a minority.[69] The Bolsheviks adjourned to Kharkov, held their own rival Congress of Soviets and – guided now by their left-wing leaders – moved to seize power in all major cities. Sovnarkom judged the moment appropriate for intervention. Troops were dispatched from Petrograd under the leadership of V. A. Antonov-Ovseenko into the Ukraine. Bolstered by local Red Guards, they eased the maintenance of soviet power in several areas and, on 26 January 1918, entered Kiev. The Ukraine was Red at last.[70]

Policy statements took a new turn. Federation, previously a word spat out even by Lenin (who was the Bolshevik leader favouring the gentlest treatment of the national question), became part of current parlance. On 3 December Lenin had drafted a 'Manifesto to the Ukrainian People', published in *Pravda* two days later, which announced the hope that a federal agreement could be worked out between Russia and the Ukraine.[71] The Ukrainian Bolshevik leftists, who regarded such suggestions as an undesirable concession to nationalism, were displeased.[72] But they needed Petrograd's support and succumbed to Lenin's pressure; and the knowledge of their electoral weakness in the Ukraine dissuaded them from disobedience to the Bolshevik Central Committee.[73]

The idea of federation was generalised in the 'Declaration of Rights of the Toiling and Exploited People', written by Lenin for presentation to the Constituent Assembly. The Soviet state, he declared, should be founded 'on the basis of a free union of free nations as a federation of Soviet republics'.[74] This was a declaration, not a decree; and the decrees themselves were in any case more declarative than decree-like. Practical regulations were undefined. None the less, a sea-change in Lenin's attitude had occurred. It was among the earliest changes of direction on major policy undertaken by him after the October Revolution. Nation-based territorial units had been his previous aim, and he had argued for them with an intemperate vigour. In conceding the federal principle, he not untypically gave no explanation of the reasons; indeed no acknowledgement was given that a concession had been made. The behind-the-scenes calculations and debates are not yet documented. But the result, undoubtedly, was a recognition that the 'national movement' was becoming stronger in several places of the old empire. Nor did

Bukharin and the Bolshevik left have a practical alternative. Their only 'policy' was constituted by the objectives of European socialist revolution and a United States of Europe.[75] In 1917, this offered no recipe for action in the former Romanov lands. But inaction had never been a Bolshevik virtue; and Lenin skilfully advocated a practical plan which at least had the merit, in the eyes of Bolshevik leftists, of seeking the retention of a multinational state.

The Ukraine had been the key region, but was far from being the only region of importance to Sovnarkom's survival. Mensheviks held authority in Georgia, and their opposition to the October Revolution meant that the Georgian Menshevik leadership acted as if they were independent: they would submit themselves only to a legitimately-elected Constituent Assembly. Bolsheviks came to power in Baku, in Azerbaidzhan (as it was coming to be called); but the local Moslem parties and influences grew in the surrounding countryside: the chances of an anti-Russian alliance was growing. In Armenia, the zeal to break with Russia was weaker; but the Bolsheviks held little influence and would have only weakened their position if concessions to national feeling had not been forthcoming. In Siberia, the Socialist Revolutionaries were attempting to set up an autonomous state administration. To the north west, Estonian and Lithuanian national movements were being roused. Even in Belorussia, where ethnic differentiation between Belorussians and Russians was frail and where the menace posed by the Germans was the greatest concern for the population, the beginnings of a campaign for autonomy were noted.[76]

The national surge among Estonians and Latvians was linked to support for the Bolsheviks in Russia. In Estonia, the Tallin Soviet announced the inception of 'soviet power' in November. The Congress of Soviets in Latvia, which was already under partial occupation by the Germans, did the same in mid-December 1917.[77] This was a success for Lenin; but it was exceptional, and the broader and more optimistic expectations he had described to the April Party Conference were being dashed. The set-backs of November and December made him less generous in his promises to the non-Russian regions. He had never touted secession as an end in itself; it had always been his assumption that the offer of secessionist rights would sooner or later bring Russians and non-Russians together voluntarily in a single multinational state as well as ignite an anti-imperialist explosion in the colonies of Germany, France and Britain. His disappointments hardened his policy: no plebiscites on national aspirations would be held on Soviet-governed territory; and the idea that the interests of the working class, as distinct from the nation as whole, in each non-Russian region should be paramount was increasingly used as a device to maintain the borders of the old empire. The Romanov lands were not seething with anti-Russianism. Social and economic issues, rather than the composition of the Kiev administration, continued to preoccupy Ukrainian peasants. Similar tendencies were observable elsewhere. Yet nationalist feelings were undeniably growing in fervour; and the signs were few that a robust pro-Sovietism pervaded the non-Russian regions. Even the goal of federation would not be achievable except by means of military force.[78]

POLITICAL REPRESSION

Sovnarkom's main worries of the moment were concentrated on Russia. The administration, joined by the Left Socialist Revolutionaries, was already involved in acts of political repression. In the last two months of 1917, Spiridonova's comrades were the only party which did not suffer directly at the hands of the Bolsheviks. Attentive observers of Lenin before the October Revolution can hardly have been surprised. He had written in favour of dictatorship. He had urged the need for a system of civil rights and judicial procedures which expressly discriminated against the bourgeoisie; and he had described all parties to the right of the Bolsheviks as mere appendages of the Kadets and their pro-bourgeois interests. He had eulogised force as the midwife of history's successful revolutions.[79]

But it was only after the October Revolution that most people who supported the Bolsheviks became fully aware of his ferocity. Lenin had hitherto adjusted his rhetoric in order to allay any feelings that a government under his leadership would produce a national bloodbath. He had written only rarely about the usefulness of terror as a means of consolidating a revolutionary administration; and he had often done this without using the word 'terror'.[80] Viktor Nogin, on resigning his post as People's Commissar of Internal Affairs, predicted that the Soviet government would steadily move towards terrorist techniques if the Bolsheviks refused to form a broad socialist coalition.[81] Yet there was no Bolshevik anathema on the application of mass terror. On the contrary, Lenin approved its use by the Jacobins in the French Revolution; and, at the Third Party Congress in 1905, the Bolsheviks displayed a willingness to resort to it in Russia if the need appeared to arise.[82] Lenin's approval of mass terror was accompanied by a rejection of the populist-terrorist tactic of assassinations of individual state officials as a means of bringing about a crisis of the Romanov state. He thought such a tactic wasted the energies of the revolutionary movement. But his attitude, even to 'individual terror', was flexible. In 1905, when the Romanov state was already enveloped in a deep political crisis, he encouraged the killing of individual state officials as heartily as did the Socialist Revolutionaries. His previous disapproval of the tactic had been based on purely pragmatic considerations.[83]

Even so, he had specifically stated in summer 1917 that he only expected to have to arrest '50–100' leading industrialists and bankers.[84] There is no firm evidence available that Lenin and colleagues such as Trotski were hell-bent, before the October Revolution, on instigating a campaign of summary arrest and execution of large numbers of people who had committed no crime but who happened to belong to a social category deemed politically inimical to the regime. Lenin made threats on political opponents quickly after the seizure of power. But he avoided the blatant advocacy of terror made by Trotski as early as 1 December: 'You wax indignant at the naked terror which we are applying against our class enemies, but let me tell you that in one month's time at the most it will assume more terrible forms, modelled on the terror of the great French revolutionaries. Not the fortress but the guillotine will await our enemies.'[85]

Systematic summary repression which did not go as far as gross physical maltreatment or capital punishment occurred with not only the sanction but even the straightforward encouragement of the central Soviet authorities in the first month of Soviet power, and several weeks before the establishment of the All-Russian Extraordinary Commission for Combating Counter-Revolution, Speculation and Sabotage (or, as it appears in its Russian acronym: the Cheka), which is rightly regarded as the forerunner of today's KGB. Such repression was undertaken by organs which, at Lenin's direction, were kept deliberately unaccountable for their actions. The facility of Lenin's resort to terror raises a question about the sincerity of his pre-October statements. Had he really believed that the dimensions of repression would be low? It cannot be discounted that, as a utopian thinker, he had been temporarily convinced that resistance to Bolshevism would be small and that he would 'need' to use little violence. He may well also have failed to consider his future administration's methods in practical detail. It is also true that the scale of terror was raised only gradually by Lenin. And yet, when all is said in his favour, it is striking how easily, quickly and frequently he came to conclusions that Sovnarkom had to amplify its repressive zeal. The suspicion must be strong that he had always known that he would deploy greater violence than he was willing to recognise before October 1917.

Several Bolshevik leaders expected that the People's Commissariats of Internal Affairs and of Justice would preside over law and order, but Lenin had other ideas. He admired the Military-Revolutionary Committee's ruthlessness in rooting out saboteurs, speculators and opponents of the regime; and he knew how little control over its activities was exercised by the Petrograd Soviet. (It was no accident that the Committee contained several Bolsheviks, including Felix Dzierzynski, who were to lead the Cheka). At a Sovnarkom session under Lenin's chairmanship on 15 November, a decision was taken to transfer various matters from the People's Commissariat of Internal Affairs to the Military-Revolutionary Committee.[86] This session just happens to have been documented and published. But a series of parallel *ad hoc* order-enforcement agencies – to call them organs of agencies of law-enforcement would be a linguistic travesty – sprang up in the first month of Soviet power; less is known about their activities, not least because little constraint was placed on them in the fulfilment and recording of their tasks. Lenin encouraged them and protected them against complaints.[87]

Admittedly, the Bolshevik Central Committee and Sovnarkom were not hallucinating when they talked of enemies who planned or could reasonably be expected to plan armed opposition towards the Bolsheviks. The Bolsheviks had seized power; they could scarcely anticipate a pat on the back from their foes. There is a 'road to Dublin' aspect to this argument; for no one had forced Lenin and Trotski to grasp power in the way they did: they could hardly demand sympathy for their subsequent dilemmas. Even so, Lenin left nothing to chance. He implicitly endorsed Cromwell's dictum that, while it is good to strike while the iron is hot, it is better to make it hot by striking. Closures of non-Bolshevik newspapers continued. Criticisms were directed at the Decree on the Press – or 'Lenin's decree', as it was sometimes called – in the Central Executive

Committee of the Congress of Soviets. Lenin brushed them casually aside.[88] He supported Dzierzynski and the Military-Revolutionary Committee in all their actions. The application of restrictions on acceptable political discourse was only a part of Dzierzynski's business. He and his associates hunted out 'speculators' flouting the grain-trade monopoly. Squads were also sent out to round up looters and drunkards.[89] Civil servants refusing to co-operate with the new regime found themselves in trouble with the Military-Revolutionary Committee.[90]

The uncontrolled actions of such agencies induced complaints not only from other political parties but also from the general public. Yet it was military opposition which caused the Bolsheviks the greatest anxiety. On 9 November, orders were given for the arrest of the Committee for the Salvation of the Motherland and the Revolution. Its members included not only liberals but also several Mensheviks and Socialist Revolutionaries; all of them sought the forcible overthrow of Bolshevism.[91] The scope of permissible repression widened. On 16 November, Sovnarkom decided, on balance, not to incarcerate Milyukov.[92] But by 28 November this inhibition had disappeared: Lenin signed a Sovnarkom announcement that all members of the Kadet party, regardless of their opinions and activity as individuals, were to be treated as 'enemies of the people' and placed outside the law.[93]

The regularising of order-enforcement agencies was becoming a practical necessity. On 6 December, Dzierzynski was asked by Lenin at Sovnarkom to draft measures for the establishment of a new body. With a civil service strike again in prospect, Dzierzynski got down to work quickly and his draft was passed by Sovnarkom the following day. Dzierzynski made no pretence of an interest in 'justice': Cheka was required to conduct an unrelenting struggle without heed of legal niceties, or of the number of innocent victims.[94] This momentous decision was made almost casually. The Cheka's formation was not even dignified by the passing of a Sovnarkom decree; and no reference was made to the official legislative body, the Central Executive Committee of Congress of Soviets.[95] The speed of Lenin's turn to repressive measures leaves little doubt that before October he had been holding back in public about his intentions. An ideological thread linked his 1905 statements on terror with his post-October practice. The licence he granted to the Military-Revolutionary Committee and, later, to the Cheka does not demonstrate a veritable lust for terror. And yet he certainly did not find terror entirely unpalatable. When other leading Bolsheviks sought to restrain Dzierzynski, Lenin freed him to follow his repressive instincts.

GERMANY AND THE ALLIES

The messages issuing from Sovnarkom and its chairman continued to be euphoric, and the elevated mood persisted even while the lurch down into repressive measures steepened; there were few Bolsheviks remaining inside the party who did not have highly unrealistic notions about what could be accomplished in the Russia of 1917. Those who had a more realistic judgement, such as Kamenev and Zinoviev, had resigned their leading positions; and others were like Stalin who, although they had always doubted that Europe was as yet truly pregnant with revolution, kept their worries to themselves. Yet Lenin, too, was pondering the excessive optimism of the Bolshevik left with growing agitation; he was relieved, in early December, when Zinoviev resumed his Central Committee seat.[96]

His worries were acute about international relations. Even the leftists at the Sixth Party Congress had acknowledged that an offensive revolutionary war was not feasible; and the creation of a People's Commissariat of External Affairs under Trotski indicated an awareness that diplomacy retained its usefulness even if Trotski predicted that he would be able to 'shut up shop' after publishing the secret treaties of Nikolai II. Lenin had never claimed that a German socialist revolution was certain to occur literally on the morrow of the Russian socialist revolution. He had also been vague about how to set about encouraging such a revolution in Germany, short of engaging in a revolutionary war. His main specific proposals had been for Russian soldiers to fraternise with German soldiers on the Eastern front, and for the Soviet government to enter serious negotiations for a general 'democratic peace'. On 7 November, therefore, Sovnarkom instructed General Dukhonin, Commander-in-Chief of the Russian armed forces since the Provisional Government's last days, to parley with the German High Command with the purpose of bringing about an armistice throughout Europe. On 8 November Trotski informed Western ambassadors in Petrograd about the Soviet government's commitment to the achievement of such an armistice.[97] Dukhonin procrastinated and was replaced by the Bolshevik N. V. Krylenko. Russian troops were encouraged to fraternise over the trenches with German troops. Trotski's *coup de théatre et de guerre* was to carry out the promise to publish Nikolai II's treaties. At last it was revealed that the Allies, who had advertised their democratic intentions in the war, were planning a redivision of whole regions of the world in the event of a military victory for the Russians, the French and the British.[98]

Naturally, there was no positive response from the Allies about the armistice proposal; and on 14 November it was agreed by the Soviet and German authorities to initiate negotiations for a separate truce on the Eastern front.[99] Lenin and Trotski issued a proclamation blaming the Allied powers for compelling them to take the step.[100] The embarrassment of governments in London and Paris was matched only by their rage at the run of events. Trotski's associate, A. A. Ioffe, led the Soviet diplomatic team at the talks with the Germans in the border town of Brest-Litovsk. The Germans, keen to be able to release troops from service on the Eastern front for combat on the Western front, were enthusiastic negotiators. On 2 December a separate armistice was signed.[101]

The Allied governments perceived that unofficial contact with Sovnarkom was vital to inhibit Russia's complete disengagement from the War. Trotski met with their various representatives in Petrograd[102] Lenin, either because of preoccupation with domestic affairs or else because he wished others to be tainted with involvement in such unpleasant duties, held himself aloof. The separate armistice with the Germans, furthermore, called for the inception of talks about a permanent peace. Trotski was already pondering aloud whether the Russians could carry on fighting if Germany failed to have its expected socialist revolution. He still thought a revolutionary war would have to be fought if all else failed; but his appreciation of the difficulties was notable.[103] Lenin, meanwhile, persisted in his silence about revolutionary war.[104] He and Trotski at least agreed that, for the moment, the talks with the Central Powers at Brest-Litovsk should be used as an instrument for spreading Soviet propaganda to the workers and soldiers of Germany. The ingenuity of the new diplomacy of the Bolsheviks was countered by the subtlety of the German and Austrian negotiators. Far from being embarrassed by the Soviet demand for 'national self-determination' as the principle to underlie any general peace in Europe, German Foreign Secretary Ricard von Kühlmann employed it to undermine the Bolsheviks' pretensions to sovereignty over most of the old Russian empire. Consultations of popular opinion in the Ukraine and in regions of the Baltic provinces and the Transcaucasus would predictably fail to produce pro-Bolshevik majorities.

Nor did the diplomats of the Central Powers have sleepless nights about the requirement that they too should offer self-determination to regions under their occupation. They could easily demand that the Allies should do the same; and they expected that the result would thus be that they would avoid giving up any territory. The German military command found such scheming to be uncongenially indirect. But Kühlmann and his Austrian counterpart Count Czernin persuaded them that there was a likelihood of transferring troops from the Eastern to the Western front; and that diplomatic feints were necessary for the achievement of this objective.[105] The Brest-Litovsk peace conference proper opened on 9 December. The Soviet delegation was headed by A. A. Ioffe, who resembled Trotski inasmuch as he was a left-wing Marxist who had joined the Bolshevik party only in 1917. Ioffe's early optimism was confounded. The German negotiators revealed that the principle of national self-determination would require that Sovnarkom disclaimed sovereignty over non-Russian areas in the old Russian empire.[106]

Lenin entered a trough of agitation. The evidence from the trenches on the Eastern front moved him profoundly. The Bolshevik peace policy called on soldiers to help to end the war by fraternising with German soldiers and spreading the revolutionary contagion to the enemy armed forces; but Russian peasants-in-uniform preferred simply to desert. Soon, not only revolutionary enthusiasm among the Russian soldiers would be lacking, but the Russian soldiers too. Ioffe and the Soviet delegation perceived the virtues in extending the conference proceedings.[107] On 18 December, Lenin came to Sovnarkom with a motion stressing the need to prepare Petrograd's defences.[108] On the same day he broke his silence about 'revolutionary war', and still gave the impression of being committed to such a war as a contingency policy.[109] Yet his work among delegates from the army committees the day before showed that he entertained severe doubts. It had been on 17 December that he issued a questionnaire to discover the army's combat readiness. Could the Germans really be resisted, and for how long? Would a collapse of the peace conference be accompanied by mass desertions? Was agitation in favour of revolutionary war sensible? Would the army, if given a vote, give its approval to a separate peace? The response of the delegates confirmed Lenin's fears, and indeed suggested that he might not be pessimistic enough.[110] The precise time of Lenin's change of heart is unknown. It cannot be ruled out that it occurred before October; but proof is unavailable.[111] Certainly from mid-December, however, he was seriously considering whether to pull Russia out of the war by a separate peace. Unlike Trotski, he had never made a point of stressing that the Russian socialist revolution would be lost if socialist revolutions failed to break out in central and western Europe. But he shared the assumption that, without revolutions in other major European states, Russia's revolutionary project would be crippled.[112] So Lenin's mental shift was not lightly undertaken. He knew it to be a potentially catastrophic retreat. There is an unknown factor here: the extent of political contacts and 'understandings', if any, between Lenin and the Berlin government. The Germans had had an interest in helping the Bolsheviks to take power, and rejoiced in the news of the October Revolution. But whether the Berlin government stretched out a helping hand to Lenin in the last two months of 1917 is undiscoverable from available documents (although the German diplomats at Brest-Litovsk acted as if they were offering little concession, monetary or political, to the Bolsheviks).[113]

At any rate, Lenin kept his changing ideas out of the public gaze. Trotski argued that as yet the Central Powers had presented no ultimatum and that the most appropriate tactic was to prolong negotiations in the hope that a German socialist revolution might occur.[114] Yet Lenin also wished to plan carefully for the contingency that such a revolution would not come to Sovnarkom's rescue and that a separate peace might prove necessary. Bolshevik leaders, while showing an awareness in summer 1917 of the difficulties of fighting a revolutionary war, had never suggested that the alternative option, namely a separate peace, was acceptable.[115] They had always believed that, if it came to a choice between a separate peace and a war of revolutionary defence, no Bolshevik should sign a treaty with the Germans. The Left Socialist-Revolutionaries, to a man and woman, were implacably opposed to a separate peace. There was no substantial party in the country which would accept a deal with Berlin and Vienna. The Mensheviks and the Socialist Revolutionaries were unappeasably hostile to any separate deal with Germany and Austria-Hungary. If Lenin was going to change his party's policy, the political campaign would make the struggle for *The April Theses* seem child's play. Trotski in the meantime was sent to Brest-Litovsk to replace Ioffe, who had not acquitted himself well as a negotiator. The fate of the October Revolution hung in the balance.

On 20 December 1917 the German peace terms were clarified. The Soviet government was asked to relinquish claims to sovereignty over Poland and the Baltic region and to accept a German military occupation of those regions.[116] No date for a reply from Petrograd was set, but Lenin foresaw that Trotski's delaying tactics might soon prove insufficient. On 24 December 1917, Lenin set out for a few days' rest in a sanatorium near the Usikirkka village railway station.[117] It could hardly be, and undoubtedly was not, much of a holiday. Krupskaya was to recall that he spent most of his time thinking and reading about politics. He was plotting how to present his volte-face on the idea of a separate peace to his fellow Bolsheviks. His notes give a clue to the direction of his thought. Among the themes for future articles he wrote: 'In the first place, vanquish the bourgeoisie – and then fight the bourgeoisie abroad'.[118]

In such a fashion he would try to sublimate disappointment with the failure of international policy to a commitment to take up the revolutionary struggle in even greater earnest at home. He eulogised civil war, claiming such a war to be 'uniquely legitimate, uniquely just and uniquely sanctified'.[119] Trotski firmly opposed such a reorientation and secured Lenin's continued support for his procrastinatory tactics with the delegations of Germany and Austria-Hungary at Brest-Litovsk. On the way from Petrograd, even he had viewed the empty trenches with horror. How could a revolutionary war be fought without an army? But he kept these worries from Kühlmann and Czernin, and his intellectual brilliance dazzled them for several days. Yet the German and Austrian representatives were not free agents; they had to answer to Hindenburg and Ludendorff. The military ultimatum could not be delayed for ever. But Trotski felt that the Bolsheviks and Left Socialist Revolutionaries had no option but to prolong the talks and call the bluff of the Central Powers, hoping against hope that the German workers would rise against the Kaiser or that a debilitating mutiny would occur among the German forces on active service; and, for the moment, it was Trotski's policy which guided the Soviet negotiators. Lenin, with difficulty, bided his time. He had yet to make his decisive impact on the issue that had played so great a role in the Bolshevik advance on power: the issue of war and peace.

DARKENING THOUGHTS

Intimidating developments at Brest-Litovsk did not dispel the optimism of the Bolshevik leaders in either Petrograd or the provinces. Lenin continued to call for working-class initiative, to welcome factory workers in person to the Smolny Institute and to proclaim the ultimate objectives of communism. His domestic political strategy in 1917, before the seizure of power, had been a combination of the revolution from above with the revolution from below. He had never satisfactorily explained precisely how to effect such a combination; but his propounding of the general strategy, for all its theoretical gaps and subterfuges, did not lack sincerity.

Strongly-held doctrines were not peculiar to the Bolsheviks among Russian political parties in the revolutionary period. They had all of them suffered, to a greater or lesser extent, under the Romanov monarchy; and their ideas and assumptions were solidified by the pressure of years of persecution. The question has been asked why Lenin failed to make a more realistic assessment of his party's capacities in the first months after the October Revolution.[120] By 1921, he was willing, through the New Economic Policy, to grant a relaxation of the state grain-trade monopoly and allow peasants to sell the post-tax surplus after the harvest on the private market. The purpose was to facilitate the resurgence of exchange of goods between town and countryside. Why did Lenin not attempt this in the winter of 1917–18? Would this not have limited the social basis for counter-revolution? Would not the pressures for the Bolsheviks to become more authoritarian have been smaller? Such questions beg several further questions. The number of employed factory workers in 1921 had fallen to a third of the number in October 1917; and the army in 1921 was being demobilised, whereas in 1917 the outbreak of either a protracted civil war or a war against foreign aggressors was a strong possibility. Workers in armaments factories and soldiers needed to be fed, and had to be fed mainly by the efforts of governmental institutions. Lenin and Sovnarkom could scarcely forego a large proportion of the tradeable grain surplus in the circumstances.[121]

Yet the Bolsheviks did not entertain a second thought (or even a first one) about introducing greater latitude for trading on the private market. The central party leadership was a collective of Marxist believers. They were nearly as averse to commerce based on principles of personal profit as Moslems and Jews are to the consumption of pork; it took years of civil war to break down the walls of their ideological inhibition; and even then the walls were reconstructed by the end of the 1920s. Moreover, a 'capitalist government' had set up the state grain-trade monopoly before the Bolsheviks seized power. The Bolsheviks, as far-left socialists, were highly unlikely to regard a relaxation of controls on capitalism as an immediately desirable priority. The entire project of socialist revolution would otherwise seem to them to have a weak rationale.[122]

In addition, Lenin was an extremist by the standards of most non-Bolshevik Russian socialists, but his policies on several socio-economic issues remained decidedly moderate in comparison with those of many colleagues. Nikolai Bukharin, N. Osinski and other Bolshevik leftists were elaborating an agrarian policy involving the rapid collectivisation of peasant households.[123] Poor Lenin! He it had been in the 1890s who had urged upon Russian Marxists that capitalism in the countryside had achieved a high level of development. Left-wing Bolsheviks concluded that this justified the transfer of all agricultural soil into the hands of socialist collective farms run by agronomists and wage labourers, and they pushed hard for the local party committees to adopt their policy.[124] Pity for Lenin is, consequently, scarcely in order. Even in *The April Theses* he had fudged the topic of 'model farms' and allowed Bolsheviks on the left to think that he and they were at one about agrarian policy.[125] He had been clearer about his attitude to 'workers' control',[126] suggesting that he did not envisage the ejection of existing managers from the factories. Factory-workshop committees, in his opinion, should supervise and not replace management. Yet others disagreed. Bukharin's supporters sought the transformation of the factory-workshop committees into managerial bodies. The struggle over industrial policy was only just beginning.[127]

The hypothesis that Lenin had sufficient authority to introduce the ideas of 1921 in 1917 badly misconstrues the ideological nature of Bolshevism after the October Revolution; it also neglects the party's organisational disjointedness and localism. The lower-level committees could not yet be trampled down by the Central Committee. The controversy over a separate peace with Germany and Austria-Hungary in the first three months of 1918 was about to show how easy it was for regional, provincial and city party committees to ignore the central leadership's demands.[128]

The revolutionary élan persisted. Streets were painted red; poster art flourished. New public buildings, statues and other adornments were planned. Workers' educational groups were formed. Painters and poets, as well as scholars and literary intellectuals, conducted new cultural experiments. A new world where the workers and peasants would be masters was being talked about. The notion that an authentic social transformation from capitalism into socialism involved the promotion and participations of 'the masses' was widely held. Local political pride was rampant. The Saratov City Soviet, having replaced the agencies of the Provisional Government, declared: 'Our commune is the beginning of the world-wide commune. We, as the leaders, assume full responsibility and fear nothing.'[129] Party committee members and activists were not immune from the euphoria, either. Bolsheviks everywhere swept into the soviets, trade unions and factory-workshop committees; the purely internal work of the party was neglected. Hierarchical obedience in public institutions was rare; the administrative framework of the soviets was poorly co-ordinated. Sovnarkom began to dispatch 'plenipotentiaries' to unplug local bottlenecks or override local opposition. But the trend was as yet frail; and the centralism advocated by all leading Bolsheviks, including the leftists who simultaneously and contradictorily wanted to grant maximum power to factory-workshop committees, was not accepted in practice.[130]

And yet the huge problems in the economy, in domestic politics and international relations, were growing huger. Kamenev, Zinoviev, Milyutin and other Bolshevik rightists had warned about the dangers of aggravating them; and Lenin, who had scoffed at the rightists' warnings in October 1917, began to share their sentiments. On 4 November 1917 he announced to the Petrograd Soviet: 'Our deficiency consists in the fact that our soviet organisation has not yet learnt to administer, that we hold too many meetings.'[131] The eulogist of mass participatory politics was finding massed gatherings increasingly tiresome. He also objected to the internal inefficiencies of the soviets and the other public organisations. It would, he suggested, no longer be enough to introduce 'account-keeping and supervision' into their operations; there would need to be *'competition* in the section of organisational successes'.[132] By this he meant that soviets should compete with each other in eradicating chaos. Quite how such competition could take place was not spelled out.[133] But the proposal, which was not made public, indicated that his hyper-elevated ideas of the pre-October period were decreasingly seen by him to be adequate.[134]

Similarly, he stressed the need not to alienate 'educated people'.[135] He had believed, before 1917, that the techniques of 'bourgeois culture' should be retained in the socialist revolution; his opposition to Bogdanov's dismissive attitude and to vague talk about 'proletarian culture' had been deep.[136] In *The State and Revolution* too he had accepted the requirement to retain the services of 'specialists'.[137] Yet it had not been a topic of emphasis. [138] Even more impressive are the neglected shifts in Lenin's attitude to the working class. He had to be cautious with any adverse public comment on the 'proletariat'. Yet privately he was exasperated by what he perceived as growing lack of co-operation from the groups of labourers. In December 1917 he considered that printing workers, by going on strike, were behaving 'like hooligans':[139] he favoured arresting them if their strikes continued. The fact that the print-workers were interested in the protection of freedom of expression for non-Bolshevik political parties was a strange ground for dubbing them hooligans, but Lenin rampantly expanded the category of imprisonable people. He jotted down the thought that 'no crook (including those who are simply fed up with work) should walk the streets in freedom but should be locked up in prison or should be serving out a sentence of forced labour of the heaviest kind'.[140] The wording here is so vague that it could have included workers as well as the rest of the population. By mid-January 1918, as the breakdown in industry continued, he edged nearer to publicising his concerns. He openly urged that the factories be cleared of 'tramplike and semi-tramplike elements imbued with the single desire to "scrounge around" and then move on'; and that too many persons in existing enterprises had taken jobs merely to avoid conscription.[141]

Yet his most jolting commentary, for those who had discerned only the libertarian aspects of his ideas before October, came in his statements on labourers in the armaments factories. These he designated as 'privileged workers' who were exercised only by their sectional interests (which, presumably, involved a continuation of the war and therefore were counterposed to Lenin's policy for a separate peace).[142] His comments had some basis in reality. But to tar so many workers with the same brush, to cast doubts on their motives and to do so with such contempt overturned much said by him about the working class in the months before the seizure of power. It had roots in his horrified and belated recognition of the dimensions and nature of the economic crisis; it was also traceable to the subordinate role he had always placed on the workers as a social class whenever they acted at variance with his policies.

His declarations about the peasants were, in contrast, calm and benign. He coined a slogan for action. Bolsheviks, he declared, should seek 'to help the labouring peasant, avoid offending the middle peasant and compel the rich peasant'.[143]. He continued to assert that there was sufficient food in the country. This was indeed true. Yet he also persisted, more dubiously, with his claim that it was only capitalism, greed and speculation that caused the food-supplies problems. 'Kulaks' were the scapegoat in his speeches and writings; he was reverting more and more frankly to the idea, which had been held largely in abeyance in summer 1917, that the peasantry should be treated as an internally-differentiated social category. Thus Lenin made a quick return to the themes of class war and of the attack on the richer peasants. He spoke with growing openness about the need for stern measures, declaring on 14 January 1918: 'Until we apply terror to speculators, shooting them on the spot, nothing will turn out right.'[144] On 28 January he talked of the necessity to squeeze money out of the kulaks.[145] He failed to recognise the impact of objective general difficulties with trade, transport and finance. Nor did he indicate how 'kulaks' were to be categorised. It was more difficult even than before to pick them out since land redistribution had led to a levelling-out of landholdings. The armed emissaries dispatched from certain town soviets to seek out hoarded grain were bound to clash with not only the minority of 'rich' households but those millions in the middling category. Lenin before October had advocated ideas resting on an alliance between workers and peasants. A central link in his strategical chain was being torn asunder.

10 The Obscene Peace: January to March 1918

THE CONSTITUENT ASSEMBLY

The October Revolution's repercussions endure in many forms: the political map of Europe was lastingly affected. It has been tempting to treat the Russian revolutionary events as if they were entirely independent of the situation in the rest of the world and as if Russia, while having an impact on other countries, did not in her turn register their impact. Yet the October Revolution did not take place in a void. The Soviet state was created in the midst of the First World War, and Russia and her empire had been a major combatant power from its beginning. The attempt to put an end to the fighting, through the Decree on Peace presented by Lenin on 26 October 1917, was not followed by a pan-European socialist revolution. As night follows day, it was certain that Russian withdrawal from the conflict would attract unpleasant consequences from abroad. The Allies were bound to be enraged by Russia's refusal to maintain operations on the Eastern front. Germany's rulers, never having been distinguished for their international altruism, would predictably exploit the weakness of Russian defences to the utmost. If revolutions failed to occur in Europe, the chances of Sovnarkom's survival were intimately linked to the question of whether any foreign capitalist power had the resources and opportunity to intervene militarily in Russia. No Russian army in 1917–18 could have repelled the armed might of either the Germans or the Allies if such might had been turned on them in concerted fashion.

Thus the absence of revolutionary explosions in Europe, as Lenin was to concede,[1] meant that his regime's fortunes depended ultimately on a factor beyond its control: the continued mutual exhaustion of the Central Powers and the Allies in the War. Should the armies of Hindenburg and Ludendorff suddenly collapse on the fields of Flanders, there was no military reason why the British,

French and American forces should not sweep through to the Urals. Only their political and economic problems might impede premiers Lloyd George, Clemenceau and Wilson. Should, on the other hand, Marshal Pétain and General Haig prove incapable of resisting further German onslaughts on the Western front, there was even less cause to suppose that Petrograd and Moscow would not swiftly be subjugated to Berlin.

The victorious progress of Bolshevism before October 1917 could not permanently obscure these supreme military issues. The party's political triumph in Russia too was being called into question in the first winter after the Bolshevik-led revolution. The Constituent Assembly results began to become available in late November. Lenin's name had been on several successful lists put forward by the Bolsheviks; and, in accordance with the then current system of proportional representation, he chose to be returned as one of the deputies for the Baltic fleet.[2] Seldom has a parliament acquired a member so disdainful of his achievement in being elected. Only in the pre-October months of 1917 had he ever spoken warmly about a Constituent Assembly; and even then it was mainly with the purpose of undermining public confidence in the Provisional Government's will to convoke the Assembly.[3] He had no abiding fondness for institutions elected by universal suffrage. His manipulativeness and lack of public candour was so extreme that, while the Second Congress of Soviets of Workers' and Soldiers' Deputies was in session, he implored his Bolshevik Central Committee colleagues to announce a postponement of the Constituent Assembly elections.[4] This was a natural corollary of his admission to the Central Committee on 10 October that the Constituent Assembly would not side with the Bolsheviks. Yet he had not stated this outside the Central Committee's sessions, and his central colleagues overruled his proposed tergiversation on 26 October, arguing that it would damage the party politically.[5]

The Assembly elections had been difficult to arrange, and voting in some places had to be spread over several weeks. Even today it is impossible to offer a definitive computation of the number of seats gained by each respective party. Data are available for 703 Assembly deputies, 380 of which, a clear majority, were Socialist Revolutionaries. Only 168, or 22 per cent, were Bolsheviks; they had suffered a massive defeat. Their only consolation was the poor showing of the Mensheviks, who received only eighteen deputies. The Kadets obtained merely fifteen.[6]

After such a result it might have seemed natural for Viktor Chernov and his Party of Socialist Revolutionaries to form the government, doubtless in coalition with their Menshevik friends. Admittedly, the Socialist Revolutionaries' triumph was not evenly-distributed across the country. In industrial cities and in places with large army garrisons the Bolsheviks held the upper hand; and the Boishevik party acquitted itself well also in those rural regions from which the peasantry tended to migrate in search of seasonal work in nearby factories. But peasant Russian general – and Russia was demographically still mainly a backward, agrarian society – voted for the Socialist Revolutionaries. The loyalty of the villages to 'their' party was unshaken by the months of its association with the Provisional Government. And only 39 Left Socialist Revolutionaries were elected to the Constituent Assembly.[7] The Bolsheviks had never expected to win the election outright: even in his 'optimistic' pronouncements on the party's electoral prospects in advance of the seizure of power in Petrograd, Lenin had calculated that collaboration with the Left Socialist Revolutionaries would be necessary.[8] And yet no Bolshevik before October is recorded as having anticipated the scale of the actual defeat. Lenin's worst fears during the Second Congress of Soviets of Workers' and Soldiers' Deputies were fulfilled.

Bolshevik spokesmen argued that the Assembly arrangements had been unfair to them. The elections had been held quickly after the October Revolution, too quickly for the popularity of Sovnarkom's social and economic reforms to be transformed into direct political support for the Bolsheviks in the countryside. Lenin and his associates also complained that the lists of electoral candidates had been drawn up before the split in the Party of Socialist Revolutionaries. The consequence was an under-representation of the Left Socialist Revolutionaries at the Assembly, since the electorate was widely unable to vote specifically for them or even to know who they were. Furthermore, it was pointed out that the Party of Socialist Revolutionaries, despite having won the Assembly elections, was riven by internal disputes. The problem was not confined to the split with the Left Socialist Revolutionaries; there were also divisions between the Party of Socialist Revolutionaries and its local committees in the non-Russian areas. The formation of a workable government by such a party would have been exceedingly difficult.

The dilemma of the Bolsheviks and the Left Socialist Revolutionaries remained: what to do about the Constituent Assembly as elected? An alliance of their fractions in the Assembly would not produce a majority; and the Sovnarkom coalition partners could not form a government by weight of numbers. Nor were there sufficient deputies from the other parties who might be persuaded to throw in their lot, even at the last minute, with the Soviet authorities. Stalin's idea, as explained to Sovnarkom on 19 November, was to postpone convocation for as long as possible.[9] But indefinite postponement was no more practical than Lenin's original proposal of a prolonged delay in holding elections. Sovnarkom moved inexorably towards a cruder solution: dispersal of the Assembly when it finally met. On 20 November, at Stalin's instigation, a press campaign against the Assembly was projected. Trotski was to be drawn in as chief propagandist. A show of force was planned, and the presence of Kronstadt sailors in Petrograd was to be strengthened.[10] The date of convocation was finally set for 5 January 1918, but the mode and timing of the violent dispersal were left open. Lenin recognised that caution had to be exercised with regard to his own party members (who were not universally in favour of the Assembly's suppression), to some among his Left Socialist Revolutionary allies and to a general population which might not take kindly to the infringement of its newly-obtained democratic rights.

Anti-Assembly opinion among Bolsheviks and Left Socialist Revolutionaries was already hardening. The idea of being ejected from governmental office appealed to few of them, especially in Petrograd. On 21 November 1917, it was decreed that all constituencies should have the right to recall and replace their Assembly deputies.[11] On 23 November, the commission charged with organising the Assembly elections was arrested.[12] On 26 November, Sovnarkom announced that the Assembly would not be considered quorate until 400 of its members had arrived in Petrograd. On 12 December, Lenin successfully called for the reselection of the Bureau of the Bolshevik fraction in the Assembly on the grounds that a sterner attitude towards the Assembly was appropriate: nothing was being left to chance.[13]

By 1 January he was considering measures to deal with the expected trouble when the Constituent Assembly convened. It was an eventful day. He also met with Bolshevik leaders who had returned from the Ukraine;[14] he spoke on the phone with the American Ambassador in Petrograd.[15] In addition, Fritz Platten had arrived in the capital. Platten's assistance as an intermediary between Lenin and the German government in March had put Lenin permanently in his debt,[16] and Platten was invited to spend the day with him as he travelled from meeting to meeting. They attended a massed gathering of soldiers, where Lenin also talked to the British journalist Albert Rhys Williams.[17] Platten, Lenin and Lenin's sister Mariya got back into their chauffeur-driven car to go to supper in the Smolny Institute. On the way, at 7.30 pm, a group of right-wing officers lay in wait and the car was fired upon. Platten flung himself across Lenin's body to save him from injury, and was hit in the hand by a bullet. The would-be assassins escaped. Lenin and his sister were unharmed and Platten's flesh wound was treated.[18] Yet Lenin refused to be deflected from his tasks. At eight o'clock he reported briefly to Sovnarkom on his misadventure and proceeded to chair the various discussions on military clashes on the Romanian sector of the Eastern front, and on revolutionary tribunals, on the annulment of loans contracted by Nikolai II's government.[19] Resilience under fire!

Nor did he relent in his aims for the Constituent Assembly. On 3 January 1918 the announcement was made on Sovnarkom's behalf that the Constituent Assembly would be acceptable only if it supported 'soviet power'.[20] This was the code for a stipulation that Sovnarkom, under Bolshevik and Left Socialist-Revolutionary leadership, should be ratified as the legitimate government and that the Socialist Revolutionaries and Mensheviks should not demand to form a cabinet. The apparent wish for compromise veiled a will to crush all opposition entirely.[21]

Sovnarkom's measures had the desired effect of electrifying the atmosphere of intimidation. The disposition of troops in the capital, together with the banning of street demonstrations, indicated to all who had eyes to see that Sovnarkom would dissolve the proceedings. Artillery units surrounded the Tauride Palace as the deputies entered on the morning of 5 January.[22] A demonstration held by supporters of the Assembly, who naïvely supposed that the Bolsheviks would not use force upon fellow socialists, was fired upon. Twelve years after Bloody Sunday almost to the day, discontented citizens in Russia's capital city were being slaughtered by the authorities for having the temerity to exercise what they took to be their rights. Scores of demonstrators were killed; the hospitals were crowded with the wounded victims.[23] The proceedings in the Tauride Palace were delayed until mid-afternoon. Shvetsov, the oldest deputy in the Assembly, was chosen to open the session, but he was brusquely pushed aside after a few minutes by Sverdlov, who demanded that the Assembly should adhere to the policies of Sovnarkom. Uproar broke out. Lenin chirpily intervened to propose the singing of the 'Internationale'; and it is a sign of the disorientation of the Socialist Revolutionaries that they accepted his proposal instead of pressing on with substantive matters of state.[24] (It was also a very rare example of Lenin using quasi-humorous behaviour to achieve a political end.)

Lenin's jauntiness could not prevent Chernov's election as the Assembly's Chairman. Chernov read out his projects on the transfer of land to the peasantry and the launching of a peace initiative. The Bolshevik Nikolai Bukharin and the Left Socialist Revolutionary Izaak Shteinberg, speaking for the Sovnarkom coalition, again demanded the Assembly's recognition of soviet power. Tsereteli rose to oppose them, and commotion ensued. The Socialist Revolutionary agenda was accepted by a vote on the floor, and the Bolsheviks and the Left Socialist Revolutionaries walked out in protest. Chernov continued the debates. By late evening he was reading out the details of legislation that he now perceived the Bolsheviks would stop him implementing. He refused to prorogue the proceedings until morning.[25]

Meanwhile Lenin, conferring with the Bolshevik fraction, decided that there should be no second session of the Assembly.[26] Orders were issued forbidding the Palace guard to attack the opponents of Sovnarkom as they left the building; earlier in the day a Bolshevik supporter had pointed his rifle at the unfortunate Shvetsov as he was speaking. But parallel instructions were given to close down the first session. At around four o'clock in the morning on 6 January 1918, sailor A. G. Zheleznyakov announced on behalf of the Tauride Palace guard that his comrades were 'fatigued' and were about to switch off the lights.[27] A forlorn group of anti-Bolshevik Constituent Assembly delegates left the Palace, never to return. None were molested, to their surprise, since rumours existed that Chernov would be assassinated as he left the building. The Bolsheviks had won the struggle. Lenin could at last relax. At the Assembly itself on 5 January he had been nervous; his aide V. D. Bonch-Bruevich later recalled: 'Lenin was agitated and was paler than ever before . . . He clenched his fists and began to scan the entire hall with burning eyes.'[28] But he had recovered his poise after sensing the weakness of the opposition. He affected to be bored while Chernov was addressing the gathering. This was not Lenin's characteristic demeanour: he usually maintained an attentive posture at public meetings. Evidently he was out to humiliate as well as to defeat the Socialist Revolutionaries and Mensheviks. Perhaps he was getting his own back for the derision he had suffered at their hands when, at the First Congress of Soviets of Workers' and Soldiers' Deputies in June 1917, he had exclaimed that his party was willing to rule Russia alone.[29]

Whatever the explanation, a terrible threshold had been crossed. The only freely-contested multi-party elections ever to have been held in Russia had been 'invalidated' by force of arms. Lenin's self-restraint could not disguise the momentousness of the occasion. With or without Lenin's actions, there would probably have been civil war in Russia after the Provisional Government's demise. But the destruction of the Constituent Assembly, which was ratified by a decree of Sovnarkom on 6 January, ensured that the anti-Bolshevik armies would be stronger than they might otherwise have been.

Many Socialist Revolutionaries were to fight against the Reds, not because they shared the aims of generals from the old imperial regiments but in pursuit of rectifying the great wrong done to their party at the Tauride Palace. The Bolsheviks had talked increasingly about civil war since coming to power, but they claimed that it was the Kadets and their allies who were bent on unleashing military conflict. Bolsheviks could no longer appear plausible with such talk, yet their confidence was strengthened by the feeling that they were the makers of a successful revolution. In addition, the ease of the Assembly's dispersal inhibited further opposition among Bolsheviks to the retention of a coalition of only two socialist parties in Sovnarkom. The numerical weakness of Left Socialist Revolutionaries at the Assembly meant that they were even less disposed to mourn its passing; and many were like P. P. Proshyan in participating in the acts of violence to suppress those who wished to keep the Assembly open. No sooner had the dispersal taken place, moreover, than the Sovnarkom coalition was swept into tumultuous discussions about foreign policy; and the memory of the events of 5–6 January 1918 quickly faded from the minds of Bolshevik and Left Socialist-Revolutionary leaders. It burned bright in the minds of Constituent Assembly deputies who had come to Petrograd demanding fair political treatment and the chance to bring Bolshevik rule peacefully to an end. They returned from the Tauride Palace feeling lucky to be alive. Their current aim was to establish a government of Assembly deputies in the Volga region and to seek the military removal of the Bolsheviks from power throughout Russia.

SOVNARKOM'S CHAIRMAN

Yet Lenin had an arsenal of self-confidence. He had sufficient for himself, and could share out the remainder among those of his associates who vacillated. The scampering ebullience of the man takes the breath away. His limited experience as an administrator – he had not even been a local government official – did not deter him. Possibly his practical innocence helps to explain his cockiness. There was in any case no respite after the Constituent Assembly. As soon as he had achieved his objective, he turned calmly to deal with the alliance with the Left Socialist Revolutionaries. Here he operated with much deftness. Letters to their leader, M. V. Spiridonova, were felinely charming.[30] Negotiations were agreeably undertaken and accomplished. Lenin's plan was simple: to lull the Left Socialist Revolutionaries into a false sense of security about their weight of importance in the coalition.[31]

The Third All-Russian Congress of Soviets of Workers', Soldiers' and Cossacks' Deputies had been arranged to start in the second week of January so that pressure might be exerted upon the Constituent Assembly should it remain in session.[32] The Bolsheviks would predictably dominate it since they held even more town and city soviets than in October 1917. The Third Congress of Soviets of Peasants' Deputies was scheduled to convene in the same week. In fact, the division between Socialist Revolutionaries and Left Socialist Revolutionaries had become so deep that two fully separate Congresses of Soviets of Peasants' Deputies were held simultaneously. Lenin proposed that the Congress called under the auspices of the Left Socialist Revolutionaries should fuse itself with the Bolshevik-dominated Congress of Soviets of Workers', Soldiers' and Cossacks' Deputies and that a joint Central Executive Committee should be created. The tactical beauty of this, from the Bolshevik party's standpoint, was that the overwhelming majority of the country's population were peasants and that Sovnarkom would therefore come to appear as representative of the lower social classes in general and not just the workers and the urban poor. At the same time, the Left Socialist Revolutionaries were not going to be accorded any greater number of seats in Sovnarkom itself than before. Bolshevik hegemony would be preserved. The Left Socialist Revolutionaries were as naïve about the Bolshevik central leadership's ruthlessness as the Socialist Revolutionaries had been about Lenin's disregard for the rights of the Constituent Assembly; but at the time they thought the deal worth making since the Bolsheviks were willing to offer them compromises on the single act of legislation, then under preparation, that most interested them: the Basic Land Law. Thus Spiridonova felt that she had achieved a fair share of the political bargain.[33]

Not that Lenin's planning lacked an idealistic aspect. At times he could be carefree, sounding as if he could hardly believe his luck to be Premier of the world's first socialist state. When he came to address the unified Third All-Russian Congress of Soviets of Workers', Soldiers' and Cossacks' Deputies on 11 January 1918, he announced that the Soviet republic had good cause for celebration: it had already lasted five days longer than the Paris Commune of 1871. Amidst all the difficulties of politics and the economy he could still find reasons for cheer.[34]

But he could and did control his emotions, upbraiding those colleagues who would not learn to behave in a business like fashion. Governing, for Lenin, was a serious enterprise and duty. Latecomers to Sovnarkom sessions were fined.[35] (Was this not evidence of his economic determinism? Were there really no other ways of establishing punctuality?). He also tried to insist upon a clear agenda at meetings, and chose aides such as V. D. Bonch-Bruevich and N. P. Gorbunov for their fastidiousness as well as their energy. Even so, no aide could match Lenin's energy: very few of them from the early days of Sovnarkom remained in post at the time of Lenin's death; he had long since worn them out.[36] Lenin had imbibed enough of the revolutionary spirit to allow fellow People's Commissars to raise subjects not previously tabled for discussion,[37] but his instinct was to reinforce order and orderliness. He would even refuse to greet long-lost friends, such as L. B. Krasin, during sessions. Lenin strove to pervade each session of Sovnarkom with an aura of austerity; only at the end, sometimes well after midnight, would he allow himself the pleasure of social intercourse.[38] His associates had often noticed his schoolmasterly techniques as an orator. In Sovnarkom his style of command was similarly reminiscent of the schoolroom, and he prohibited smoking at the green baize table.

This appears less extraordinary nowadays, when such bans are common in public institutions, than it did then. Few phenomena of the October Revolution are more comic than the surreptitiousness of Dzierzynski in trying to evade notice while indulging his craving for cigarettes. Dzierzynski was a survivor of Siberian penal servitude and the head of the Cheka; his name was enough to frighten the enemies

of Bolshevism. And yet, at Sovnarkom sessions, he would creep off
to the stove at the side of the room and puff secretly up the flue.[39]

In the intervals between Bolshevik Central Committee meetings,[40]
Sovnarkom was the major centre of power in the country. Lenin tried
to direct its entire work. This involved detailed supervision of a range
of activities. Trotski and Stalin were invaluable collaborators, and
the skills of the Bolshevik ex-undergrounders at central and local
levels of government ought not to be forgotten. But the butterfly
attitudes of some of them left much to be desired from an
organisational standpoint. Yuri Larin's penchant for drawing up
highly ambitious schemes on paper, which had not the slightest
chance of realisation, was notorious. A bruising of the sensibilities of
the dreamier party stalwarts was inevitable. Unlike Trotski and
Stalin, however, Lenin succeeded in doing this without giving
lifelong offence. Trotski's past as an anti-Bolshevik and his obvious
talent (and, worse still, his knowledge of his talent) counted against
him. Stalin's abrasiveness was to become an issue of intra-party
significance in 1919. Of the other prominent Bolsheviks, both
Zinoviev and Kamenev had compromised themselves by their so-
called 'strike-breaking' in October 1917; and younger leaders such as
Bukharin and Pyatakov, who were taken seriously by Lenin before
1917 and who were to figure in his 'testament' of 1922, lacked
Lenin's prestige and authority.[41]

As for the other People's Commissars, there were certainly many
outstanding figures. Sovnarkom was the best-educated or, at least,
the most intellectually-engaged government in history; it was also
filled with people of practical initiative. The likes of Rykov, Tomski
and Shlyapnikov should not be underestimated simply because their
skills as theorists were frail. Alas, such assumptions are yet another
example of the blight cast by intellectual snobs like Trotski upon
accounts of Soviet history. When all is said and done, however, none
of these practical administrators rivalled Lenin. He could equal them
all in every department of activity; and he was, in addition, the
party's founder and outstanding theorist.

He was now loved by the entire party and its supporters. He had
the kudos of being the Revolution's successful leader and, after the
assassination attempt, he wore the crown of the near-martyr. His
family, as usual, was supportive. Krupskaya, sharing his flat in the
Smolny Institute, worked ceaselessly in her own right while tending
to his daily needs. Lenin's sister Anna and her husband, Mark
Elizarov, were close at hand to give moral support.[42] Their rooms

were modest, and both Lenin and Krupskaya took care to avoid advertising their relative material comfort to the general population. He still visited workers' districts despite the attempt on his life, and gave little attention to the special security arrangements made for him. He acted like all the other People's Commissars even though, as the second shooting in August 1918 showed, he would remain a prime target for terrorism: to the horror of his aides, he continued to take occasional strolls around Petrograd. The 'normality' of daily life was important enough to him to seem worth the risks; and he wanted to observe material and social conditions for himself. While on holiday in late December, he had stayed with the families of colleagues. Sovnarkom's premier relaxed with the children, playing hide-and-seek around the house and getting down on his knees to hide under the table as part of the fun.[43]

Not that Lenin lived a life that was normal for most inhabitants of the Soviet republic. He and Krupskaya had house servants. Lenin satisfied his bibliophilia by constructing an extensive private library around the walls of his small study. He could order any book he wanted from any Russian library.[44] Nor does Lenin's liking for children demonstrate that he was basically just an 'ordinary person'. Most people do not possess his ability to countenance the arrest and execution of thousands of individuals without proof of their criminal guilt. Lenin, had many likeable personal traits; but he also had some exceedingly unpleasant and unusual ones.[45]

THE FORMULATION OF POLICIES

The political symbiosis of Lenin the Bolshevik and Spiridonova the Left Socialist Revolutionary laid a premium on the rapid promulgation of a Basic Land Law. Peasants and Bolsheviks had tolerated each other in late 1917, and the Decree on Land had been well received. But a more solid basis was required. Sovnarkom had taken care to avoid giving offence to the peasantry. A system of direct, progressive taxation had been a Bolshevik aim in the pre-October months and D. P. Bogolepov prepared draft legislation which was accepted by Sovnarkom on 24 November.[46] It was quickly recognised that any new fiscal system would meet with popular suspicion. The Left Socialist Revolutionaries were nervous about peasant feelings and on 6 December the new tax law was amended to allow local soviets to exempt the poorer sections of the population from all taxation.[47] The Basic Land Law had to be approached with similar circumspection. Committees, commissions and informal forums of discussion sprang up in profusion. The Left Socialist Revolutionary A. L. Kolegaev was influential. Bolsheviks and Left Socialist Revolutionaries knew they had to reach a compromise loaded in favour of the Left Socialist Revolutionaries if there was to be any point in the continued coalition. Lenin's indefinite concept of 'model farms' was quietly shelved; and, for a while, the Bolshevik leftists were induced to refrain from mass collectivisation.[48] The Basic Law 'On The Socialisation Of The Land' was passed on 27 January 1918.[49]

This title signified that nationalisation was no longer a Bolshevik short-term aim. The Left Socialist Revolutionaries also successfully stipulated that the peasants should receive land according to the number of mouths to feed in each household. The Bolsheviks had wanted to base transfers of property to a greater extent with an increase of productivity in mind; but the need to reconcile their partners in Sovnarkom forced them to give way.[50]

They were also taken aback by the effects of land redistribution, especially the reduction in the number of wealthier peasants in terms of landholdings.[51] Lenin had always hoped to keep the middle peasants, who had suddenly become an overwhelming majority, on the party's side. This meant that Bolshevism also had to forgo an insistence on retention of the large estates in integral form; and that the agricultural wage labourers, as distinct from poor peasants, were not supported as strongly as the Bolsheviks had originally desired.[52] Lenin won a few minor battles. The Basic Law stated that the local soviets should be empowered to oversee the redistribution of the land even though it was tacitly conceded that no interference with the peasants in any village would be undertaken. He also inserted the point that the ultimate objective of the coalition's agrarian policy was 'the collective system of agriculture'.[53] The difficulty was that the peasants did not react to the sanctioning of the land's transfer in a spirit of gratitude. Food supplies continued to diminish. In February 1918, when the Basic Law was issued, the official bread ration in Petrograd was dropped to merely two ounces a day.[54] The return to their native villages of hundreds of thousands of peasant conscripts, whose acquaintance with the Bolshevik programme was closer than that of the normal rural population, made little difference. Local soviets from January 1918 started to dispatch armed squads into the countryside in quest of grain.[55] Sovnarkom desisted from comprehensive forcible requisitioning, and Lenin's occasional talk of an anti-speculator terror was not yet a systematic and lasting policy. A. G. Shlikhter was instructed to gather supplies of industrial goods and set out for western Siberia by train to exchange the goods for grain.[56]

The Bolshevik inclination towards using violence against the peasantry, which is traceable to the manipulative attitude to peasants traditional in Bolshevik thought,[57] was emerging, but the army which would be necessary to suppress peasant discontent, was not yet formed. Sovnarkom encouraged demobilisation of several regiments in late 1917. The pre-October commitment to demilitaris-ing industrial production and switching to output for the civilian market was also being fulfilled; and Sverdlov engineered the closure of Bolshevik party committees in the Russian army on the Eastern front.[58] Yet military conflict, in civil war and in foreign anti-Bolshevik crusades, was expected. From February 1918 a series of instructions were issued which led within weeks to the creation of the Workers' and Peasants' Red Army.[59]

Measures were passed to exert control over industry and banking. On 14 December 1917, Lenin and the People's Commissar of Finances, G. Y. Sokolnikov, legislated for the nationalisation of all banks.[60] Six weeks later, on 21 January 1918, the Soviet authorities unilaterally annulled the foreign and domestic loans incurred by Nikolai II and the Provisional Government.[61] These two steps offered a mixture of control and relief. Sovnarkom could in any case expect no help or indulgence from the Allies. The snag was that industrial production remained on its steeply downward track. The total output value in 1918 fell to nearly a half of the value in 1917.[62] Lenin and his colleagues breathed fire about the future fate of capitalism and capitalists. The exodus of the middle and upper social classes abroad became a torrent. Shutdowns of enterprises continued. Thirty-eight per cent of large factories were closed in the first ten months of Soviet power.[63] A state-managed industrial sector seemed to most Bolshevik leaders the cure for this problem. Before October 1917, Lenin had sketched a process of gradual nationalisation,[64] and subsequently convinced associates that caution was needed in the winter of 1917-1918 despite the impatience of Bukharin and other leftists. Individual large factories were nationalised, not whole industries. But Bukharin and Osinski pressed for the creation of a general body to co-ordinate the process and obtained Lenin's consent.[65] On 5 December 1917 a decree was issued for the creation of the Supreme Council of the National Economy.[66]

The Council's ameliorative impact on the industry and trade was negligible. Symptoms of desperation entered governmental pronouncements. Unskilled workers were encouraged to return to their villages while the economic crisis lasted.[67] Industrial decline was tacitly acknowledged as virtually unavoidable. Even Lenin was accepting the sober predictions of his associate, V.P. Milyutin, before October 1917.[68] There were still Bolsheviks who drew up plans for a perfectly-functioning system of complete economic management, as Lenin irritably noted. The real material plight grew ever worse.

'Workers' control' was not abandoned as a policy; a statute on the principle was passed on 14 November 1917.[69] Yet the rights of factory-workshop committees were vigorously trimmed. Such committees had their own national hierarchy; but Sovnarkom found the trade unions more amenable to government control and, in 1918, stealthily provided them with authority over the factory-workshop committees.[70] Bolshevik leftists, who combined arch-centralism of outlook with demands for uninhibited power for workers' representatives on the shop floor, denounced this as a betrayal.[71] But Sovnarkom faced them down. It helped Lenin, perhaps, that Bukharin had no answer to the problem of disorder on the railways. Few Bolsheviks objected when Aleksandr Shlyapnikov was appointed commissar with extra-legal powers to restore an operational network. The railways were militarised, and railwaymen who failed to submit to the disciplinary code were liable to the sternest punishments.[72] There was a long tradition in Bolshevism which held that the party should guide rather than automatically follow the workers. Working-class moods were not to be lodestars of policy. This menacing condescension had been largely, but not wholly, submerged in Bolshevik pronouncements before October 1917. It returned to prominence as the depth of the economic crisis was registered by Sovnarkom and as the hopes of succour from fraternal socialist revolutions lessened. The doctrines of *What Is To Be Done?* acquired a new potency; material pressures and ideological inclinations were joined in a powerful compound.

Nevertheless, funds were given to establish cultural organisations which would train workers to take advantage of the opportunities available under Sovnarkom's aegis. The Bolshevik leaders did not enjoy the compulsion they were applying to the working class; they assumed that, in time, the workers would understand the requirements of the situation and would support the party. A People's

Commissariat of Enlightenment was installed under A. V. Luna-charski (who had initially resigned on hearing that the Kremlin treasures were being looted in the October seizure of power, but then returned to post).[73] Lenin's old adversary, Aleksandr Bogdanov, strongly disapproved of what he regarded a a premature attempt at the transition to socialism; and the dispersal of the Constituent Assembly appalled him. And yet he saw the chances of applying his ideas about 'proletarian culture' and secured resources for an organisation known by its acronym of Proletkult.[74] And skilled and literate workers assumed positions in the administration of the young Soviet state.

THE CENTRAL COMMITTEE IN DISPUTE

Lenin's restlessness with Trotski's tactic of 'neither war nor peace' grew sharply in 1918. On 7 January, a day after the Constituent Assembly's closure and six days after the assassination attempt, the two Bolshevik leaders conferred while Trotski briefly took leave from Brest-Litovsk. The terms offered to the Soviet delegation by Germany and Austria-Hungary, especially the proposal that the armies of the Central Powers would maintain their occupation in Poland, Lithuania and the Baltic region, had provoked a furious reaction in the local committees of the Bolshevik party. Most regional and city party committees felt that the Brest-Litovsk negotiations should be broken off and a 'revolutionary war' be undertaken.[76] Lenin reluctantly accepted that his proposal for a separate peace would not receive favour; and he agreed to what he regarded as the second-best tactic: that Trotski should still apply the 'neither war nor peace' formula in the hope that either a German socialist revolution would occur, or the German High Command would not carry out its military threats.[77]

On 8 January, Lenin could ascertain the strength of the internal party opposition when he addressed sixty three leaders of the Bolshevik fraction to the Third Congress of Soviets of Workers', Soldiers' and Cossacks' Deputies. His 'Theses on the Question of a Separate and Annexationist Peace' were considered outrageous. Only fifteen voted in favour of Lenin's proposal: a massive defeat.[78] Yet Lenin was used to being in a minority, and reminded his opponents that he had been execrated by Bolshevik leaders in 1907 when he had recommended participation in the State Duma elections. And yet he had eventually won the struggle for participation.[79] It was also a comfort to him that only thirty-two out of sixty-three members in the fractional gathering of the Third Congress of Soviets, a very narrow majority, voted directly for war. Sixteen supported Trotski's tactic.[80] A wedge existed between two tendencies of opinion hostile to a separate peace; and Trotski had confided that, in the event of a German invasion, Lenin could count on his vote in favour of a separate peace.[81] For Lenin, this demonstrated that Trotski was not yet ready to face up to reality. But he could perceive opportunities to win him over. Lenin regarded a German invasion as a certainty, and believed that the possibility existed that the Germans might press deeper into Soviet territory than was projected in their peace terms. Estonia might well fall under German occupation. 'In any event,' Lenin argued with Trotski, 'I stand for the immediate signature of peace, it is more secure.'[82]

The crucial arena for debate among Bolsheviks was the Central Committee. Undeterred by defeat at the Congress of Soviets fractional gathering, Lenin restated his case on 11 January. He reminded the Central Committee that Bolshevism had never objected to defence in absolute terms and that the 'socialist republic' needed to be defended. It was indeed an 'obscene peace',[83] he conceded, that was being proposed with Germany. But it would give time for the Bolsheviks to 'strangle' the Russian bourgeoisie and to prepare an army for a future revolutionary war – he made no pretence of being a pacifist. Meanwhile Germany was 'pregnant' with revolution; the signature of a treaty with Ludendorff and Hindenburg would not harm the prospects of international revolution.[84]

Bukharin, the left's major theorist, preferred revolutionary war to a separate peace. But he had always recognised the practical difficulties and wanted, for the moment, to allow Trotski's policy of prolonging the negotiations to continue;[85] and Moisei Uritski, who had worked shoulder to shoulder with Lenin over the Constituent Assembly, maintained that Lenin was now guilty of the same Russo-centrism in foreign policy that had played him false in 1915.[86] Lenin was obviously not the only Bolshevik leader who could point to another Bolshevik leader's past failings. Dzierzynski went further: Lenin was doing in international relations what Zinoviev and Kamenev, the so-called revolutionary 'black-legs', had done in domestic policy in the October Revolution.[87] Only Stalin and Zinoviev spoke up strongly on Lenin's side (even though, when Stalin said that 'there is no revolutionary movement in the

West', his pessimism was much deeper than Lenin would allow himself).[88] On the other hand, the proposal for revolutionary war found only two supporters; the more cautious tactical counsel of Bukharin prevailed among the leftists.[89] The vote in favour of procrastinating and hoping for the outbreak of a German socialist revolution was passed by twelve against one.[90] This attitude was confirmed by a joint session of the Bolshevik and Left Socialist-Revolutionary Central Committees on 13 January.[91]

On 1 February, the Bolshevik Central Committee reconvened. A. Lomov, for the left, demanded a Party Conference to settle policy.[92] Conferences, being less authoritative bodies than Congresses, according to the party's traditions, could be called more quickly; and since the left already held so many local committees it would be easy to defeat Lenin. Therefore Zinoviev called instead for a full Party Congress, which ought to involve the open election of delegates at mass meetings. A Congress was agreed upon.[93] But the left managed to obtain a Central Committee session with local representatives on 3 February, and again the policy of dragging out the negotiations was approved. Yet signs appeared that Lenin was gaining ground: five participants now voted in favour of a separate peace.[94] Moreover, both Bukharin and Uritski agreed that such a peace was 'permissible' if the Germans simply broke off negotiations.[95] Their anti-Lenin arguments were not as unequivocal as they might have been. There was also vacillation in their approach; for simultaneously they refused to agree or disagree that such a peace would also be 'necessary'.[96]

At Brest-Litovsk, time was running out for the Soviet delegation. The Germans and Austrians indicated on 10 February that their patience was exhausted; and Trotski, in a last-ditch effort at calling the bluff of the Central Powers and stirring up political trouble among their own populations, announced simply that the Soviet republic was withdrawing from the war. Sovnarkom, he declared, would not sully itself with the signature of a separate peace but would not resume the war either.[97] On 16 February, after conquering their incredulity, the Central Powers announced that an offensive would be resumed on the Eastern front on 18 February. Lenin urged a rapid reconvening of the peace talks and, if the Germans were still willing, the signature of a treaty on the terms specified in December 1917. The Central Committee met, with Trotski in attendance, on 17 February. No one, to Lenin's relief, would any longer press the case for an immediate declaration of revolutionary war. And yet Trotski adamantly refused to accede to a separate peace until the German offensive had happened (and even until it became clear whether the working classes of the Central Powers would rise against an invasion of the Soviet republic). Trotski's middle course was passed by six votes to five.[98] Lenin had come within inches of political victory in the Central Committee. Pushing the left into a corner about their Marxist assumptions, he cunningly tabled the question whether a peace treaty with 'imperialist Germany' was 'acceptable in principle'. Everyone agreed that it was acceptable. He also posed the problem as to what would happen if the German army attacked and there was no revolutionary 'upsurge' in Germany. Trotski, being prised out of his 'neither war nor peace' position, declared that in such a contingency he would favour a separate peace. Lenin won the debate on this hypothetical situation, which was shortly to become reality, by six out of eleven votes. Only Ioffe voted against. Bukharin and his friends abstained.[99]

Lenin's forensic and philosophical skills were tugging the Central Committee closer towards him. But the military timetable of the Central Powers cut short his success: on 18 February, Trotski had bad news to report to the Central Committee. The German High Command, tired of the diplomatic parleying at Brest-Litovsk, had broken off negotiations. The Central Committee meeting was abruptly terminated in confusion.[100] A second meeting was held on the same evening, when Trotski relayed even worse information. The town of Dvinsk, only six hundred kilometres from Petrograd, had fallen to the Germans. Petrograd was at their mercy. Lenin's comment to the leftists was mordant: 'History will say that you gave away the revolution.'[101]

The choice between revolutionary war and a separate peace could no longer be avoided; the German offensive had brutally destroyed the basis of Trotski's tactics. Bukharin chose war even if it were only to be a defensive and, inevitably, unsuccessful war. He stuck to official Bolshevik policy as expressed before the October Revolution. He and his associates asserted that, whereas he had been willing to accept a situation of peace on the Eastern front if the Germans simply agreed to stop fighting, he could not bring himself to approve the formal signature of such a peace. A spontaneous separate peace between the soldiers of the two sides was one thing; a treaty was entirely another. This fine distinction did not win him the necessary support and the voting went against him by seven to five. Lenin had achieved his long-pursued majority in the Central Committee. The decision was made to 'approach the German government with a proposal of the immediate conclusion of peace'.[102] Trotski was now on Lenin's side. Nerves of steel would still be required; nobody in the Bolshevik Central Committee knew whether the Central Powers, once their armies had started moving and found the resistance to be so feeble, would agree to halt. Information about opinion at the German Court and in the High Command was scanty.

Trotski, meanwhile, was wavering. On 22 February, he reported to the Central Committee that military aid was presently being offered by representatives of the British and French governments. Trotski favoured acceptance, and the vote went in his favour by six to five. Bukharin was among his opponents, objecting that Trotski's proposal represented collusion with Anglo-French imperialism. Having remained in the Central Committee after the vote in favour of a separate peace, he chose this occasion to resign his membership of it.[103]

And yet the Central Committee's position had to be resolved. The respective policies of Lenin and Trotski, mutually contradictory, had to be reassessed. The Germans again supplied extreme pressure. After the fall of Dvinsk they announced a set of expanded demands. The Soviet republic was asked to disclaim sovereignty over the entire Ukraine, Belorussia and the Baltic region. This would involve a massive loss of demographic, industrial and agricultural resources. The republic would be confined to central, northern and south-eastern Russia and the territory to the east. Russia would also have to demobilise, and would be compelled to protect the interests of German entrepreneurs. Sverdlov revealed the grim news to the Central Committee on 23 February, and Trotski explained that an answer to the German ultimatum had to be given by seven o'clock on the morning of the next day.[104] This time, he asserted that since a divided party could not undertake a concerted war effort, he could not vote for revolutionary war. He added that he was unconvinced by Lenin's reasoning; but his own self-justification lacks cogency since he had agreed conditionally to a separate peace on 18 February. Lenin, while suspecting him of posturing, declined to respond. Trotski's abstaining vote was what counted. Bukharin continued to oppose. Even Stalin vacillated, saying that it might be possible to start negotiating again.[105] Lenin was horrified and threatened to leave Sovnarkom and the Central Committee: 'These terms must be signed. If you don't sign them, you are signing the death warrant for Soviet power within three weeks.'[106] Lomov struck back: 'It is necessary to take power without V. I. [Lenin]. It is necessary to go to the front and do everything possible.'[107]

But Lenin could see he would win. He maximised his support by stressing that, whatever he might be compelled to agree to in the treaty, he would seek to 'prepare a revolutionary war'. Seven Central Committee members against four, with four abstentions, took his side.[108] The left-wingers under Bukharin collectively resigned from their posts in government and party.[109] Yet Lenin's victory was complete in the Central Committee. The obscene peace, the separate and annexationist peace, was to be signed.

PARTY POLEMICIST

Vital as it was to control the Central Committee, however, Lenin did not yet control the entire political system: the various organs of power were rivals to each other. Institutional polyarchy persisted. The Bolsheviks, wanting results at almost any cost, heeded little about the means. Soviets, trade unions, factory-workshop committees, and party organs: these were infused with Bolshevik personnel who were instructed to get on with the job at hand. Wherever deficiencies appeared in an institution's activity, moreover, another institution was encouraged to retrieve the situation. This sometimes involved the creation of entirely new bodies, such as the Cheka and the Supreme Council of the National Economy. Functional demarcation was not a priority.[110] Such an attitude was operable so long as two major conditions were met: firstly, that the Bolsheviks in the various public institutions were more or less agreed on policy; and second, that the Left Socialist-Revolutionaries were not at variance with the Bolsheviks. Neither condition was met from January 1918 when rifts opened on the issues of war and peace. Naturally this pushed leading Bolsheviks back into the central body where they could resolve their own disagreements on policy definitively and without interference from other parties. The Brest-Litovsk dispute was not the first example of this after the October Revolution. The argument over coalition with the Mensheviks and Socialist Revolutionaries in November 1917 had involved a similar recourse to the Central Committee; but the three months of controversy over the proposed separate peace with Germany and Austria-Hungary were more intense and set a powerful precedent for subsequent developments.[111]

The party as a whole resumed greater importance when the Brest-Litovsk negotiations were discussed. While the battle raged in the Central Committee, Bolsheviks at lower levels was riven by conflict. Lenin recognised that the central party leadership's authority was not limitless and that further struggles would be necessary if the party was to follow the newly-adopted central policy. He himself had threatened to resign from the Central Committee when he was making no headway with his struggle for a separate peace; and he had been determined to have the freedom to campaign more openly among the party's rank-and-file membership. And throughout January and February 1918 he had contributed weighty articles to *Pravda* putting the case for the signature of a separate peace treaty.[112]

In the Central Committee he had been helped by factors of personality. He had always had a psychological edge over Bukharin and the left. Bukharin, when finally infuriated by his leader's behaviour in 1916, wrote to him timidly expressing regret that bad blood had come between them. Lenin had not written such a message to Plekhanov in the dispute of 1900.[113] In addition, the leftists had nobody of his stature as a dominant revolutionary figure. He had instigated the October seizure of power and established the new government's policies and institutional arrangements. Only Trotski came near to him in prestige as a pre-eminent Soviet statesman; but even Trotski could have no claim to recognition as the Bolshevik party chief. Lenin also had boundless self-confidence in his own judgements, and was supremely articulate in pronouncing them. He had a knack of taking a finely-balanced decision and presenting it as if no other decision was conceivable for proper-thinking socialists. There was much menace in his political style. When he did not get his way, he threatened to cause disruption until others fell in line with him; and his behaviour in the factional squabbles of the pre-war years demonstrated that this was no idle threat. The Left Communists had no such figure. There was talk among them of dropping Lenin from the government and even of imprisoning him if this alone would guarantee the retention of a policy hostile to a separate peace. This talk, incidentally, was to be used against several of them in Stalin's show-trials of the late 1930s. But in 1918 it was just talk. No moves were made to implement the intention.[114]

Lenin, by contrast, was someone who could confront a difficult situation and take responsibility for the outcome. 'Duty' was a frequent word in his vocabulary. This is not to say that Lenin was incapable of being irresponsible; several of his policy proposals in 1917 were cases in point. But his international policy of 1918 came out well in comparison with the suggestions of his Left Communist opponents. He constantly derided what he regarded as mere 'rhetoric', as the politics of the kindergarten. Phrase-mongering, he declared (with impressive disregard for his own penchant for utopian phrases in the pre-October months), had to be abandoned.

Lenin also had the advantage of possessing a strong group in the central party apparatus. Sverdlov, after an initial inclination towards revolutionary war, sided with Lenin. Stasova, too, eventually backed him. These two shaped the contents of the Secretariat's correspondence in the direction of acceptance of Lenin's policy.[115] Even the preparations for the Seventh Party Congress were dealt with less than even-handedly. Lenin and his friends were old hands at manipulating lists of delegates. The invitations were sent out at the last moment; and there are grounds for thinking that they were aimed mainly, if not exclusively, at addresses likely to supply a pro-Lenin delegation.[116] Organisational manipulation was not the only reason for the advance of the Leninists before the Party Congress. Another was the series of speeches given by Central Committee supporters in the rest of the country.[117] Kamenev and, above all, Zinoviev were tireless orators; and Zinoviev had even less compunction than Lenin in sinking to nasty innuendoes and defamation in order to win debates.[118] His proven skills as a polemicist made Lenin, who had always had a soft spot for 'Grisha', forgive everything that had happened between them in October 1917. Lenin cannot have been wholly displeased when Zinoviev unleashed a furious assault on Trotski's vacillatory demeanour in the Brest-Litovsk dispute even after Trotski had disowned the proposal for revolutionary war: it was important that Trotski was warned not to change his mind yet again.[119]

Such attacks served to emphasise Lenin's unique position of leadership in the party. A sort of reverence for him was growing by 1918. Zinoviev, despite having plenty of party and governmental business to occupy him, was collecting material for a short biography of Lenin;[120] and it was recorded that at a national soviet gathering, as the proceedings drew to a close, a delegate rose to his feet to proclaim that 'the entire Russian revolution showed that undoubtedly comrade Lenin is the sole person of genius among us.'[121] Stasova wrote to local party organisations declaring her unbounded admiration for his qualities as an orator.[122] Certainly Central

Committee member Artem is known to have switched sides in the debates, not because he was particularly swayed by the argument, as out of a faith in the man who had led the October Revolution.[123] Many Bolshevik opponents experienced inhibitions in attacking him. For example, G. I. Safarov denied that Lenin's faction were describable as 'collaborators' with imperialism.[124] Few critics, after the early tirades in the privacy of the Central Committee in January, castigated Lenin personally. It was not unknown for Zinoviev to be derided as Lenin's 'errand boy'; but Lenin himself was usually left alone.[125]

Even without this adulation, however, Lenin would have been in a better situation to win the debate in the party as a whole than his opponents supposed. Even before the October Revolution the leftists perceived that a military offensive against Germany was extremely unlikely to be feasible. By 1918 many could see that a defensive war, too, would probably not be successful. Their policies embodied ideological purity and practical despair. Thus the Urals regional party committee condemned the Brest-Litovsk treaty while explicitly recognising the futility of hoping to survive a continued war with the German army.[126] The sheer impracticality of the Left Communists, as they were becoming known, played into Lenin's hands. While refusing to advocate a separate peace, some of them were also advocating the de-militarisation of factory production.[127] In addition, there could be no revolutionary war if only the local Bolshevik committee members were in favour of fighting it. Left Communists were essentially volunteer military commanders without military experience and, worse still, without soldiers. In their hearts, they knew this only too well. Hence their otherwise odd belief that, when it came to a fight with the Germans, the Russian peasants would enlist *en masse*. Left Communists, as Bolshevik radicals, would normally have turned first to the workers. But they knew they would be rebuffed by 'people who had been spiritually and physically tormented in the course of a four-year war'.[128] Even the provision of adequate food to their armed units was beyond the capacity of the Left Communists in Ivanovo-Voznesensk.[129]

It is against this background that the swing towards Lenin has to be assessed. A survey of town and city soviets at the beginning of January 1918 revealed an anti-Lenin majority, but in subsequent weeks the balance of opinion steadily changed. It is true that, by the end of February, many regional and province-level party committees – perhaps even a majority – held fast in opposition to the peace treaty.[130] But the frequency of conferences at the local level had declined in recent months; and quite possibly the Left Commmunists had been reluctant to hold elections in the party for fear of losing their numerically predominant position. Their commitment to intra-party democracy was no firmer than Lenin's. So Lenin's instinctive feeling was realistic that his policy had a great chance of acceptance if open discussions were held and if those party rank-and-filers who were likely candidates for conscription in a revolutionary war were made aware of the implications. Without Lenin, the Brest-Litovsk treaty would probably not have been signed; and the Germans might well have invaded all Russia. But Lenin had a tide of mass opinion running his way, and no Russian politician knew better how to exploit his advantages.

THE SEVENTH PARTY CONGRESS

The Seventh Party Congress met in Petrograd's Tauride Palace from 6–8 March 1918. Most Central Committee members had to travel back to Moscow since the capital had been transferred to there when the military emergency became acute. Petrograd was chosen for the Party Congress so as to affirm that the Central Committee's mood was neither downcast nor defeatist. The proceedings lasted less than three full days: the shortest ever held by the party. The number of delegates, too, remains the smallest: only thirty-six attended the opening session on 6 March (although forty-seven with voting rights are reckoned to have been present later in the Congress).[131] Sverdlov chaired, and at the preliminary meetings had secured agreement for rules of procedure enabling him to direct business vigorously.[132] At the opening session there was no time to do more than listen to Sverdlov's organisational report on the Central Committee. He claimed in particular that the number of party members had reached 300,000.[133]

The second (and penultimate) day started with Lenin's political report. Lenin analysed 'the extraordinary ease' of the party's 'triumphal procession' to power in 1917.[134] Success, according to Lenin, had been possible only because 'international imperialism' was temporarily distracted from intervening in Russia.[135] In 1918 the Bolsheviks faced not the ineffective 'bands of Kerenski' but the might of Germany. Russia had a semi-industrialized economy which had been devastated by the war; she lacked even an army. 'A peaceful domestic pet,' asserted Lenin, 'has been lying side by side with a tiger.'[136] Safety for the Soviet republic would come about only through 'an all-European revolution'. Meanwhile, the Bolsheviks would have to retreat. They might even have to move the capital to Vladivostok, on the Pacific coast. Political as well as spatial retreat had to be accepted. Just as Lenin's Bolshevik followers had swallowed their pride by participating in Stolypin's emasculated Third State Duma in 1907, so now they ought to conclude a separate peace with Germany and Austria-Hungary. A refusal to do so would merely be playing at being 'supermen' and listening to 'fairy stories'. Bolshevik leftists were like the Polish noblemen of former times who died in a beautiful pose, saying: 'Peace is a disgrace, war is honour.'[137] Lenin argued that a peace treaty would give a 'breathing space'. He did not predict its duration. But he promised his opponents that, should circumstances turn in the party's favour, he would break the treaty without compunction. Thus he conveyed a combative impression even while advocating an immediate acceptance of defeat.[138]

Bukharin's co-report justifiably denied that his group had under-estimated the difficulties that would be faced after the October Revolution.[139] He acknowledged that defeats for socialism might be at hand, and agreed that no Russian army could crush the German forces on the Eastern front. He even declared that he would be willing to sign a separate peace if there was a guarantee that it would endure and would give the opportunity for the political and military preparations in Russia to assist the ultimate 'overthrow of international capital'. An aggressive 'revolutionary war' in the given circumstances was 'impossible'. What Bukharin had in mind was a defensive partisan campaign against the Germans wherever their forces invaded.[140]

This meant that Bukharin, contrary to what has usually been written about him,[141] put forward a far from confident alternative to Lenin's policy. Lenin was lucky to face such opponents. Neverthe-less, Bukharin's attack on his case inflicted some damaging wounds. Lenin was gambling on obtaining a lengthy breathing space, on the Germans abiding by their word, on the inability of the two military coalitions in the War to come together to strangle the young Soviet republic in its cradle. Nothing in the current situation gave assurance that his bet would be successful.[142] It was highly unlikely, in Bukharin's estimation, that the breathing space would be sufficient to facilitate economic reconstruction and military preparedness. So why bend the knee to the German high command at Brest-Litovsk? Surely the answer was to train the proletariat for a 'crusade' against imperialism.[143] The speeches by Lenin and Bukharin lasted two hours, and the ensuing debate was adjourned until the third session on the evening of 6 March. M.S. Uritski noted sarcastically that Lenin would sign a separate peace even if it was destined to last only a couple of days.[144] Like other Bolshevik leftists, Uritski was horrified both by the compulsory evacuation of the recently-conquered Ukraine and by the compulsory demobilisation of the Russian army. And yet not even Uritski claimed that victory in a revolutionary war was probable; but he expressed a preference for military defeat over sheer 'chaos'.[145]

Zinoviev retorted that the leftists spoke more from the emotions than from the head, and he reminded the Congress that Bukharin was not absolutely opposed to a separate peace. He congratulated the leftists on their good fortune that, being the Congress minority, they did not have the responsibility of taking onerous decisions.[146] This was a different Congress from all previous ones. There had always been dangers in the life of an underground revolutionary, but Congresses before 1917 had neither increased nor diminished these dangers through their decisions. The Seventh Congress proceedings were a life-and-death matter from beginning to end.

A.S. Bubnov stood up for the left, arguing that their case of today was simply Lenin's of yesterday. He drew attention to the strikes in Austria and Germany; and, like Bukharin, he called only for a defensive partisan form of warfare.[147] But the Left Communists were hopelessly divided. One of them, I.T. Smilga, denied that the necessary peasant support would be forthcoming.[148] But they held their heads high in debate: Karl Radek justifiably maintained that the Left Communist case had persistently been misrepresented. He denied that he thought the German socialist revolution would break out within a day or two.[149] He could easily have mentioned that it had been Lenin, not Radek, who had claimed that a mere change of party leadership in Germany could have brought the workers on to the streets for revolutionary action. This was a polemical opportunity that would not have been missed by Lenin if the roles had been reversed. G.Y. Sokolnikov sided with Radek, but criticised Bukharin's proposal for partisan warfare.[150] The fissures on the party's left impeded a unified assault on Lenin; and Sverdlov felt no need to ration the contributions from the leftists.[151] Trotski, whose cause was already lost, asked for the floor only half-way through the session; he stoutly defended the activity of the Soviet delegation to the peace talks and repeated that he had abstained from voting in the Central Committee because he did not believe that a revolutionary war could be fought if the party was divided by factionalism. But he unexpectedly urged the Congress to vote for a spatial withdrawal without the accompaniment of a formal treaty; and he pleaded that, if the Congress none the less was intent on a treaty, no peace should simultaneously be signed with the Ukrainian Rada.[152] Twisting and turning, he added that he was not urging the Congress to refuse to ratify the treaty.[153]

Trotski also helped Lenin by declaring contempt for the leftist plan for partisan warfare conducted with 'the knives of Pskov peasants' instead of rifles and artillery.[154] D. B. Ryazanov was less charitable to Lenin's group, accusing Sverdlov of closing down the party's organisations in the old army solely in order to make it harder for the party to resist the proposal for a separate peace.[155] Sverdlov met this with a flat denial (even though Ryazanov was probably right).[156] T. D. Sapronov complained that provincial delegates had not yet been given the floor.[157] Several speakers followed, including the prominent leftists N. Osinski and Aleksandra Kollontai; but their speeches added little to what had already been said. No one could suggest that the left-wing case had been muffled at the Congress itself.[158]

At the fourth session, on 8 March, provincial delegates were given their say. V. F. Stozhok from the Donbass opposed Lenin's policy; O. I. Rozanova from Yaroslavl supported it. Maskov, a Urals delegate, came over to Lenin's side despite having been mandated to advocate revolutionary war.[159] Sapronov and V. A. Shumailov, both leftists, stuck to their mandates.[160] Debate was ended, and Bukharin's closing speech predicted that the 'breathing space' would not be realised and that Lenin would soon have to adopt the position of the Bolshevik left.[161] Lenin replied that, if it had not been for Bukharin, the Central Committee would have chosen its current sensible policy earlier. Abrasively, he added: 'To declare war on Germany now would mean giving in to the provocation of the Russian bourgeoisie.'[162] A report from the Congress mandate commission ensued. This was a lively affair since the fiddling of mandates was a traditional party pastime. The commission's Chairman G. I. Boki, noting that the Kronstadt delegate claimed to represent 3,500 party members, doubted that even 500 Bolsheviks remained in the naval garrison.[163] Thereupon the Congress returned to the discussion of the Brest-Litovsk peace treaty and, as expected, confirmed Lenin's pro-peace motion as the basis of its resolution.[164] The clause-by-clause discussion was boisterous and chaotic. Ryazanov intervened to denounce Trotski for having ordered the execution of six innocent citizens some days previously.[165] Trotski ignored him and proceeded to offer amendments to Lenin's motion. He wanted to say that the signature of the peace was 'permissible' rather than 'necessary'. And where Lenin had spoken generally about a breathing-space before 'the attack of the imperialists', Trotski wanted to mention 'the inevitable and imminent attack'. He also argued against signing a treaty with the Rada.[166] All his amendments were repudiated.[167]

Until then no one had given a thought to possible reactions from the German high command. Zinoviev pointed out how vital it was to take up the matter. The motion called for 'the most energetic, mercilessly decisive and draconian measures to raise the self-discipline and discipline of the workers and peasants of Russia'; it declared that 'a liberationist, patriotic socialist war' was unavoidable, and that universal military training should be put in hand.[168] The Congress therefore decided to pass Lenin's resolution but to withhold it from publication. Instead a short announcement on the ratification of the peace would appear in the official Soviet press.[169] Even at this stage, however, several delegates tried to reactivate debate on the resolution's contents. Trotski's supporter, N. N. Krestinski, complained that the clauses failed to express approval for the negotiating policy of the Brest-Litovsk delegation in 1917–18; and Trotski defended his abstention in the crucial votes in the Central Committee.[170] Zinoviev, denying that the resolution on war and peace had implied criticism of Trotski, offered his own additional motion which welcomed the work done at Brest-Litovsk to expose the plans of 'the German imperialists'; Krestinski responded with another motion asserting that the delegation's tactics had been 'correct'. Both motions were passed.[171] Yet Zinoviev and Trotsky became very agitated. Zinoviev argued that only his resolution should stand, since Krestinski's majority had been the smaller.[172] Trotski, his pride dented, proposed a motion actually condemning the Brest-Litovsk delegation's tactics as 'mistaken'. By these indirect means he sought to get the Congress to give him a vote of approval. To his satisfaction, his own motion was rejected; but the flurry of re-balloting led also to a repudiation of Krestinski's already-accepted resolution.[173]

This sting in the tail of the main debate showed how tactless and imprudent Trotski could be, and how fiercely Zinoviev wished to do him down. Lenin held himself aloof from the wrangling. He had won what he had come to the Congress to win. That was sufficient for him. There was no need to humiliate Trotski. On the contrary, there was every reason to keep Trotski in the Central Committee. The episode gave further reinforcement to Lenin's position as patriarch of his party.

The fifth and last session began in the evening of 8 March. Lenin gave a joint report on two further issues: the revision of the party programme and the change of the party's name. His aim was to incorporate sections in the programme to highlight the differences between the Bolsheviks and most other adherents of the Second International. The themes of *The State and Revolution* were rehearsed. Lenin, denouncing 'bourgeois democratism', called for a new type of democracy based on the Russian soviets.[174] His difficulty came about with the writers of three competing projects: Nikolai Bukharin, V.M. Smirnov and G.Y. Sokolnikov. These leftists had wanted to scrap all vestiges of the reform proposals in the existing party programme on the grounds that they had been formulated in 1903 with a future bourgeois revolution rather than a socialist revolution in mind. Lenin, emphasising that the Bolsheviks were still 'only at the first transitional phase between capitalism and socialism', wanted to retain the old proposals.[175] In a nutshell, he believed that the programmatic offerings of Bukharin and his associates revealed excessive optimism about how much reform had already been achieved and how much more could be achieved in the near future. He also urged that, since there were contrasting as well as common features among European industrial countries, the programme should continue to refer to Russian specificities.[176]

Such arguments had their roots in the Lenin–Bukharin dispute of 1915–16, and Lenin saw that they were irresolvable in this last Congress session. He proposed the transference of the revision of programme to either a Congress-selected commission or to the Central Committee.[177] Bukharin still wanted his say at the Congress. While 'subscribing to Lenin's every word in his characterisation of the state', he called for a definition of socialism. Lenin's vague references to the nationalisation of the means of production lacked the necessary concreteness.[178] When debate shifted to the question of the party's name, however, Bukharin spoke strongly on Lenin's side; and the Congress voted to redesignate the party as the

Russian Communist Party (Bolsheviks) in order to distinguish it from other Marxist parties in Russia and elsewhere.[179] The Congress set up a seven-person commission to compose the party programme definitively. It was divided equally between Lenin's and Bukharin's supporters, with Trotski holding the balance between them.[180]

The collaborative atmosphere was dispelled by the elections to the Central Committee. Sverdlov proposed to cut the membership down from twenty-one to fifteen, since a smaller number would make decision-making easier. The Congress presidium proposed a list including some leftists. Yet M. S. Uritski announced that the leftists would not join the Central Committee.[181] Zinoviev asserted that the whole course of the Congress had indicated that there was 'no serious danger of a split'. Uritski replied that the leftists did not rule out the possibility of co-operation in the future, especially when revolutionary war re-entered the agenda. Lenin pleaded with the leftists, arguing that diversity of opinions was good for the Central Committee.[182] Yet the leftists were adamant. Reluctantly they agreed to vote in the election of the Central Committee, but declined to accept membership. Lenin and Trotski, with thirty-four votes, had most support. Trotski's success signalled his meteoric rise in the Bolshevik party. Sverdlov and Zinoviev obtained thirty-three votes. But even Bukharin gained thirty-two.[183] His objection to joining the Central Committee was the sole matter at the Seventh Party Congress where victory failed to go to Lenin. But it was a small and only temporary triumph for Bukharin. Perhaps because they were bemused by the last-minute flurry in the proceedings, the Congress ended at twenty minutes past midnight without the usual rendition of the 'Internationale'.[184]

Lenin, despite his brave face, knew that troubles remained in store for the Soviet republic. His triumph at the Party Congress had damaged relations with the Left Communists, and the Left Socialist Revolutionaries were destined to leave Sovnarkom. In broader political terms, too, he was threatened. Workers in increasing numbers were challenging the party's measures and methods. Conflicts between the peasantry and the local soviets were intensified. State institutions and power, shaken in the February Revolution against Emperor Nikolai II and paralysed throughout the Provisional Government's rule, had not recovered its previous control over society even though the Bolsheviks had used violence on a vast scale. And in south-eastern Russia, the Socialist Revolutionaries were mustering to establish an alternative Russian government consisting of deputies from the dispersed Constituent Assembly. Anti-Bolshevik regimes had sprung up in the Transcaucasus and counter-revolutionary armies were being formed in south Russia and Siberia to overthrow Sovnarkom. International problems were acute: Germany could not be trusted even after the Brest-Litovsk treaty, and the Allies, furthermore, were already planning armed intervention in Russia.

If anyone could lead the fight against the regime's enemies it was Vladimir Ilich Lenin. Before the February Revolution, he had been a factionalist and a theorist. He made virtually no effort to attract support among those subjects of the Emperor who were not already convinced revolutionaries. Lenin did not push for the foundation of popular Marxist newspapers, and he failed to develop the promise he had once exhibited as a lively and accessible pamphleteer. He sought influence among Marxists. He did not control the Bolshevik faction and, in the First World War, his contacts with its members in the Russian empire became extremely frail and intermittent. Outside the faction, furthermore, he remained a deliberately disruptive politician (as socialist leaders in the rest of Europe noted with displeasure). Nevertheless, at the level of political philosophy, he markedly influenced his own Bolsheviks even though they objected to his divisive tirades; and, as often as not, it was Lenin who set the agenda for Bolshevik debates even if he did not always win them. Nor should it be concluded that his organisational impact was negligible. He had the inestimable advantage that the maintenance of a foreign-based apparatus was important for Bolsheviks in the Russian empire. Thus the Okhrana, by arresting revolutionaries and severely constricting the freedoms of the illegal labour movement, made a Lenin possible.

And so he survived, acquiring the prestige of a veteran and a major thinker among Bolsheviks. His anti-tsarist credentials were impeccable. Lenin, like his comrades, also found much to detest in the whole political and economic order of pre-war Europe, and his rage reached a peak of intensity in the First World War. He was in his way a visionary, with the fire of an Old Testament prophet. He genuinely wanted a better (nay, a perfect) world for mankind; and he was convinced that Marxist doctrines provided an unrivalled tool to analyse reality, and predict and determine the future.

No less than Elijah and Isaiah, however, he lacked tolerance. His Marxism evinced a fanaticism which was common in varying degrees among Bolsheviks – and it was alloyed with non-Marxist doctrines and impulses which he did not acknowledge. Bolshevism was not the originator of all ideas of dictatorship. The idea that the oppressive tsarist order should be followed immediately by an order which foreswore authoritarianism had a long tradition in Russian revolutionary attitudes before the Bolsheviks existed; and it was not confined to the Russian empire either. Lenin's framework of Marxism was very elastic. He perennially criticised those Marxists who adopted notions developed outside the boundaries of conventional European Marxism, but this seldom stopped him from being similarly exploratory. On many questions of Russian politics and economics, furthermore, he developed ideas which were combatively expressed. When he insisted that the Bolsheviks should address the national question, he took risks with his own reputation among them. There can be no doubts about his high intellectual potential in the pre-war period. But his thought in general remained patchy and ill-elaborated. To take just two examples: his agrarian theories flew in the face of much evidence he chose to ignore; his answer to the national question overlooked defects pointed out to him at the time.

Such debates could have dragged on interminably if the monarchy had not suddenly been overthrown in February 1917. It was this revolution that made Lenin, for the first time, into a figure in world politics. He quickly became not only the leader of a party but also master of a government. Lenin, for most of his opponents outside the Bolshevik party, *was* the October Revolution. Yet this was an exaggerated image; Russian military defeat and economic collapse were not caused by him and his party, and the Provisional Government was falling headlong before its dissolution. Nevertheless, his towering reputation reflected a real superiority of impact over his colleagues and his party: no one matched him in importance.

Yet he had to handle internal party politics carefully. On some occasions he yielded to his Central Committee; on others he was expressing an existing widespread mood in his party. Even so, he wielded a crucial influence on the fashioning of the party's policies, on the hastening of its decision to overthrow Kerenski, and on the fixing of the framework of Sovnarkom's decrees. He emerged as a skilled public politician. He learned to address mass meetings and to adjust ideas in quest of popular acceptance: he also fudged many policies. He managed, too, to appeal at last both to sophisticated far-left socialist intellectuals and to ordinary factory workers. He was an inspiring leader. Sections of his analysis were brilliant, but his argumentation was marred by poorly elaborated, incoherent and reckless projections. Not only intolerance but also self-deception drove him on; he shared in the utopian visions of the revolutionary era. Nevertheless he, as an intellectual claiming to act from considered premises, had little excuse since commentators in other parties, and even in his own, predicted the consequences of his measures. Civil war was more the making of Lenin than of any other single person. Multitudes of revolutions had occurred in the old Russian empire in 1917, and Lenin had always said that they were easily compatible. Yet the socio-economic requirements of urban Russia clashed with what was demanded by the countryside. The inter-ethnic rivalries were another source of immense conflict. Lenin's policies misjudged the enormity of the old Russian empire's crisis.

And so a broadly-based socialist government did not take place in late 1917. The chances of the prolonged survival of such a regime, linking Bolsheviks with Mensheviks and Socialist Revolutionaries, had never been large; but Lenin was prominent in preventing the attempt from being made. He brushed aside all criticism with the declaration that the policies of the Mensheviks and the Socialist Revolutionaries had had their opportunity in government before the October Revolution, and they had failed. Lenin still hoped against hope that Russian workers and peasants would 'from below' make a mass participatory system and that European socialist revolution would occur. In the meantime, the authoritarian side of his thinking won out steadily over the democratic side. He would not take opposition lying down. And yet it was far from being obvious in March 1918 that Lenin would be able to secure his Soviet state in power and live to pursue his plans for socialist revolution in Russia and the rest of the world.

Notes

As in Volume One, the system of transliteration used in the chapters is modified in the endnotes to conform with the conventions of the SEER in respect of authors' names and the titles of their works in Russian. The abbreviations used in the endnotes are as follows:

BK	*Vladimir Il'ich Lenin. Biograficheskaya khronika* (Moscow, 1970–1982) vols 1–12.
Bol'sheviki	M. A. Tsyavlovskii (ed.), *Bol'sheviki: dokumenty po istorii bol'shevizma s 1903 po 1916 god byvsh. Moskovskogo okhrannogo otdeleniya(Moscow 1918).*
BWW	O. Gankin and H. H. Fisher (eds) *The Bolsheviks and the World War. The Origin of the Third International* (eds), (Stanford, 1940).
DSV	*Dekrety sovetskoi vlasti,* vol. 1 (Moscow, 1957).
DVP	*Dokumenty vneshnei politiki SSSR,* vol. 1, (Moscow, 1959).
DZB	H. Lademacher (ed.), *Die Zimmerwalder Bewegung. Protokole und Korrespondenz* (The Hague, 1967).
IA	*Istoricheskii arkhiv* (Moscow, 1955–1962).
ITsKPSS	*Izvestiya Tsentral'nogo Komiteta Kommunisticheskoi Partii Sovetskogo Soyuza* (Moscow, 1988–).
KPSS	*Kommunisticheskaya partiya v rezolyutsiyakh i resheniyakh s"ezdov, konferentsii i plenumov TsK,* vol. 1, *1898–1917* (Moscow, 1970).
KVI	'Protokoly VI (Prazhskoi) Vserossiiskoi konferentsii RSDRP', *VIKPSS,* 1988, part 1 (no. 5); part 2 (no. 6); part 3 (no. 7).
KVII	*Sed'maya (aprel'skaya) vserossiiskaya konferentsiya RSDRP (bol'shevikov). Petrogradskaya obshchegorodskaya konferentsiya RSDRP (bol'shevikov). Aprel' 1917 goda. Protokoly* (Moscow, 1958).
Letters	T. Dan, *Letters (1899–1946),* B. Sapir (ed.) (Amsterdam, 1985).
LS	*Leninskii sbornik* (Moscow–Leningrad, 1924–).

Perepiska	*Perepiska sekretariata TsK RSDRP(b) s mestnymi 1 partiinymi organizatsiyami. Sbornik dokumentov* (Moscow, 1957).
PR	*Proletarskaya revolyutsiya* (Moscow, 1921–40).
PSS	*Polnoe sobranie sochinenii V. I. Lenina* (Moscow, 1958–1965) vols 1–55.
PU	Yu. Ya. Makhina, (ed.) *Perepiska sem'i Ul'yanovykh, 1883–1917* (Moscow, 1969).
PTsK̄	*Protokoly Tsentral'nogo Komiteta RSDRP(b): avgust 1917 g.–fevral 1918 g.* (Moscow, 1958).
PV	R. C. Elwood (ed.), *Vserossiiskaya Konferentsiya Ros. Sots. -Dem. Rab. Partii 1912 goda together with Izveshchenie o Konferentsii Organizatsii RSDRP* (London, 1982).
RPG	R. P. Browder and A. Kerensky (eds), *The Russian Provisional Government. Documents* (Stanford, 1961).
RPP	*Resheniya partii i pravitel'stva po khozyaistvennym voprosam*, vol. 1, *1917–1928* (Moscow, 1967).
SII	*Vtoroi sez'd RSDRP. Protokoly. Iyul'–avgust 1903* (Moscow, 1959).
SIII	*Tretii sez'd RSDRP. Protokoly. Aprel'–mai 1905 goda* (Moscow, 1959).
SIV	*Chetvertyi (Ob"edinitiel'nyi) sez'd RSDRP. Protokoly. Aprel' (aprel'–mai) 1906 goda* (Moscow, 1959).
Stalin, *Sochineniya*	I. V. Stalin, *Sochineniya* (Moscow, 1946–1951).
SV	*Pyatyi (Londonskii) sez'd RSDRP. Protokoly. Aprel'-mai 1907 goda* (Moscow, 1963).
SVI	*Shestoi s"ezd RSDRP (bol'shevikov). Avgust 1917 goda. Protokoly* (Moscow, 1958).
SVII	*Sed'moi ekstrennii sez'd RKP(b). Mart 1918 goda. Stenograficheskii otchet* (Moscow, 1962).
Trotskii, *Sochineniya*	L. D. Trotskii, *Sochineniya* (Moscow, 1925–1927) vols 1–21.
UB	L. Hass (ed.) *Unbekannte Briefe, 1912–1914* (Zürich–Cologne, 1967).
UNE	'Utro novoi epokhi', *Voprosy istorii KPSS*, part 1 (no. 10, 1987); part 2 (no. 11, 1987) part 3 (no. 2, 1988) part 4 (no. 4, 1988).
VIKPSS	*Voprosy istorii KPSS* (Moscow, 1962–).
VL	N. K. Krupskaya, *Vospominaniya o Lenine* (2nd edn) (Moscow, 1968).
Vospominaniya	G. E. Zinov'ev, 'Vospominaniya', *Izvestiya Tsentral'nogo Komiteta Kommunisticheskoi Partii Sovetskogo Soyuza,* 1989: part 1 (no. 5); part 2 (no. 6); part 3 (no. 7).
VVIL	*Vospominaniya o V. I. Lenine* (Moscow, 1968–69) vols 1–5.
ZIL	I. I. Skvortsov-Stepanov, *et al.*, (eds) *Zapiski Instituta Lenina* (Moscow, 1927) vols 1 and 2.

CHAPTER 1: ALL OR NOTHING

1. It ought to be added, however, that he felt he had a special political vocation. See the discussion on page 11.
2. See Volume One of this trilogy, *The Strengths of Contradiction* (London, 1985) pp. 189–90.
3. See I. Getzler, *Martov: A Political Biography of a Russian Social Democrat* (Cambridge, 1967) p. 128.
4. *PSS*, vol. 19, 198–9.
5. Idem, pp. 202–4.
6. Idem, p. 205.
7. Idem, p. 414.
8. Idem, vol. 20, pp. 25–6.
9. See Volume One, pp. 107–8, 115–16 and 186–7 for earlier manifestations of this phenomenon.
10. See below, pp. 108.
11. See N. Cherevanin, Agrarnyi vopros na Ob″edinitel′nom Sezde RSDRP in *Krest′yanstvo i sotsial-demokratiya* (Moscow, 1906) p. 5. This is just one example among many such references to Lenin.
12. Nor was it at the height of his influence throughout 1917: see this volume, pp. 179, 203 and 213–14.
13. This attitude to Lenin among Bolsheviks was as old as Bolshevism: see Volume One, pp. 108, 112 and 188–90. Lenin was also vigorously taken to task for his behaviour at the Prague Conference in January 1912: see this volume, pp. 20–1 and 25
14. *PSS*, vol. 20, pp. 256–61.
15. Idem, pp. 303–4.
16. Idem, p. 335.
17. Lenin's relations with Polish Marxists are taken up in greater detail on pp. 25–9.
18. *PSS*, vol. 20, pp. 42–4.
19. Idem, pp. 253–5.
20. Idem, pp. 270–1.
21. Idem, pp. 157–60; 'Izveshchenie o Konferentsii Organizatsii RSDRP', in *PV*, part 2, pp. 3–4.
22. See *PSS*, pp. 54–5, 57.
23. Trotski is mentioned about seventy times in idem, vol. 19, pp. 192–424; vol. 20, pp. 1–406; vol. 21, pp. 1–120: these pages cover the years 1910 and 1911. I have excluded from this calculation those references which simply repeat Trotski's name after mentioning it earlier in the same paragraph (or indeed on the same page or clutch of pages) when the same point is simply being reiterated or amplified by Lenin.
24. Idem, vol. 20, p. 96.
25. Idem, p. 96. This epithet was first used in an article of January 1911 (which was not published at the time). Lenin stuck to the usage mainly in his letters to Bolsheviks. If it seems strange that Lenin did not appreciate the racial echoes here, it may be that he assumed that all

social-democrats were anti-racists, and that he felt free to deploy a term which anyway was not intrinsically obnoxious. Undoubtedly the rest of his career is unblemished as a fighter against ethnic prejudice.

26. The strength of Lenin's conscious anti-chauvinism will be considered in Volume Three.
27. See G. Zinov'ev, *Voprosy taktiki. Po povodu petitsionnoi kampanii"* (Ideal: Paris, 1912), especially, pp. 14, 25 and 28 for a virulent attack on Trotski's position. Trotski continued to defend himself against misrepresentation through to the beginning of the First World War: 'Parlamentarizm i rabochii klass', *Bor'ba* (St Petersburg) no. 1, 22 February 1914, pp. 31–5.
28. Ibid.
29. Ibid., p. 28; Lenin, *PSS*, vol. 21, p. 31.
30. L. Trotskii, *Parlamentarizm i rabochii klass,* loc. cit., pp. 32, 35.
31. See *PSS*, vol. 20, fn. 105 (pp. 476–7).
32. *PSS*, vol. 21, pp. 5–7.
33. Ibid., pp. 5, 273, 302–3.
34. See G. Swain, *Russian Social Democracy and the Legal Labour Movement* (London, 1983) pp. 4–7.
35. See V. S. Dyakin, *Krizis samoderzhaviya, 1895–1917* (London, 1984) p. 397.
36. See G. Swain, *Russian Social Democracy and the Legal Labour Movement*, p. 247.
37. See A. Gerschenkron, 'Agricultural Policies and Industrialisation: Russia, 1861–1917', *Cambridge Economic History of Europe*, vol. 6, part 2 (Cambridge, 1966) p. 149.
38. See P. Gatrell, 'Industrial Expansion in Tsarist Russia, 1908–1914', *Economic History Review*, no. 1 (1982) pp. 105–7.
39. See O. Crisp, *Studies in the Russian Economy before 1914* (London, 1976) pp. 34–5.
40. See P. I. Lyashchenko, *Istoriya narodnogo khozyaistva SSSR* (Moscow, 1952), vol. 3, chs 12 and 13.
41. See L. H. Haimson and R. Petrusha, 'Two Strike Waves in Imperial Russia, 1905–1907, 1912–1914', in L. H. Haimson and C. Tilly (eds.), *Strikes, Wars and Revolutions in International Perspective. Strike Waves in the Late Nineteenth and Early Twentieth Centuries* (Cambridge, 1989) p. 107.
42. See C. Rice, *Workers and the Russian Socialist Revolutionary Party through the Revolution of 1905–1907* (Macmillan: London, 1988) pp. 199–200.
43. There has been some confusion about this in Western, though not Soviet, literature. But the publication of the Prague Conference minutes leaves little doubt about the Bolshevik commitment to working in the legal labour movement: see pp. 21–3.
44. Particularly valuable evidence, coming from Bolsheviks talking among themselves without thought of publication, is found in *KVI*, part 1, pp. 46, 49–50, and 53; and part 3, p. 39. See also the police report in M. Tsyavlovskii, *Bol'sheviki*, pp. 90–1.
45. G. K. Ordzhonikidze, *Stat'i i rechi* (Moscow, 1956) pp. 4–5.

46. See *KVI*, part 2, pp. 52 and 56–7; part 3, pp. 33–4. See also this volume, pp. 20–1.
47. See p. 20–2 and 23–4.
48. See *KVI*, part 2, pp. 53 and 55.
49. See N. V. Nelidov and P. V. Barchugov, 'Leninskaya shkola v Long-zhyumo', *IA*, no. 5, 1962, p. 37.
50 Ibid.
51. *KVI*, part 1, p. 46.
52. Police report reproduced in M. Tsyavlovskii, *Bol'sheviki*, pp. 90–1.
53. *KVI*, part 2, pp. 49–51 for the reports of Prague Conference delegates.
54. See Swain, *Russian Social Democracy and the Legal Labour Movement*, pp. 116–9.
55. *PSS*, vol. 19, p. 287.
56. See Trotski's figures in R. C. Elwood, *Russian Social-Democracy in the Underground. A Study of the RSDRP in the Ukraine, 1907–1914* (Assen, 1974) p. 36.
57. *PSS*, vol. 24, p. 34.
58. Idem, p. 35.
59. Idem, p. 40.
60. See the rousing note sounded in idem, vol. 22, pp. 72–3.
61. L. Trotskii, 'K edinstvu – cherez vse prepyatsviya', *Pravda* (Vienna), no. 12, 3(16) April 1912. See Lenin's response in *PSS*, vol. 20, p. 335.
62. Idem; and L. Trotskii, 'Parlamentarizm i rabochii klass', *Bor'ba*, no. 1, 22 February 1914, p. 35.
63. See note 61.
64. See R. C. Elwood, *Russian Social-Democracy*, pp. 60–6.
65. *KVI*, part 2, p. 52.
66. Idem, p. 50.
67. See C. Read, *Religion, Revolution and the Russian Intelligentsia, 1900–1912* (Macmillan: London, 1979) p. 81.
68. Even in his notebooks he seldom mentioned Nietzsche: see *PSS*, vol. 28, p. 181; vol. 29, p. 341.
69. See Lenin's response in idem, vol. 23, p. 115.
70. G. Zinoviev, 'Vospominaniya', *ITsKKPSS*, 1989, no. 7, p. 171.
71. Ibid.
72. *PSS*, vol. 23, pp. 71 and 72–3.
73. Idem, vol. 48, pp. 23–4.
74. Idem, p. 24.
75. See the difficulties of Lenin as communicated to Maksim Gorki, idem, pp. 33–4.
76. Discussions of this kind continued through the First World War: see this volume, pp. 35–6
77. *PSS*, vol. 48, p. 33.
78. Idem, p. 34.
79. Idem, vol. 7, pp. 129–203.
80. *KVI*, part 2, p. 50.
81. *PSS*, vol. 21, p. 178 contains the only public reference to Rasputin by Lenin before Rasputin's assassination in 1916.

82. *Idem*, vol. 21, p. 126.
83. *Idem*, vol. 22, pp. 19–20.
84. *Idem*, vol. 23, pp. 20–1.
85. See J. Pallott, 'Agrarian Modernization on Peasant Farms in the Era of Capitalism', in J. H. Bater and R. A. French (eds.), *Studies in Russian Historical Geography*, vol. 2 (London, 1983) pp. 441, 445.
86. See, for example, *PSS*, vol. 25, p. 92. See also Volume One, pp. 161–5.
87. See the commentary on Cherevanin's contribution in A. Yu. Finn-Enotaevskii, 'Neurozhai i ego posledstviya', *Prosveshchenie*, (St Petersburg) no. 2, January 1912, p. 66. I have been unable to trace Cherevanin's comments on this specific issue; but for his general analysis of pre-war Russian agriculture see his 'Agrarnyi vopros na Ob'edinitel'nom Sezde RSDRP' in *Krest'yanstvo i sotsial-demokratiya* (Moscow, 1906) pp. 1–37.
88. Ibid.
89. *PSS*, vol. 19, pp. 327.
90. N. Cherevanin, *Krest'yanstvo*, p. 23.
91. *PSS*, vol. 19, pp. 323–44; *LS*, vol. 39, pp. 43–4.
92. *PSS*, vol. 27, pp. 135, 142, 180.
93. See Volume One, pp. 159–65.
94. *PSS*, vol. 21, pp. 237–46.
95. Idem, pp. 237–46
96. *Idem*, vol. 24, pp. 20–1.
97. *PSS*, vol. 21, pp. 288–91.
98. *PSS*, vol. 21, p. 291.
99. See this volume, pp. 54–5.
100. *PSS*, vol. 21, pp. 366–8.
101. *PSS*, vol. 22, pp. 26–7. It is true that he also made a study of I. M. Kuzminykh-Lapin's figures on the trends in the average working day; but this was mainly a piece of statistical criticism: *PSS*, vol. 22, pp. 28–9.
102. *PSS*, vol. 25, pp. 19–20.
103. See Volume One, pp. 160–3.
104. Ibid.
105. *KVI*, part 3, p. 45.
106. See A. Walicki, *A History of Russian Thought from the Enlightenment to Marxism* (Oxford, 1979) pp. 144–51.
107. See R. Service, 'Russian Populism and Russian Marxism: Two Skeins Entangled' in R. P. Bartlett, *Studies in Russian History and Thought* (Keele, 1984) pp. 235–40; and Volume One, pp. 159–62.
108. For an opposite interpretation, stressing the unilinear development of Lenin's pre-war thinking, see N. Harding, *Lenin's Political Thought*, vol. 1, passim.
109. See this volume, Chapters 9 and 10.
110. See for example N. Poulantzas, *Political Power and Social Classes* (London, 1973).
111. *ITsKKPSS*, no. 4, 1989, pp. 158–9; *PSS*, vol. 21, pp. 37–51.

112. *PSS*, ibid.
113. On the ramshackle nature of the administration see H. Rogger, *Russia in the Age of Modernisation and Revolution, 1881–1917* (London: Longmans, 1983) pp. 54–6.
114. See R. Service, *The Russian Revolution, 1900–1927* (Macmillan: London, 1986) pp. 17–19.
115. G. K. Ordzhonikidze, *Stat'i i rechi* (Moscow, 1956) pp. 4–5; *PSS*, vol. 21, p. 8.
116. *PSS*, ibid.
117. *KPSS*, vol. 1, pp. 313–21.
118. See R. C. Elwood, Introduction to *PV*, pp. xx-xxi.
119. Ibid.
120. See idem, pp. xxv-xxviii.
121. *KVI*, part 1, pp. 42, 44–5.
122. So, too, was the so-called Seventh Party Conference in April 1917: see this volume, p. 169.
123. See the account by R. C. Elwood in PV, *p. xxi.*
124. A. K. Voronski, *The Waters of Life and Death* (London, 1936) pp. 301–2.
125. See Elwood, *PV*, p. xxi. It ought to be added that the Vperedists were willing to send an observer; but this was not the same as a full delegate: ibid. .
126. See G. Zinov'ev, *Vospominaniya*, part 1, p. 191.
127. See the comments by Lenin and Ordzhonikidze in *KVI*, part 2, p. 62.
128. On Malinovski and the damage he did to the Bolsheviks, see this volume, pp. 48–50.
129. I infer this from the résumé of his planned ripost to Zevin by Lenin: *KVI*, part 1, p. 43.
130. Idem, p. 45.
131. Idem, part 2, p. 51.
132. Idem, part 1, p. 52
133. Idem, part 2, p. 52.
134. This can be inferred from Lenin's speech in idem, pp. 52–3. It is a pity that the seven sheets of paper from the notebook of the Conference minutes are now said to be missing. The contents of some of those speeches must have been extremely critical of Lenin since his speech consists entirely of a reply to such criticisms.
135. Idem, p. 53.
136. Idem, p. 53.
137. Idem, pp. 55 and 57.
138. Idem, pp. 56–7.
139. Idem, part 3, p. 33. The second quotation from Ordzhonikidze comes from Lenin's speech in answer to Ordzhonikidze: ibid.
140. Ibid.
141. Idem, part 2, p. 58 ff. and p. 63 ff.
142. Idem, part 3, p. 33.
143. Idem, p. 34.
144. Idem, p. 35.
145. *PV*, part 1, pp. 30–1.

146. *KVI*, part 3, p. 38.
147. Idem, p. 39.
148. Ibid.
149. Idem, p. 40.
150. Idem, p. 41.
151. *PSS*, vol. 21, p. 485.
152. Ibid.
153. *PV*, part 1, pp. 22–3.
154. *KVI*, part 3, p. 48.
155. Idem, p. 49.
156. Idem, p. 51; *PV*, part 1, p. 28.
157. *PV*, part 1, pp. 21–2.
158. Idem, p. 15.
159. *KVI*, part 2, p. 47.
160. *PV*, part 1, p. 29.
161. Idem, p. 30.
162. Idem, pp. 30–1.
163. It ought to be added, however, that we cannot be sure that Lenin did not want to window-dress the nature of the Conference by having a non-Bolshevik on the Central Committee. But other delegates, certainly, felt stronger about the need to avoid giving unnecessary offence to other factions: see this volume, pp. 39–40.
164. *KVI*, part 3, p. 53–4.
165. See this volume, pp. 39–40.
166. *PSS*, vol. 21, p. 214.
167. See R. C. Elwood, Introduction to *PV*, p. xxviii.
168. *PV*, part 2, pp. 28–9.
169. *KVI*, part 1, p. 47.
170. Idem, part 3, p. 33.
171. See this volume, p. 25.
172. See Volume One, p. 165.
173. See R. A. Ermolaeva and A. Ya. Manusevich, *Lenin i pol'skoe rabochee dvizhenie* (Moscow, 1971) pp. 76–7.
174. See Volume One, pp. 110–1.
175. See R. A. Ermolaeva and A. Ya. Manusevich, op. cit., p. 76.
176. N. Krupskaya, *VL*, p. 139. See also J. P. Nettl, *Rosa Luxemburg* (London, 1966), vol. 2, pp. 557–60.
177. *SV*, pp. 587–8.
178. *SV*, pp. 87 and 627–8.
179. See J. P. Nettl, op. cit., vol. 2, pp. 396–404. See also the archival citations in R. A. Ermolaeva and A. Ya. Manusevich, op. cit., pp. 170 and 239.
180. See J. P. Nettl's account of the evolution of Polish Marxist thought on this question, *op. cit.*, vol. 2, pp. 566–7.
181. See this volume, pp. 156 and 225.
182. Unpublished archives cited in R. A. Ermolaeva and A. Ya. Manusevich, op. cit., p. 233; see also Lenin, *PSS*, vol. 19, p. 271.
183. F. Dan, *Letters*, pp. 231 and 235. See also Lenin's rueful comments in *PSS*, vol. 20, pp. 479–81; and J. P. Nettl, op. cit., vol. 2, pp. 578–80.

184. *PSS*, vol. 21, p. 355; vol. 24, p. 213. See also R. A. Ermolaeva and A. Ya. Manusevich, op. cit., pp. 197–207 and 255; Nettl, op. cit., vol. 2, pp. 575–6.
185. See R. A. Ermolaeva and A. Ya. Manusevich, op. cit., pp. 232–4.
186. See A. Martynov's complaints about 'our little Machiavelli' in idem, p. 277. See also J. P. Nettl, op. cit., vol. 2, pp. 380–3.
187. See the archival reference cited in R. A. Ermolaeva and A. Ya. Manusevich, op. cit., p. 255.
188. See idem, p. 380.
189. See R. A. Ermolaeva and A. Ya. Manusevich, op. cit., pp. 277–8.
190. See archival sources cited in idem, pp. 281–2.
191. See J. P. Nettl, op. cit., vol. 2, p. 563.
192. See idem, pp. 288–9, 301.
193. See R. A. Ermolaeva and A. Ya. Manusevich, op. cit., p. 259.
194. See idem, p. 289.
195. See J. P. Nettl, op. cit., pp 586–7; R. A. Ermolaeva and A. Ya. Manusevich, op. cit., pp. 288–9.
196. See archival sources cited in R. A. Ermolaeva and A. Ya. Manusevich, p. 330.
197. See Yu. V. Bernov and A. Ya. Manusevich, *V Krakovskoi emigratsii. Zhizn' i deyatel'nost' V. I. Lenina v 1912–1914 gg.* (Moscow, 1988) p. 14.
198. Nor is it mentioned in the main textbooks of party history: see L. B. Schapiro, *The Communist Party of the Soviet Union* (London, 1960) p. 125–30; P. N. Pospelov et al., *Istoriya Kommunisticheskoi Partii Sovetskogo Soyuza* (Moscow, 1971) pp. 141–4.
199. See Volume One, p. 165.
200. *PSS*, vol. 21, p. 134.
201. See this volume, pp. 71–2.
202. See this volume, pp. 73.
203. See this volume, pp. 105, 108 and 137–8.
204. See this volume, pp. 108 and 138.
205. See Volume One, pp. 33–7, 161–5.
206. *PSS*, vol. 23, p. 43.
207. See R. Service, *The Bolshevik Party in Revolution. A Study in Organisational Change* (Macmillan: London, 1979) pp. 34–5.
208. See D. Geary, *Karl Kautsky* (Manchester, 1987) pp. 64–8.
209. See Volume One, pp. 110–11.
210. See his advice to Zinoviev in *PSS*, vol. 30, p. 386.
211. See G. Lichtheim, *Marxism: An Historical and Critical Study* (London: Routledge & Kegan Paul, 1967) pp. 188–9.
212. *PSS*, vol. 22, pp. 221–2.
213. Ibid.
214. Idem, vol. 23, pp. 93–4.
215. Ibid.
216. Idem, pp. 18–19.
217. See Volume One, pp. 63–4.
218. V. A. Karpinskii, *Vladimir Il'ich za granitsei v 1914–1917 gg.*, ZIL, vol. 2 (Moscow, 1927) pp. 94–5.

219. See also Lenin's editorial calculations about typefaces in *LS*, vol. 39, p. 130.
220. *PSS*, vol. 22, pp. 279–80.

CHAPTER 2: STORMS BEFORE THE STORM

1. See Chapter 1, pp. 8 and 18.
2. *PSS*, vol. 55, p. 324.
3. N. Krupskaya, *Pedagogicheskie sochineniya*, vol. 11 (Moscow, 1963) p. 134: letter to V A. Karpinski in Geneva.
4. Ibid.
5. See the discussion about the difficulties of dating the arrival of the couple in Yu. V. Bernov and A. Ya. Manusevich, *V krakovskoi emigratsii*, pp. 19–20.
6. *LS*, vol. 2, p. 471.
7. *PSS*, vol. 48, p. 84.
8. *VL*, p. 187. See this volume, pp. 11–12 for the background to *Pravda*'s foundation.
9. See the account by Bernov and Manusevich, op. cit., p. 41.
10. See this volume, pp. 12 and 19.
11. See the archival quotation in *KPSS* (1966) no. 5, p. 116.
12. *PSS*, vol. 48, p. 84.
13. This was N. Krupskaya's phrase: *VL*, p. 203.
14. *PSS*, vol. 48, pp. 72, 107: letters to L. B. Kamenev.
15. This is based on a perusal of the record presented in *BK*, vol. 2, pp. 616–69 and vol. 3, pp. 1–8.
16. F. Dan, *Letters*, p. 286.
17. See I. Getzler, *Martov*, (op. cit.) p. 119.
18. *PSS*, vol. 48, p. 172.
19. Idem, p. 175.
20. See Yu. U. Bernov and A. Ya. Manusevich, op. cit., p. 141. See also *PSS*, vol. 55, p. 339.
21. *BK*, vol. 48, p. 211.
22. See W. Jedrzejewicz, *Pilsudski: A Life for Polamd* (Orbis: London, 1982) pp. 42–3.
23. G. E. Zinov'ev, *Vospominaniya*, part 2, p. 193.
24. See Jedrzejewicz, op. cit., pp. 48.
25. See *idem*, pp. 48–51; N. Davies, *God's Playground. A History of Poland*, vol. 2, *1795 to the Present* (Oxford, 1981) p. 376. I am grateful to Norman Davies for advice on twentieth-century Galicia.
26. *PSS*, vol. 48, p. 177.
27. Idem, vol. 55, p. 343.
28. Idem, vol. 48, p. 201.
29. *BK*, vol. 3, pp. 69–172.
30. N. Krupskaya, *VL*, p. 211; G. Zinov'ev, *Vospominaniya*, part 2, pp. 193–5.

31. *BK*, vol. 3, pp. 52–172.
32. This is not to say that the Bolsheviks in the years immediately before the First World War were in good organisatonal shape: see this volume, pp. 63 and 64.
33. V. T. Loginov *et al.*, 'Adresnye knigi TsK RSDRP (1912–1917 gg.)', *IA*, no. 3, 1959, pp. 33–42.
34. 'Perepiska TsK RSDRP s mestnymi partorganizatsiyami', *IA*, no. 1, 1957, p. 16.
35. See this volume, p. 22, for the Prague Conference's decision to give additional influence to Central Committee members based in Russia.
36. See this volume, p. 64.
37. 'Deyatel'nost' TsK RSDRP po rukovodstvu gazetoi "Pravda"', *IA*, no. 4, 1959, pp. 48, 50.
38. Ibid.
39. See this volume, p. 40, for the occasion of the fraction's split.
40. See R. C. Elwood, 'Lenin and *Pravda*, 1912–1914', *Slavic Review*, no. 2, 1972, pp. 369–70.
41. *PSS*, vol. 48, p. 78.
42. *Iz epokhi Zvezdy i Pravdy, 1911–1914 gg.*, vol. 3 (Moscow, 1924) p. 243.
43. *PSS*, vol. 48, p. 95.
44. See the comments in R. C. Elwood, 'Lenin and *Pravda*', loc. cit., p. 365.
45. The opposite view is taken by R. C. Elwood, ibid. It has to be remembered that the phenomenon of editors turning down manuscripts, even commissioned manuscripts, is not a rare one on most newspapers.
46. *PSS*, vol. 48. p. 162. See also this volume, p. 46.
47. *Iz epokhi 'Zvezdy' i 'Pravdy'*, vol. 3, p. 203.
48. The last issue, no. 9, was made in July 1912. The motivations of even the date of the closure decision remain undivulged.
49. *KPSS*, vol. 1, p. 367. See the discussion in R. C. Elwood, 'Lenin and *Pravda*', loc. cit., pp. 369–70.
50. See R. C. Elwood, idem, p. 372.
51. See idem, p. 373–5.
52. *KPSS*, vol. 1, pp. 391–5; *PSS*, vol. 24, pp. 81–3.
53. *PSS*, vol. 22, pp. 208 and 284.
54. See L. Haimson, 'The Problems of Urban Stability in Urban Russia, 1905–1917', *Slavic Review*, December 1964, part 1, pp. 631–2.
55. *PSS*, vol. 22, p. 284.
56. See *IA*, no. 6, 1958, p. 11.
57. See this volume, pp. 40 and 65.
58. See this volume, p. 63.
59. *PSS*, vol. 24, p. 59. Please note that the 'national question' (or, in Russian, *natsional'nyi vopros*) was conducted about the 'nationalities' (*natsional'nosti*), a vaguer and more comprehensive term than 'nations' (*natsii*).
60. Idem, pp. 58–9.
61. *KPSS*, vol. 1, pp. 446–7.
62. *PV*, part 2, p. 42. The August gathering, however, did not unequivocally support the concept of 'national–cultural autonomy' as Lenin

polemically suggested. The gathering was too divided on the question to say any more than that the concept did not cut 'directly across' the principle of national self-determination.

63. O. Bauer, *Die Nationalitätenfrage und Sozialdemokratie* (Vienna, 1907). See Lenin's notes on ch. 7, apparently taken in 1912: *LS*, vol. 40, pp. 292–4.
64. O. Bauer, op. cit..
65. *PSS*, vol. 23, p. 210: this came in a 'project platform' translated into Latvian and published in August 1913.
66. See, for example, *PSS*, vol. 25, pp. 259, 263.
67. Bauer, *Die Natonalitätenfrage*, pp. 137–8.
68. *PV*, part 2, p. 42.
69. See this volume, pp. 25–6. See also J. Nettl, *Rosa Luxemburg*, vol. 2, appendix 2, pp. 842–62.
70. *PSS*, vol. 25, pp. 260–3 in Lenin's main work on the national question: *O prave natsii na samoopredelenie*.
71. Idem, vol. 23, pp. 318–9: *Tezisy po natsional'nomu voprosu*.
72. N. Zhordaniya, 'Natsional'nyi vopros, *Bor'ba* (St Petersburg), no. 2, 18 March 1914, pp. 26, 30.
73. S. Semkovskii, 'Uproshchennyi marksizm v natsional'nom voprose', *Novaya rabochaya gazeta* (St Petersburg), no. 71, 31 October 1913. See also his fuller treatment in the pamphlet *Natsional'nyi vopros v Rossii* (Petrograd: Kniga, 1917), especially pp. 10 and 18–19. Inidentally, Semkovski rejected the argument of Bauer's friend Karl Renner that the problem of ethnic intermingling was smaller and less troublesome in the Russian empire than in Austria-Hungary: op. cit., p. 10.
74. This matter will be resumed in Volume Three.
75. N. Zhordania, 'Natsional'nyi vopros', op. cit., p. 26.
76. See this volume, p. 74. For an early rejection of their views in detail see his letter to S. G. Shaumyan, 6 December 1913: *PSS*, vol. 48, p. 233.
77. See this volume, pp. 110 and 174–5.
78. *PSS*, vol. 23, p. 316. See also idem, vol. 24, p. 59.
79. Idem, vol. 23, p. 315.
80. Idem, vol. 48, p. 173. See also his letter to I. A. Pyatnitskii, January 1913, idem, vol. 48, p. 147.
81. Idem, vol. 23, pp. 315–16.
82. 'Kriticheskie zametki po natsional'nomu voprosu', reprinted in *PSS*, vol. 24, p. 128.
83. Idem, vol. 25, p. 277.
84. Idem, vol. 23, p. 315.
85. 'Natsional'nyi vopros i sotsial-demokratiya', *Prosveshchenie* (St Petersburg) (1913) no. 3, pp. 50–62; no. 4, pp. 22–41; no. 5, pp. 25–36.
86. Idem, no. 3, pp. 52–60.
87. Idem, no. 5, pp. 31, 36.
88. *PSS*, vol. 48, p. 173.
89. Idem, vol. 25, pp. 259–60 and 263.
90. Ibid.

91. See this volume, pp. 284 and 287.
92. *PSS*, vol. 27, p. 256.
93. See this volume, pp. 286–7.
94. See I. Getzler, *Martov*, pp. 66–7.
95. *SII*, p. 371. See also I. Getzler, op. cit., p. 81.
96. *PSS*, vol. 12, pp. 36–7.
97. See Volume One, p. 135.
98. See idem, p. 185.
99. See G. Zinov'ev, *Vospominaniya*, part 2, p. 195.
100. See S. F. Cohen, *Bukharin and the Russian Revolution. A Political Biography, 1888–1938*, (London, 1974) p. 18. For Bukharin's case, as stated to Lenin, see his letter in *ITsKKPSS*, no. 4, 1989, pp. 206–7.
101. See the explanation of the general difficulties of unmasking offered by Zinov'ev in *Vospominaniya*, part 2, pp. 187–8 and 192–6.
102. See this volume, pp. 20 and 39–40.
103. N. Krupskaya, *VL*, p. 222.
104. M. Tsyavlovskii, *Bol'sheviki*, pp. 97–8.
105. *PSS*, vol. 48, p. 172. This letter was printed in its entirety in the fifth edition of Lenin's collected works; it was written some time before the end of March 1913.
106. See this volume, pp. 326–7. See also the report of Lenin's evidence to the commission of enquiry into the Malinovski affair, *Izvestiya* (Petrograd), no. 94, 17 June 1917.
107. See *PSS*, vol. 48, p. 293.
108. Idem, p. 294.
109. Zinov'ev, *Vospominaniya,* op. cit., pp. 196, 198.
110. 'Perepiska TsK RSDRP c mestnymi partiinymi organizatsiyami v gody novogo revolyutsionnogo pod'ema', *Istoricheskii arkhiv*, no. 1, 1957, p. 37: letter to V D. Vegman. The Russian term was *duratskaya vykhodka*.
111. Ibid.
112. *PSS*, vol. 49, p. 194. See also this volume, p. 154, for the moment when the scales fell from Lenin's eyes.
113. *PSS*, vol. 49, p. 261.
114. A rule of thumb was applied in the respective debates on the so-called 'national question' and the question of imperialism and militarism. The first was treated as relating mainly to Europe, especially to plans for the areas presently governed by the Habsburgs and the Romanovs. The second was implicitly thought to refer to issues appertaining to the non-European and predominantly overseas possessions (or semi-possessions) of Europe's great powers. Consequently, although socialist projects for Bohemia or the Ukraine were integrally connected with the imperial problems of Vienna and St Petersburg, they were usually subsumed under the discussions of the 'national question' rather than of the question of imperialism and militarism. This is not to say that the debaters were unaware that the questions were closely linked; on the contrary, Lenin and his adversaries were acutely conscious that approaches to one question affected attitudes to the other. See this volume, pp. 41–6.

115. *Prosveshchenie*: see especially part 2 in no. 9, pp. 36–44 and part 3 in no. 10, pp. 28–41.
116. R. Luxemburg, *Die Akkumulation des Kapitals. Ein Beitrag zur ökonomischen Erklärung des Imperialismus* (Berlin, 1913), translated by A. Schwarzschild as *The Accumulation of Capital* (London, 1951), esp. chs pp. 29, 33; K. Radek, *Das deutsche Imperialismus und die Arbeiterklasse* (Bremen, 1911), reprinted in his *In Den Reichen Der Deutschen Revolution, 1909–1919. Gesammelte Abhandlungen* (Munich, 1921), esp. pp. 63–132.
117. See the account by D. Geary in *Karl Kautsky* (Manchester, 1987) pp. 48–50.
118. See idem, pp. 50 and 53.
119. On imperialism in general terms, see *PSS*, vol. 2, p. 98. This is one of the few sustained comments in the first two volumes of the fifth edition of the collected works. For an account of the reasons for the eruption of debates on militarism and imperialism among European socialists, which had smouldered for some years, in 1907 see J. P. Nettl, *Rosa Luxemburg*, vol. 1, pp. 396–404.
120. *PSS*, vol. 3, pp. 592–4.
121. Idem, vol. 4, pp. 379, 381.
122. See, for example, idem, vol. 5, pp. 82–3, 325; and vol. 7, p. 170.
123. Idem, vol. 8, p. 173: flysheet *K russkomu proletariatu*.
124. Idem, p. 170.
125. See G. Lichtheim, *Marxism. An Historical and Critical Study* (London, 1967) pp. 355–6.
126. An implicit acknowledgement of Luxemburg's pre-eminence is offered in the citation of the unpublished memoir of A. V. Lunacharski in R. A. Ermolaeva and A. Ya. Manusevich, *Lenin i pol'skoe rabochee dvizhenie*, p. 170.
127. See ibid. See also Lenin's recollections in *PSS*, vol. 16, p. 73: 'Mezhdunarodnyi kongress v Shtutgarte' (from *Proletarii*).
128. Ibid.
129. See Ibid.
130. See Lenin's note in *PSS, vol. 16, pp. 75–6.*
131. See 'Mezhdunarodnyi kongress v Shtutgarte', loc. cit., p. 72; and also vol. 17, pp. 189–90, 192 and 194.
132. Idem, pp. 177–80 and 182.
133. Idem, pp. 188–9.
134. Idem, pp. 228–9: Sobytiya na Balkanakh i v Persii.
135. Idem, vol. 22, p. 198. For other pieces on international relations before 1912 see also his 'Kongress angliiskoi sotsial-demokraticheskoi partii' (1911) in idem, vol. 20, p. 231.
136. See the translation by T. Bottomore, *Finance Capital. A Study of the Latest Phase of Capitalist Development* (London, 1981).
137. Idem, esp. pp. 94–6, 120, 191–2, 225, 263, 309, 319–20, 321–2, 331, 334–5.
138. See this volume, pp. 114.
139. Hilferding, op. cit., p. 368.
140. See this volume, p. 115.

141. K. Radek, *Der deutsche Imperialismus und die Arbeiterklasse*, in loc. cit., p. 72. I am grateful to Jyrki Iivonen for drawing my attention to this work.
142. Idem, p. 139.
143. Idem, pp. 63, 85–91, 96–7, 132, 147.
144. *LS*, vol. 39, p. 89.
145. See D. Geary, *Karl Kautsky*, op. cit., pp. 54–5.
146. *The Accumulation of Capital*, especially, pp. 419–67. See also this volume, p. 115.
147. Idem, p. 13.
148. *LS*, vol. 38, pp. 88–91.
149. *Accumulation of Capital*, p. 317.
150. *LS*, vol. 21, esp. p. 361.
151. Idem, vol. 38, p. 86.
152. *PSS*, vol. 48, 148–9 and 173: letters to A. Pannekoek and L. B. Kamenev.
153. See for example *PSS*, vol. 23, p. 144; vol. 24, p. 89, 125. 154. Idem, vol. 25, p. 261.
155. Idem, p. 76.
156. *PSS*, vol. 47, pp. 98–9, 315.
157. *BK*, vol. 2, p. 337.
158. G. Haupt, *Correspondance entre Lénine et Camille Huysmans, 1905–1914* (Paris, 1963) p. 57; *PSS*, vol. 19, p. 126.
159. See this volume, p. 2.
160. *PSS*, vol. 48, p. 335.
161. *BK*, vol. 2, p. 584.
162. *PSS*, vol. 48, p. 335.
163. *BK*, vol. 2, p. 601; *Voprosy istorii KPSS*, 1960, no. 5, p. 179.
164. *LS*, vol. 38, p. 41 (letter to K. Kautsky, dated 6 June, New Style,); *BK*, vol. 2, p. 616; *VIKPSS*, 1960, no. 5, p. 179.
165. *BK*, vol. 2, p. 628; *LS*, vol. 38, p. 42.
166. *LS*, vol. 38, p. 46–7; D. Geyer (ed.) *Kautskys russisches Dossier: deutsche Sozialdemokraten als Treuhänder des russischen Parteivermögens, 1910–1915* (Frankfurt/New York, 1981).
167. Idem, p. 47.
168. *Pis'ma P. B. Aksel'roda i Yu O. Martova, 1901–1916*, (Berlin, 1924) p. 217; *LS*, vol. 38, p. 145.
169. Idem, vol. 38, pp. 57, 61 and 63.
170. Idem, p. 70.
171. Idem, p. 74.
172. Idem, p. 84.
173. Idem, pp. 96, 113, 134.
174. Idem, pp. 136, 144.
175. See also *PSS*, vol. 24, pp. 189–91, 211–13, 230–2.
176. *UB*, pp. 128–9.
177. Idem, pp. 48–9, 121.
178. Idem, pp. 53, 130.
179. Idem, p. 121.
180. *UB*, p. 47, 117–18.

181. *LS*, vol. 38, p. 133.
182. Idem, vol.8, p. 158–9; vol. 39, pp. 110–19.
183. *UB*, pp. 59–60, 148–9.
184. *PSS*, vol. 25, p. 391: Central Committee report of June 1914.
185. See R. C. Elwood, 'The Congress That Never Was: Lenin's Attempt to Call a "Sixth" Party Congress in 1914', *Soviet Studies*, no. 3, 1979, pp. 346–7. This article is as yet the only substantial work on the endeavour to call the Congress.
186. See 'Zasedaniya Tsentral'nogo Komiteta', *VIKPSS*, no. 4, 1957, p. 115.
187. Idem, p. 117.
188. Idem, p. 116.
189. *PSS*, vol. 25, p. 420.
190. Idem,p. 247.
191. Idem,p. 250.
192. See L. H. Haimson, Problems of Urban Stability, part 1, p. 627.
193. See idem, p. 631.
194. 'Perepiska TsK RSDRP c mestnymi partiinymi organizatsiyami v gody novogo revolyutsionnogo pod'ema, *IA*, no. 1, 1957, p. 26.
195. Ibid.
196. Idem, pp. 19, 21.
197. See the Okhrana report reproduced in 'Podgotovka s'ezda bol'shevistskoi partii v 1914 godu, *IA*, no. 6, 1958, p. 9; see also p. 11 for a similar comment in the same report.
198. See idem, p. 11.
199. See H. Hogan, 'The Reorganisation of Work Processes in the St Petersburg Metal-Working Industry, 1901–14', *Russian Review*, no. 2, 1983, p. 171.
200. See T. Hasegawa, *The February Revolution: Petrograd, 1917* (Seattle, 1981) p. 82.
201. 'Adresnye knigi TsK RSDRP (1912–1917 gg.)', *IA*, no. 1, 1959, pp. 15–26.
202. See VVIL, vol. 2, p. 342; G. I. Petrovskii, *Nash mudryi vozhd.'* (Moscow, 1970) p. 18.
203. See the resolution reproduced in 'Deyatel'nost' TsK RSDRP po rukovodstvu gazetoi 'Pravda'', IA, no. 4 (1959) pp. 42 , 43.
204. Idem, p. 50.
205. Ibid.
206. *PSS*, vol. 48, p. 272. See also R. C. Elwood, 'Lenin and *Pravda*', loc. cit., pp. 373–6; and this volume, p. 36.
207. *PSS*, vol. 48, p. 272.
208. See this volume, p. 41. See also M. A. Moskalev, *Byuro Tsentral'nogo Komiteta v Rossii* (Moscow, 1964) pp. 220–30.
209. See this volume, p. 40; and Volume One, p. 149, 153.
210. *PSS*, vol. 25, p. 402.
211. See this chapter, note 182.
212. *PSS*, vol. 48, p. 297.
213. Idem, p. 293.
214. Idem, pp. 297, 300, 313.
215. Idem, pp. 299, 301.

216. Gankin and Fisher, *BWW*, p. 160.
217. *PSS*, vol. 48, p. 308; Gankin and Fisher, *BWW*, p. 106; G. Haupt (ed.), *Correspondance*, p. 131.
218. See this chapter, note 182.
219. A. Kiselev, 'V iyule 1914 g. (Iz vospominanii)', *PR*, no. 7 (1924) p. 42.
220. Idem, p. 42.
221. *PSS*, vol. 48, p. 160.
222. See L. Haimson, Problems of Social Stability, part 1, loc. cit., pp. 640–2.
223. See this chapter, note 220.

CHAPTER 3: *AD EXTIRPANDA*

1. See this volume, pp. 66.
2. 'Vospominaniya', *ITsKKPSS*, no. 5 (1989) p. 197.
3. See J. Joll, *The Origins of the First World War* (London, 1984) p. 203. It might be mentioned that a draft article was been published for the first time in the fifth edition of Lenin's collected works which, according to the editors (who adduce no evidence), was written between 15, 18 July 1914 and which included the section heading: 'War between Austria and Serbia'. This item, however, was not worked up by Lenin into a full article; nor does it reveal any presentiment of the scale of the military conflict across Europe: see *PSS*, vol. 25, p. 4.
4. See this volume, pp. 53–4.
5. See *PSS*, vol. 48, pp. 107–8, 114.
6. N. Krupskaya, *VL*, p. 224.
7. S. Bagotskii, 'V. I. Lenin v Krakove i Poronine', *VVIL*, vol. 2, p. 324; *LS*, vol. 2, p. 173.
8. Bagotskii, 'V. I. Lenin', ibid.
9. Idem, p. 325.
10. Ibid. The first printed call for the foundation of a new International comes in 'Zadachi revolyutsionnoi sotsial-demokratii v evropeiskoi voine', August 1914, reproduced in *PSS*, vol. 26, p. 5.
11. This term may well have had a brilliantly contemptuous resonance for French-speaking intellectuals; but it is doubtful whether less well-educated Russia-based activists will have understood it.
12. V. Karpinskii, 'Vladimir Il'ich za granitsei v 1914–1917 gg. po pis'mam i vospominaniyam, *ZIL*, vol. 2, pp. 72–3. See also A P. Yakushina, *Lenin i zagranichnaya organizatsiya*, pp. 249–50.
13. See I. Getzler, *Martov*, pp. 139–40.
14. *DZB*, vol. 1, p. 82.
15. See S. H. Baron, *Plekhanov: the Father of Russian Marxism*, (London, 1963) p. 323.
16. *DZB*, vol. 1, pp. 94, 152–3.
17. See the memoir of Jan Hanecki in *LS*, vol. 2, p. 173. The text of Lenin's telegram is reproduced here.

18. *BK*, vol. 3, p. 268.
19. *LS*, vol. 2, pp. 176–7.
20. *Idem*, p. 176.
21. *Idem*, p. 179.
22. Ibid.
23. *BK*, vol. 3, p. 270.
24. *LS*, vol. 2, p. 180.
25. *Idem*, p. 181, 186.
26. *BK*, vol. 3, p. 271. Unfortunately the details of his reading are not reproduced in this source.
27. See *PSS*, vol. 31, p. 176: Greulich was numbered by Lenin among the so-called 'social-chauvinists'.
28. *LS* , vol. 2, p. 186.
29. I have been unable to establish why he lacked a passport. Possibly he had been unable to renew one legally in the pre-war period because of his hunted status with the Russian authorities.
30. *BK*, vol. 3, p. 273.
31. M. M. Kharitonov, Iz vospominanii in *ZIL*, vol. 2 (1927) p. 115.
32. Ya. Ganetskii, 'V poiskakh arkhivov V. I. Lenina (otchet o poezde v Pol'shu po porucheniyu Instituta Lenina), *LS*, vol. 2, p. 467. I have weighed the first volume of Lenin's *PSS*. If such a volume may be considered to be of average weight, then ten hundredweights would constitute 640 volumes. Obviously Lenin had had a comfortable working environment in Galicia.
33. Ibid.
34. *PSS*, vol. 49, p. 2.
35. V. T. Loginov *et al.,* 'Adresnye knigi TsK RSDRP (1912–1917 gg.), *loc. cit.*, pp. 33–42; Zinov'ev, *Vospominaniya*, part 2, p. 200; *Izvestiya* (Petrograd), no. 94, 17 June 1917 .
36. A. E. Senn, *The Russian Revolution in Switzerland, 1914–1917* (University of Wisconsin: Madison, Milwaukee and London, 1971) pp. 11–14.
37. *PSS*, vol. 49 , p. 3; *LS*, vol. 11, pp. 95–6.
38. *PSS*, vol. 26, pp. 1–7.
39. V. Karpinskii, 'Vladimir Il'ich za granitsei', loc. cit., p. 72.
40. *PSS*, vol. 26, p. 1.
41. *Idem*, p. 2.
42. V. Karpinskii, 'Vladimir Il'ich za granitsei', loc. cit., pp. 73–4.
43. *PSS*, vol. 26, p. 6.
44. On his difficulties with the party in the emigration and in Russia, see this volume, pp. 88–9 and 122–5.
45. *PSS*, vol. 8, pp. 170–4.
46. P. Maslov, *Ekonomichskie prichiny mirovoi voiny* (Moscow, 1915) pp. 5, 21, 22, 33;' Ekonomicheskoe znachenie voiny dlya Rossi'i, *Samozashchita. Marksistskii sbornik* (Petrograd) no. 1 (1916) pp. 32–3.
47. See the understated memoir by V. A. Karpinskii, 'Vladimir Il'ich za granitsei', loc. cit., pp. 85–6; and compare it with the trenchant letter from him to Lenin in September 1914: *LS*, vol. 11, pp. 255–7.
48. F. N. Samoilov, *Po sledam minuvshevo* (Moscow, 1954) pp. 263–4.

49. For evidence of Lenin's caution *vis-à-vis* the Swiss authorities in *PSS*, vol. 49, p. 8.
50. See A. E. Senn, *The Russian Revolution in Switzerland*, p. 17.
51. *PSS*, vol. 26, p. 334.
52. Idem, vol. 49, p. 9.
53. V. A. Karpinskii, 'Vladimir Il'ich za granitsei', p. 8. The information that most copies were sent to fellow migrs is given on the basis of cited party archives (unfortunately without reproducing them) by A. P. Yakushina in *Lenin i zagranichnaya organizatsiya RSDRP*, p. 268.
54. *LS* , vol. 11, pp. 255–7.
55. *PSS*, vol. 26, p. 21.
56. Ibid.
57. N. Bukharin, 'Pamyati Il'icha', *Pravda*, no. 17 (2948), 21 January 1924.
58. *PSS*, vol. 26, p. 59.
59. Idem, p. 40.
60. F. Il'in, 'Otryvok iz vospominanii', *ZIL*, vol. 1, pp. 126–7.
61. He had, of course, been disrespectful at strictly party meetings. Even so, his invective in wartime was much stronger. He no longer called him 'comrade' but 'the speaker' (*dokladchikom*): Il'in, 'Otryvok iz vospominanii', p. 127.
62. See also this volume, p. 98.
63. Il'in, op. cit., pp. 126–7.
64. PSS, vol. 26, p. 31.
65. Ibid.
66. L. M[artov], 'Mir', *Nash golos*, no. 19, 3 October 1914; L. Trotskii, 'Voennaya katastrofa i politicheskie perspektivy', *Nashe slovo*, no. 180, 2 September 1915, as reprinted in his *Sochineniya*, vol. 9, p. 151. I am grateful to Brian Pearce for advice over several years about attitudes to the Great War among Russian Marxists.
67. See I. Getzler, *Martov*, pp. 139–40.
68. Nevertheless it must be conceded that Karl Liebknecht too came to use such phraseology: *DZB*, vol. 1, p. 55. Further research, however, is needed on the slogans used with the German social-democratic left.
69. See I. Getzler,*Martov*, op. cit., p. 145.
70. *PSS*, vol. 26, p. 349. There was, however, the glimmering of a softer attitude to Trotski, especially after his criticism of Chkheidze: unsigned article (by G. Zinov'ev?), 'Chkheidze-Tsimmerval'd-Gyusmans-Gvozdev', *Sotsial-demokrat*, no. 52, 25 March 1916. But see also this volume, p. 70.
71. See the nomenclature used in *DZB*, vol. 1, p. 45; *ITKKPSS*, no. 11, 1989, p. 199.
72. G. L. Shklovskii, 'Tsimmerval'd', *PR*, no. 5 (40), 1925, pp. 141–2.
73. *PSS*, vol. 27, pp. 389, 392, 393–4, 412.
74. Idem, vol. 26, pp. 237, 265.
75. Idem, p. 319. See also idem, pp. 215, 219.
76. Idem, p. 223.
77. Idem, p. 317.

78. Idem, p. 218, 221.
79. See D. Kirby, *War, Peace and Revolution: European Socialism at the Cross-Roads* (London, 1986) pp. 3–5.
80. Ibid.
81. See C. E. Schorske, *German Social-Democracy, 1905–1917: the Development of the Great Schism* (Harvard: New York, 1955) p. 288–90.
82. *PSS*, vol. 26, pp. 243, 246.
83. P. Maslov, *Ekonomicheskie prichiny mirovoi voiny*, p. 36.
84. A. Martynov, *Mezhdunarodnost' na zapade i na vostoke* (Petersburg–Moscow, 1916), pp. 44.
85. G. Plekhanov, 'Eshche o voine', *Sovremennyi mir*, bk 8 (1915) pp. 244–5.
86. L. Trotskii, 'God voiny', *Nashe slovo*, no. 156, 4 August 1915 as reprinted in his *Sochineniya*, vol. 9, pp. 220–1; N. I. Bukharin, letter to N. K. Krupskaya in *ITsKKPSS*, no. 1 (1989) p. 208.
87. See this volume, p. 85.
88. A. Martynov, *Mezhdunarodnost'*, p. 43.
89. On Robert Michels, see this volume, pp. 30–1. For Michelsian arguments in Lenin's two works under review, see *PSS*, vol. 26, pp. 228, 243, 248, 322.
90. Idem, vol. 27, p. 14.
91. G. Zinov'ev, *O prichinakh krakha germanskoi sotsial-demokratii*, (Petersburg [*sic*]: 1917; written earlier, in wartime, in Switzerland) part 1, p. 6.
92. Idem, part 3, esp. pp. 15, 23.
93. *PSS*, vol. 26, p. 252.
94. See this volume, p. 31.
95. *PSS*, vol. 26, p. 341. See also the 'admission' of this in 'Posle Tsimmerval'da' (unsigned editorial), *Sotsial-demokrat*, no. 52, 25 March 1916.
96. R. Pearson, *The Russian Moderates and the Fall of Tsarism* (London, 1977), chapter 4.
97. A. G. Shlyapnikov, *Kanun semnadtsatogo goda* (Moscow, 1922) part 2, p. 44.
98. See this volume, pp. 123–4.
99. See this volume, p. 150.
100. See this volume, p. 110; and *ITsKKPSS*, no. 11, 1989, p. 208. See also S. Cohen, Bukharin and the Russian Revolution, op. cit., pp. 23–4.
101. M. Syromyatnikova, 'Bernskaya konferentsiya zagranichnykh organizatsii RSDRP(b) 1915 g.', *PR*, no. 5 (1925) pp. 150–2.
102. *KPSS*, vol. 1, pp. 415–6.
103. *PSS*, vol. 26, pp. 161–7 for the Berne Conference's resolutions.
104. Gankin and Fisher, *BWW*, p. 222.
105. See *PSS*, vol. 27, p. 280. See also this volume, p. 111.
106. See S. Cohen, *Bukharin and the Russian Revolution*, op. cit., pp. 38–9.
107. *PSS*, vol. 49, pp. 131, 155, 160.
108. V. A. Karpinskii, 'Vladimir Il'ich za granitsei', pp. 75–82; *PSS*, vol. 49, pp. 11, 32–34, 37–8, 39–41 (for 1914).

109. See S. Cohen, *Bukharin*, op. cit., pp. 36–7.
110. See idem, pp. 36, 38.
111. See D. Kirby, *War, Peace and Revolution*, pp. 75–7.
112. See I. Getzler, *Martov*, pp. 144–5; Kirby, *War, Peace and Revolution*, pp. 69–75.
113. *PSS*, vol. 49, pp. 82–4.
114. See Volume One, pp. 178–81.
115. *PSS*, vol. 48, p. 324; idem, vol. 49, p. 31.
116. Idem, vol. 29, pp. 323–32; for an example of his linguistic zeal see p. 329.
117. G. Plekhanov, 'Eshche o voine', *Sovremennyi mir*, no. 8, 1916; L. Martov, *Kant s Gindenburgom, Marks s Kantom. (Iz letopisi ideinoi reaktsii)* (Petrograd, 1917).
118. *PSS*, vol. 29, pp. 316–22.
119. Idem, p. 161.
120. See note 117.
121. Y. Martov, *Kant s Gindenburgom*, pp. 8, 9, 11, 13. This work of Martov's shows that, for all his differences with Lenin, there was still much that bound them together even on questions of ethics. At least in theory; in practice Martov took a very different tack.
122. *PSS*, vol. 29, pp. 161, 248.
123. Idem, p. 162. This aphorism is conventionally mistranslated through neglect of the significance of the perfective gerund *ponyav*.
124. See L. Kolakowski, *Main Currents of Marxism*, vol. 2, *The Golden Age*, (trans. by P. S. Falla: Oxford, 1978) p. 462.
125. *PSS*, vol. 29, pp. 163–4.
126. Idem, p. 131.
127. See Volume One, pp. 180–1.
128. See idem, *p. 181.*
129. *PSS*, vol. 29, pp. 172–3, 193.
130. See Volume One, pp. 144, 182–3.
131. *PSS*, vol. 29, pp. 146.
132. Idem, pp. 112, 256.
133. On the paradoxical absence of such an approach in his earlier writings, see Volume One, p. 183–4.
134. Idem, vol. 28, pp. 308, 309 (where he contemptuously dismisses R. Hilferding as a 'Kantian') and p. 424 (where he despises G. Schulze-Gaevernitz as 'a scoundrel, a Kantian'); and vol. 29, p. 71 (where he admires L. Feuerbach's supposed 'joke at Kant's expense').
135. See his introduction to the second edition, *PSS*, vol. 18, p. 12.
136. *PSS*, vol. 29, p. 160; see also idem, pp. 72, 144, 162.
137. Idem, p. 257.
138. Idem, pp. 249, 286, 322.
139. Idem, p. 248.
140. Idem, p. 322.
141. See J. P. Scanlan, *Marxism in the USSR. A Critical Survey of Current Soviet Thought* (Ithaca and London: Cornell University Press, 1985), chapters 1–4.
142. On the other hand, see L. Kolakowski, *Main Currents*, vol. 2,

pp. 463–4, where the case is made that there are subtleties in Lenin which are absent from Engels in the interpretation of Hegel.
143. *PSS*, vol. 29, p. 330.
144. See Volume One, p. 89. For a later comment, in the draft article 'Towards The Question of the Dialectic', see idem, vol. 29, p. 330 (on 'the useful dream').
145. D. I. Pisarev, *Sochineniya*, vol. 3 (Moscow, 1963) pp. 147–51.

CHAPTER 4: WAR'S DIVISIONS

1. See this volume, p. 82.
2. *PSS*, vol. 26, p. 50.
3. Idem, vol. 49, p. 378. The inverted commas were used by Lenin in his statement.
4. Ibid.
5. See her conversation as recorded in L. H. Haimson (ed.), *The Making of Three Russian Revolutionaries. Voices from the Menshevik Past*, (Cambridge, 1987) p. 124.
6. See R. H. MacNeal, *Bride of the Revolution. Krupskaya and Lenin* (Ann Arbor: Michigan, 1972) p. 172.
7. See idem, pp. 136–7.
8. At the time of writing it is predominanantly the non-historians, whether novelists or journalists, who have criticised Lenin directly.
9. See Krupskaya's letter of 6 May 1923, in *ITsKKPSS*, no. 4 (1989) p. 179
10. See, for example, *PSS*, vol. 49, p. 57
11. *PSU*, vol. 338.
12. *PSS*, vol. 49, p. 3.
13. Idem, pp. 178–9.
14. *PSS*, vol. 26, p. 300; see also idem, p. 113.
15. See this volume, pp. 82–4. See also Lenin's expression of continued wartime admiration for Kautsky's pre-war *Weg zur Macht: idem*, pp. 98–9.
16. *PSS*, vol. 30, p. 328.
17. Idem, p. 306.
18. Idem, p. 140.
19. Ibid.
20. See D. Kirby, *War, Peace and Revolution*, pp. 75–7.
21. See idem, pp. 69–75.
22. See I. Getzler, *Martov*, pp. 144–5.
23. See C. Schorske, *German Social-Democracy*, pp. 297–305.
24. *BZD*, vol. 55.
25. L. D. Trotskii, *Moya zhizn'. Opyt avtobografii*, vol. 1, p. 285.
26. *BZD*, vol. 1, p. 54.
27. Idem, pp. 45–9.
28. A. Senn, *The Russian Revolution in Switzerland*, p. 84.

29. *PSS*, vol. 49, pp. 115–16, 128–9.
30. *BZD*, vol. 1, p. 45–9.
31. *PSS*, vol. 49, p. 78.
32. Idem, vol. 26, pp. 383–5. See also another draft, apparently a later one, pp. 282–5.
33. The original is unpublished; but it is discussed in citational detail in Ya. G. Temkin, *Lenin i mezhdunarodnoe sotsial-demokratii, 1914–1917* (Moscow, 1968) pp. 193–4. See Lenin's criticisms, which also help to reconstitute Radek's proposals for us: *PSS*, vol. 49, pp. 125.
34. See note 33.
35. Idem, vol. 49, p. 115. See also his letter to Kollontai expressing similar sentiments, idem, p. 117.
36. *PSS*, vol. 49, pp. 316–7.
37. Idem, pp. 100, 104–6.
38. See the archive-based discussion in Ya. Temkin, *Lenin i mezhdunarodnoe rabochee dvizhenie*, pp. 201–2.
39. *DZB*, vol. 1, pp. 51–2.
40. *LS*, vol. 38. , p. 167.
41. Ibid.
42. *DZB*, vol. 1, pp. 55–6.
43. Idem, pp. 73–9 and 80.
44. Idem, pp. 84, 93, 117–26.
45. Idem, pp. 128, 129.
46. Idem, pp. 133, 137.
47. Idem, p. 141.
48. Idem, pp. 144, 146–7
49. Idem, pp. 149–50.
50. Idem, p. 169
51. *PSS*, vol. 49, pp. 93 (where Zinoviev was criticised for too light a treatment of *Our Word*).
52. G. Zinoviev, *O prichinakh krakha germanskoi sotsial-demokratii*, parts I-III (printed in full under the auspices of the Central Committee.) This work was based on his wartime researches.
53. *PSS*, vol. 49, p. 86. See also idem, vol. 49, pp. 208–9, 210–1.
54. Idem, p. 88.
55. Idem, p. 90.
56. *LS*, vol. 11, pp. 134–5.
57. Idem, p. 135.
58. See I. Deutscher, *Trotsky: The Prophet Armed*, pp. 236–8.
59. On worries about Lenin's earlier indulgence to Malinovski, see this volume, p. 49–50.
60. 'Tezisy Bukharina, predlozhennye im na bernskoi konferentsii zagranichnykh sektsii RSDRP, 27 fevralya 1917 g', *PR*, no. 1 (1930) (96) p. 44. Like Trotski, however, they accepted it on condition that it specifically anticipated a socialist, not a capitalist, United States of Europe: see Bukharin's letter to Krupskaya in the first weeks of 1915: *ITsKKPSS*, no. 11, 1989, p. 208.
61. M. Kharitonov, 'Iz vospominanii', *ZIL*, vol. 2, p. 120; *PSS*, vol. 26, p. 161.

62. *PSS*, vol. 30, p. 356. The outbreak of the February Revolution was to mean that this article remained in the form of unpublished notes.
63. Idem, p. 354.
64. See the account by A. E. Senn, *The Russian Revolution in Switzerland*, p. 39.
65. *PSS*, vol. 26, pp. 352–3, 354.
66. Idem, p. 352.
67. Idem, vol. 27, pp. 379, 383, 393–4.
68. See the English translation in O. Gankin and H. H. Fisher, *BWW*, pp. 236–9.
69. See D. Smart (ed. and trans.), *Pannekoek and Gorter's Marxism* (London: Pluto, 1978), passim.
70. *PSS*, vol. 30, pp. 227–8.
71. Idem, vol. 49, pp. 194–5.
72. Ibid.
73. This is deducible from *PSS*, vol. 27, p. 280.
74. Ibid.
75. Idem, pp. 299–300. See also *PSU*, p. 427.
76. *PU*, p. 427.
77. *PSS*, vol. 27, p. 280.
78. M. Tsyavlovskii, *Bol'shevik*, pp. 87–8.
79. Ibid.
80. See S. Cohen, *Bukharin*, p. 40.
81. This is conventionally translated, in reverse order of words, as Imperialism and the World Economy. See M. Haynes, *Nikolai Bukharin and the Transition from Capitalism to Socialism* (Croom Helm: London, 1985) p. 17.
82. *PSS*, vol. 27, p. 97.
83. Idem, p. 301, 312, 343, 350
84. Idem, vol. 28, p. viii (editorial note).
85. Idem, p. 382.
86. Idem, vol. 27, pp. 252, 302, 310; vol. 28, p. 207; vol. 49, p. 259.
87. Idem, vol. 27, p. 310.
88. Idem, vol. 49, p. 344; *PSU*, p. 419.
89. See his insistent remarks to his intermediary with the publishers, M. N. Pokrovski: *PSS*, vol. 49, p. 259.
90. See D. K. Fieldhouse, *Economics and Empire, 1830–1914* (London: Weidenfeld & Nicolson, 1973) pp. 53–4.
91. See V. Ya. Laverychev, *Gosudarstvo i monopolii v dorevolyutsionnoi Rossii* (Moscow, 1982), passim.
92. See Fieldhouse, *Economics and Empire*, op. cit., pp. 41, 44–8.
93. *PSS*, vol. 28, p. 594.
94. See Lenin's preface to the French and German editions of 1920: idem, vol. 27, p. 307.
95. See this chapter note 92.
96. *PSS*, vol. 27, p. 412.
97. See D. K. Fieldhouse, *Economics and Empire*, op. cit.
98. *PSS*, vol. 27, pp. 379, 383, 393–4.
99. Idem, pp. 378, 383.

100. Idem, vol. 28, p. 65.
101. Idem, vol. 27, p. 324. This point is also implicit in Lenin's introduction to N. Bukharin's *The World Economy and Imperialism*.
102. *PSS*, vol. 27, p. 367, 397.
103. *LS*, vol. 11, p. 352.
104. *PSS*, vol. 27, pp. 397–8, 403.
105. Idem, p. 398.
106. See this volume, p. 82
107. See this volume, pp. 120–1.
108. *Sotsial-demokrat*, no. 58, 31 January 1917. This editorial does not seem to have been written by Lenin himself. But, as editor, he must presumably have approved of it.
109. *PSS*, vol. 30, p. 243.
110. Ibid.
111. Ibid.
112. Idem, p. 190.
113. Idem, pp. 187–8.
114. 'Rossiiskaya sotsial-demokratiya i russkii sotsial-shovinizm', first published in *Kommunist*, no. 1–2 (1915) and reprinted in G. Zinoviev and N. Lenin (sic*)*, *Protiv techeniya. Sbornik statei iz 'Sotsial-Demokrata', 'Kommunista' i 'Sbornika sotsial-demokrata'* (Petrograd, 1919) p. 183.
115. Idem, p. 180. This is the best rendering I can propose for *soldatskii, feodal'nyi*. In fact *soldatskii* carries a slightly condescending connotation, being used instead of the more usual *militaristicheskii*.
116. Ibid.
117. P. Maslov, *Ekonomicheskie prichiny mirovoi voiny*, pp. 5, 21–2, 33, 46; 'Ekonomicheskoe znachenie voiny dlya Rossii', *Samozashchita*, no. 1, 1916, pp. 32, 36.
118. A. Ermanskii [*sic*], *Marksisty na rasput'i: o sbornike 'Samozashchita'* (Petrograd–Moscow, 1916).
119. See this volume, p. 246.
120. See this volume, p. 116.
121. See this volume, pp. 116–17
122. *PSS*, vol. 27, p. 280; vol. 33, pp. 329–30.
123. See Volume One, pp. 129–30.
124. A. G. Shlyapnikov, *Kanun semnadtsatogo goda*, part 2 (Moscow-Leningrad, 1923), p. 13.
125. *PSS*, vol. 27, p. 280.
126. Idem, vol. 30, p. 111.
127. See Volume One, p. 130.
128. On Martov, see *PSS*, vol. 27, p. 92; on Luxemburg, *LS*, vol. 38, p. 163.
129. See Volume One, pp. 130–1.
130. *PSS*, vol. 27, pp. 91.
131. Idem, vol. 30, p. 16: reproduction of article in Sbornik *'Sotsial-demokrata*, no. 1 (1916).
132. *Sotsial-demokrat*, no. 58, 31 January 1917.
133. See this chapter notes 131, 132.
134. On the problem of continuity, however, see this volume, pp. 156–7.

135. *PSS*, vol. 27, p. 61.
136. Idem, vol. 27, p. 27.
137. *PU*, vol. 49, p. 361.
138. V. T. Loginov, *IA* (1959) no. 1, pp. 15–25 reproduces the addresses in full.
139. V. T. Loginov, *IA* (1959) no. 3, pp. 38–42. I ought to add that there were a further three Russian addresses in the book; but all three were dubbed as 'personal' and not to be used for political communications: ibid.
140. Ibid.
141. Ibid.
142. See Moskalev's quotation from unpublished archives in his *Byuro TsK*, p. 270.
143. See *BK*, vol. 3, pp. 432–592. A qualification must be inserted here: namely that some Ulyanovs, particularly Lenin's sisters Anna and Mariya, were deeply involved in Bolshevik politics. Consequently letters to relatives were not always about purely family matters. Anna was largely running the Russian Bureau in Petrograd in winter 1915–16: *PSU*, p. 416. Nevertheless the point about the paucity of Lenin's dispatches to wartime Russia stands.
144. *BK*, vol. 3, pp. 432–592.
145. The full list is S. A. Spandaryan, L. B. Kamenev, A. G. Shlyapnikov, I. V. Stalin, L. N. Stark (who turned out to be a police agent) and two other persons (presumed to be Bolsheviks) who remain unidentified: ibid.
146. See this chapter note 144.
147. See *Sotsial-demokrat*, no. 53, 13 April 1916.
148. *IA* (1958) no. 1, p. 219.
149. *PU*, p. 364.
150. Idem, p. 398.
151. *BK*, vol. 3, p. 265 ff. . It must be added that until free access to Soviet party archives is granted we shall not know for sure how accurate these statistics really are.
152. See M. A. Moskalev, 'Byuro TsK', p. 254.
153. For a wartime piece by L. B. Kamenev see 'O krushenii Internatsionala', *Letopis'* (Petrograd), no. 4, April 1916, especially p. 180, where he states, in Aesopian style, that the current war will lead Germany to a socialist order. The idea that Lenin and Kamenev were at daggers drawn after Kamenev's trial in 1915 is disproved by the fact of their continued amicable correspondence: see, for example, the evidence that Lenin sent him a postcard in exile, *BK*, vol. 3, p. 438.
154. See M. A. Moskalev, op. cit, p. 258.
155. *PSU*, p. 411.
156. Idem, p. 416.
157. M. A. Moskalev, *Byuro,* p. 258.
158. See M. Djilas's account of a conversation with V. M. Molotov in 1944 about co-ordination among Bolsheviks in the First World War: *Memoir of a Revolutionary* (New York, 1973) p. 388. I am grateful to Geoffrey Swain for pointing me towards this unlikely source.

159. *Sotsial-demokrat*, no. 56, 6 November 1916.
160. Ibid.
161. See the skeptical numerical review in R. Service, *The Bolshevik Party in Revolution*, op. cit., p. 43.
162. But see an unusually full local account in *Sotsial-demokrat*, no. 51, 29 February 1916.
163. *LS*, vol. 39, p. 150.
164. *PU*, pp. 411, 416, 421.
165. Idem, p. 362: report by A I. Elizarova-Ulyanova. On Kamenev's position, see also M. Tsyavlovskii, *Bol'sheviki*, p. 153.
166. *Sotsial-demokrat*, no. 51, 29 February 1916
167. Ibid.
168. *PSU*, p. 363.
169. Idem, p. 428.
170. *PSS*, vol. 49, p. 192.
171. Idem, pp. 260–1.
172. See, for example, idem, p. 82. This term is much more abusive in Russian than in English, and was even more so in Lenin's day. Until his archives are accessible, we shall not definitively know whether he used similar language regularly before the war; but the presently published evidence suggests a crudification in 1914–1916.
173. *LS*, vol. 11, p. 219.
174. *PU*, p. 422.
175. See, for example, idem, pp. 292–3.
176. Idem, pp. 338, 423,
177. Idem, p. 355.
178. *BK*, vol. 4, pp. 58–9.
179. *PSS*, vol. 49, p. 340.

CHAPTER 5: UNSEALED MESSAGES

1. See T. Hasegawa, *The February Revolution* pp. 215–23 and 239–42.
2. *PSS*, vol. 26, p. 221.
3. 'O separatnom mire', idem, vol. 30, pp. 184–91. It should also be noted that even this article was dedicated more to international relations than to internal politics.
4. See especially his reaction to the Junius Pamphlet of Rosa Luxemburg, *PSS*, vol. 30, p. 1.
5. Idem, vol. 28,p. 602.
6. *LS*, vol. 100, p. 219.
7. Idem, p. 222.
8. *PSS*, vol. 49, p. 361.
9. Idem, vol. 30, p. 202.
10. Idem, vol. 49, p. 149.
11. Idem, vol. 55, p. 367. See also idem, p. 365.
12. Idem, vol. 49, p. 377.
13. For a brief survey, see R. Service, *The Russian Revolution*, pp. 26–8.

14. See idem, p. 27.
15. Ibid.
16. See this volume, p. 233. See also N. Stone, *The Eastern Front* (London, 1975) pp. 208–9.
17. See L. Siegelbaum, *The Politics of Industrial Mobilisation in Russia, 1914–1917: A Study of the War-Industry Committees* (London, 1983) pp. 79–80.
18. See T. Hasegawa, *The February Revolution*, pp. 187–91.
19. 'Chkheidze i ego fraktsiya – posobniki 'gvozdevskoi' partii', *Sotsial-demokrat*, no. 53, 13 April 1916.
20. See M. Ferro, *The Great War, 1914–1918* (London, 1973) pp. 99 and 109–10.
21. K. Radek, 'The Song Is Played Out', trans. in J. Riddell, *Lenin's Struggle for a Revolutionary International. Documents: 1907–1916. The Preparatory Years*, pp. 374–5; V.I. Lenin, 'Irlyandskoe vosstanie 1916 goda' in *Itogi diskussii o samoopredelenii*, reprinted in *PSS*, vol. 30, pp. 52–6.
22. See the letter to Zinoviev of November (?) 1915 in idem, vol. 49, p. 167. For Lenin's enduring worries about Grimm, see idem, vol. 30, p. 293. Lenin even wondered, before the Kienthal Conference, whether to continue drafting material with Radek: idem, vol. 49, pp. 188, 199.
23, *DZB*, vol. 1, p. 273. Lenin and Radek themselves had to agree to avoid public exacerbation of their own disagreements about 'Russian and Polish affairs': *PSS*, vol. 49, pp. 181–2.
24. See J.P. Nettl, *Rosa Luxemburg*, op. cit, vol. 2, pp. 614–16, 621–3 and 628–9.
25. *DZB*, vol. 1, p. 273.
26. See Ya. G. Temkin, *Lenin i mezhdunarodnoe rabochee dvizhenie*, p. 387, note 52 for a detailed elucidation of the Conference participants' list.
27. *DZB*, vol. 1, p. 273.
28. Idem, p. 274.
29. Idem, p. 284
30. Idem, pp. 307–8.
31. Idem, p. 309.
32. Idem, p. 310.
33. Ibid.
34. Idem, pp. 313–16.
35. Idem, pp. 319–20.
36. Idem, pp. 321–3.
37. Idem, pp. 325–36, esp. p. 335.
38. See the quotation in Ya. G. Temkin, *Lenin i mezhdunarodnoe rabochee dvizhenie*, op. cit., p. 399.
39. *DZB*, vol. 1, pp. 345 and 347–8.
40. Idem, p. 345.
41. Idem, p. 362.
42. Idem, p. 365.
43. Idem, p. 366.
44. Idem, p. 372.
45. Ibid.

46. Idem, pp. 374, 376.
47. A. Balabanoff (ed.), *Die Zimmerwalder Bewegung, 1914–1919* (Frankfurt am Main, 1969) pp. 41–4. See also *DZB*, vol. 1, p. 378.
48. A. Balabanoff, *Die Zimmerwalder*, op. cit., pp. 42, 43.
49. See the Zimmerwald Left's (unsuccessfully-proposed) draft resolution reproduced in translation in J. Riddell (ed.), *Lenin's Struggle*, pp. 511–12.
50. *DZB*, vol. 1, p. 377.
51. See the exchanges in idem, vol. 1, pp. 377–9, 388.
52. On Switzerland, see *PSS*, vol. 30, pp. 219–20.
53. Idem, vol. 26, p. 354. See this volume, p. 121–2.
54. See this chapter, note 53.
55. This acknowledgement of the superior (in Marxist terms) socioeconomic development of Germany continued even after the February Revolution, when he called for the inception of a transition to socialism in Russia. See also this volume, p. 224.
56. See this volume, p. 141.
57. *LS*, vol. 12, pp. 419, 421, 429.
58. Ibid.
59. *PSS*, vol. 28, p. 478.
60. N. Bukharin, 'K teorii imperialisticheskogo razboinicheskogo gosudarstva', *Revolyutsia prava. Sbornik pervyi* (Moscow, 1925) pp. 5–32.
61. *PSS*, vol. 30, p. 397.
62. Idem, pp. 281, 299, 314 (on industrialised Europe); and p. 344 (on Russia).
63. Idem, p. 347. The English term 'petty gentry' does not fully capture the contemptuous savour of the diminutive noun *dvoryanchiki*.
64. Idem, vol. 49, p. 294.
65. See idem, vol. 33, p. 367, editorial note 367.
66. Idem, p. 128.
67. Idem, p. 158.
68. Idem, p. 264.
69. Idem, p. 128.
70. Idem, p. 162; see also pp. 288, 198.
71. He did not consider this in his notes at the time; and even in *The State and Revolution*, written later in 1917, he addressed the theme only sketchily: see this volume, p. 220.
72. Idem, p. 228.
73. Idem, p. 172.
74. Idem, pp. 170, 172, 226, 228, 264.
75. Idem, pp. 226, 228, 292.
76. Ibid.
77. Idem, pp. 228, 230.
78. Ibid.
79. Idem, pp. 154, 212, 214, 226, 228.
80. Idem, pp. 212, 230.
81. Idem, p. 230. See also idem, pp. 172, 174, 226, 228.
82. Idem, p. 186.
83. Idem, p. 214.

84. See the comprehensive account of T. Hasegawa in *The February Revolution*, chs 12–17.
85. See idem, chs 18, 19.
86. See idem, chs 22–25.
87. *PSS*, vol. 49, p. 399.
88. Idem, p. 398.
89. Ibid.
90. Ibid.
91. Idem, pp. 399–400.
92. Ibid.
93. This is given in a postscipt to the letter: idem, p. 403.
94. This is usually referred to as 'a sketch of theses'; but in fact it does not take the form of theses and appears more like the preliminary draft of an article or public lecture: see idem, vol. 31, pp. 1–6.
95. Idem, p. 2.
96. See volume one, pp. 129–30.
97. See this volume, pp. 26.
98. *PSS*, vol. 31, p. 5.
99. Idem, p. 7.
100. Idem, pp. 1, 7.
101. See A. H. Wildman, *The End of the Russian Imperial Army*, vol. 1, *The Old Army and the Soldiers' Revolt* (Princeton, 1980) pp. 228–43.
102. See L. Lande, 'The Mensheviks and the Provisional Government', in L. H. Haimson (ed.), *The Mensheviks. From the Revolutions of 1917 to the Second World War* (Chicago, 1974) pp. 15–20.
103. *PSS*, vol. 49, p. 402.
104. A. Shlyapnikov, *Semnadtstayi god* (Moscow, undated), vol. 1, p. 129. See also D. A. Longley, 'Divisions among the Bolsheviks', *Soviet Studies*, no. 2 (1972) p. 67.
105. See D. A. Longley, *Soviet Studies*, op. cit.,pp. 65–6.
106. 'Protokoly i rezolyutsii Byuro TsK RSDRP (b) (Mart 1917 g.)', *VIKPSS*, no. 3 (1962) p. 153.
107. A. Shlyapnikov, *Semnadstsatyi god*, vol. 2, pp. 179–80.
108. 'Protokoly i rezolyutsii Byuro TsK', loc. cit., pp. 146, 148.
109. See D. A. Longley, *Soviet Studies*, op. cit., pp. 70–3.
110. *PSS*, vol. 31, pp. 17 and 19–20.
111. Idem, p. 22.
112. Idem, p. 21.
113. Idem, pp. 30, 33.
114. Idem, p. 30.
115. Idem, p. 44.
116. Idem, p. 53.
117. Idem, p. 56
118. *Pravda*, nos. 14–15, 21–22 March 1917.
119. See Lenin's own references in *PSS*, vol. 31, pp. 34, 69, 74, 75; vol. 49, pp. 409, 412, 413.
120. Idem, p. 401.
121. See the various working drafts in Idem, vol. 31, pp. 478–86.
122. *LS*, vol. 38, p. 187.

123. Idem, pp. 187–90.
124. For Kamenev's similar critique of Lenin, see this volume, p. 166.
125. See S. H. Baron, *Plekhanov*, op. cit., p. 343.
126. See below, p. 184..
127. See S. Cohen, *Bukharin and the Russian Revolution*, op. cit., p. 44; and I. Deutscher, *Trotsky: The Prophet Armed*, op. cit., p. 246.
128. *PSS*, vol. 31, p. 119.
129. V. A. Karpinskii, 'Vladimir Il'ich za granitsie v 1914–1817 gg.', *ZIL*, vol. 2, p. 106.
130. Ibid.
131. Idem, p. 105.
132. See I. Getzler, *Martov*, op. cit., pp. 147–8.
133. See idem, p. 148; and A. Senn, *The Russian Revolution in Switzerland*, pp. 225–6.
134. Karl Radek recorded that Lenin believed that Grimm was exploiting the discussions as a way of initiating multilateral negotiations for an end to the First World War itself. Lenin was particularly incensed when Grimm blurted out that Fritz Platten, Grimm's fellow negotiator and a person enjoying Lenin's confidence, was a 'bad diplomat'. For Lenin, Platten's intransigence betokened sound commitment and Grimm's complaint mere megalomania. See 'V plombirovannom vagone', *Pravda*, no. 91, 20 April 1924, p. 4. See also Lenin's irascible comments in *PSS* vol. 49, pp. 322–4, 356–7, 359–60, 379–80 and 397.
135. See A. Senn, *The Russian Revolution in Switzerland*, op. cit., p. 226.
136. See *LS*, vol. 2, pp. 383–93; and H. Guilbeaux, *Vladimir Il'ich Lenin* (Leningrad, 1925) p. 161.
137. *BK*, vol. 4, p. 36.
138. See I. Getzler, *Martov*, op. cit., p. 148.
139. In fact the total cannot be regarded as definitive; there may have been either slightly more or slightly fewer passengers.
140. N. Krupskaya, *VL*, pp. 278–9.
141. See *PSS*, vol. 31, p. 57.
142. Idem, p. 94.
143. Idem, p. 91.
144. Idem, p. 56.
145. See A. Senn, *The Russian Revolution in Switzerland*, p. 228.
146. K. Radek, 'V plombirovannom vagone', *Pravda*, no. 91, 20 April 1917, p. 4.
147. Ibid.
148. Ibid.
149. Ibid.
150. Ibid.
151. Ibid.
152. Ibid.; Ya. S. Ganetskii, 'Ot fevralya k oktyabrui', *VVIL*, co. 2, p. 376.
153. K. Radek, op. cit., loc. cit.
154. Ibid.
155. Ibid.
156. *PSS*, vol. 49, p.434.
157. G. Zinov'ev, 'Vospominaniya', part 2, p. 201.

158. Ibid.
159. Ibid.
160. F. F. Raskol'nikov, 'Priezd tov. Lenina v Rossiyu', *PR*, no. 1 (1923) p. 221.
161. N. Sukharov, *Zapiski o revolyutsii*, vol. 3, p. 36.
162. *PSS*, vol 31, p. 44.
163. M. Sawer's excellent article on Lenin's strategy in 1916–1917 tends to portray a natural and inevitable development of his strategical thinking from his new notions of the nature of the socialist state (1916) to his demand for socialist revolution in Russia itself (March 1917). Obviously there was a possible link, but not a logically necessary one. See 'The Genesis of *State and Revolution*', *Socialist Register* (1977) pp. 217–19.
164. *PSS*, vol. 30, p. 344. See this volume, p. 139.
165. Idem, p. 44 (in the third 'Letter from Afar').
166. See Volume One, pp. 131–2.
167. See this volume, pp. 115–16.
168. For a different opinion, presenting Lenin as first and foremost a theorist who proceeded to practical policies only after careful and comprehensive consideration of all the theoretical ramifications, see N. Harding, *Lenin's Political Thought*, (London, 1981) vol. 2.
169. This did not mean that he could not also be aggressive when trying to constrain his own leftists to become cautious: see this volume, pp.317–30.
170. *PSS*, vol. 31, pp. 113–14.
171. Idem, pp. 114–15.
172. Idem, p. 114.
173. Idem, p. 115.
174. Ibid.
175. Idem, p. 116.
177. Ibid.
178. Idem, vol. 31, p. 115
179. Ibid.
180. A brilliant description of the rhetorical devices used by Lenin in the theses is given in *LEF*, no. 3 (1924).
181. *PSS*, vol. 31, pp. 114, 115.
182. See this volume, note 180; see also R. Service, 'Introduction' *What is to be Done?* (London: Penguin, 1988) pp. 26–30 for a brief account of his style in earlier works.
183. Idem, p. 114.
184. Ibid.
185. Ibid.
186. Idem, p. 115.
187. Idem, p. 116.
188. Compare, for example, the fourth and fifth theses, loc. cit., p. 115. In the fourth, only workers' soviets are mentioned, even though the context is not primarily urban; in the fifth, all the various types of soviets occur in a list. This ambiguity was not fully cleared up until after the October Revolution: see this volume, p. 228.

189. To be fair to him, Lenin opened thesis six as follows: 'In the agrarian programme a switching of the centre of gravity to soviets of farmworkers' deputies': ibid. But elsewhere he used other formulations, including both the poorest peasants and the peasantry as a whole respectively: ibid. See also this volume, p. 225.
190. See his oral explanation of his theses on 4 April 1917: *PSS*, vol. 31, p. 109.

CHAPTER 6: THERE IS SUCH A PARTY!

1. It did not permanently remain so; but monarchism, after the killing of the imperial family in 1918, became a declining political force.
2. See G. J. Gill, *Peasants and Government in the Russian Revolution* (London, 1979) pp. 28–44.
3. See W. G. Rosenberg, *Liberals in the Russian Revolution. The Constitutional Democratic Party, 1917–1921* (Princeton, N.J., 1974) pp. 127–8.
4. See R. Service, *The Russian Revolution*, pp. 31–2.
5. See *idem*, p. 32.
6. See this volume, p. 216.
7. This is not to say that Bolshevism and popular aspirations were identical, or that either Bolshevism and popular aspirations were internally undifferentiated and clearly definable items.
8. See this volume, p. 184.
9. The notion that Kamenev and Stalin were pro-Menshevik in March is universal in current monographs in the USSR and the West; but, as I seek to show, it begs the question why they persisted in calling themselves Bolsheviks and – when the division between Bolsheviks and Mensheviks took permanent organisational form – they stayed with the Bolsheviks.
10. 'Protokoly Vserossiiskogo (martovskogo) soveshchaniya partiinykh rabotnikov (27 marta–2 aprelya 1917 g.)', part 1, *VIKPSS*, no. ,(1962) pp. 114, 121. (Part 2 of these Minutes were published in no. 6 (1989) of the same journal.)
11. See this chapter, note 9.
12. *Idem*, part 1, p. 112.
13. *Idem*, part 1, p. 121; and *idem*, part 2, p. 134.
14. See the speeches by Goloshchekin (idem, part 1, p. 117), Vasil'ev (p. 117); and Skrypnik (p. 118).
15. *Idem*, part 2, p. 135.
16. *Idem*, p. 139.
17. *Idem*, p. 140.
18. *Idem*, p. 139.
19. *Idem*, p. 135; M. N. Tsapenko (ed.), *Vserossiiskoe soveshchanie sovetov* (Moscow–Leningrad, 1927) p. 106.
20. N. Sukhanov, *Zapiski o revolyutsii*, op. cit., vol. 3, pp. 27–36.

21. N. A. Uglanov, 'O Vladimire Il'iche Lenin (v period 1917–1922 gg.', *ITsKKPSS*, no. 4 (1989) p. 192.
22. *LS*, vol. 7, p. 308.
23. Idem, pp. 307–8.
24. N. A. Uglanov, 'O Vladimire Il'iche Lenine', op. cit., p. 192.
25. See the archival reference (without quotation) by E. N. Burdzhalov, 'O taktike bol'shevikov v marte–aprele 1917 goda', *Voprosy istorii*, no. 4 (1956) p. 51.
26. *Pravda*, no. 26, 7 April 1917.
27. Yu. Kamenev, 'O tezisakh Lenina', *Pravda*, no. 30, 12 April 1917.
28. P. F. Kudelli (ed.) *Pervyi legal'nyi Petersburgskii komitet bol'shevikov v 1917 g.* *Sbornik materialov i protokolov zasedanii Peterburgskogo komiteta i ego ispolnitel'noi komissii za 1917 god* (Moscow–Leningrad, 1927) p. 88.
29. We need more data on local Bolshevik committees; but Soviet historians with access to archives have been unable to discover cases of immediate support for Lenin. See, for example, the pioneering work of E. N. Burdzhalov, 'O taktike bol'shevikov', op. cit.
30. The fact that he returned while scores of Bolsheviks were in Petrograd after attending the March 1917 all-Russian national soviet gathering must obviously have helped him.
31. *Pravda*, no. 28, 9 April 1917.
32. See R. Service, *The Bolshevik Party*, pp. 53–4.
33. See idem, p. 54.
34. Ibid.
35. See Idem, pp. 53–4.
36. Ibid.
37. See the minutes as recorded in the first part of the book devoted to the Seventh Conference itself: *KVII*, pp. 12, 37.
38. Idem, p. 14.
39. Idem, p. 57.
40. Idem, pp. 14 (K. I. Shutko on the commune), 17 (G. I. Safarov on land nationalisation).
41. See esp. S. Y. Bagdatev's comments in idem, pp. 17–8.
42. Idem, p. 20.
43. Idem, p. 37.
44. Ibid.
45. See this volume, pp. 202–5 and 229–37.
46. *KVII*, p. 16.
47. See this volume, p. 215.
48. See W. Rosenberg, *Liberals in the Russian Revolution*, pp. 106–11.
49. *Pravda*, no. 37, 21 April 1917.
50. See S. P. Knyazev *et al.*, *Petrogradskie bol'sheviki v oktyabr'skoi revolyutsii* (Leningrad: Leninzdat, 1957) p. 100. See also this volume, p. 171.
51. See Rosenberg, op. cit., pp. 113–14.
52. *KVII*, p. 326–30.
53. Idem, p. 63.
54. Idem, pp. 65–6.

55. Idem, pp. 67–8.
56. Idem, p. 75.
57. Idem, p. 77.
58. Idem, p. 69, 72.
59. Idem, pp. 72–3.
60. Idem, pp. 80–1.
61. Idem, p. 85.
62. Idem, p. 91.
63. Idem, p. 98.
64. There is a tendency in both Soviet and Western historiography to dwell on the undoubted discrepancies between Lenin and Kamenev in March and April 1917; but this has led to a neglect of the issues that united them. There were reasons of policy that kept Kamenev as a Bolshevik.
65. *KVII*, p. 84.
66. See Volume One, pp. 134–6.
67. *KVII*, p. 84.
68. Idem, p. 85.
69. Idem, esp. p. 67; and *Pravda*, no. 39, 23 April 1917.
70. *KVII*, p. 79.
71. Idem, p. 93.
72. See idem, p. 112 for Lenin's rejection of Trotsky's 1905 formula, 'Without the tsar, and a workers' government'. Bubnov's statement was not tackled explicitly.
73. Idem, p. 112. Editorial note 99 in idem, p. 352 states that Milyutin and I. A. Teodorovich were added to the seven commission members.
74. Idem, p. 115.
75. Idem, pp. 118–9.
76. Idem, pp. 122, 128. The voting figures were 140 in favour of the Lenin–Kamenev resolution with only eight abstentions; it appears that there were no votes directly against. The resolution is given in idem, pp. 248–50.
77. Idem, p. 145.
78. Idem, p. 172.
79. Idem, pp. 173–4.
80. The final resolution also specified that the party protested against the slur that 'we sympathise with a separate peace' with Germany and Austria-Hungary: idem, p. 243.
81. Idem, p. 177.
82. Idem, pp. 177–8.
83. Idem, p. 185.
84. Idem, p. 188.
85. Idem, p. 189.
86. Idem, p. 190.
87. Idem, p. 192.
88. Idem, p. 191; *Pravda*, no. 13, 19 March 1917 (Kalinin) and no. 32, 14 March 1917 (Stalin).
89. *KVII*, p. 192.

90. Even so, it is significant that no one had the foresight to place the agrarian question earlier on the agenda sheet. On the other hand, at least there had been a prior debate in the Conference's specially-arranged 'agrarian section'. Unfortunately the section's personal composition is not known.
91. Idem, pp. 210–2.
92. Idem, p. 212.
93. Idem, p. 213.
94. Idem, p. 219.
95. Idem, p. 226.
96. Idem, p. 227.
97. Idem, p. 228.
98. Idem, p. 322.
99. Idem, p. 324. Zinoviev, despite some minor disagreements (and he had always had some such) with Lenin, may be taken to be speaking on behalf of both himself and Lenin at this stage.
100. Idem, p. 228.
101. Idem, p. 228.
102. Idem, pp. 232–4.
103. See W. H. Roobol, *Tsereteli. A Democrat in the Russian Revolution* (The Hague: Nijhoff, 1976) pp. 119–22.
104. See R. Abraham, *Alexander Kerensky: First Love of the Revolution* (London, 1987) pp. 142–3.
105. I. Getzler, *Kronstadt, 1917–1921. The Fate of a Soviet Democracy (Cambridge, 1983) pp. 88–9.*
106. *PSS*, vol. 32, pp. 195–7; *Pravda*, no. 73, 4 June 1917.
107. See W. H. Roobol, *Tsereteli;*, pp. 121–3 and 157–8.
108. See P. V. Volobuev, *Ekonomicheskaya politika Vremennogo pravitel'stva* (Moscow, 1962) pp. 68–70, 253, 288–99, 303–5.
109. See M. Perrie, 'The Peasantry' in R. Service (ed.), *Politics and Society in the Russian Revolution* (Macmillan, London; forthcoming), chapter 1.
110. *BK*, vol. 4, pp. 145–268.
111. See this volume, pp. 239–40, for a discussion of problems of communication in the party. Lenin's draft, unpublished at the time, is reproduced in *PSS*, vol. 31, pp. 40–2.
112. *PSS*, vol. 32, pp. 40–1.
113. *Pravda*, no. 51, 7 May 1917: front-page editorial.
114. Ibid.
115. *PSS*, vol. 31, pp. 40–2.
116. On the Military Organisation's significance, see A. Rabinowitch, *Prelude to Revolution. The Petrograd Bolsheviks and the July 1917 Uprising* (Indiana University Press: Bloomington-London, 1967) pp. 54–6.
117. See idem, pp. 56–60.
118. See J. H. L. Keep, *The Russian Revolution: A Study in Mass Mobilisation* (London, 1976) pp. 131–2.
119. *PSS*, vol. 31, p. 267.
120. See A. Rabinowitch, *Prelude to Revolution*, op. cit., pp. 68, 74, 77.

121. D. A. Chugaev *et al.* (eds) *Revolyutsionnoe dvizhenie v Rossii v mae-iyune 1917 g. Iyun'skaya Demonstratsiya* (Moscow, 1959) p. 485.
122. Idem, p. 486.
123. Ibid.
124. See A. Rabinowitch, *Prelude to Revolution*, op. cit., pp. 58–9. See also *Perepiska*, vol. 1, p. 13.
125. See A. Rabinowitch, *Prelude to Revolution*, op. cit., p. 67.
126. See idem, p. 77.
127. See idem, pp. 72–3.
128. See A. M. Sovokin, 'K istorii iyun'skoi demonstratsii 1917 g.', *VIKPSS*, no. 5, 1966, p. 49.
129. See A. Rabinowitch, op. cit., pp. 77–8.
130. *Pravda*, no. 80, 13 June 1917.
131. See A. Rabinowitch, *Prelude to Revolution*, op. cit., p. 84.
132. See idem, pp. 85–94.
133. See idem, pp. 97–8.
134. P. F. Kudelli (ed.), *Pervyi legal'nyi Peterburgskii komitet*, pp. 185–99. See also the record of M. S. Kedrov in his *Velikaya sotsialisticheskaya revolyutsiya: sbornik vospominanii* (Moscow, 1957) pp. 77–8 for Lenin's speech to the All-Russian Conference of Bolshevik Military Organisations. This speech does not appear in any of the editions of Lenin's collected works, not even the fifth. See also *ZIL*, vol. 2, p. 49.
135. See M. S. Kedrov, *Velikaya sotsialisticheskaya revolyutsiya*, op. cit., loc. cit.. See also *PSS*, vol. 32, pp. 363–4.
136. B. Farnsworth, *Alexandra Kollontai. Socialism, Feminism and the Bolshevism* (Stanford, 1980) pp. 76–80.
137. See *Rabochaya gazeta*, no. 79, 13 June 1917 for a typically critical but non-abusive article on Lenin: 'Lenin–Milyukov'.
138. See this volume, pp. 239–40, for commentary on the levels of understanding of Lenin by his contemporary public.
139. *PSS*, vol. 32, p. 21.
140. *BK*, vol. 4, p. 171.
141. *BK*, vol. 4, p. 181.
142. *Sotsial-demokrat*, no. 65, 26 May 1917.
143. The Mensheviks really had no towering single figure in 1917. Tsereteli, Chkheidze, Dan, Martov, Potresov: each had his own outlook on policies and his own followers in the party.
144. *BK*, vol. 4, p. 156. For example, see *idem*, pp. 151, 159, 165, 168.
145. Nevertheless even some Bolsheviks had felt that there was some reason for complaint about Lenin's special status among them: see Volume One, p. 134.
146. F. Ström, *I stormig tid* (Stockholm, 1942) pp. 197–8. I am grateful to David Kirby for drawing this source to my attention and translating it.
147. *BK*, vol. 4, pp. 145–268.
148. See, in general, A. V. Lunacharskii, *Revolyutsionye siluety*.
149. On Lenin's multilayered presentation of his strategy, see this volume, especially pp. 239–40.
150. N. Uglanov, 'O Vladimire Il'liche Lenin, op. cit., p. 193.

151. See the reproduced extracts in I. M. Dazhina, 'Leninskie istoki zhizni i bor'by', *VIKPSS*, no. 3 (1987) pp. 71–2.
152. *BK*, vol. 4, pp. 55–272.
153. See this volume, pp. 280.
154. *BK*, vol. 4, pp. 145–208.
155. *SVI*, p. 41: report by I. D. Smilga.
156. Ibid.
157. See R. Service, *The Bolshevik Party*, op. cit., p. 43.
158. But see this volume, pp. 219–22, for the commentary on Kautsky in *The State and Revolution*.
159. See 'Liberdan' in *Sotsial-demokrat* (Moscow), no. 141, 25 August 1917.
160. V. R. Menzhinskaya, 'Sverdlov v fevral'skoi revolyutsii in N. V. Nelidov (ed.), *Ya. M. Sverdlov: sbornik vospominanii i statei* (Leningrad, 1926) pp. 87–91; *Perepiska sekretariata*, vol. 1, pp. 6–102.
161. See R. Service, *The Bolshevik Party*, pp. 58–9.
162. *KVII*, p. 323.
163. L. Trotskii, *Sochineniya*, vol. 8, p. 251.
164. See, for example, this volume, pp. 219–20
165. *Pravda*, no. 60, 18 May 1917.
166. See J. D. Biggart, 'Aleksandr Bogdanov and the Revolutions of 1917', *Sbornik*, no. 10 (1984) p. 9.
167. *Pravda*, no. 60, 18 May 1917.
168. Unsigned editorial, 'Chkheidze i ego fraktsiya – posobniki 'gvozdevskoi' partii', *Sotsial-demokrat*, no. 53, 13 April 1916.
169. See L. Trotskii, *Chto dal'she? (Itogi i perspektivy)* (Petersburg [sic], 1917), esp. his defence of the theory of 'permanent revolution' on p. 6.
170. *Pravda*, no. 60, 18 May 1917.
171. See S. A. Smith, *Red Petrograd. Revolution in the Factories* (Cambridge, 1983) pp. 145–8.
172. See P. V. Volobuev, *Ekonomicheskaya politika*, pp. 288–99.
173. See Gill, *Peasants and Government* pp. 109–10.
174. See R. A. Wade, *The Russian Search for Peace, February to October 1917* (Stanford, 1969) pp. 89–91.
175. *Novaya zhizn'*, no. 54, 21 June 1917; *ZIL*, vol. 2, p. 49.
176. *ZIL*, loc. cit., ibid.
177. See A. Rabinowitch, *Prelude to Revolution*, op. cit., pp. 123–5.
178. See idem, p. 127.
179. See idem, p. 133.
180. I am indebted to the late Dr R. W. Biagi for conversations over several years about the implications of Lenin's medical condition.
181. See Volume One, pp. 114–5.
182. *BK*, vol. 4, p. 266.
183. For a discussion of the dating see A. Rabinowitch, *Prelude to Revolution*, op. cit., pp. 136–7.
184. See idem, pp. 142–4.
185. See idem, pp. 144–9.
186. See idem, p. 156.
187. See idem, p. 157.

188. See idem, pp. 161–2.
189. See idem, pp. 171–2.
190. V. S. Voitinskii, 'Gody pobed i porazhenii', op. cit., p. 193; N. Sukhanov, *Zapiski o revolyutsii*, op. cit., vol. 4, p. 391.
191. G. E. Zinov'ev, *God revolyutsii* (Gosizdat: Leningrad, 1926) pp. 189–90.
192. See A. Rabinowitch, *Prelude to Revolution*, op. cit., p. 175.
193. V. D. Bonch-Bruevich, *Na boevykh postakh fevral'skoi i oktyabr'skoi revolyutsii* (Moscow, 1931) p. 72.
194. M. Savel'ev, 'Lenin v iyul'skie dni', *Pravda*, 17 July 1917.
195. N. I. Podvoiskii, *God 1917* (Moscow, 1958) p. 62.
196. See A. Rabinowitch, *Prelude to Revolution*, p. 183.
197. L. D. Trotskii, *Moya zhizn'. Opyt avtobiografii* (Berlin, 1929) vol. 2, pp. 32–3.
198. See A. Rabinowitch, *Prelude to Revolution*, p. 192.
199. See I. Getzler, *Martov*, op. cit., pp. 155–6.
200. *Pravda*, no. 99, 5 July 1917.
201. See A. Rabinowitch, *Prelude to Revolution*, op. cit., pp. 204–5.
202. See idem, p. 207.
203. See ibid.
204. See the invaluable memoir of N. I. Podvoiski in 'Voennaya organisatsiya TsK RSDRP(b) i voenno-revolyutsionnyi komitet 1917 g.', *Krasnaya letopis'*, no. 6 (1923) p. 84. No minutes of the Central Committee meeting have been published.
205. See the account by A. Rabinowitch, *The Bolsheviks Come To Power* (New York, 1976) pp. 30–2.
206. See this volume, pp. 149–150
207. *Bez lishnikh slov*, no. 1, 11 July 1917.
208. S. Ordzhonikidze, 'Lenin v iyul'skie dni', *Pravda*, 28 March 1924.
209. See Volume One, p. 24.
210. See this volume, p. 147.
211. See A. Rabinowitch, *The Bolsheviks Come to Power*, op. cit., p. 33.
212. See *Petrogradskaya gazeta*, 7 July 1917.
213. See A. Rabinowitch, *The Bolsheviks Come to Power*, op. cit., p. 33.
214. *BK*, vol. 4, pp. 287–8.
215. G. Zinov'ev, 'Lenin v iyul'skie dni', *PR*, 1927, nos. 8–9 (67–8) p. 70.
216. I repeat this joke with the permission of its author, Professor Walter Pintner of Cornell University.
217. For a detailed account of Stalin in particular, see R. Slusser, *Stalin in October*, pp. 175–6.
218. Later in summer the Central Committee was able to resume its own newspaper's publication, but had to avoid calling it *Pravda*.
219. *BK*, vol. 4, p. 305.
220. *PSS*, vol. 49, p. 444.
221. See Rabinowitch, *The Bolsheviks Come to Power*, pp. 94–104.
222. *PSS*, vol. 34, pp. 443–4.
223. *BK*, vol. 4, p. 315. This new pseudonym was to prove to be one of the last that he had to invent for himself since within weeks he was premier of the Soviet state.

224. This was not an unusual touch of vanity among revolutionaries: the St Petersburg Marxists in the mid-1890s had group photogrphs taken even though the Okhrana was searching them out.
225. A. V. Shotman, 'Lenin v podpol'e (iyul' – oktyabr' 1917 goda, *VVIL*, vol. 2, pp. 424–5.
226. Idem, p. 319.
227. See this volume, p. 211–12.
228. See R. MacNeal, *Bride of the Revolution*, pp. 180–1.

CHAPTER 7: THE FIRE NEXT TIME

1. See R. Service, *The Bolshevik Party in Revolution*, chapter 2.
2. See idem, pp. 42–49.
3. *PSS*, vol. 34, p. 2.
4. Idem, pp. 2 and 5.
5. See the account by A. M. Sovokin, 'Rasshirennoe soveshchanie TsK RSDRP(b), 13–14 iyulya 1917 g.', *VIKPSS*, no. 4, 1959, pp. 125–38.
6. S. Ordzhonikidze, Il'ich v iyul'skie dni, *Pravda*, 28 March 1924.
7. *KVII*, p. 291.
8. See this volume, p. 228.
9. See the account by A. Rabinowitch, *The Bolsheviks Come to Power*, op. cit., p. 60.
10. G. Sokol'nikov, 'Kak podkhodit' k istorii oktyabrya', in *Za leninizma: sbornik statei* (Moscow–Leningrad, 1925) p. 165.
11. *PSS*, vol. 34, p. 17.
12. Ibid.
13. *Vtoraya i tret'ya petrogradskie obshchegorodskie konferentsii bol'shevikov v iyule i oktyabre 1917 goda. Protokoly* (Moscow–Leningrad, 1927) pp. 64–8. See also the reconstruction of the background by R. M. Slusser, *Stalin in October. The Man Who Missed the Revolution* (Baltimore, 1987) pp. 165–71
14. *Vtoraya i tret'ya petrogradskie obshchegorodskie konferentsii*, pp. 17 and 69–70.
15. Idem, p. 165.
16. Idem, p. 88.
17. *PSS*, vol. 34, p. 16. This qualification is omitted from the informative account in R. M. Slusser, *Stalin in October*. Its insertion is vital in order to demonstrate that, just as Stalin could be pushed towards Lenin, so Lenin was propellable towards his critics.
18. See this Chapter, note 6.
19. *PSS*, vol. 34, p. 17.
20. The exact number of delegates who eventually arrived remains uncertain: see *SVI*, p. 294 (editorial note).
21. See A. Rabinowitch, *The Bolsheviks Come To Power*, op. cit., pp. 83–4. The account by Rabinowitch is the fullest on the Sixth Party Congress; it naturally concentrates on questions relating to the seizure

of power. In this résumé of the Congress debates I shall be focusing on political and socio-economic aspects which throw light on Lenin's position and ideas. Although Lenin was not present at the Congress, it is important to look at its debates inasmuch as they provide one of the few opportunities to assess his ideas by the gauge of the general opinion of central and local Bolshevik leaders. Clearly, we need a comprehensive monograph on Bolshevik opinion in 1917.

22. See S. Ordzhonikidze, *SVI*, pp. 30–1; and V. Volodarski, idem, p. 32.
23. *BK*, vol. 4, p. 304: the archival evidence is cited, but not quoted.
24. See the textological analysis of A. M. Sovokin, 'Rezolyutsiya VI s''ezda partii "O politicheskom polozhenii"' in G. A. Trukan *et al.* (eds), *Istochnikovedenie istorii Velikogo Oktyabrya. Sbornik statei* (Moscow, 1977) pp. 11–25.
25. Presumably this was the last time that such informality was evident. Even at the hectic Seventh Party Congress in March 1918 the main reports were well-prepared in advance.
26. *SVI*, p. 20.
27. Idem, p. 21, 25.
28. Idem, p. 36.
29. Idem, p. 71. 30. Idem, p. 89.
31. Idem, p. 101–2, 104.
32. Idem, pp. 104–5.
33. Idem, pp. 106–7.
34. Idem, p. 108.
35. Idem, pp. 109–10.
36. Idem, pp. 111–12.
37. See I. Getzler, *Martov*, p. 155.
38. *SVI*, p. 115.
39. Idem, pp. 116–17.
40. Idem, p. 119.
41. Idem, p. 122. Stalin also defended his reference to 'the poorest peasantry' by claiming that its validity had long ago been established by Lenin: idem, p. 123.
42. Idem, p. 124, 136.
43. Idem, p. 136.
44. Idem, p. 142.
45. Idem, p. 145.
46. Idem, p. 151.
47. Idem, pp. 152–4.
48. He did not say this in his Congress report, possibly because he supposed that the war question lay outside his remit. On 26 June, however, he had emphasised the need for civilianisation at the Third All-Russian Conference of Trade Unions: D. Koenker (ed.), *Tret'ya vserossiiskaya konferentsiya professional'nykh soyuzov 20–28 iyunya 1917 goda. Sterograficheskii otchet* (New York–London, 1982) pp. 294–5, 299–300. Both his Party Congress report and his earlier Trade Union Congress report displayed a wider understanding of the country's economic problems than had until then been attained by Lenin.

49. *SVI*, p. 151.
50. Idem, p. 156.
51. Idem, p. 158.
52. Idem, p. 162.
53. Idem, p. 163.
54. Idem, p. 14, 162. See also this volume, pp. 179.
55. This debate, which is carried idem, pp. 166–92, has an importance for the history of the party; but in order to economise on space I have omitted it from the present discussion, not least because it had little connection with the life of Lenin. It will be resumed as a theme in Volume Three.
56. Idem, p. 192, 238. For the Seventh Congress debate on the programme, see this volume, pp. 331.
57. *SVI*, pp. 196–8.
58. See this volume, pp. 318–21.
59. *SVI*, p. 243.
60. Idem, p. 249.
61. Idem, p. 250.
62. Idem, p. 252.
63. See this volume, p. 176.
64. *PSS*, vol. 34, p. 32.
65. See J. Channon, chapter 'The Landed Gentry' in R. Service (ed.), *Society and Politics in the Russian Revoluion* (Macmillan: London, forthcoming).
66. See G. Gill, *Peasants and Government*, pp. 92–7, 100–1. See also Lenin's thoughts in *PSS*, vol. 34, p. 91.
67. See W. Rosenberg, *Liberals in the Russian Revolution*, pp. 212–18.
68. See A. Rabinowitch, *The Bolsheviks Come to Power*, pp. 110–16.
69. See idem, p. 118–28.
70. See R. Service, *The Bolshevik Party*, esp. p. 43.
71. *PSS*, vol. 34, pp. 49 and 51.
72. Idem, p. 221.
73. Idem, pp. 135–6.
74. Idem, p. 135.
75. Idem, pp. 138–9.
76. See, for example, 'Odin iz korennykh voprosov revolyutsii' in idem, pp. 200–7; 'Russkaya revolyutsiya i grazhdanskaya voina' in idem, pp. 214–28; 'Zadachi revolyutsii' in idem, pp. 229–38. The precise date of the composition of these articles is unknown. They were published between 14 and 27 September 1917.
77. Idem, pp. 239–41, 242–7.
78. Idem, p. 239.
79. Idem, p. 244.
80. *PTsK*, p. 55.
81. *Rabochii put'*, no. 9, 13 September 1917. See also immediately below for the Central Committee's continuing use of Lenin's articles from the days when he urged a 'compromise' with the Mensheviks and the Socialist Revolutionaries.
82. *PTsK*, p. 49.

83. Ibid.
84. *PSS*, vol. 34, p. 262.
85. 'Iz rechi tov. Bukharina na vechere vospomianiiv 1921 g.', *PR*, no. 10, 1921, p. 319.
86. See this chapter, note 76.
87. *PSS*, vol. 34, p. 262.
88. Here I heartily agree with A. Rabinowitch's argument in 'Lenin and Trotskij' in F. Gori (ed.)), *Pensiero e Azione Politica di Lev Trockij* (Florence, 1983), vol. 1.
89. See I. Getzler, *Martov*, p. 158.
90. See W. Rosenberg, *Liberals in the Russian Revolution*, op. cit., pp. 241–5.
91. See A. Rabinowitch, *The Bolsheviks,* op. cit., pp. 226–8.
92. See J. Keep, *The Russian Revolution*, op. cit., esp. chapters 6, 8, 11.
93. See P. V. Volobuev, *Ekonomicheskaya politika Vremennogo pravitel'stva*, p. 289.
94. See idem, pp. 442–3.
95. See M. Perrie, chapter 'The Peasants' in R. Service (ed.), *Society and Politics in the Russian Revolution*.
96. He needed copies of the first in both German and Russian editions, and of the second in Russian: *PSS*, vol. 49, p. 460.
97. The final chapter, which was to be devoted to the Russian historical experience in 1917, was never completed. Only the first two sentences were written: idem, vol. 33, p. 120.
98. See idem, pp. 5–22.
99. Idem, p. 28.
100. Idem, p. 30. Lenin repudiated Kautsky's notion that the civil service and the standing army were somehow 'a parasite on the body' of bourgeois society. These institutions, according to Lenin, were vital bastions of that society.
101. Idem, p. 37. *The Civil War in France* was written in 1871; and Marx and Engels, as Lenin noted (ibid.), quoted the phrase in their 1872 edition of the *Communist Manifesto*.
102. *PSS*, vol. 33, p. 41: the quotation comes from Marx's *Civil War in France*.
103. Idem, pp. 41–2: again the quotation comes from Marx's *Civil War in France*.
104. Idem, p. 44.
105. Idem, p. 45.
106. Idem, pp. 44, 49.
107. Idem, p. 58.
108. Idem, pp. 61–2. It is important to note that Marx never explicitly interpreted the Commune in such a fashion. Lenin made his own gloss here without announcing the fact. Kautsky, by contrast, had always had objections to notions of 'primitive democracy': see M. Salvadori, *Karl Kautsky e la Rivoluzione Socialista, 1880–1938* (Feltrinelli: Milan, 1976) pp. 140–56; and D. Geary, *Karl Kautsky*, pp. 73–85. He continued to have them after the publication of *Lenin's State and Revolution*: see this volume, pp. 221–2 Lenin, too, had

earlier, scoffed at notions of 'primitive democracy': see Volume One, pp. 92–3.

109. PSS, pp. 63 and 65–6. Kautsky is not named in this passage, but throughout *The State and Revolution* his views are picked out for special blame by Lenin. Presumably it would have been embarrassing for Lenin to cite pre-1914 examples of Kautsky's statism if only because no glimmer of criticism of Kautsky had appeared in Lenin's own pre-1914 work: Lenin and Kautsky had had a similar attitude to the revolutionary state before the First World War. Lenin offered *obshchina* as the nearest Russian rendering of Engels's term: idem., pp. 65–6.

110. Idem, pp. 66–7.

111. Idem, pp. 88 and 90.

112. Idem, p. 88.

113. Idem, p. 95. Thus Lenin makes a distinction between socialism and communism with the latter as the later stage. The socialist stage itself, however, is not clearly articulated; in particular, Lenin does not specify whether the dictatorship of the proletariat and socialism are to be regarded as co-extensive. This issue has been resolved in favour of demarcating the two concepts by Lenin's successors. Party programmatic ideas since 1919 have claimed that the dictatorship of the proletariat was a first and separate stage.

114. Idem, p. 106.

115. Idem, p. 110.

116. Idem, pp. 113–14. By bringing the Kautsky–Pannekoek dispute into the discussion in this context, Lenin manages to avoid seeming to have 'misjudged' Kautsky before 1914. But in fact that dispute, as Lenin's own text indicates, took place in 1912: see ibid. See also this volume, pp. 85–6.

117. Idem, p. 116.

118. Idem, p. 112.

119. See this volume, pp. 140.

120. On the other hand, they certainly discussed party strategy after the October Revolution: see this volume, pp. 318ff.

121. Martov's ideas are best expressed in his articles written in the first half of 1919. The articles were originally published from April 1919 onwards and were brought together in a posthumous collection entitled *Mirovoi bol'shevizm* (F. Dan (ed.), Berlin, 1923). This collection includes an 'appendix', which is constituted by Martov's article 'Marks i problema proletarskoi diktatury', first published in *Rabochii Internatsional* in 1918. Kautsky's book, *The Dictatorship of the Proletariat* appeared in German in 1918 and is still available in English translation (Ann Arbor, 1964). Martov has been poorly served in English translations, and his post-1917 theoretical onslaught on *The State and Revolution* has been all but totally ignored in other countries also. The notable and valuable exception is V. Strada's Italian edition of *Mirovoi bol'shevizm* ('World Bolshevism') published as *Bolscevismo mondiale* (Turin, 1980). Strada makes the point that the Western neglect of Martov's work has led to the framework of debate on the

consequences of the October Revolution being unduly influenced by the framework imposed by the Bolsheviks themselves, especially Lenin, Stalin and Trotski.

For an introduction to post-October Menshevik thought on the actual events of Soviet history, as contrasted with Bolshevik theory, see L. H. Haimson (ed.), *The Mensheviks*, ch. 4 *et seq.* Martov, even in his 1918 articles, while supplying original anti-Lenin arguments of his own, acknowledged the importance of Kautsky's *The Dictatorship of the Proletariat*. The similarity of viewpoint was not complete. Martov was reluctant to abandon the idea of 'the dictatorship of the proletariat' even though he understood it very differently from Lenin. Kautsky, after Lenin's tirades of 1917, rejected the idea altogether.

122. K. Kautsky, *The Dictatorship of the Proletariat*, p. 75.
123. V. Strada, *Bolscevismo mondiale,* p. 89.
124. Idem, p. 59. Martov also cited Engels's remark in the same introduction that socialists in power would need to 'amputate' only the 'worst sides' of the contemporary bourgeois state: idem, pp. 56–7.
125. *PSS*, vol. 33, p. 70.
126. *Bolscevismo mondiale*, p. 59.
127. See for example, K. Kautsky, *Dictatorship of the Proletariat*, pp. 9, 44.
128. See Martov's comments in *Bolscevismo mondiale*, pp. 72–4.
129. See this volume, p. 220.
130. See this volume, notes 129 and 130.
131. For Blanqui, see *Bolscevismo mondiale*, p. 43; for Weitling, see K. Kautsky, *The Dictatorship of the Proletariat*, op. cit., p. 21.
132. See Volume One, pp. 29, 35, 38, 99, 135.
133. See also this volume, pp. 156–8 and 232–3.
134. K. Kautsky, *Dictatorship of the Proletariat*, pp. 76–7.
135. Idem, p. 75. See also the related argument of Martov in *Bolscevismo mondiale*, op. cit., pp. 89–90.
136. *Bolscevismo mondiale*, p. 36; K. Kautsky, *Dictatorship of the Proletariat*, p. 33 and 75–6.
137. *Bolscevismo mondiale*, sect. 3; K. Kautsky, *Dictatorship of the Proletariat*, chs 9, 10 for analyses of post-October Bolshevik policies.
138. K. Kautsky, *Dictatorship of the Proletariat*, op. cit., pp. 32–3.
139. *Bolscevismo mondiale*, p. 36 ,
140. *PSS*, vol. 33, pp. 86–91.
141. Idem
142. Lenin mistook the situation by failing to see that the adaptability of the workforce to new jobs, via training, involved an increase in functional specialisation.
143. K. Kautsky, *Dictatorship of the Proletariat*, op. cit., pp. 31, 45.
144. See preceding section of the volume, passim.
145. *PSS*, vol. 33, p. 50.
146. An alternative notion, suggested by N. Harding in his second volume on *Lenin's Political Thought*, holds that Lenin's thinking had an internal coherence and a basically finished quality. Subsequently, A. J. Polan, in *Lenin and the End of Politics* (London, 1984), has contended

that the adverse consequences of the October Revolution flowed in large measure from a 'negative' factor: namely Lenin's aversion to normal considerations of politics and politicking. Again I feel that this is to present too coherent and elaborate of version of *The State and Revolution*. Nevertheless I agree with Polan that the 'negative factor' counted in subsequent history, and that Harding's predominant emphasis on circumstantial post-October factors outside the Bolshevik party's capacity to predict or control is misplaced. Yet the best approach is surely to take both types of factor into account and to avoid monocausal explanations. It will also be readily apparent, from the account given here (especially pp. 222–3 and 225), that Lenin's book was not merely implicitly authoritarian (as Polan contends) but was also 'positively' such. In sum, the book was a hotch-potch – and a dangerous one at that.

147. For a different view, see N. Harding, *Lenin's Political Thought*, op. cit., ch. 6 and A. Polan, *Lenin and the End of Politics*, op. cit., passim.
148. See this volume, pp. 235 and 246–7.
149. See this volume, p. 216.
150. *PSS*, vol. 31, p. 50.
151. Idem, p. 334.
152. Idem, vol. 32, p. 31.
153. Idem, vol. 34, p. 5.
154. For references for the months after the April Conference see *PSS*, vol. 31, p. 461; vol. 32, p. 76, 197.
155. Idem, p. 134.
156. *PSS*, vol. 34, p. 135, 217, 295, 373, 411. A similar formulation was 'the dictatorship of the proletariat and the poorest peasants': see idem, pp. 206–7. Another was 'the dictatorship of the proletariat and the poorest layers of the peasantry': see idem, p. 394.
157. This erroneous proposition is yet another indication of the distortive consequences of trying to understand Bolshevism solely through the prism of grand treatises without reference to the specific time and circumstances of publication.
158. The fact that *The State and Revolution* so frequently referred to dictatorship and was written in July–August 1917 does not disprove this contention. For ths work was not 'public' until 1918; and in any case it was not aimed at the general reading public but at Bolshevik activists.
159. *PSS*, vol. 34, pp. 134, 135, 206–7, 217, 295, 373, 394, 411.
160. I am referring here to *Pravda* and the other central Bolshevik organs which were its successor after July but were disallowed from using the *Pravda* masthead after the closure of the paper's offices. Unfortunately, little is yet known about this aspect of the ideological orientation of Bolsheviks in the towns outside the capital in 1917.
161. *Pravda*, no. 51, 7 May 1917.
162. See I. Stalin, *Sochineniya*, op. cit., vol. 3. Until we have a fully reliable edition of Stalin's works it will not be clear what he wrote in 1917; but none of those *Pravda* articles as yet attributable to him contain summons to dictatorship.

163. It ought nevertheless to be added, in connection with L. Trotski, that he happily wrote about the need for 'terror' and 'iron repression'; but references to 'dictatorship' were few: see his *Chto zhe dal'she? (Itogi i perspektivy)* (Petersburg [*sic*], 1917) pp. 23–4.
164. This is a central premise of *The State and Revolution*: see this volume, pp. 217–18.
165. See *PSS*, vols 31–32, 34.
166. See, for example, the references given in this chapter, note 159.
167. 'O vragakh naroda', *Pravda* article, no. 75, 7 June 1917.
168. Ibid.
169. 'Grozyashchaya katastrofa i kak s nei borot'sya, *PSS*, vol. 174.
170. Idem, pp. 14, 20, 27, 44–6, 67 and 80.
171. See this volume, p. 120; and *PSS*, vol. 31, pp. 64–5, 197, 250; vol. 34, pp. 208, 240.
172. Idem, vol. 31, 250; vol. 34, pp. 205, 343.
173. Idem, vol. 34, p. 36.
174. Idem, p. 403.
175. Idem, p. 37.
176. Ibid.
177. This calculation was first made by S. Mahoney in his unpublished Oxford University M. Phil dissertation (1987), Political Theory in Context: the Significance of *State and Revolution* in Lenin's Political Thought and Policy, p. 84. I am grateful to him for permission to cite his discovery.
178. See this volume, pp. 202–4.
179. See, for example, *Tret'ya vserossiiskaya konferentsiya professional'-nykh soyuzov,* op. cit., pp. 313–4. See also N. A. [*sic*], 'Krizis vlasti', *Rabochaya gazeta*, no. 44, 30 April 1917; and' Kak lenintsy boryutsya s razrukhoi' (unsigned editorial), idem, no. 68, 1 June 1917.
180. See for example his article 'Finlyandiya i Rossiya', *Pravda*, no. 46, 2 May 1917.
181. Ibid.; and 'Ukraina', *Pravda*, no. 82, 15 June 1917.
182. *PSS*, vol. 32, pp. 352. For similar sentiments see idem, pp. 286, 341–2.
183. Idem, pp. 341–2, 352.
184. Idem, p. 286.
185. *Rabochaya gazeta*, no. 57, 16 May 1917.
186. On the Congress discussions see *Izvestiya*, no. 95, 18 June 1917.
187. See the project of the Menshevik Conference section in *Rabochaya gazeta*, no. 57, 16 May 1917.
188. S. Semovskii, *Natsional'nyi vopros v Rossii* (Kniga: Petrograd, 1917) p. 19. See also this volume, p. 41.
189. See idem, pp. 18–19.
190. The proviso should been entered that Lenin, especially with his contemptuous references to the 'Liberdans' of the anti-Bolshevik socialist leadership, continued nevertheless to criticise Liber; but the criticisms related to matters of general state policy and not specifically to the 'national question'.
191. *Izvestiya*, no. 93, 16 June 1917.
192. See the resolution passed by the April Party Conference, *KVII*, p. 252.

193. This topic will be dealt with in Volume Three of this trilogy.
194. 'Programma mira', unsigned editorial in *Rabochaya gazeta*, no. 27, 9 April 1917.
195. See this volume, pp. 175–6, for Lenin's remarks at the Seventh Conference; see also 'Finlyandiya i Rossiya', *Pravda*, no. 46, 2 May 1917; 'Est' li put' k spravedlivomu miru?, idem, no. 75, 7 June 1917; 'Zadachi revolyutsii', *Rabochii put'*, no. 21, 10 October 1917.
196. Ibid.
197. The four were: 'Finlyandiya i Rossiya', *Pravda*, no. 46, 2 May; 'Est' li put' k spravedlivomu miru?', idem, no. 75, 17 June; 'Ukraina', idem, no. 82, 15 June; and 'Ukraina i porazhenie pravyashchikh partii Rossii', idem, no. 84, 17 June. For his other comments, see in particular his remarks on a revised party programme in *PSS*, vol. 32, p. 142 and vol. 34, pp. 378–80; his newspaper journalism in idem, vol. 32, p. 199 and vol. 34, pp. 233–4; his speech to the First All-Russian Congress of Workers' and Soldiers' Soviets, idem, vol. 32, p. 286. Even with the addition of these comments his output on the national question was small in 1917. It is salutary to remember this in view of the danger of according a disproportionate attention to his views because of excessive attention to specific texts.
198. *PSS*, vol. 34, 378, 380.
199. Idem, p. 379.
200. *Pravda*, no. 75, 7 June 1917.
201. Ibid.
202. For example, there were no articles (so far as I know) which were markedly different from Lenin's about nationalities policies before the October Revolution. This marks a contrast with the behaviour on the land question: see this volume, p. 236.
203. See the chapter by S. F. Jones, The Non-Russian Nationalities, in R. Service (ed.), *Society and Politics in the Russian Revolution*, op cit.
204. Ibid.
205. See *PSS*, vol. 34, pp. 173–4 for a typically stinging attack on capitalist greed, fraud and corruption. Moral denunciation was common to Marxists describing the behaviour of capitalists: K. Marx's *Capital* is the supreme example. But Marx also argued that capitalism compelled capitalists to act as they did; and there is little trace of precisely such argumentation in Lenin's writings in 1917.
206. See Volume One, pp. 34–5, 41–3.
207. 'Ischezlo dvoevlastie?', idem, no. 62, 20 May 1917 as reprinted in *PSS*, vol. 32, p. 128. .
208. See his report in *Tret'ya konferentsiya profsoyuzov 1917*, p. 294.
209. 'Grozyashchaya katastrofa i kak s nei borot'sya', *PSS*, vol. 34, p. 194.
210. This subject will be resumed in Volume Three.
211. 'Zapugivanie naroda burzhuaznymi strakhami', *Pravda*, no. 48, 4 May 1917 as reprinted in *PSS*, vol. 32, p. 19.
212. 'Neminuemaya katastrofa i bezmernye obeshchaniya', *Pravda*, no. 59, 17 May 1917, reprinted in *PSS*, vol. 32, p. 210.
213. *PSS*, vol. 32, p. 44.
214. Idem, p. 107.

215.   Idem, pp. 195–7. The case for this interpretation of Lenin is given by S. A. Smith in *Red Petrograd*, pp. 153–5. It must be added, however, that Lenin did not always go out of his way to stress that he did not have it in mind to supplant managerial staff entirely. He must have perceived the advantages of a degree of verbal imprecision (since he knew that several Bolshevik leftists wanted a more radical policy).

216.   *PSS*, vol. 32, p. 293.

217.   Idem, p. 240.

218.   Yet it was mainly after the October Revolution that N. Bukharin specified his policies: see his *Programma kommunistov (bol'shevikov)* (Volna: Moscow, 1918) pp. 27–35.

219.   See this volume, pp. 315–16.

220.   *PSS*, vol. 32, p. 76.

221.   Idem, vol. 31, p. 168.

222.   Idem, vol. 32, p. 313; vol. 34, pp. 168–70.

223.   The only occasion when Lenin used the term 'state capitalism' positively between the February and October Revolutions occurred in a *Pravda* article of 4 June 1917 (*PSS*, vol. 32, p. 293–4). But he did not trumpet it as a major party goal or as an essential and prominent basis of his thinking. On the contrary, the comment came only in response to to criticisms of the Bolsheviks on the grounds that they seemed to be hoping to take a route to socialism via state capitalism. Lenin's words were therefore solely reactive; they were not repeated until after the October Revolution.

       It may still be that state capitalism was part of his plans even before the October Revolution. This argument is implied by N. Harding, *Lenin's Political Thought*, vol. 2, pp. 73–81. But Lenin did not make this clear at the time, and sometimes he offered ideas which were wholly anti-capitalistic. Two conclusions are possible: either he deliberately omitted to deploy the term 'state capitalism' for the reasons I have suggested; or else he was undecided or even merely incoherent; indeed both conclusions are simultaneously possible (and, in my view, probable).

224.   *PSS*, vol. 34, pp. 168–71, 175–9

225.   *PSS*, vol. 32, pp. 112–13.

226.   *PSS*, vol. 32, p. 106.

227.   Idem, p. 197.

228.   *PSS*, vol. 32, pp. 196–7, 293

229.   Idem, vol. 33, pp. 44–5. Let it be noted, however, that this statement occurred in *The State and Revolution*, which was not published until 1918.

230.   See Volume One, pp. 65–70.

231.   *Tret'ya vserossiiskaya konferentsiya professional'nykh soyuzov 1917 goda*, pp. 294–5, 304, 450; Milyutin, *KVI*, p. 151–2.

232.   *PSS*, vol. 32, p. 182.

233.   *Pravda*, no. 51, 7 May 1917.

234.   Idem, no. 48, 4 May 1917.

235.   *PSS*, vol. 32, p. 169.

236. This theme is picked up in detail in the author's 'Lenin's Agrarian Economics' in 1917 in Linda Edmondson and Peter Waldron (eds), *Economy and Society in Russia, 1860–1930. Essays for Olga Crisp* (London; forthcoming). Traditional accounts, basing themselves on Lenin's announcement of the abandonment of the 'land nationalisation' slogan in August, fail to draw attention to the earlier implicit abandonment.
237. *PSS*, vol. 34, pp. 115–16.
238. 'Model farms' as such, however, ceased to be mentioned publicly by Lenin until after October 1917.
239. *PTsK*, p. 38.
240. On the other hand, he continued to refer to the need for the new revolutionary government's power to rest upon the specific support of workers and poor peasants: see this volume, p. 225.
241. *PSS*, vol. 34, p. 115.
242. Idem., pp. 115–16. It must be noted that a shift in emphasis had occurred, with Lenin stating the 'the end of the rule of capital' would nevertheless be initiated by the party's policies in government: Ibid. For Lenin's detailed argumentation at the First Congress of Peasants' Deputies on the subject of the continued development of exploitative economic relationship, even if the peasants were able to institute their own agrarian reform in accordance with their own wishes, see this volume, pp. 235–6.
243. *PSS*, vol. 34, pp. 428–9.
244. *RPG*, vol. 3, pp. 1485–6.
245. Even so, we should keep in mind the thinness of our knowledge about the peasantry's acquaintance with Bolshevik policies. It may be that the peasants came to hear about them mainly indirectly, namely from deserting soldiers, until after the October Revolution and the promulgation and dissemination of the Decree of Land. Further research is needed.

CHAPTER 8: TO ALL THE PEOPLES

1. It is, as we shall see, rather hard to decide when he was restraining himself and when he was restrained by his colleagues. This is always a problem for political historians, and especially so with subjects such as Lenin who kept their innermost feelings so closely guarded. Nevertheless, self-restraint may reasonably be assumed to have played at least some part. Possibly, but not certainly, we shall know more when (and if) the central party archives are opened up.
2. See R. Service, *The Bolshevik Party*, pp. 45–6.
3. This theme is developed in the remaining pages of this chapter; see also this volume, pp. 224–30.

4. This did not stop him from portraying the Bolsheviks as the sole firm defenders of Russia against Germany in September and October 1917: see this volume, p. 247.
5. After all, he was a 'defeatist' until the February Revolution. But see also this volume, pp. 247, for the undercurrents of patriotic appeal in Lenin's statements in September 1917.
6. See this volume, p. 104.
7. The qualification ought to be made to this rather sweeping remark that the Bolshevik party's central organ was not devoid of commentary on diplomatic shifts: see K. R(adek?), 'Massovye stachki v Germanii', *Pravda*, no. 47, 3 May 1917. Articles also appeared on the fall of Riga in August 1917, but centred mainly on the possible connivance of the Provisional Government in letting the German armed forces move along the Baltic littoral: see L. T(rotskii), 'Kogda zhe konets proklyatoi boine', *Rabochii*, no. 10, 1 September 1917. None of these articles, however, came from Lenin.
8. *PSS*, vol. 32, p. 96.
9. Idem, vol. 31, pp. 326, 336, 341, 450: these references to strikes were all made in April 1917.
10. Idem, vol. 34, pp. 272, 275, 340, 386–7, 393, 395, 407.
11. See, for example: 'K. R(adek?), 'Massovye stachki v Germanii', *Pravda*, no. 47, 3 May 1917; unsigned editorial, 'Revolyutsiya rastet vo vsem mire', *Pravda*, no. 52, 9 May 1917. The newspapers did not, however, make foreign news (as opposed to prognostication about the European socialist revolution) a major regular item.
12. *PSS*, vol. 31, pp. 319, 326, 336. For other references, different only in phrasing, see *idem*, vol. 32, p. 54 and vol. 34, p. 340. See also note 11; and the unsigned editorial, 'Revolyutsiya i mir' in *Rabochii put'*, no. 8, 12 September 1917.
13. Idem, vol. 34, pp. 272, 275, 407.
14. The nature of Lenin's communications with Radek has been obscured by the continued speculation about Radek's possible activities as a link-man with agents of the German government. Be that as it may, Radek was an important source of information about political developments outside Russia.
15. The difficulties of obtaining reliable information were not greatly alleviated immediately after the October Revolution.
16. Thus in a lecture on 14 May 1917 he stated *en passant* that only imperialist motives had induced the USA to enter the war: *PSS*, vol. 32, p. 98. This lecture did not quickly reach a wider public than his audience on the day; it was published only in 1929. The other main statement by Lenin on the USA came in a *Pravda* article of 9 May, where he declared that the already difficult food-supplies situation in Germany would be aggravated by the American military involvement. This was only a glancing remark, not a lengthy analysis: see *PSS*, vol. 32, p. 54. In addition, Lenin typically referred to the influence of 'Anglo-French capital' on Russian politics. Only exceptionally did he mention the American factor. For a rare example of the latter see idem, vol. 31, p. 326.

17. Plekhanov, in particular, was even more strongly convinced that Russia could expect only the very worst in the event of a German victory: see 'Nasha taktika', *Edinstvo*, no. 18, 20 April 1917.
18. This is based on a reading of *PSS*, vols 31–34.
19. I have been unable to find references in Lenin's collected works to Woodrow Wilson between the February and October Revolutions. *Pravda*, too, virtually completely avoided the subject.
20. For examples of the contempt felt by the Mensheviks for Lenin's predictions and the policies based on them, see the unsigned editorials in *Rabochaya gazeta*: 'K vosstanovleniyu Internatsionala', no. 54, 12 May 1917; 'Itogi', no. 55, 13 May 1917; 'V bor'be za mir', no. 73, 6 June 1917. See also Nik. [*sic*] Andreev, Voina i sotsializm, no. 73, 6 June 1917.
21. *PSS*, vol. 31, p. 114. See also G. Zinov'ev, Bratat'tsya li dal'she, *Pravda*, no. 49, 5 May 1917.
22. *PSS*, vol. 34, p. 148.
23. See, for example, idem, vol. 32, p. 72, 271.
24. Idem, p. 72.
25. See, for example, his *Chto zhe dal'she. (Itogi i perspektivy)* (Priboi; Petersburg [*sic*], 1917) p. 6.
26. See this volume, pp. 109 and 175–6.
27. See this volume, p. 84.
28. *PSS*, vol. 32, p. 72.
29. Idem, p. 274.
30. Idem, p. 288.
31. In mid-May he wrote a pamphlet, *War and Revolution*, declaring that the Bolsheviks would be in favour of war if no revolution occurred in Germany; but publication was delayed until after Lenin's death. It cannot therefore be adduced as evidence that the general public knew what Lenin's intentions were. See *idem*, vol. 32, pp. 77–102.
32. See, for example, A. Ulam, *Lenin and the Bolsheviks*, p. 353–4.
33. See notes 29, 30.
34. See his explicit denial of any such intention: *PSS*, vol. 32, p. 287.
35. See *idem*, vol. 32, p. 272 ff. and vol. 34, *passim*.
36. See R. Service, *The Bolshevik Party*, p. 43.
37. The treatment of the theme of private intra-Bolshevik discussions would be enhanced if archival access was to be granted. At the moment we are dependent upon published documentary sources and upon memoirs written long after the events.
38. *PSS*, vol. 34, p. 121.
39. See Nota Bene (N. Bukharin), 'The Imperialist Robber State', translated and reprinted from *Jugend-Internationale*, no. 6, 1 December 1916 in O. Gankin and H. H. Fisher, *BWW*, especially p. 239; and L. D. Trotskii, 'Natsiya i khozyaistvo', *Nashe slovo*, no. 135, 9 July 1915, reprinted in *Sochineniya*, vol. 9, (Moscow–Leningrad, 1927) p. 214, and his 'God voiny', *Nashe slovo*, no. 156, 4 August 1915 in idem, p. 220; and his 'K novomu godu', *Nashe slovo*, no. 1, 1 January 1916 in idem, p. 226.
40. See this volume, pp. 167–8.

41. See, above all, the local soviet electoral campaign recommendations in *Pravda*, no. 51, 7 May 1917.
42. For exceptions see the unsigned article 'Vneshnaya politika russkoi revolyutsii', *Pravda*, no. 81, 14 June 1917; and G. Zinov'ev, 'V chem vykhod', *Rabochii*, no. 2, 5 September 1917 (where he stated that the Bolsheviks would have to continue the war if the German government were to refuse their peace terms). For denials about an intention to sign a separate peace, see Kamenev's speech to the First All-Russian Congress of Soviets of Workers' and Soldiers' Deputies in *Pravda*, no. 77, 9 June 1917; the editorials in idem, no. 81, 14 June 1917; no. 84, 17 June 1917; and no. 85, 18 June 1917
43. See this volume, pp. 317 *et seq.*
44. *PSS*, vol. 34, p. 347.
45. For the 'errand-boy' reference see idem, vol. 31, p. 18 from the first of the *Letters from Afar*. For analogous references see idem, pp. 16, 17, 19, 21, 30, 50–1, 63, 70, 72. The last such reference occurred in *The Tasks of the Proletariat in Our Revolution*, written on 10 April, where 'Anglo-French capital' was described as 'the protector and owner of Russian capital'; but this already indicated a shift away from looking at Russian capital as being wholly subordinate to foreign interests: see idem, p. 153.
46. See this volume, p. 119.
47. See W. Rosenberg, *Liberals in the Russian Revolution*, p. 119.
48. It behoves us to remember that his cognitive capacity, while being large, was yet finite.
49. See, for example, idem, vol. 31, p. 158. For the same and for similar wording see idem, pp. 251, 261, 291, 297–8, 343, 407, 454; vol. 32, p. 384; and vol. 34, pp. 206, 347. Nevertheless, Lenin also referred to the impact of 'Anglo-American capital' (idem, vol. 32, p. 407) as well as of 'Anglo-French and American bank capital' (idem, vol. 31, p. 326).
50. See P. V. Volobuev, *Ekonomicheskaya politika Vremennogo pravitel'-stva*, pp. 288–99.
51. *PSS*, vol. 32, p. 365.
52. See note 47 above.
53. *PSS*, vol. 34, p. 389.
54. Idem, vol. 32, p. 177.
55. I should like to stress that Lenin never explicitly used such vocabulary of patriotism. But it was increasingly implicit in his critique of Kerenski. For one of the possible reasons why he inclined in this direction see the following section of this chapter.
56. See especially *Bez lishnikh slov*, no. 1, 11 July 1917 and no. 3, 27 July 1917: both issues contain nothing other than the anti-Bolshevik campaign.
57. For a measured account of the growth of the legend in 1917, see A. Rabinowitch, *The Bolsheviks Come To Power*, pp. 17–20. See also Alfred Senn, 'The Myth of German Money', *Soviet Studies*, no. 1 (1976) p. 84 for a lively and sceptical study of possible German subsidies to the Bolsheviks before Lenin's return in April.

58. For an account of the importance of the timing of the American forces' disembarkation in France, see B. Pearce, *How Haig Saved Lenin* (London, 1987) p. 84.
59. 'Kak my doekhali': *PSS*, vol. 31, pp. 119–21; vol. 32, p. 422, 424–6. This last statement was published only posthumously.
60. Idem, vol. 32, p. 422.
61. Idem, p. 415.
62. Z. A. Zeman and W. B. Scharlau, *The Merchant of Revolution. The Life of Alexander Israel Helphand (Parvus)* (Oxford, 1965) pp. 227–8.
63. Z. A. B. Zeman (ed.), *Germany and the Revolution in Russia, 1915–1918: Documents from the Archives of the German Foreign Ministry* (Oxford, 1958) pp. 70 (doc. 71) and 94 (doc. 94).
64. *Bez lishnikh slov*, no. 1, 11 July 1917.
65. Z. A. B. Zeman (ed.), *Germany and Revolution*, p. 93 (docs. 91 and 92).
66. See Volume One, p. 81.
67. See the account by R. Pipes, *Struve: Liberal on the Left, 1870–1905* (Harvard, 1970) pp. 250–5.
68. Needless to say, Lenin could not have spelled out such reasoning since he would always have been unable to acknowledge the Bolshevik-Berlin financial link. I am putting words into his mind; but they are entirely in line with his own.
69. The attitudes of Bolshevik rank-and-filers to this and many other questions are as yet obscure; but, as ever, we should not presuppose that Lenin's policy coincided closely with those of everyone else in his party. Further research is required, especially in the archives.
70. See this volume, p. 197.
71. See F. Fischer, *German War Aims in the First World War* (London, 1967).
72. See A. Senn, *The Myth of German Money*, p. 84.
73. See M. Ferro, *The Great War*, p. 99.
74. Aleksinski continued his accusatory campaign after 1917, in emigration: see *Du tsarisme au communisme* (Paris, 1923) pp. 23–31. He also co-authored a book of purported 'revelations' of Lenin's sexual adventures: A. Beucher and G. Alexinsky, *Les amours secrètes de Lénine* (Paris, 1937).
75. Whether the Central Committee, or one of its entrusted members, kept records which might help the historian is not known. Thus the opening of the archives would not necessarily resolve our problems.
76. See W. B. Scharlau and Z. A. Zeman, *Merchant of Revolution*, passim.
77. E. D. Stasova, *Vospominaniya* (Moscow, 1969) p. 133.
78. See R. Service, *The Bolshevik Party in Revolution*, ch. 2.
79. *BK*, vol. 4, pp. 358–9.
80. See Yu. N. Flakserman, '10 oktyabrya 1917 goda', in *Petrograd v dni velikogo Oktyabrya: vospominanii uchastnikov revolyutsionnykh sobytii v Petrograde v 1917 g.* (Leningrad, 1967) p. 266.
81. A. Kollontai, 'V tyur'me Kerenskogo', *Katorga i ssylka* (1927) no. 7(36) pp. 25–53.
82. *PTsK*, p. 84.

83. Even Lenin's speech appears in a précis of less than three hundred words: idem, pp. 84–5.
84. *PTsK*, p. 85.
85. Ibid.
86. Ibid.
87. Ibid.
88. Ibid.
89. Ibid.
90. Idem, pp. 87–92.
91. Ibid.
92. Idem, p. 86.
93. See the account by A. Rabinowitch in *The Bolsheviks Come To Power*, p. 206.
94. This rejection is implied by its absence from the meeting's final, pithy resolution: ibid.
95. L. Trotskii, *O Lenine (Materialy dlya biografa)* (Moscow, 1924) p. 70.
96. *PTsK*, p. 86.
97. P. A. Lebedev, 'Fevral'–oktyabr' v Saratove', *PR*, no. 10, 1922, pp. 251–2. But see also V. P. Antonov-Saratovskii, 'Oktyabr'skie dni v Saratove' in idem, pp. 279–80.
98. *PTsK*, pp. 88 and 92.
99. Idem, p. 93.
100. A.A. Ioffe, 'Kanun oktyabrya. Zasedanie v 'Lesnom'', *ITsKKPSS*, no. 4, 1989, p. 203.
101. Ibid.
102. *PTsK*, p. 94.
103. See this volume, pp. 212–13.
104. See Volume One, pp. 88–93.
105. *PTsK*, p. 94.
106. Idem, p. 95.
107. Idem, pp. 95–6.
108. Idem, p. 96.
109. Idem, p. 97. It is this sort of comment that makes me doubt that accounts which assume the existence of clear-cut left-versus-right arguments in the Bolshevik Central Committee somewhat mislead. Even several rightists were ready for a fight with the Provisional Government.
110. Ibid.
111. Idem, pp. 97–8.
112. Idem, p. 98.
113. Idem, pp. 98–9.
114. Idem, p. 99.
115. Idem, pp. 100–3.
116. Ibid.
117. Idem, p. 100.
118. Idem, p. 104.
119. Ibid.
120. Ibid.

121. See A. Rabinowitch, *The Bolsheviks Come To Power*, pp. 232–3.
122. P. N. Podvoiskii, 'O voennoi deyatel'nosti V. I. Lenina', *VIKPSS* (1957) no. 1, p. 33. See the excellent discussion in A. Rabinowitch, *The Bolsheviks Come to Power*, op. cit., pp. 234–5, 349–50.
123. P. N. Podvoiskii, 'O voennoi', op. cit., p. 37.
124. *PTsK*, pp. 95–102.
125. P. N. Podvoiskii, 'O voennoi', op. cit., p. 37.
126. Idem, pp. 37–8.
127. See E. A. Lutskii, 'Zasedanie TsK RSDRP(b), noch'yu 24–25 oktyabrya 1917 g.), *VIKPSS*, 1986, no. 11, pp. 89–90.
128. *Novaya zhizn'*, no. 156, 18 October 1917.
129. *PTsK*, p. 114.
130. Idem, p. 115.
131. Idem, p. 114.
132. See A. Rabinowitch, *The Bolsheviks Come to Power*, pp. 224–5.
133. See idem, p. 243.
134. *Rabochii put'*, 24 October 1917.
135. *BK*, vol. 4, p. 394.
136. See for example *Delo naroda*, no. 185, 20 October 1917.
137. *PSS*, vol. 49, p. 453.
138. *PTsK*, p. 118.
139. F. Dan, 'K istorii poslednikh dnei Vremennogo pravitel'stva', *Letopis' revolyutsii*, no. 1, 1923, pp. 161–76.
140. M. V. Fofanova, 'Poslednee podpol'e' in *Ob Il'iche: vospominaniya pitertsev* (London, 1970) p. 348.
141. *PSS*, vol. 34, p. 436.
142. Idem, p. 435.
143. Idem, vol. 49, p. 453.
144. E. A. Rakh'ya, Moi vospominaniya o Vladimire Il'iche, *VVIL*, vol. 2, p. 432.
145. Idem, p. 433.
146. See A. Rabinowitch, *The Bolsheviks Come to Power*, pp. 268–72.
147. See idem, pp. 272–82.
148. This, of course, had an immense practical and symbolic significance which is frequently overlooked: see this volume, p. 264.
149. V. P. Milyutin, *O Lenine* (Leningrad, 1924) pp. 4–5; E. A. Rakh'ya, 'Moi vospominaniya', op. cit., p. 434.
150. See V. P. Milyutin, *O Lenine*, ibid.
151. See E. A. Lutskii, 'Zasedanie TsK', op. cit., p. 89.
152. See ibid.
153. See ibid. ; and *PSS*, vol. 35, p. 23–27.
154. See V. P. Milyutin, *O Lenine*, op. cit.; L. D. Trotskii, *Moya zhizn'*, vol. 2, p. 59.
155. See note 154 above.
156. *PSS*, vol. 35, p. 1.
157. *Pravda*, 29 October 1917.
158. Rabochaya gazeta, no. 196, 26 October 1917. The Russian phrase describing the reaction to Lenin's name was *nesmolkaemye*

aplod [*ismenty*]. The fact that this was reported by a hostile newspaper, run by Mensheviks, indicates the warmth of the anticipation of Lenin's arrival.

159. Ibid.; and N. Sukhanov, *Zapiski o revolyutsii*, vol. 6, pp. 174–5.
160. *Rabochaya gazeta*, no. 196, 26 October 1917.
161. See N. Sukhanov, *Zapiski o revolyutsii*, op. cit.
162. *Rabochaya gazeta*, no. 196, 26 October 1917.
163. J. Reed, *Ten Days That Shook The World* (Boni Lightfoot: New York, 1919) pp. 86–7.
164. *Rabochaya gazeta*, no. 196, 26 October 1917.
165. *Pravda*, 29 October 1917.
166. See I. Getzler, *Martov*, p. 162; A. Rabinowitch, *The Bolsheviks Come to Power*, op. cit., p. 292.
167. See the data assembled in A. F. Butenko and D. A. Chugaev (eds.), *Vtoroi vserossiiskii s"ezd rabochikh i soldatskikh deputatov: sbornik dokumentov* (Moscow, 1957) pp. 386–98.
168. See A. Rabinowitch,*The Bolsheviks Come to Power*, op. cit., pp. 292–3.
169. See idem, p. 296.
170. See idem, p. 303.
171. *BK*, vol. 5, p. 3.
172. See E. A. Lutskii, 'Zasedanie TsK', p. 90; *BK*, vol. 5, p. 2.
173. *BK*, vol. 5, p. 6.
174. The proclamation (in Russian, *obrashchenie*) is reprinted in *RPP*, p. 11.
175. Ibid.
176. Idem, pp. 11–12. It is interesting to note that the proclamation not once expressly mentioned 'industry'.
177. Idem, p. 12. This is a curious formulation, seeming to be a shorthand term for the old Russian empire. For, strictly speaking, it would otherwise have excluded, for example, Poland. Either haste or the desire for literary vigour probably explains the choice of words. It would seem altogether too suspicious an interpretation to suggest that Lenin's formulation was a deliberate, early attempt to limit the scope of national self-determination he wished to offer through his government.
178. Ibid.
179. The account by E. H. Carr in his *The Bolshevik Revolution*, vol. 3 (London, 1953) pp. 9–20 remains a most subtle analysis of the Decree's contents.
180. Idem, p. 13. Lenin was using two main terms to refer to nation: *natsiya* and *narodnost'*.
181. Ibid.
182. Idem, p. 12.
183. Idem, pp. 12–14, 183. For example, the nearest Lenin got to talking of European imperialist powers was his reference to 'strong and wealthy nations': *idem*, p. 13.
184. See S. Page, *Lenin and World Revolution*, pp. 84–5.
185. *RPP*, p. 13.
186. Idem, pp. 12, 13.
187. Idem, p. 14.

188. Of course, difficulties in establishing contact with the rest of Europe remained even in the first year of Soviet rule.
189. *RPP*, p. 15.
190. Ibid.
191. Idem, p. 16.
192. Idem, p. 16.
193. See idem, p. 15.
194. The translation as 'enactment' for *postanovlenie* is used so as to distinguish it from 'decree' for *dekret*: idem, p. 17.
195. Idem, pp. 17–18.
196. Draft in *PSS*, vol. 35, pp. 51–2.
197. *RPP*, pp. 18–22.
198. See this volume, esp. pp. 315–16.
199. *RPP*, pp. 23–4.
200. See idem, p. 24.

CHAPTER 9: THE VIEW FROM PETROGRAD

1. *PSS*, vol. 34, pp. 239–41.
2. See this volume, pp. 254–6.
3. At least there is nothing in Kemenev's speech on 16 October or in his subsequent *Novaya Zhizn'* article of 18 October to suggest that he foresaw Lenin's tactic with precision: see *PTsK*, pp. 99–100 and 115–16.
4. This is not to say that they were without tactical subtlety or without the ability to postpone the pursuit of particular ends. On the contrary, they were also masters of flexible political leadership.
5. See A. F. Butenko and D. A. Chugaev (eds), *Vtoroi vserossiiskii s"ezd sovetov*, pp. 389–98.
6. R. A. Abramovich, *The Soviet Revolution, 1917–1939*, (New York, 1962) pp. 104–5.
7. *PTsK*, p. 122.
8. *Protokoly TsK*, p. 127.
9. Idem, p. 123.
10. Idem, pp. 124–5.
11. Idem, p. 126.
12. Idem, p. 122.
13. See the lengthy footnote no. 156 in idem, pp. 271–2. The minutes of the meeting, though extant, have not been published. For Kamenev's own account to the Bolshevik Central Committee, which gives several details, see idem, p. 124.
14. Idem, p. 125.
15. Idem, pp. 126–7.
16. Idem, p. 130.
17. Ibid.

18. See I. Getzler, *Martov*, pp. 168–70 for an account of the Vikzhel talks.
19. *Protokoly TsK*, p. 131 and Note 173 on p. 275 (which contains a previously unpublished record of the voting in Lenin's handwriting; it was omitted from the subsequently published fifth edition of the collected works (*PSS*).
20. *PSS*, vol. 35, p. 50.
21. Idem, pp. 48–9.
22. *Protokoly TsK*, p. 135.
23. Idem, p. 136.
24. Idem, pp. 136–7.
25. See the report on Trotski in *Isvestiya*, no. 217, 5 November 1917.
26. I. N. Steinberg, *In the Workshop of the Revolution* (Gollancz, London: 1955) pp. 46–7.
27. See J. Keep, *The Russian Revolution*, pp. 315–16.
28. See O. H. Radkey, *The Sickle Under the Hammer. The Russian Socialist Revolutionaries in the Early Months of Soviet Rule* (Columbia, 1963) pp. 97–109.
29. Idem, pp. 226–53.
30. The break-up of the coalition will be dealt with in Volume Three.
31. See the account in R. Service, *The Bolshevik Party*, op. cit., pp. 69, 74–5, 77–8, 81–2, 102–3, 105–6, 109.
32. See idem, p. 77.
33. See, for example, 'K naseleniyu', *PSS*, vol. 35, pp. 65–7.
34. Ibid.
35. *Perepiska*, vol. 2, p. 3.
36. See J. Keep, *The Russian Revolution*, pp. 353–6.
37. *UNE*, part 1, p. 5; part 2, pp. 60, 61; part 3, p. 95. Needless to add, the Sovnarkom minutes do not tell the whole story of assistance from Petrograd to the provinces. Informal, off-the-record instructions played a great part. The Military-Revolutionary committee sent out its commissars too. But the overall impression of the Sovnarkom Minutes is not excessively distorted.
38. See report of Balashov in 'Protokoly 3-i Moskovskoi oblastnoi konferentsii RSDRP (b) 1917 goda', *PR*, no. 10 (105) (1930) pp. 107–8.
39. See J. Keep, *The Russian Revolution*, p. 362.
40. Ibid., résumé, ch. 26.
41. See 'Protokoly 3-i Moskovskoi oblastoi konferentsii', op. cit., pp. 112–14.
42. See J. Keep, *The Russian Revolution*, op. cit., chs. 26, 27.
43. L. Trotskii, 'Politicheskie siluety', *Sochineniya*, vol. 8, p. 249; K. T. Sverdlova, *Yakov Mikhailovich Sverdlov* (Moscow, 1957) p. 348.
44. The practical factors, of course, were not alone in explaining Lenin's indifference to procedural legalism; an ideologically-conditioned casualness was also at work. This was especially obvious in the absence of restraints on the powers of the Cheka: see this volume, pp. 289–93.
45. *Pravda*, no. 194, 19 December 1917.
46. *BK*, vol. 5, pp. 24–166.
47. See R. Service, *The Bolshevik Party*, op. cit., pp. 58–9 and 75–6.

48. See J. Channon, 'The Bolsheviks, Land Reform and the Peasantry', unpublished Essex conference paper (May 1984) p. 4.
49. M. Mayzel, *Generals and Revolutionaries. The Russian General Staff During the Revolution: A Study in the Transformation of Military Elite* (Osnabruck, 1979) pp. 173–7) and 193–203.
50. N. Krupskaya, *VL*, p. 341.
51. See V. P. Danilov, *Dokolkhoznaya derevnya*, pp. 286–7, 295.
52. See idem, pp. 106–8.
53. *PTsK*, p. 118.
54. *PSS*, vol. 35, p. 11. An exigent perusal of this wording might question whether, by offering this right only to the peoples inhabiting Russia, Lenin was refusing it to the non-Russian regions of the Romanov lands. Such an interpretation is implausible in view of the other decrees of October–December 1917; and the form of words, while probably coming naturally from a Russian, is surely mainly the result of hasty compilation.
55. Idem, pp. 13–14.
56. *DSV*, vol. 1, p. 40.
57. See this volume, p. 231.
58. See this volume, p. 230–1. There is no evidence, despite post-1945 Soviet claims, that Lenin had the slightest intention of recognising the permanent independence of Finland; his policy on national self-determination was instrumentalist, and he expected nations and nation states eventually to disappear: see this volume, p. 46.
59. *PSS*, vol. 35, p. 90. See A. F. Upton, *The Finnish Revolution, 1917–1918* (Minnesota, 1980) p. 141.
60. See idem, p. 147.
61. Ibid.
62. See idem, p. 197.
63. Polish–Soviet relations will be treated in Volume Three.
64. See this volume, pp. 130 and 232.
65. See this volume, pp. 46, 110 and 175.
66. See R.Pipes, *Formation of the Soviet Union*, p. 115.
67. *UNE*, part 1, p. 5.
68. See R. Pipes, *Formation of the Soviet Union*, p. 119.
69. See idem, p. 121.
70. See idem, p. 124–6.
71. *PSS*, vol. 35, p. 143.
72. See the theses in 'Oblastnoi s'ezd RSDRP (b-kov)', *Letopis' revolyutsii* (1926) no. 5, pp. 76–7.
73. See D. A. Chugaev *et al.*, *Istoriya natsional'no-gosudarstvennogo stroitel'stva v SSSR*, vol. 1, *Natsionalno-gosudarstvennoe stroitel'stvo v SSSR v perekhodnyi period ot kapitalizma k sotsializmu (1917–1937 gg.)* (Moscow, 1968) pp. 69–71.
74. *PSS*, vol. 35, p. 221.
75. See this volume, p. 110.
76. See R. Pipes, *The Formation of the Soviet Union*, pp. 73–4.
77. See A. Ezergailis, *The 1917 Revolution in Latvia* (Boulder, 1974) chap 4.

78. This theme will be treated in greater detail in Volume Three.
79. See this volume, pp. 217 and 222–4.
80. See this volume, pp. 226–7.
81. See G. Leggett, *The Cheka. Lenin's Secret Police. The All-Russian Extraordinary Commission for Combating Counter-Revolution and Sabotage (December 1917 to February 1922* (Oxford, 1981) p. 5.
82. See Volume One, p. 135.
83. See idem, pp. 76, 145.
84. See this volume, pp. 227.
85. This topic will be resumed in Volume Three of this trilogy.
86. See the document in *UNE*, part 1, p. 31.
87. See G. Leggett, op. cit., pp. 87–9.
88. See idem, p. 5.
89. See idem, p. 14.
90. See idem, pp. 14–15.
91. See idem, p. 15.
92. *UNE*, op. cit., part 1, p. 5.
93. See G. Leggett, *The Cheka*, p. 13.
94. See idem, p. 17.
95. See idem, p. 18.
96. On Zinoviev's earlier resignation see this volume, p. 277.
97. *DVP*, vol. 1, (Moscow, 1959) pp. 15–17.
98. See S. Page, *Lenin and World Revolution*, op. cit., p. 86.
99. Idem, pp. 26–7.
100. Idem, pp. 28–30.
101. Idem, pp. 47–52.
102. See R. Debo, *Revolution and Survival: the Foreign Policy of Soviet Russia, 1917–18* (Liverpool, 1978) pp. 36–46.
103. L. Trotskii, *Sochineniya*, vol. 3, part 2, pp. 211–17. R. Debo, in his informative chapter on the subject, contends that Trotski's speech indicated a change of analysis about the prospect of waging a revolutionary war: *Revolution and Survival*, op. cit., pp. 47–8. As I have tried to show in the survey of the Sixth Party Congress proceedings, it was, in fact, common among Bolsheviks to argue that a revolutionary war would not be an easy option: see this volume, p. 205.
104. Again, Debo's account emphasises Lenin's silence as if it were a new factor in the political developments; but, in fact, he had been silent for some months before the October Revolution: see this volume, pp. 244–5.
105. See I. Deutscher, *Trotsky: The Prophet Armed*, pp. 363–4.
106. See idem, p. 359.
107. See idem, p. 360.
108. See, for example, *PSS*, vol. 35, p. 181.
109. Ibid.
110. Idem, pp. 179–80. See also E. N. Gorodetskii, 'Demobilizatsiya armii v 1917–1918 gg.', *Istoriya SSSR*, no. 1 (1958) pp. 15–19.
111. See this volume, pp. 245–6.
112. See this volume, p. 139.

113. The book by Z. E. B. Zeman and W. B. Scharlau, *The Merchant of Revolution*, op. cit., is notably silent on the chronology of the alleged financial subsidies from Berlin to the Bolsheviks.
114. See I. Deutscher, *Trotsky: The Prophet Armed*, op. cit., pp. 371–2.
115. See this volume, p. 205.
116. See I. Deutscher, *Trotsky: The Prophet Armed*, op. cit., p. 362.
117. *BK*, vol. 5, p. 155.
118. *PSS*, vol. 5, p. 189. Another projected article was the following; '"Separate peace", its danger and its possible significance. Is a separate peace "an agreement" ("collaboration") with the imperialists'; see idem, p. 188. It might be objected that my interpretation does not take into account yet another projected article, 'How must revolutionary war "be prepared"?'. This wording might be taken to signify that Lenin was planning to describe precisely how a revolutionary war could instantly be got ready; but, in fact, we ought to remember that, even while signing the Brest-Litovsk treaty in March 1918, Lenin explicitly refused to foreswear the need to prepare a revolutionary war in the longer term: see this volume, p. 322.
119. *PSS*, vol. 34, p. 192: an article unpublished until 1929; written 24–17 December 1917.
120. R. A. Medvedev argues the case for Lenin's having missed a real opportunity in 1917–18 in *The October Revolution* (London, 1979).
121. See the arguments in R. Service, *The Russian Revolution* p. 57.
122. See ibid.
123. See Yu. Larin, 'Sovety batratskikh deputatov', *Rabochii put'*, no. 20, 26 September 1917. See also N. Bukharin, *Programma kommunistov*, op. cit., pp. 30–33.
124. See R. V. Daniels, *The Conscience of the Revolution. Communist Opposition in Soviet Russia* (London, 1960), pp. 81–91.
125. See this volume, p. 205.
126. See S. A. Smith, *Red Petrograd*, pp. 155–6, for further discussion of this theme.
127. See idem, pp. 228–9.
128. See this volume, pp. 158 and 173–4.
129. W. Mosse, 'Revolution in Saratov (October–November 1917)', *Slavonic and East European Review* (October 1981) p. 57.
130. See R. V. Daniels, *The Conscience of the Revolution*, Op. cit., pp. 81–91
131. *PSS*, vol. 35, pp. 62–4. The phrasing on meetings is perjorative in the Russian original: '. . . *my slishkom mnogo mitinguem*'.
132. See his article, unpublished until 1929 but written between 24 and 27 December 1917, 'How to organise competition?': idem, pp. 195–205.
133. See idem.
134. See this volume, pp. 225–8 and 232–4.
135. *PSS*, vol. 35, p. 202.
136. See Volume One, pp. 182–3.
137. See this volume, p. 223.
138. For a different view, emphasising continuity in Lenin's thought in 1917–1918, see N. Harding, *Lenin's Political Thought*, vol. 2, chs 8, 9.
139. *PSS*, vol. 35, p. 204.

140. Idem, p. 203.
141. Idem, p. 275.
142. Idem, p. 276.
143. Idem, p. 64.
144. Idem, p. 311
145. Idem, pp. 330–1.

CHAPTER 10: THE OBSCENE PEACE

1. *SVII*, p. 11.
2. *PSS*, vol. 50, p. 14.
3. See this volume, p. 227.
4. L. D. Trotskii, *O Lenine. Materialy dlya biografii*, pp. 91–2.
5. Ibid.
6. See O. H. Radkey, *The Election to the Russian Constituent Assembly* (Harvard, 1950) p. 21.
7. See ibid. .
8. *PSS*, vol. 34, p. 266.
9. *UNE*, part 2, 67. See also idem, p. 60.
10. Idem, p. 67.
11. *Pravda*, 24 November 1917.
12. M. Vishnyak, *Dan' proshlomu* (New York) pp. 328–30.
13. *DSV*, vol. 1, p. 159.
14. *BK*, vol. 5, p. 168.
15. Idem, p. 169.
16. See this volume, p. 151.
17. *BK*, vol. 5, p. 170.
18. M. I. Ul'yanova, *O Lenine* (4th edition: Moscow, 1971) pp. 84–5.
19. *BK*, vol. 5, p. 171.
20. See Fel'shtinskii, *Bol'sheviki i levye esery*, p. 86.
21. See this volume, pp. 227–8.
22. See Fel'shtinskii, *Bol'sheviki i levye esery*, op. cit., p. 90.
23. See ibid.
24. See M. Vishnyak, *Dan' proshlomu,*, p. 363.
25. See Fel'shtinskii, *Bol'sheviki i levye esery,*, pp. 96–8.
26. See idem, pp. 98–9.
27. *Vserossiiskoe Uchreditel'noe sobranie* (Moscow–Leningrad, 1930) p. 110.
28. V. D. Bonch-Bruevich, 'Vospominaniya o V. I. Lenine, 1917–1924', *Izbrannye Sochineniya* (Moscow, 1963), vol. 3, p. 135.
29. See this volume, p. 181.
30. *PSS*, vol. 50, p. 29.
31. This does not mean that Lenin had already decided upon a rapid rupture of the link with the Left Socialist Revolutionaries. Quite the contrary; he wanted them with the Bolsheviks in coalition. But he also wished to preserve the Bolshevik party's dominance in the relationship.
32. See Fel'shtinskii, *Bol'sheviki i levye esery*, p. 78.

33. See *Tretii vserossiiskii sovetov rabochikh, soldatskikh i krest'yanskikh deputatov* (Petersburg, 1918) pp. 111. See also Spiridonova's speech in *idem*, p. 46.
34. *Idem*, p. 21.
35. See T. H. Rigby, *Lenin's Government. Sovnarkom, 1917–1922* (Cambridge, 1979) pp. 34, 72.
36. This topic will be resumed in Volume Three.
37. See Y. H. Rigby, *Lenin's Government*, pp. 69–70.
38. Ya. Gindin, *Vospominaniya o V. I. Lenine* (Moscow, 1973) p. 9.
39. See T. H. Rigby, *Lenin's Government*, op. cit., p. 74.
40. The division of functions and power between the central bodies of party and government is a complex topic which will be resumed in Volume Three. But see also 'From Polyarchy to Hegemony: The Party's Role in the Construction of the Central Institutions of the Soviet State, 1917–1919', *Sbornik*, 1984, no. 10, *passim*.
41. This theme, so important in the political struggles after Lenin's death, will be resumed in Volume Three.
42. N. Krupskaya, *VL*, pp. 334–5.
43. Ya. Berzin, *Partiya bol'shevikov v bor'be za kommunisticheskii internatsional* (Moscow, 1931) p. 111.
44. This continued to be a major source of pleasure for him through to his death.
45. In most ways, a comparison between Lenin and Hitler is odious. But it is worth recalling, however, that Hitler, too, was attracted to children, but this did not stop him from massacring every Jewish and gypsy boy or girl who fell into the hands of the Gestapo.
46. *UNE*, part 2, p. 66; part 3, p. 93, 100.
47. *DSV*, vol. 1, pp. 141–2 and 549–50.
48. This theme is resumed in Volume Three. But see also this volume, pp. 269–70.
49. *DSV*, vol. 1, pp. 406–9.
50. See Lenin's comments in *PSS*, vol. 41, p. 37 about the compromise with the Left Socialist Revolutionaries.
51. See V. P. Danilov, *Dokolkhoznaya sovetskaya derevnya*, op. cit., chapter 2.
52. See E. H. Carr, *The Bolshevik Revolution*, op. cit., vol. 2, pp. 35–41.
53. *DSV*, vol. 1, pp. 407, 408.
54. See D. Mandel, *The Petrograd Workers and the Soviet Seizure of Power. From the July Days, 1917, to July 1918* (London, 1984) p. 111.
55. See J. Keep, *The Russian Revolution*, op. cit., p. 431.
56. See S. Malle, *The Economic Organisation of 'War Communism, 1918–1921* (Cambridge, 1985) pp. 326–7.
57. See Volume One, esp. pp. 131–2, 161–5.
58. See R. Service, *The Bolshevik Party*, p. 71.
59. See S. M. Klyatskin, *Na zashchite Oktyabrya. Organizatsiya regulyarnoi armii i militsionnoe stroitel'stvo v Sovestkoi republike, 1917–1920*, (Moscow, 1965), ch. 1.
60. *PPR*, vol. 1, p. 28.
61. Idem, p. 31.

62. This was a portent of things to come: industrial output collapsed through to 1921.
63. See E. V. Gimpel'son, '*Voennyi kommunizm*': *politika, praktika, ideologiya* (Moscow, 1973) p. 34.
64. See this volume, pp. 233–4.
65. *UNE*, part 1, p. 6.
66. *RPP*, vol. 1, p. 23.
67. See A. G. Rashin, 'Dinamika promyshlennykh kadrov SSSR za 1917–1958 gg.' in D. A. Baevskii (ed.), *Izmeneniya v chislennosti i sostave sovetskogo rabochego klassa* (Moscow, 1961) p. 9.
68. See this volume, p. 234.
69. *RPP*, vol. 1, pp. 25–6.
70. See S. Smith, *Red Petrograd*, pp. 216–22.
71. See S. Cohen, *Bukharin*, pp. 69–72.
72. See Smith, *Red Petrograd*, op. cit., p. 249.
73. See S. Fitzpatrick, *The People's Commissariat of Enlightenment. Soviet Organisation of education and the Arts under Lunacharsky* (Cambridge, 1970) pp. 14–25.
74. See J. Biggart, Alexander Bogdanov and the Revolutions of 1917, *Sbornik*, no. 10, 1984, pp. 8–10.
75. See E. V. Gimpel'son, *Velikiii Oktyabr' i stanovlenie sovetskoi sistemy upravleniya narodnym khozyaistvom (noyabr' 1917–1920 gg.)* (Moscow, 1977) pp. 282–5.
76. See Service, *The Bolshevik Party*, pp. 76–83.
77. L. Trotskii, *O Lenine*, pp. 80–1.
78. *PTsK*, p. 168; *PSS*, vol. 35, pp. 243–52.
79. *PSS*, vol. 35, p. 253.
80. *PTsK*, p. 168.
81. Trotskii, *O Lenine*, p. 81.
82. *PSS*, vol. 35, p. 225.
83. *PTsK*, p. 168.
84. Idem, pp. 168–9.
85. Idem, pp. 169–70.
86. Idem, pp. 170.
87. Idem, p. 172.
88. Idem, pp. 171, 172.
89. Idem, p. 173.
90. Ibid.
91. The minutes of this meeting are said to be lost: *PTsK*, fn. 205, p. 283.
92. Idem, p. 175. Please note that this is the first date in this volume registering the adoption of the new Gregorian calendar in official Russia; the date according to the old calendar would have been 19 January. The rest of the dates in this volume follow the Gregorian calendar.
93. *PTsK*, pp. 175–9.
94. Idem, pp. 190–1.
95. Ibid.
96. Ibid.
97. See I. Deutscher, *Trotsky: The Prophet Armed*, pp. 80–2.

98. Idem, pp. 194–5.
99. Ibid.
100. Idem, pp. 197 amd 199.
101. Idem, p. 201.
102. Idem, pp. 203–4.
103. Idem, pp. 206, 208.
104. Idem, p. 211.
105. Idem, p. 212.
106. Idem, p. 213.
107. Idem, p. 214.
108. Idem, p. 215.
109. Idem, p. 216. Bukharin himself did not have a governmental post.
110. See R. Service, 'From Polyarchy to Party Hegemony', *Sbornik*, no. 1 (1984) pp. 77–90.
111. This is not to say that the Central Committee decided all major issues of policy after January–March 1918; on the contrary, the Central Committee's role declined somewhat immediately afterwards, partly because of the walkout by the Left Communists and partly because of the intensification of the Civil War in the second half of 1918. See ibid.
112. See, for example, 'O revolyutsionnoi fraze', *Pravda*, no. 31, 21(8) February 1918.
113. See this volume, p. 80; see also Volume One, pp. 82–4.
114. On the talk, see *PTsK*, p. 214.
115. *Perepiska sekretariata*, vol. 3, p. 23. But note that the Left Socialist Revolutionaries were themselves garbling their reports: see R. Service, *The Bolshevik Party*, p. 82.
116. See C. Duval, 'Yakov Sverdlov: Founder of the Bolshevik Party Machine' in R. C. Elwood (ed.), *Reconsiderations on the Russian Revolution* (Slavica Press, 1976) pp. 226–7. But see also R. Service, *The Bolshevik Party*, fn. 53, p. 226.
117. The ability to win over mass party meetings continued to be a crucial asset in intra-Bolshevik politics: see the account of the trade union controversy of 1920–21 in R. Service, *The Bolshevik Party*, pp. 148–52.
118. See idem, pp. 150–1.
119. *SVII*, pp. 129–31.
120. See G. Zinov'ev, *N. Lenin. Vladimir Il'ich Ul'yanov. Ocherki zhizni i deyatel'nosti* (Petrograd, 1918).
121. *Pyatyi vserossiiskii s'ezd sovetov rabochikh, krest'yanskikh, soldatskikh i kazach'ikh deputatov. Stenograficheskii otchet. Moskva, 4–10 iyulya 1918 g.* (Moscow, 1918) p. 201.
122. *Perepiska*, vol. 3, p. 23.
123. For his speech of support, see *PTsK*, pp. 172–3.
124. *Ural'skii rabochii* (Ekaterinburg) no. 58/155, 31 March 1918.
125. See V. Gorev's comments in *Golos naroda* (Tula) no. 7, 13 January 1918.
126. *Ural'skii rabochii* (Ekaterinburg) no. 33/130, 27(14) March 1918.
127. Idem, no. 12/109, 18 January 1918. It ought to be added that this was at a time when it was widely believed by Bolsheviks that Trotski would

be able to string along the German and Austrian diplomats at Brest-Litovsk until such time as revolution broke out in central Europe. Nevertheless the advocacy of transferring industry to civilian-goods output was breathtakingly risky for persons who might shortly expect to have to wage war.

128. Idem, no. 24/121, 15 February 1918.
129. *Rabochii krai* (Ivanovo), no. 44/129, 26 April 1918: report by soviet guberniya executive committee's military department leader P. Baturin.
130. See R. Service, *The Bolshevik Party*, p. 79.
131. *SVII*, pp. 1, 201–3.
132. Idem, pp. 191–3.
133. Idem, p. 4.
134. Idem, p. 8.
135. Idem, p. 11.
136. Idem, p. 13.
137. Idem, pp. 13, 16, 21.
138. Idem, pp. 21–2, 23.
139. Idem, p. 24.
140. Idem, pp. 26, 34–5.
141. The overstatement of Bukharin's differences with Lenin is contained even in detailed monographs on him such as S. Cohen, *Bukharin and the Russian Revolution*, op. cit., pp. 61–9. On the other hand, Cohen's chapter on the Brest-Litovsk controversy is innovative in highlighting the differences among the Bukharin and left Bolsheviks: see idem, pp. 71–2.
142. *SVII*, pp. 27, 28, 32.
143. Idem, pp. 35.
144. Idem, p. 41.
145. Idem, pp. 42–4.
146. Idem, p. 44, 46.
147. Idem, pp. 50–1.
148. Idem, p. 56.
149. Idem, p. 57.
150. Idem, p. 64.
151. Idem, p. 66, 68, 72.
152. Idem, p. 70. Sverdlov gleefully welcomed this equivocation: idem, p. 80.
153. Idem, p. 70.
154. Ibid.
155. Idem, p. 76.
156. Idem, p. 77.
157. Idem, p. 81.
158. Idem, pp. 82–90. Nevertheless the freedom of expression at the Congress was, as we have seen, preceded by a preliminary manipulation of the Congress mandates which meant that the leftists stood little chance of victory: see this chapter, pp. 324.
159. Idem, pp. 95, 97 and 99.
160. Idem, pp. 99–100.
161. Idem, p. 101–6.

162. Idem, pp. 110, 114.
163. Idem, p. 115.
164. Idem, p. 121.
165. Ibid.
166. Idem, p. 122.
167. Idem, p. 124.
168. Idem, pp. 125, 175–6.
169. Idem, p. 125.
170. Idem, p. 128–9.
171. Idem, p. 129–31.
172. Idem, p. 131.
173. Idem, pp. 133, 137.
174. Idem, p. 138.
175. Idem, p. 141.
176. Idem, p. 147–8.
177. Idem, p. 146.
178. Idem, pp. 150–1.
179. Idem, p. 158. The Russian word here for Russian was *Rossiiskaya*, emphasising – as had the party's earlier name – that the party hoped to unite all the peoples of the old Russian empire.
180. Idem, p. 163.
181. Idem, pp. 164–5.
182. Idem, pp. 166–7.
183. Idem, p. 170.
184. Idem, p. 172.

Index